DOMINION OVER
PALM AND PINE

RETHINKING CANADA IN THE WORLD
SERIES EDITORS: IAN MCKAY AND SEAN MILLS

Supported by the Wilson Institute for Canadian History at McMaster University, this series is committed to books that rethink Canadian history from transnational and global perspectives. It enlarges approaches to the study of Canada in the world by exploring how Canadian history has long been a dynamic product of global currents and forces. The series will also reinvigorate understanding of Canada's role as an international actor and how Canadians have contributed to intellectual, political, cultural, social, and material exchanges around the world.

Volumes included in the series explore the ideas, movements, people, and institutions that have transcended political boundaries and territories to shape Canadian society and the state. These include both state and non-state actors, and phenomena such as international migration, diaspora politics, religious movements, evolving conceptions of human rights and civil society, popular culture, technology, epidemics, wars, and global finance and trade.

The series charts a new direction by exploring networks of transmission and exchange from a standpoint that is not solely national or international, expanding the history of Canada's engagement with the world.

http://wilson.humanities.mcmaster.ca

DOMINION OVER PALM AND PINE

A History of Canadian Aspirations in the British Caribbean

Paula Hastings

McGill-Queen's University Press
Montreal & Kingston · London · Chicago

ISBN 978-0-2280-1129-3 (cloth)
ISBN 978-0-2280-1130-9 (paper)
ISBN 978-0-2280-1285-6 (ePDF)
ISBN 978-0-2280-1286-3 (ePUB)

Legal deposit third quarter 2022
Bibliothèque nationale du Québec

Printed in Canada on acid-free paper that is 100% ancient forest free (100% post-consumer recycled), processed chlorine free

This book has been published with the help of a grant from the Canadian Federation for the Humanities and Social Sciences, through the Awards to Scholarly Publications Program, using funds provided by the Social Sciences and Humanities Research Council of Canada.

Funded by the   Financé par le
Government   gouvernement
of Canada   du Canada

Canada Council Conseil des arts
for the Arts   du Canada

We acknowledge the support of the Canada Council for the Arts.

Nous remercions le Conseil des arts du Canada de son soutien.

Library and Archives Canada Cataloguing in Publication

Title: Dominion over palm and pine : a history of Canadian aspirations in the British Caribbean / Paula Hastings.

Names: Hastings, Paula, author.

Series: Rethinking Canada in the world ; 11.

Description: Series statement: Rethinking Canada in the world ; 11 | Includes bibliographical references and index.

Identifiers: Canadiana (print) 20220199132 | Canadiana (ebook) 20220199191 | ISBN 9780228011309 (paper) | ISBN 9780228011293 (cloth) | ISBN 9780228012856 (ePDF) | ISBN 9780228012863 (ePUB)

Subjects: LCSH: Canada – Foreign relations – Caribbean Area. | LCSH: Caribbean Area – Foreign relations – Canada. | LCSH: Caribbean Area – History – 19th century. | LCSH: Caribbean Area – History – 20th century. | CSH: Canada – Foreign relations – 1867-

Classification: LCC FC251.C37 H37 2022 | DDC 327.710729 – dc23

This book was designed and typeset by Peggy & Co. Design in 11/14 Adobe Garamond Pro.

For Mike

CONTENTS

FIGURES

ACKNOWLEDGMENTS

The research and writing of this book would not have been possible without the support of many people and institutions. At Duke University, where the manuscript started life as a doctoral dissertation, I was especially fortunate to work under the supervision of the late John Herd Thompson. John's indefatigable kindness, intellectual generosity, and writing talent never ceased to amaze me. I am lucky to have known him. Susan Thorne and Barry Gaspar, two of my committee members, were also crucial to the book's genesis. Susan offered ongoing encouragement and never let me lose sight of the broader imperial context of my project. I thank Barry for our countless discussions about Caribbean history; I hope the profound impact of those discussions is evident in the book. I am grateful, too, for the intellectual insights and professional guidance of Sally Deutsch, Thavolia Glymph, Anna Krylova, Jane Moss, Gunther Peck, Philip Stern, and, at the University of North Carolina at Chapel Hill, Miles Fletcher and Michael Hunt. My fantastic grad student comrades – Mitch Fraas, Reena Goldthree, Sebastian Lukasik, Christina Ramos, Jacob Remes, Felicity Turner, Kristin Wintersteen, Maren Wood, and Jenny Wood-Crowley – provided much-needed levity and friendship.

Dominion over Palm and Pine received generous funding from several sources. I thank the Social Sciences and Humanities Research Council of Canada, the American Council of Learned Societies, the Andrew W. Mellon Foundation, the International Council for Canadian Studies, the London Goodenough Association of Canada, and the Australian Historical Association. At Duke University, I was fortunate to receive funding from the Graduate School, the (now unfortunately defunct) Center for Canadian Studies, the Department of History, the John Hope Franklin Humanities Institute, the Center for Latin American and Caribbean Studies, and the Department of Women's Studies (now named the Department of Gender, Sexuality and Feminist Studies).

For their research assistance, I am grateful to librarians and archivists at Duke University, the University of the West Indies at St Augustine, the National Library of Jamaica, and the University of the West Indies at Mona; Oxford University, Cambridge University, the National Archives of the United Kingdom, the Parliamentary Archives (London), Durham University, the National Library of Scotland, and the London School of Economics; the Directorate of History and Heritage at Canada's Department of National Defence, Library and Archives Canada, Dalhousie University, Cape Breton University, Nova Scotia Archives and Records Management, the Whitney Pier Historical Museum, the Centre d'histoire La Presqu'île (Vaudreuil-Dorion), McGill University, the Provincial Archives of Ontario, the University of Toronto, the Sun Life Insurance Company of Canada Corporate Archives (Mississauga), and the Provincial Archives of Manitoba.

During my SSHRC postdoc at the University of Manitoba, colleagues in the Department of History, St John's College, and wider Winnipeg helped push the manuscript along in various ways. I owe thanks to Allison Abra, Ryan Eyford, Gerald Friesen, Erin Millions, Robert Penner, and especially Adele Perry. Since my arrival at the University of Toronto, many colleagues have offered professional and institutional guidance, including Dan Bender, Heidi Bohaker, Li Chen, Connie Guberman, Franca Iacovetta, Steve Penfold, Ian Radforth, Natalie Rothman, and Jo Sharma. Kamal Hassan, Monica Hretsina, Ashfak Khan, Urooj Khan, and Minda Nessia provided crucial administrative support.

The feedback of colleagues, reviewers, and editors at various stages of the revision process improved the manuscript considerably. Sean Mills and Adele Perry read an early version, and their thoughtful comments helped guide its direction. More recently, Sarah-Jane (Saje) Mathieu and Steve Penfold read the entire book, providing invaluable substantive and stylistic suggestions. Susan Colbourn read several chapters and offered an incisive critique that pushed me to sharpen one of the book's central arguments. Funké Aladejebi encouraged me to reflect more critically on the deeply rooted genealogy of racialized thinking that sustained white Canadian prerogatives in the Caribbean over time. Alongside Saje, Steve, Susan, and Funké, several colleagues gave generously of their time to read one or more chapters for a virtual book workshop in December 2020. I thank Dimitry Anastakis, Husseina Dinani, Nick Fast, Lee Frew, Brian Gettler, Sean Mills, Melanie Newton, Steve Rockel, Natalie Rothman, Alissa Trotz, and Tamara Walker for their questions, insights, and guidance. At McGill-Queen's University Press, Kyla Madden expertly shepherded the manuscript through the many stages of publication. I am grateful for her judicious advice and sustained interest in the book. Two anonymous reviewers carefully read the manuscript and offered several helpful suggestions for improvement. Kathleen Fraser and Elli Stylianou kindly answered endless questions about images, maps, and formatting. Maureen Garvie combed the manuscript with her keen editorial eye, strengthening the prose throughout.

Earlier versions of chapters 2 and 3 were published in "Rounding off the Confederation: Geopolitics, Tropicality, and Canada's 'Destiny' in the West Indies in the Early Twentieth Century," *Journal of Colonialism and Colonial History* 13, no. 2 (August 2013), and "Territorial Spoils, Transnational Black Resistance, and Canada's Evolving Autonomy during the First World War," *Histoire Sociale/Social History* 47, no. 94 (June 2014): 443–70. I am grateful to these journals for their permission to reproduce portions of this work. Thanks to Edd Uluschak are also in order for allowing me to reproduce one of his cartoons, and to Robert Cronan, who made the maps.

While I don't wish to replicate the first-book tendency to acknowledge everyone who has crossed my path since kindergarten, I do want to go back to my MA years at Carleton University. If it were not for the intellectually rich and supportive environment in Carleton's Department of History, my life would have played out very differently. I am indebted to David Dean, Bruce Elliott, Norman Hillmer, Brian McKillop, James Opp, Pamela Walker, and John Walsh. Norman's formidable scholarship and teaching on Canada's role in the world left an indelible mark.

Finally, I am grateful for the unwavering support of friends and family. Thank you to Tharwat Awamleh, Wes Farris, Rick and Myrna Pears, Joan Stalzer, Erin Stokes, Felicity Turner, Julie Crum-Vendeiro, the late Christine Winer, Phil and Ute Winer, and Maren Wood. Without my parents, Paul and Arline, this book never would have seen the light of day. Their love, encouragement, and financial support made everything possible. My father is not here to see the book in print, but the intellectual curiosity, integrity, and sense of right he instilled are hopefully evident throughout. Margaret and Bill Crum provided a warm home-away-from-home in Virginia, where Margaret's radiant positivity lifted me up on many occasions. She, too, is not here to see the book, but her glow is with me still. I am tremendously thankful for my sister Ruthie and her family – Marc, Paul, and Alexandra – and our many Vancouver adventures. My children, Esmé, Izzy, and Xander, brilliant new life on the path from dissertation to book, have brought unprecedented love and joy into my world. At long last, Mommy's book is done. Mike Crum, my partner and best friend, endured endless stories about the unrelenting hubris of Canadian expansionists for over a decade. His love and humour kept me strong. This book is dedicated to him.

DOMINION OVER PALM AND PINE

In the interests of the Empire, and especially in view of the early completion of the Panama Canal, it is expedient that there should be full reciprocity of trade, and, if possible, close political union between the Islands of the British West Indies, Newfoundland, and the Dominion of Canada ... Then [we] would have the resources of the British Empire developed, and a dominion over palm and pine.

> William N. Ponton, president of the Associated Boards of Trade of Ontario, resolution presented at the Eighth Congress of the Chambers of Commerce of the British Empire, 11–14 June 1912, London, UK

God of our fathers, known of old,
Lord of our far-flung battle line,
Beneath whose awful hand we hold
Dominion over palm and pine –
Lord God of Hosts, be with us yet,
Lest we forget – lest we forget!

> Rudyard Kipling, "Recessional" (first stanza), 1897

Introduction

IMAGINING A DOMINION
OVER PALM AND PINE

Soon ... we shall become an integral part of a nascent nationality spreading from the Atlantic to the Pacific. But our territorial expansion does not seem likely to stop there ... the still grander scheme of uniting the West Indian Colonies with the Dominion of Canada is beginning to loom up, and it is apparently only a matter of a short time when it will take new shape and form, and become an accomplished fact.

Amor De Cosmos, *Victoria Daily Standard*, 9 March 1871

Amor De Cosmos wrote these words a few months before British Columbia entered Confederation in July 1871. Born William Alexander Smith to a loyalist family in Nova Scotia, De Cosmos settled in Victoria in 1858, soon establishing himself as an eccentric journalist and political reformer. In the years before he was elected British Columbia's second premier in 1872, De Cosmos was instrumental in bringing about the colony's federation with Canada. He imagined the British North American union and the eventual absorption of Britain's Caribbean colonies as steps in a process of territorial expansion and consolidation that would nourish the "British American nationality," advance the cause of nation building, and ultimately enable Canadian independence. With the union of Nova Scotia, New Brunswick, and the Canadas in 1867, the appropriation of Hudson's Bay territory and the old North-Western territory in 1869–70, the imminent absorption of British Columbia, and high hopes for the future inclusion of Prince Edward Island, Newfoundland, and the British Caribbean, Canada was, in De Cosmo's assessment, playing its part in the "grand drama" of global expansionism.[1]

Variations of De Cosmos's vision have captured the imagination of settler Canadians throughout the country's history. Not long after Confederation, Canada's first nationalist organization promoted a political association with the British Caribbean colonies. A proposal 150 years later, in 2016, to "adopt" the Turks and Caicos Islands was among the many resolutions discussed at the New

Democratic Party's (NDP) annual convention in Edmonton.[2] In the intervening years, the idea of Canada absorbing one or more Caribbean territories recurred frequently. In the late nineteenth and early twentieth centuries, it emerged in the expansionist fervour generated by the settler state's push westward, Europe's scramble for territory in Africa, Asia, and the South Pacific, and the seizure of Cuba, Puerto Rico, and the Philippines by the United States in the Spanish-American War. It persisted in the wake of America's expanding presence in the Caribbean during the two world wars and the Cold War. Its proponents advanced union as Canada's imperial and later Commonwealth responsibility in light of Britain's retreat from the western hemisphere and Canada's evolving sovereignty. They saw it as a solution to Cold War anxieties about Caribbean vulnerability to communist infiltration, especially after the collapse of the West Indies Federation in 1962. They believed union would bring Canada commercial self-sufficiency, international prestige, and, in the latter half of the twentieth century, a tourist paradise.

Unionism ebbed and flowed against the backdrop of Canada's long-established and developing ties with the Caribbean. Businesses in Montreal, Toronto, and especially the Maritime cities of Halifax, Yarmouth, and Saint John imported sugar, fruit, coffee, dyewoods, and spices and exported flour, fish, lumber, and a growing number of manufactured products. From the late nineteenth century, several Canadian banks and life insurance and investment companies expanded in the region, including the Bank of Nova Scotia, the Royal Bank of Canada, and the Sun Life Assurance Company. Transportation companies like Canadian National Steamships, Pickford and Black Steamship Company of Halifax, and Montreal's Ocean Dominion Steamship Corporation forged ocean links. Canadian businessmen established railways and utility companies in the Caribbean and Latin America, in the latter specializing in hydroelectricity, tramways, lights, and telecommunications.[3] With an ongoing scarcity of employment opportunities at home, many African Caribbeans migrated to Canada to work as industrial labourers in Sydney, Montreal, and Toronto, porters on the Canadian Pacific Railway, and domestic workers in rural and urban homes across the country. Others came north to attend university, join family already resident in Canada, or enlist in the Canadian military during the two world wars.[4]

After the Second World War, Canadian investment in the British Caribbean swelled. The Aluminum Company of Canada's bauxite enterprises in British Guiana, Jamaica, and Trinidad were Canada's largest investment in the region, exceeding C$300 million by 1967.[5] Canadians invested in the production of several other commodities in the British Caribbean, from shoes and blankets to typewriters and transistor radios.[6] Canada pledged development aid to the region in 1958 and 1966 and was a founding member of the Caribbean Development Bank in 1969.[7] Canada's tourist traffic to the Caribbean increased dramatically from the 1960s, as did Canadian investment in the region's tourist industry.[8] Under Canada's racially restrictive immigration policies, Caribbean migration to Canada was slight in the immediate postwar decades. Between 1955 and 1966, approximately three thousand British Caribbean women arrived in Canada under the federal government's targeted program to recruit domestic workers. Following immigration reforms in 1962, 1967, and 1976, British Caribbean immigrants to Canada, as a proportion of total Canadian immigration, increased dramatically from .69 per cent in the 1950s to 11 per cent in the 1970s.[9]

Dominion over Palm and Pine explores the history of unionism in the broader context of these asymmetrical relationships. This asymmetry was rooted in the divergent yet deeply intertwined colonial histories of Canada and the Caribbean. These colonies were connected nodes in the triangular trade in European manufactures, enslaved Africans, and raw materials from the Americas that produced enormous economic and racial disparities not only between European metropoles and their colonies but among and within the colonies as well. In addition to their participation in African chattel slavery for over two hundred years, European settlers in northern North America built ships to transport abducted Africans to the Americas, invested in Caribbean enterprises that depended on enslaved humans, supplied fish to Caribbean planters to feed their captives, and purchased sugar, rum, and other goods produced on slave plantations.[10]

European occupation, Indigenous dispossession, and the exploitation of land and labour characterized both the Canadian and British Caribbean colonies. But French and British pursuits in northern North America and the Caribbean diverged in significant ways, particularly from the seventeenth century. In the former context, European interest centred on the fur trade and the exploration, missionary work, and settlements that gradually grew up around it. The French and British empires came to see colonization and settlement as a way to claim sovereignty over the land, but settlements grew slowly well into the eighteenth century. In the 150 years after Britain's conquest of New France in 1760, successive waves of migrants arrived from the United States (white, enslaved and free Blacks), Ireland, Britain, and continental Europe. A significant but smaller number of Chinese, Japanese, South Asian,

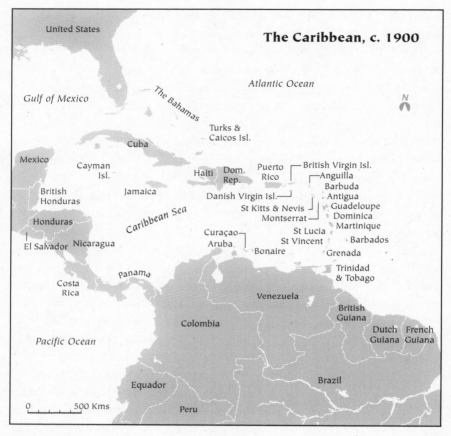

Fig. 0.1   Map of the Caribbean, c. 1900. Copyright Robert Cronan

and African Caribbeans also migrated to Canada, most of them arriving from the mid-nineteenth to the early twentieth century. Canada had become a so-called British settler colony whose substantial European majority expelled Indigenous peoples and appropriated their lands. In 1911, people of British and French descent made up the bulk of the population (54 and 29 per cent, respectively), and 97 per cent of the total population was of European descent. Indigenous peoples comprised roughly 1.5 per cent of the population.[11]

The British Caribbean comprised in the main plantation-based colonies repopulated with enslaved African and indentured South Asian labourers and their descendants. As the most prosperous overseas possessions of Britain and France into the late eighteenth century, the region was a site of intense

European conflict.[12] By the end of the Napoleonic Wars in 1815, Britain's territories in the Caribbean region included the Bahamas and Jamaica; the British Virgin Islands, Anguilla, Barbuda, Antigua, St Kitts, Nevis, Montserrat and Dominica (sometimes grouped as the Leeward Islands); St Lucia, Barbados, St Vincent, Grenada, Trinidad, Tobago (sometimes grouped as the Windward Islands); British Guiana (now Guyana) on the northern coast of South America; and British Honduras (now Belize) in Central America.[13] Colonial officials often grouped Bermuda, a long-time British colony about 650 miles off the coast of North Carolina, with the British Caribbean as well.

Following the emancipation of enslaved peoples in the British Empire in the 1830s, planters and colonial governments struggled to secure enough labour. From 1838 to 1917, more than half a million South Asians and approximately eighteen thousand Chinese migrated to the British Caribbean as indentured labourers, the majority going to British Guiana and Trinidad.[14] With the exception of Bermuda, Barbados, and the Bahamas, the white population (which varied by class and ethnic origin within and across the colonies), rarely exceeded 10 per cent from the eighteenth century. In the census of 1911 Jamaica's Black population comprised 75.8 per cent of the total population, "coloured" 19.6 per cent, and white 1.88 per cent. In British Guiana, the figures for the same year were 42.9 per cent South Asian, 39 per cent Black, 10.2 per cent "mixed," 3.4 per cent Portuguese, 2.3 per cent Amerindian, and 1.3 per cent European.[15] The centuries-old idea that tropical climates were unsuitable for white settlement gained currency from the mid-nineteenth century with the rise of racial determinism.[16] Yet despite their small numbers, whites controlled the region's economic resources.[17]

While settler Canadians gradually established the institutions, infrastructures, and industries necessary to develop sustainable societies with increasing populations, the British Caribbean colonies were purposely underdeveloped in the colonial period. The singular objective of the plantation economy was to generate wealth for the metropole.[18] These distinct economic priorities and the racial constructs that European colonizers contrived to sustain them engendered different constitutional trajectories. In the late 1830s, for example, crises of governance arose in both the Canadas and post-emancipation Jamaica. In the Canadas, the Colonial Office conceded democratic reforms that eventually culminated in responsible government, but denied parallel concessions in Jamaica. While the ethnic makeup of the island's Legislative Assembly transformed in the 1840s and '50s with the election of more Jews and Black Jamaicans, British policy-makers deemed

Jamaica "unfit" for responsible government. They believed the island's racial composition necessitated a system of "benevolent guardianship." The "iconography of dependency," writes historian Thomas Holt, "formerly applicable to individual slaves, came to characterize whole societies." The ethnic division in the Canadas – between French and English Canadians – aroused concern at Whitehall, but it was understood as a protean division. French Canadians were white; they could be assimilated into British culture. The imperial government rendered blackness, on the other hand, an immutable obstacle to constitutional progress.[19] Racial determinism and violent colonial rebellions in India (1857) and Jamaica (1865) hardened notions of racial difference in the empire and generated an enduring impulse to differentiate colonies along racial lines.[20] As the imperial government assisted the British North American colonies in drafting the terms of an autonomous federation in 1866, it reinstated direct rule in Jamaica, thereby circumscribing the island's autonomy. The British Caribbean colonies would not achieve political independence for almost a century after Canada, commencing with Jamaica and Trinidad and Tobago in 1962.

In the midst of this emergent racial divide in the nineteenth century and its enduring salience well into the twentieth, English-speaking Canadians and especially those of British descent defined their national becoming, their evolution in the British Empire-Commonwealth, in relation to the empire's non-white dependencies. They assessed a colony's capacity for self-government in racial terms, often interpreting their own country's constitutional development as a product of "Anglo-Saxon" ingenuity.[21] White Britons at home and abroad insisted upon dominion status for Canada, Australia, New Zealand, and Newfoundland in 1907, excluded non-white colonies from imperial conferences until the First World War, and restructured the Colonial Office in 1925 to hierarchically differentiate countries of white settlement from non-white dependencies.[22] Canada rejected imperial citizenship schemes and enacted racially discriminatory immigration policies to maintain (the myth of) white homogeneity for nearly a century after Confederation. As the old Commonwealth of white dominions gave way to an expanded, racially diverse Commonwealth after the Second World War, and many British Caribbean colonies moved toward independence, white settler Canadians adopted new strategies to maintain the international order's racial status quo.

Dominion over Palm and Pine is a transnational history concerned first and foremost with what unionism reveals about Canada as a project of rule within and beyond the country's borders.[23] For a great many settler Canadians,

the Caribbean was central to Canada's future. I argue that the history of
unionism complicates our understanding of three familiar phenomena in
settler Canadian history: expansionism and its entangled history with nation
building, the struggle for sovereignty, and Canada's evolving status on the
world stage. Narratives of Canadian expansion typically commence with
the appropriation of the Hudson's Bay territory in 1869–70, the annexation
of British Columbia in 1871, Prince Edward Island two years later, and the
Arctic territory in 1880, and protracted efforts to bring Newfoundland into
the union, eventually realized in 1949. It is usually taken for granted that
this Atlantic-to-Pacific-to-Arctic mandate defined the geographical limits of
settler Canadians' territorial aspirations.[24] The history of Canadian designs on
the Caribbean tells a different story. Unionists were convinced, particularly
in the period before the Second World War, that the country's continued
development hinged on the acquisition of tropical territory. Canada, temperate
and frigid, was territorially incomplete. The country had no Florida, Louisiana,
or California, nor a Hawaii, Philippines, Cuba, or Puerto Rico. The US
example purportedly demonstrated that the thriving commerce necessary for
national growth followed lines of longitude, not of latitude. Trade agreements
could address this imbalance somewhat, but they were subject to change by
future governments and left Canada and especially the British Caribbean
vulnerable to demands for trade concessions and possible retaliation from
the United States.

Drawing insights from postcolonial studies, I suggest that settler Canadians
defined their sovereignty and international role through the colonial encounter
and especially the racial and cultural distinctions it generated.[25] Claiming
this sovereignty hinged on an aggressive assertion of white supremacy and a
virulent denial of Indigenous sovereignty. Canadians with territorial aspirations in the Caribbean framed their claims – like settler claims to Indigenous
lands within Canadian borders – as a racial prerogative. Administering and
"developing" the region would simultaneously augment Canada's autonomy
and international profile and disavow Caribbean autonomy. Unionists drew
from a repertoire of racial concepts and assumptions to stake their claims, from
imperial geographies to racial liberalism. Delineating more than geographical
coordinates and their agricultural possibilities, "tropical" and "temperate"
regions were, in Ikuko Asaka's words, "historically specific geographies that
structured particular designs of conquest, settlement, and exploitation."[26] From
the advent of European colonialism in the Americas, the contrast between
untapped tropical abundance and the supposed indolence of "tropical races"

was "routinely used to serve a colonial purpose."[27] Unionists mobilized these racial geographies to justify their designs on the Caribbean and devise union arrangements that would restrict African Caribbeans' freedom of movement and their political rights. Racial liberalism provided further rationale to circumscribe these rights. Under union, the Caribbean colonies would be subject to what Uday Mehta has called the "not yet" phenomenon – not yet ready for greater autonomy and certainly not self-government. Acquisition of these responsibilities was "conditional on following a specific trajectory of development."[28] Until that time, Canadian unionists argued, African Caribbeans had no business involving themselves in the political life of the proposed union.

This racial impulse adapted to the shifting international context after 1945. As anti-colonial movements proliferated and Britain's Caribbean colonies won democratic reforms, approached independence, and joined the Commonwealth – theoretically on the basis of equality – the exclusionary rhetoric of racial liberalism was no longer appropriate.[29] Whiteness as a "global imperial identity" lost its salience in the capitalist West, at least explicitly. Canada's emerging human rights culture and efforts to cultivate the country's international image as a progressive, egalitarian society compelled unionists to de-emphasize race. In doing so, their efforts mirrored a central impulse within liberal internationalism to ignore rather than confront racism. This colour-blindness, argues Daniel Gorman, "buried lingering racial division within Canada" and allowed liberal internationalists to "shape Canada's self-image as a postracial state." Despite this posturing, an implicit whiteness continued to inform Canada's domestic and international policies.[30] Liberal internationalism did not, Barrington Walker reminds us, emerge in an interwar vacuum, but rather derived from the racially exclusive liberal project that ordered Canadian society from at least 1867.[31] The pursuit of global justice after 1945 was no longer tied to an imperial civilizing ethos, but it was not easily disentangled from this ethos. The paternalistic assumption that capitalism, democracy, and other Western values should be imported to the global South persisted.[32]

As the first substantive study of Canadian efforts to acquire territory in the Caribbean, *Dominion over Palm and Pine* contributes, on the one hand, to the growing body of studies that explore Canada's entanglements with the Third World.[33] Moving beyond the long-standing North Atlantic perspective of international relations history, these studies have traced a broad range of transnational relationships by way of missionaries, non-governmental organizations, and social movements, banking and mining corporations, state and cultural diplomacies, migration, and military intervention, often prioritizing Third

World perspectives.[34] The book takes a multi-perspective approach, conceiving the brokers of Canada's imperial and international histories widely and taking seriously Caribbean peoples' vital roles in the fate of union campaigns.[35] On the other hand, while the book moves beyond a North Atlantic framework, it remains sensitive to the abiding import of Britain and the United States. Indeed, I argue that unionism was a means to navigate Canada's place in the British-Empire Commonwealth and the growing preponderance of US power.

For good reason, Britain and the United States loom large in narratives of Canada's path from colony to nation to international actor. From the federation of 1867 to the 1931 Statute of Westminster that established Canada's autonomy in foreign affairs, and from Canada's involvement in military conflicts abroad (most notably the two world wars) to its role in the postwar Commonwealth, Canada's autonomy and activities in the world were a function of the country's evolving relationship with Britain. At the same time, boundary disputes, the threat of annexation to the United States, and the spectre of American economic and cultural domination on the continent posed ongoing challenges to the Canadian nation-state, often prompting a defensive response to protect Canadian sovereignty. In historical writing, these phenomena rarely intersect with the history of Canada-Caribbean relations. I suggest these histories were deeply entwined. A formal role for Canada in the Caribbean, unionists argued, would strengthen the empire by way of consolidation, allow Canada to take up a greater share of imperial responsibilities in the Caribbean in the wake of Britain's ongoing retreat, check American influence in the hemisphere, and – in the process – boost Canada's autonomy and stature in the Empire-Commonwealth and the world.

Of course, unionism never succeeded. The book gives considerable attention to the idea's ongoing popularity but also accounts for its failure. Over the course of the book, I highlight three broad categories of opposition to the various schemes. First, in Canada, though the idea was never completely marginal, it never acquired the political force to make it a priority for government. Prime ministers, members of Parliament, business leaders, and others talked a lot about the possibility, but real progress on the idea hit many barriers, from public apathy to explicit resistance, particularly among Black Canadians engaged in their own struggles against domestic racism. Second, in Britain, politicians and colonial officials often promoted the idea, but in other moments they worried that union would undermine British interests. Finally, and in many cases most importantly, while African Caribbeans entertained union from time to time – usually for commercial reasons – they were more often sceptical or decidedly opposed. Their unwillingness to embrace union was based on a variety of concerns over time, including economic arguments, opposition to Canadian racism, and political-aspirational desires for self-determination. Indeed, I argue that African-Caribbean opposition was instrumental in union's perennial failure.

Before proceeding, I should note the complicated nature of three key terms. First, in the nineteenth and twentieth centuries, white settler Canadians frequently used the words "tropics" and "tropical" to designate a geographical space falling between the Tropics of Cancer and Capricorn. It can be difficult to disentangle this literal usage from discursive representations in the historical sources. For this reason, I have decided not to place "tropical"/"tropics" between quotation marks in the text. While I explicitly address the discursive salience of the tropics (and its contrast, temperate) at various points in the book, it should be read throughout with the constructed and historically protean meanings of these terms in mind. Second, I refer to people of African descent in the British Caribbean as Black or African Caribbean(s), and their counterparts in Canada and the US as Black or African Canadians/Americans, using the terms "West Indian" and "West Indies" only when quoting historical sources or referencing historical agreements, institutions, or other bodies (e.g., West Indies Federation, West India Committee). Finally, I use the word "union" to designate the idea of a formalized political or constitutional relationship between Canada and all or parts of the British Caribbean. Many proponents of union, whom I call "unionists," used the term, though their understandings of its meaning changed over time. Sometimes it was used to refer to a customs union only; I employ the phrase "customs union" to differentiate these cases from the broader constitutional and commercial relationship most union-ists envisioned. A variety of terms were used alongside or instead of union (e.g., annexation, expansion, federation, association), which provide insight into the arrangement anticipated and are analyzed accordingly.

Dominion over Palm and Pine is structured chronologically and spans the late 1860s to the 1970s. Chapter 1 explores two consecutive campaigns for union in the decades immediately following Confederation. The union idea first emerged in 1869 in an Ontario-centred nationalist movement, styled Canada First. It was later taken up by a small group of Canadian expan-sionists in the 1880s. In both instances, unionists were invested ideologically and practically in the Canadian state's push into the Northwest, and they envisioned their designs on the British Caribbean as part of the same process. The expansionist project in the Northwest – building a railroad, dispossessing

Indigenous peoples, and repopulating the region with white settlers – was an enormous undertaking that would take many years to complete. Annexing the British Caribbean, on the other hand, a cluster of colonies already primed by Britain for production and consumption, would bring economic returns much sooner. But absorbing colonies with predominantly Black populations was at fundamental odds with the settler state's racial agenda.

Chapter 2 examines unionism's return at the turn of the twentieth century. Canada's extraordinary economic and population growth after 1896 restored settler confidence in the Northwest and generated lofty speculation about Canada's future. Proposals to expand Canada's borders to the Caribbean were not anomalous; they cohered with the settler bombast so ubiquitous in the early twentieth century. They circulated alongside projections of Canada's population reaching one hundred million by the century's end, claims that Canada's economic trajectory was more promising than that of the United States in the nineteenth century, and arguments about Canada's apparent superiority to the US and Britain. Canada might eventually take the reins of empire and reach an apex of power unheard of in modern times. I contextualize the union debates in the heady settler optimism of the period to foreground the entangled and constitutive histories of imperial aggrandizement and settler nation building.

Chapters 3 and 4 move through the First World War and the interwar period, respectively. I consider unionism's re-emergence in relation to the different yet interrelated struggles for autonomy in Canada and the British Caribbean. In both contexts, the war was crucial to these struggles. Canadians and British Caribbeans alike made tremendous contributions to the war effort, and they did so with the expectation of increased political autonomy and respect after the war. At the Imperial War Conference in 1917, Canadian prime minister Robert Borden drafted a resolution calling for greater autonomy after the war. The resolution was reaffirmed in the Balfour Report in 1926 and given constitutional weight with the Statute of Westminster in 1931. In the British Caribbean, the war had a markedly different impact. Black Caribbean servicemen faced considerable racial discrimination during the war, and their service went unrewarded. Neither respect nor constitutional concessions were forthcoming. These divergent experiences engendered oppositional responses to union in Canada and the Caribbean.

Chapter 4 examines the persistence of the union dream in the interwar decades. While the principle of self-determination and the language of equality and greater autonomy for *all* of Britain's imperial subjects gained considerable traction after the war, white racial entitlement and paternalism prevailed. Unionists continued to frame Canada's evolution in the empire and the world in relation to the stagnancy and non-evolution that ostensibly marked British Caribbean societies. While Canadian independence was not constitutionally entrenched until 1931, many Canadians of British descent emerged from the war with a new sense of sovereignty and being in the world. Unionists believed that this new status came with responsibilities. Canada was now a bona fide partner in the work of empire and should take on a greater role in developing the "dependent empire" and the British Caribbean especially. Ever anxious about US expansion in the Caribbean, unionists leveraged Canada's enhanced status to legitimize their claims.

Chapter 5 explores unionism from 1945 to the Canada-Caribbean conference in 1966. The idea had waned during the Depression and the Second World War, but it returned in the context of an expanding Commonwealth, the failed West Indies Federation (1958–62), and the Cold War. The Second World War expedited decolonization and transformed the old Commonwealth of "white men's countries" into a multiethnic one based on egalitarian principles. Canadians valued the practical aspects of an expanded Commonwealth. It provided a forum to discuss issues of international concern, counter communism, and facilitate commercial, scientific, and educational exchanges. White Canadians were less willing to embrace the principle of equality on which it was based. They held fast to the racial demarcation of empire that had structured imperial relations since the nineteenth century, thus sustaining the ideological groundwork for unionism to endure. This racial ontology and the continued preponderance of white supremacy within Canadian borders were inimical to the increasingly assertive demands for self-determination in the British Caribbean.

As Canada's ties to Britain dwindled in the 1960s, the union idea loomed up as a means to temper American power. This is the subject of chapter 6. Heightened anxieties about America's growing influence in Canada – cultural, military, and especially economic – and Canadian disgust with America's destruction in Vietnam and racial strife at home inspired a new, nationalist brand of unionism. Proponents continued to operate under the assumption that the economic and political challenges plaguing Caribbean societies required white intervention. They framed union as a benevolent proposition that would rescue Caribbean peoples from their stagnant economies and dismal living conditions, while ignoring the central role of colonialism and white supremacy in producing these circumstances. Union, they claimed, was not a self-interested gesture but rather a noble one that would enhance Canada's profile on the world stage. It was, however, wildly out of touch with British Caribbean sentiment and aspirations. Under the swell of anti-colonial, anti-racist activism in Canada and the Caribbean – bolstered by a rapidly expanding Caribbean population in Canada – the union idea floundered. In calling white Canadians to account for not only the obtuse pursuit of union but also Canada's historical and continuing complicity in colonialism, and the hypocrisy of Canada's moral posturing overseas and the rampant racism within the country's borders, African Caribbeans and Black Canadians once again exposed the facade of Canadian egalitarianism. Canada's do-gooder image was a white construct that did not hold up under Black scrutiny. Despite genuine antipathy toward racial thinking and a commitment to equality among many white Canadians, a deep-seated paternalism and an obstinate empire apologism endured.

While the book traverses a broad range of analytic terrain – political, diplomatic, social, economic, military, migration, labour – it is particularly concerned with union as a transnational cultural and racial phenomenon. I am interested in how union, as an idea, captured the imagination of its proponents across time and space, why it persisted for so long, and the circumstances that obstructed its realization again and again. Canadian unionists were part of a global community of self-styled white men's countries that emerged in the context of nineteenth-century imperialisms, a fear of global (non-white) migration, and the threat of democratic equality.[36] They mobilized the same racial hierarchies, binaries, and pretensions that abetted European and American imperialisms. Their plans for union and, by extension, Canada, were informed by the spectre of racial conflict elsewhere, especially in the United States. And the discussion generated about the racial implications of union, like the discussion of union itself, was transnational in scope. In circulating from Montreal to London to Demerara, and from Halifax to Port of Spain to Manchester, the union idea – and the racialized thinking that framed its terms – were challenged and remade.

"POSSESSING A GREAT SOUTH
AS WELL AS A GREAT WEST,"
1869–1885

On the evening of 3 March 1871, members of Halifax's Young Men's Early Closing Association filed into Temperance Hall to hear fellow Nova Scotian Robert Grant Haliburton deliver a lecture on the "Young Men of the New Dominion." A lawyer, prolific author, and amateur anthropologist, Haliburton told his audience that every man in Canada was duty bound to take up the important work of "building a great power within the Dominion." He then outlined what he saw as the principal means for attaining this mission. The development of the expansive Northwest, recently purchased from the Hudson's Bay Company, was central, but it would be some years before the region was sufficiently populated to support a thriving east-west trade. In the interim, he argued, Canada should pursue two sources of "immediate national wealth." One was digging the Baie Verte canal across the Isthmus of Chignecto, connecting the St Lawrence directly to the Bay of Fundy. The other was Canada's annexation of Britain's Caribbean colonies.[1] The aggregate imports and exports of these colonies in 1868 were almost precisely the same as those of Canada, meaning an "enormous trade of millions of dollars could be secured without cost, and in almost a few months by such a union." For Haliburton, who made this argument often, absorbing the British Caribbean was no less reasonable than incorporating the Northwest. "You can reach those Islands via New York from Ottawa in one sixth of the time that it takes to go to British Columbia; in a third of the time that a journey to Red River occupies; and even in a shorter time than is required for a visit to Newfoundland," he had stated in an earlier address. "The ocean and the St. Lawrence, are the highways nature has given us."[2]

For settler Canadians, visions of commercial, geographic, and political expansion as key nation-building processes are generally coterminous with Canada's modern borders.[3] Yet these borders and, more specifically, their contiguity, were not a foregone conclusion in the decades following

Confederation. When Canada incorporated Prince Edward Island in 1873, it had, with the exception of Newfoundland, fulfilled the expansionist provisions specified in section 146 of the British North America Act (BNA). These provisions reflected the territorial (though not uncontested) priorities of the statesmen who negotiated the terms of Confederation in 1866–67. They subsequently circumscribed the geographical parameters in which historians interpreted Canada's making. To be sure, the dream of nation stretching *a mari usque ad mare* was the dominant expansionist narrative in the rhetorical repertoire of late nineteenth-century nation building, but it was not the only one. The BNA guided but did not limit the possibilities of Canada's geographical boundaries.

A broader, more dynamic understanding of settler expansionism in the post-Confederation decades is in order. Federations, confederations, and nation-states, historians Frederick Cooper and Jane Burbank remind us, "have no defendable claim to be 'natural' units of political affinity or action." They could emerge and disappear, expand and retract, transform into empires or be absorbed by them.[4] Canada's federal structure, geographical boundaries, and even existence were "far from inevitable, but rather the product of immediate events and often short-term thinking in the Confederation era."[5] To accept uncritically that Canada reached its "natural" limits when it extended its sovereignty from the Atlantic to the Pacific (and later the Arctic) is especially problematic because it denies – or naturalizes – the state-sanctioned violence inflicted on Indigenous peoples to create these borders.[6] The sea-to-sea mandate also perpetuates a teleological narrative of national creation that obscures the mutability of political formations. It renders invisible the more geographically expansive vision of someone like Haliburton. In fact, a range of political configurations was contemplated in the post-Confederation decades. A self-governing Canada stretching from the Atlantic to the Pacific to the Arctic, content to evolve gradually within the empire, was the leading configuration. Others envisioned Canada's continental consolidation as the first step in a wider imperial federation.[7] Some saw annexation to the United States as the preferred outcome, often in pursuit of a broader agenda to unite "the Anglo-Saxon peoples."[8] Others, like Haliburton, identified union with the British Caribbean colonies as a crucial step in Canada's development and a means to consolidate the empire.

The proposed expansion southward to the Caribbean and the Canadian state's push westward were entangled priorities. The chapter begins by unpacking the dynamics of this entanglement in 1869–76 and in 1882–85. In the first instance, the union idea surfaced in an Ontario-centred collective of Canadian nationalists just as the Canadian state assumed sovereignty over the Northwest. Their commitment to union was patchy, lacked verve, and clashed with the Anglo-Saxon "nationality" at the centre of their movement. A small group of Canadian expansionists revived the cause in 1882, training their efforts on Jamaica. The idea gained limited traction in Canada, Jamaica, and Britain before taking a long hiatus in 1885. While it did not generate significant government or public support, union was not dismissed outright. It was discussed in the press, debated by intellectuals, and politely considered in Ottawa, Kingston, and London. By the mid-1880s, however, it was roundly derided. Manifold domestic problems, the stalled progress in the Northwest especially, made union with Jamaica an absurd proposition. Unionists also struggled with the question of how to incorporate Black Caribbean subjects in the federation while simultaneously denying their access to the franchise. Shifting ideas about race and racial governance in Canada and the wider British Empire tempered white settler responses to this question. Throughout this discussion, the chapter also considers the imperial and Jamaican contexts of the debate.

Canada First and the Racialized Mythology of the "New Nationality"

Haliburton was invested in Canada's development. In the 1850s and '60s, he was involved in several initiatives to further Nova Scotia's agricultural and industrial development. He advocated the province's inclusion in the federation of 1867 and, while in Ottawa in the late 1860s to promote Cape Breton's coal mining interests, he met a small group of like-minded intellectuals who were similarly concerned about Canada's future.[9] They included lawyer William Alexander Foster, poet Charles Mair, military officer and lawyer George Taylor Denison, and civil servant Henry James Morgan, all of Ontario. Seeing Confederation as a political transaction among elites, they founded the country's first nationalist organization, Canada First, to generate a broader sense of non-partisan national purpose and inspire a "Canadian nationality." The Northwest was crucial to these plans. In their racialized thinking, it was the manifest destiny of the "Anglo-Saxon race" to possess and develop the region. The Northwest was the key to Canada's future and a national cause around which (white) Canadians could rally. Their "new nationality" fused British values with distinct characteristics born of Canada's northern geography and an intransigent Anglo-Saxon nationalism.[10]

Haliburton embarked on a "New Nationality" lecture tour that took him to various cities in Ontario, the Maritimes and, late in 1869, to the Leeward Islands in the Caribbean. While in Antigua, he discussed the union idea with politicians and commercial interests from the islands. He thought the time was opportune for such a union because Colonial Office initiatives to encourage Caribbean federations – with a view to greater economic and administrative efficiency – were already underway. In 1869 the colonial secretary commissioned Antiguan governor Benjamin Pine to federate the Leeward islands – St Christopher (St Kitts), Antigua, Nevis, Dominica, Montserrat and the Virgin Islands – into a single colony with one governor and one council. Haliburton met with Pine and several leaders of the islands, who were taken with Haliburton's proposal for union with Canada. When Pine submitted his federation scheme to the imperial government in June 1870, he delivered a speech in which he romanticized a future for the Leeward Islands within a broader federation of British territory in the Americas. The proposed Leeward Islands federation "contains within itself the germ of progress and expansion" that might before long embrace "neighbouring colonies of the crown into its fold … those islands of eternal summer, but also regions whose inhabitants are refreshed and invigorated by the winter's cold."[11] The same month, St Christopher's president Alex Moir made a similar speech. Leeward Islanders should "grasp the friendly hand of the Dominion" and forge a "political and mercantile union" without delay.[12]

Haliburton had little affiliation with Canada First after he moved to England in 1871, but he continued to push the union idea. He purchased London's *St. James Magazine* and published in it articles on imperial unity and other empire-related subjects. His interest in imperial unity – which he understood as a commercial and racial (i.e., Anglo-Saxon) project rather than a political one – informed his thinking about Canada's relationship with the Caribbean. But his central concern, as it was for the next generation of imperialists at the turn of the century, was Canada's future. Independence was not something Haliburton desired nor anticipated in the near future, not least because the threat of American annexation lingered. At the same time, he was critical of British policy. He and his Canada First colleagues were particularly disturbed by the Washington Treaty of 1871, in which Britain conceded fishing rights and access to the St Lawrence River to the United States but failed to obtain analogous concessions from the US government for Canada (most notably, compensation for the Fenian raids).[13] The treaty demonstrated that Britain could not be trusted to look after Canadian interests. Haliburton thus eschewed an imperial federation that centred power in London, preferring instead some form of future imperial association or "alliance of nations" in which Canada had a voice in its own external affairs.[14]

The union proposal re-emerged a few years later in the platform of the Canadian National Association, a Toronto-based political party that grew out of Canada First. Between 1871 and 1873, Canada First's membership changed dramatically; all the founding members had moved on except William Foster. The most notable new member was Goldwin Smith, the English-born history professor who would go on to advocate Canada's annexation to the United States. In 1874, the group founded the Canadian National Association (CNA), as well as a political club on Toronto's Bay Street called the National Club, and a weekly journal, the *Nation*. They also drafted and released to the public the CNA's platform. Lingering dissatisfaction with the Treaty of Washington and a desire to secure, at some future date, Canadian representation in London, gave rise to the first plank – "British Connection, Consolidation of the Empire, and in the meantime a voice in treaties affecting Canada." The second plank called for closer trade relations with the British Caribbean "with a view to ultimate political connection."[15] Haliburton's earlier promotion of union probably resonated with Foster, who played a leading role in drafting the platform.[16] The CNA inspired the formation of a Maritime National Club in New Brunswick in 1874, whose platform similarly identified a "political connection" between Canada and the British Caribbean as one of its objectives.

The thinking behind the CNA's decision to include union with the Caribbean colonies in its platform is difficult to discern. Historians of Canada First have failed to make sense of its inclusion, probably because the archival records of the movement's central members provide little insight. To some extent, they probably envisioned this political connection as part of the larger project of imperial unity. Britain's disengagement from North America in the years 1867–71, its declining industrial power relative to Germany and the United States from the early 1870s, and growing unrest in the colonies aroused anxiety about imperial disintegration. Consolidating British territory in the Americas would presumably help ease this anxiety. To be sure, Canada Firsters valued the imperial connection: the British Empire's strength was Canada's strength, and vice versa. But they were also laying the intellectual and nationalist foundations for what they understood as Canada's ultimate rise to greatness. Their fashioning of a new nationality based on Canadian superiority foretold a future in which the empire's centre might shift from London to Ottawa.[17]

Beyond the national or imperial impulses that prompted it, Canada Firsters' interest in union was difficult to reconcile with the racially exclusive nationality they promoted. When Canada annexed the Northwest in 1870, the population was approximately 73,000. The large majority were Indigenous. Canada's annexation of the British Caribbean colonies would have brought roughly 1,238,000 new subjects under Canadian jurisdiction, the large majority of African and African-European descent.[18] The white populations in both the Northwest and the Caribbean comprised tiny minorities. These demographic realities challenged Canadian expansionism, though in different ways. Indigenous and African-descended subjects occupied different positions in New World "regimes of difference." The relationship between Europeans and Indigenous peoples centred on land, but colonizers typically imagined Black people in terms of labour.[19] White settlers would move westward, pushing Indigenous peoples to the margins of society or eliminating them through dispossession and disease. African-Caribbean peoples, on the other hand, would not be displaced. Their labour would be required in the new union. But Canada Firsters' racialized views of African-descended peoples suggested a paternal approach that was predicated on circumscribing Caribbean involvement in governing the new union.

When Haliburton returned to Canada from his lecture tour in the Leeward Islands in early 1870, hostilities were escalating in the Red River colony in the wake of Métis resistance to the impending transfer of Rupert's Land to Canada. While the Métis mobilized and formed a provisional government to negotiate with Ottawa, Canada First's propaganda campaign to popularize the idea of the Northwest in Ontario shifted to an aggressive defence of white, Anglo-Protestant dominion. Beyond the lectern and the press, they conspired in various ways to establish Anglo-Protestant dominance at Red River. They pressured the federal government to swiftly despatch an expeditionary force to secure control of the colony, founded the Northwest Emigration Society to grow the Anglo-Protestant settler community, and, following the creation of Manitoba in July 1870, tried (unsuccessfully) to secure Haliburton a judgeship at Red River to offset the influence of French judges.[20] Haliburton was outraged by what he understood as Métis defiance of Canadian authority, even though the land transfer was not official until 15 July 1870. He interpreted the confrontation – and the federal government's French language concessions in the Manitoba Act – as a serious but not insurmountable threat to Canada's future. A vast territory had been acquired,

and British settlers would soon flood the Northwest, diluting the French and
Métis populations into political insignificance.[21]

When Haliburton advanced the union idea during his lecture tour in
1870–71, he did not elaborate on the constitutional arrangement he envis-
aged. Aside from his contention that there were "no future communities to be
created" in the Caribbean as there were in the Northwest, he scarcely mentioned
Caribbean peoples. His efforts to formulate a racialized nationality for Canada,
premised on the idea of northern superiority, suggests that he anticipated
Canada taking on a paternal role in the Caribbean. In his lecture and his widely
circulated pamphlet *The Men of the North and Their Place in History*, Haliburton
argued that climate was a determinant of racial character and capabilities: "As
long as the north wind blows, and the snow and the sleet drive over our forests
and fields, we must be a hardy, a healthy, a virtuous, a daring, and if we are
worthy of our ancestors, a dominant race."[22] If climate had not "the effect of
moulding races," he reasoned, "how is it that southern nations have almost
invariably been inferior to and subjugated by the men of the north?"[23]

In a contradiction typical of colonial discourses, these climatic and
geographic constructs circulated alongside the conviction that northerners
in ill health should relocate to tropical or semi-tropical climes to convalesce.
Haliburton spent extended periods in Jamaica in the 1880s for this very reason.
His preconceptions of the island prior to his first visit in 1881, which he later
outlined in "The Black and Brown Landholders of Jamaica," are consistent
with the racialized geography he outlined in *The Men of the North*:

> I was, in common with most persons who judge of the island from
> a distance, somewhat prejudiced against the black and brown people
> of that colony. I had been led to believe that they were fast-relapsing
> into savages, and could not safely have a voice in their own affairs; that
> firm, paternal sway was the only practical way of ruling them; that,
> in consequence of their being able to acquire little holdings, either by
> purchase or by squatting, their tendency was to abjure work, raise a few
> yams and chickens, and steadily relapse into the state of listless African
> barbarism from which their ancestors were torn by slave-hunters; and
> that, whatever wages could be offered, they could not be induced to
> work on the sugar plantations – a field of labour which, therefore, must
> be abandoned, or entrusted to imported coolies; in short, that labour
> was despised and abhorred by the blacks, as a survival of the horrors
> of slavery.[24]

Haliburton's thinking about Jamaicans – an aversion to work and propensity for violence in particular – was no doubt informed by the peasant uprising at Morant Bay in October 1865 and its violent suppression by colonial authorities, which attracted empire-wide attention. But his thinking changed considerably after spending some time on the island. He was pleased to find that the people were "peaceful and law-abiding," willing to work for "a very scanty amount of wages," and that they had benefited from being small landowners, and were "in a singularly advanced state," considering their limited opportunities and the "evil influences and habits of former servitude." He nonetheless believed a paternal approach was still advisable, especially in dealing with the colony's Black labourers, who were "like children," requiring constant guidance.[25] Given his racialized worldview, Haliburton likely considered the Caribbean "communities" he referenced in his union advocacy as ones of consumption and production rather than citizenship.

Canada Firsters, like many white Canadians, identified the racial conflict in the United States as an example to be avoided. Containing Canada's Black population, chiefly by discouraging Black immigration, was seen as the best way to do so. Canada First's lifespan corresponded with a period of intense racial animosity in the United States. It emerged three years after the Civil War (1861–65) and dissolved near the end of Reconstruction (1865–77). While most British North Americans condemned American slavery before its abolition in 1865, their racialized worldviews remained largely intact. Canada Firster George T. Denison was a case in point. He not only sympathized with the secessionist South during the Civil War but also abetted the Confederate cause. He provided sanctuary for Confederate agents, exiles, and other sympathizers at his home in west Toronto and assisted efforts to purchase a steamer for Confederate use as a raider on the Great Lakes. After the war, he later entertained southern general Robert E. Lee and Confederacy president Jefferson Davis when they visited Toronto.[26] But his support for the South did not imply an anti-abolitionist stance. Denison had in fact railed against the evils of slavery in his 1860 review of the extradition case of John Anderson, an enslaved person who killed a Missouri farmer during the course of his escape to Canada West.[27] At the same time, Denison's critique of slavery was a far cry from a belief in racial equality. In 1877, he became a Toronto police magistrate and routinely discriminated against Black defendants.[28]

Canada First feared racial parity. The *Canadian Monthly and National Review*, a publication funded, owned, and operated by Canada Firsters, frequently warned of the perils of extending rights to non-white people.[29]

Enfranchising Black men, the *Monthly* claimed in November 1876, was dangerous. Blacks were "sensual, ignorant [and] passionate" and thus easily beguiled
by unprincipled politicians and interest groups.[30] Just before the American
Civil Rights Bill became law in 1875, the *Monthly* predicted its disastrous
consequences. To pass a bill "in nature's despite," compelling "the two races
to mingle in public conveyances and places of public resort," would be "to
sound the tocsin of a chronic civil war."[31]

Two of the leading members of Canada First in its later years, William
Foster and Goldwin Smith, offered similar warnings about the dangers of
granting Blacks political power. Foster cautioned readers of the Canadian
National Association's *Nation* about the base social condition and immorality
of Blacks,[32] while Smith, writing a few years after Canada First dissolved,
emphasized their intellectual limitations: "There are those who fancy that
education will turn the Negro white; but generations, probably, must lapse
before his low intellect can be brought up to the Anglo-American level. If
supreme power were in his hands, he would make the South a Hayti [*sic*]."
Citing the Black population's higher rate of growth in the US South compared
to the white population, Smith lamented the fierce "struggle for political
ascendancy" that whites would have to wage. He thought whites would
prevail, as long as they maintained strength in numbers.[33] Smith's warnings
were curious not only for his membership in an organization that advanced
union with the British Caribbean but also for his later promotion of Canada's
annexation to the United States.

The coexistence of Smith's anti-slavery and anti-Black sentiments were not
especially peculiar. Canada's history of abolition provided British Canadians
with the moral foundation to distance Canada from the taint of slavery and
rationalize their commitment to a white Canada. Upper Canada introduced
legislation for the gradual abolition of slavery in 1793, and the British government emancipated the empire's enslaved peoples in 1834. While people of
African descent had resided since the early seventeenth century in the colonies
that became Canada, the Black population increased at the conclusion of the
American Revolutionary War, as thousands of free Black loyalists (3,500) and
those enslaved by white loyalists (2,000) migrated to the Maritimes, Upper
Canada (Ontario), and Lower Canada (Quebec). During the War of 1812,
thousands of enslaved people in the United States escaped and joined the
British army, later settling in Canada. Identifying the British as "champions of
black freedom and equality" – a reputation formed during the Revolutionary
War – Black fugitives were eager to join their loyalist predecessors. The Black

population increased further in the thirty years between British emancipation in the 1830s and the American Civil War. Somewhere between thirty thousand and forty thousand Blacks (enslaved and free) migrated to British North America. The majority migrated back to the United States during and after Reconstruction, along with thousands of African Canadians. In the 1881 census, the total number of "negro" residents in Canada had dwindled to 21,394. Despite this exodus, Canada's earlier history of abolition and its space as a preferred destination for Black loyalists and a safe haven for Black fugitives nonetheless formed the basis of an enduring narrative about Canada's moral superiority to the United States.[34] The spectre of racial conflict in the republic reinforced this narrative and evinced the necessity of maintaining Canada's (mythic) whiteness.

Canada First's new nationality was based on a spurious racial logic, a mythology at fundamental odds with union and the heterogeneity of Canadian society. Of course, the union musings of the 1870s were faint and ultimately inconsequential for reasons other than the specious presumptions of the new nationality. They faded into obscurity in 1876, along with Canada First and the *Nation*. The movement failed to gain traction as a political party. It suffered from internal divisions, changes in leadership, inconsistent membership, and, as an Ontario-centred movement, a lack of national appeal. At the same time, the onset of economic depression – which saw its worst years from 1873 to 1878 – stalled the agenda central to Canada's First's national vision, the colonization project in the Northwest.[35] The union idea circulated among a small group of mostly Toronto-based Anglo-Saxon nationalists in the 1870s, with isolated whispers of interest in the Maritimes, British Columbia, and the Leeward Islands. And while it appeared in the CNA platform, there is little evidence to suggest it captured the imagination of Canada Firsters as a whole. It nonetheless reflected one of the many efforts to negotiate the terms on which Canada – as a formation both national and imperial – would take shape in the decade following Confederation.

Global Expansionism in the 1880s

If Robert Haliburton was the apostle of Canada's first annexation campaign, A. Spencer Jones was its driving force in the 1880s. Early in 1882, shareholders of the Montreal-based Planter's Bank of Canada, a newly incorporated institution chartered to conduct business in the Caribbean, advanced the idea of a Canada-British Caribbean union. The shareholders comprised a handful of prominent Montreal businessmen and politicians, including flour-mill magnate Alexander Ogilvie and financier Matthew Gault. Both men were involved with the Sun Life Assurance Company of Canada – Ogilvie as share-holder and Gault as shareholder and former managing director – which had recently expanded into the Caribbean. To promote union, they enlisted Jones as their publicist, a prolific writer who, like Ogilvie and Gault, was a staunch Conservative with strong protectionist views. Jones took up the union cause with zeal. He saw the incorporation of the Planters' Bank and the Conservative government's recent approval of a steamship subsidy to develop trade between Canada and the Caribbean as stages in a process toward Canada's ultimate absorption of the islands. The Planters' bank never made a loan or accepted a deposit, but Jones became an outspoken voice for union.[36]

As with Haliburton, Jones's interest in union took shape against a backdrop of global events and was inspired by a particular understanding of Canada's development priorities. In the years following Canada First's demise in 1876, the global trend of territorial expansion intensified. American settlers continued to push westward until the frontier closed in 1890. The European powers engaged in a contest for African territory, a process formalized at the Berlin Conference of 1884–85. Russia expanded further into central Asia, and Britain annexed Baluchistan in the continuing saga of Anglo-Russian rivalry. Japan's Meiji government annexed the Ryukyu Islands, France expanded its imperial presence in Indochina and Polynesia, and Germany did so in northeastern New Guinea and Micronesia.

At the same time, settlement colonies and emergent nation-states in the British Empire similarly sought to expand their territory and sovereignty over already occupied lands, both contiguous and non-contiguous. The Cape Colony in southern Africa annexed Griqualand West and Griqualand East. The Australian colonies and New Zealand, fearful of French and German encroachments in the South Pacific, pressured Britain to establish protectorates over several islands in the region. Many of these islands were later placed under the administration of New Zealand and the newly federated Australia, most notably the Cook Islands and Papua New Guinea, respectively. In Canada, the development of the Northwest remained a central priority for expansion-ists, would-be settlers, and the nation-state. Neither the completion of this development nor the future absorption of Newfoundland, however, were universally understood as the end point of Canadian expansion.

Born in England to white Barbadian parents, Jones was a grammar-school principal in Canada West/Ontario, from 1857 to 1868. He returned to England in the 1870s, where he promoted colonial settlement schemes for British migrants in New Zealand and later Canada. Jones's work in the first instance may have stimulated his interest in union. He worked closely with New Zealand's second premier, Julius Vogel, who was the foremost proponent of Antipodean expansion in the 1870s.[37] In 1875–76, Jones served as emigration agent for the Federal Union of Agricultural Labourers in England and later for Canada's Department of Interior. In 1876, he initiated a colonization scheme for English and Welsh settlers in Manitoba, reserving four townships for this purpose.[38] Jones understood Canadian dominion over the Northwest and the British Caribbean as dual imperatives in the project of nation building. Reflecting in the *Toronto Mail* on Prime Minister John A. Macdonald's support for the steamship subsidy, Jones asked, "Do I assume too much in believing that [Macdonald] sees with prophetic eye the period – not so distant – when we shall possess a great South as well as a great West[?]"[39] In his estimation, Macdonald was up to the task. In the 1860s, "Sir John found British North America a string of petty provinces mutually ignorant, jealous, unprogressive, and drifting by slow but sure stages to annexation to the United States." Against all odds, he confederated the provinces, "acquired for civilization the fertile and boundless wildernesses" of the Northwest, and "successfully blended all these rival and discordant elements into the fair Dominion of to-day."[40] Jones wrote to the prime minister in May 1883 to outline the benefits of union and to urge him to consider the proposal. Macdonald expressed cautious interest but advised Jones that further consideration awaited evidence of widespread Caribbean support for the scheme.[41]

Macdonald's government focused considerable energy on economic development. When he returned to power in 1878, he had imposed a protective tariff to stimulate the development of Canadian manufactures and foster east-west trade. At the same time, his government continued to expand and strengthen trade with the Caribbean. One of the Conservatives' effective rallying cries during the general election of 1882 was to encourage trade with "all the world" and with the Caribbean in particular.[42] Jones argued that expanding the scope of Canada's protective tariff to the Caribbean would broaden the market for Canadian natural products and assuage the farmers, fishermen, and lumber producers alienated by the tariff. Canadian manufacturers would enjoy new protected markets and have opportunities to initiate new industries previously unknown in Canada, such as the cultivation of silk, indigo, and other tropical products. Caribbean staple exports such as sugar and fruit would encourage the development and expansion of sugar refineries

and canning factories in Canada. The present Confederation, moreover, was
weakened by a lack of climatic variation. As a result, the east-west trade that
Macdonald sought to develop through his three-pronged national policy –
railroad development, a protective tariff, and the "peopling" of the West with
white settlers – could never be large. "Commerce in its largest developments
follows the lines of longitude, not of latitude, as is our case at present." A
reciprocity agreement with the British Caribbean colonies would address this
imbalance somewhat, but their incorporation in the Canadian federation
would secure broad and ongoing commercial interchange.[43]

   In the summer of 1884, Jones's campaign attracted wider interest in Canada,
a direct result of the trade negotiations taking place between the United States
and, on behalf of the Caribbean colonies, the British minister to Washington.
Earlier that year, the US had negotiated a trade agreement with Spain, which
removed all existing duties and tariffs between the US and Cuba and Puerto
Rico. This agreement caused alarm in Canada, as the Spanish Caribbean
ranked fifth in total dollar value of Canadian exports. The British Caribbean ranked fourth. Negotiations for a US–British Caribbean trade agreement
threatened to shut Canada out of the Caribbean market altogether.[44] Union
seemed to provide a solution. Several Canadian newspapers emphasized the
benefit to Canadian manufactures, while the Maritime newspapers emphasized
the advantages for exports of fish. The United States, the *Ottawa Free Press*
argued, was establishing a foothold in the Caribbean in order to acquire
markets for American manufactures. Why should Canada not do the same?
Annexing British Guiana and the Caribbean islands would increase Canada's
population by one-fourth – an increase that would undoubtedly benefit
Canada in general and Canadian manufacturers in particular.[45] With "sole
control of their markets," Halifax's *Morning Herald* observed, "we would
certainly have a much better market for our fish than now. At present we
have to compete on equal terms, – and in some cases, unequal terms – with
the whole world, in every island of the West Indian group, no matter what
its nationality." Union would provide Canada with "practically a monopoly"
of the British Caribbean market.[46]

   To opponents of union, the commercial drawbacks outweighed the advantages.[47] The *Gazette* (Montreal) and Toronto's *Globe* appreciated the benefits of
a more diverse economy and a wider market, but these hardly compensated for
the expenditure required to maintain the Caribbean colonies. Canada would
have to assume the responsibility for public works, the development of internal
resources, the maintenance of local militia, the administration of justice, and

payment of subsidies to the colonies.[48] Montreal's *Journal of Commerce* and the *Halifax Morning Chronicle* were more sceptical about the trade advantages. Free entry of British Caribbean sugar – currently subject to a high duty – would create a substantial loss of revenue and would harm Canada's sugar refineries, and, most significantly, the Canadian market was nowhere near big enough to consume the bulk of sugar produced in the Caribbean colonies.[49] "We cannot take free sugar from Jamaica without either depositing our revenue or putting increased duties on other articles of consumption," the *Chronicle* argued. "We cannot take from this nursemaid of the Antilles half the sweets she desires to dispose of, and she might be discontented with the discovery of our inability."[50]

Beyond the logic of commerce and sentiment, Jones saw the absorption of the British Caribbean as a natural and necessary step along Canada's path to greatness. Like his predecessors in the Canada First movement, he anticipated a future in which Canada would assume a pre-eminent position in the hemisphere and perhaps even the empire. Rampant political corruption and the rise of Jim Crow suggested the US republic might not endure. With America "torn by faction and honeycombed by corruption," Jones argued, "we are destined to be the great Anglo-Saxon power of this continent ... but to do this, we need a south as well as a west."[51] Jones was a loyal subject of the Crown and he thought union would serve British imperial interests by consolidating Britain's colonies in North America. But the mother country was in decline, had long since shifted its imperial priorities to Asia and Africa, and could no longer be counted on to look after Caribbean interests. Jones understood Canada's annexation of the Caribbean colonies as a logical development in the course of Britain's ongoing retreat from the hemisphere. He published letters on the subject in several Caribbean newspapers and established contacts with prominent men in Jamaica and elsewhere in the region. By the summer of 1884, he had won the support of a small group of Jamaican planters and merchants and absentee proprietors in Britain.

Britain's Long Retreat from the Hemisphere

Entirely different circumstances animated British Caribbean responses to the union question. Britain's commitment to free trade since the 1840s had left Caribbean products largely unprotected in the world economy. Sugar-producing colonies, unable to compete with European-grown beet sugar, were dealt a particularly serious blow. Unrepresentative and self-interested colonial governments made matters worse. Jamaica, which exemplified the political, racial, and economic turmoil rampant in the British Caribbean in the latter half of the nineteenth century, became the focal point of unionism in the 1880s. The peasant uprising in Morant Bay in October 1865 symbolized the struggle of formerly enslaved peoples, which had persisted since emancipation in 1834. While enslaved peoples were now free, the social, political, and economic structures that ordered society before the 1830s remained largely intact. The "plantocracy" and the merchant elite – aided in no small way by the colonial government – sought to maintain the pre-emancipation status quo of white privilege and Black servitude. The large majority of Jamaicans were denied representation in the island assembly and the right to vote, fair wages, and respectable working conditions and the resources to obtain freehold land.[52]

The Colonial Office in London did little to address these blatant inequalities. By 1865, as Thomas Holt has argued, the imperial government was unwilling to consider peasant proprietorship as a means to economic recovery in Jamaica. This unwillingness reflected the imperial government's preoccupation with capitalist agriculture in Jamaica but also its "inability to even conceive of an alternative economy based on Black initiative and enterprise."[53] This triumph of self-interest over humanitarian concerns was reflected in the imperial government's response to the Morant Bay disturbance. Under pressure from humanitarian and missionary groups in London, the government condemned Governor Edward Eyre's brutal excesses in quashing the riot, but reforms failed to address the inequalities that inspired the riot in the first place. Whitehall's principal concern was to establish the political conditions necessary for Jamaica's plantation economy to recover and thereby ensure the colony's financial solvency. Rather than widen the island's franchise to address the discontent caused by oligarchic rule, the government eliminated the elective assembly and expanded the powers of the governor. Extending the franchise was dismissed as impractical primarily because the populace was thought racially unfit.[54] The colonial government thereafter consisted of a legislative council with six (later nine) official and six unofficial members.

Local planters and merchants expressed discontent with these reforms soon after their implementation in 1866. They wanted more control over the island's revenue and expenditure, and they petitioned the imperial government, unsuccessfully, to restore the old representative system. The Colonial Office finally considered more substantive reforms in 1882 when the official members of the legislative council resigned in 1882 over dissatisfaction with the imperial government's ruling in the "*Florence* incident," which required Jamaica to absorb half the expenditure resulting from Governor Anthony Musgrave's erroneous detention of the vessel *Florence* in 1877.[55] In 1884, the Colonial Office conceded a majority of elected members to the legislative council, with the proviso that the imperial government retained the power to increase the number of official members if necessary.[56] In the first elections following these reforms, the monetary requirement to hold office was set so high that it restricted eligible candidates to the planter and merchant elite. No Black Jamaicans were elected, and only five council members were native to the island. At the recommendation of a royal commission, the franchise was also widened. But this too did little to increase Black Jamaican political participation. For small-scale planters, merchants, and landholders, as well as the rising professional classes who aspired to positions in government, these reforms were small consolation.[57]

In a letter to the *Colonial Standard*, Jamaica's principal anti-government newspaper, Spencer Jones assured Jamaicans that union with Canada would correct many of the wrongs afflicted by the imperial and colonial governments. Canada would restore Jamaica's legislative assembly, administer its government with funds from Ottawa, and encourage investors to develop the island's unexploited resources.[58] The *Standard* expressed interest in the idea. Union with Canada would alleviate the perils of geographic isolation and ensure that the island would no longer "be treated as a serf and an alien" by officials in London. Annexation to either the United States or Canada was inevitable, the *Standard* averred, but Canada was the preferred choice because Jamaica could remain within the empire.[59] Such an arrangement, however, should only be entered after Jamaica attained an appropriate measure of self-government. "Jamaica must be a free agent before she can dispose of her fortunes or determine her destiny," the *Standard* claimed in a different editorial.[60] Local autonomy, the *Trelawny Advertiser* concurred, must precede union with Canada.[61]

Jamaican merchant Michael Solomon, less patient about the timeline for union, became Jones's tireless ally. Born in London in 1818, Solomon moved to Jamaica early in life to live with his brother, a successful Kingston auctioneer. He later worked in two of the island's commercial firms. Active in politics, he was a nominated member of the legislative council for several years and an ardent opponent of Crown colony government.[62] He was one of the unofficial members of the council who resigned over the *Florence* incident on the grounds that "the damages were incurred in pursuance of imperial policy and objects" rather than Jamaican interests. He returned to the council as an elected member following the reforms conceded by the imperial government during the Royal Commission of 1882–84.[63]

In June 1884, Solomon travelled to London, where he discussed the proposal with Sir Charles Tupper, the Canadian high commissioner to the United Kingdom. Tupper promised him that the Canadian government would encourage any scheme to advance the interests of both Jamaica and Canada, but he warned that he "saw many and serious obstacles in the way" of federation.[64] A meeting with the West India Committee (a body comprised of absentee planters and others with commercial interests in the Caribbean) was more encouraging. Several members with commercial investments in Jamaica were persuaded by his arguments, and to advance the proposal they formed a subcommittee that passed a resolution approving "the scheme for the entrance of Jamaica as a Province into the Canadian Dominion." The subcommittee urged Solomon to place the proposal before the Jamaica Legislature without haste so that the Canadian government, assured of Jamaican support, could take up the matter in its own parliament. "In any communication Mr. Solomon may have with Sir J[ohn] Macdonald," the resolution continued, "he may be assured of the support of the Jamaica Proprietors & Merchants in Great Britain." The subcommittee also resolved that a deputation of the West India Committee would present the proposal to the colonial secretary, Lord Derby.[65]

In preparation for this meeting, the subcommittee drafted a "Memorandum on the Proposal for the entrance of Jamaica as a Province into the Dominion of Canada." The document explained the impetus for the proposal and tentatively outlined possible economic and constitutional terms. The island's proprietors and merchants were mobilized by the "restriction of the market in the United Kingdom for Jamaica Sugar in consequence of the continental bounty system, the uncertainty of the market in the United States owing to reciprocity treaties allowing the import of a considerable quantity of [Cuban and Puerto Rican] Sugar duty free, and the possibility of a growing import of Sugar into the United States from the bounty-giving countries of Europe." Union with Canada would provide a market on "some basis of permanence" and encourage investment in the sugar industry.[66]

Jamaica's customs and excise duties would form part of Canada's consolidated revenue, and in return Canada would pay Jamaica annual subsidies, absorb the costs of several government services, and assume Jamaica's debt. The memo was less clear about constitutional matters. Jamaica would maintain its own legislature and make its own special (provincial) laws, send members to the Canadian Senate and House of Commons, and be subject to the dominion's federal legislation. No mention was made of the franchise, nor to any change in Jamaica's structure of government.[67] As a strong opponent of crown colony status, Solomon no doubt envisioned a legislature with more elected members in the Legislative Council, but it is unclear whether he expected franchise reform or the return of a legislative assembly. Presumably he did, given his use of the term "province," which seemed to anticipate an equality of status within the Canadian federation. Not all provinces had legislative councils, but they all already had (or, in the case of British Columbia, were granted) responsible government and a popularly elected assembly when they entered Confederation.

At the end of August, Solomon and a group of Caribbean proprietors and merchants – including members of the Jamaica subcommittee formed in June – met with Derby to discuss conditions in the British Caribbean. When the question of a "closer connection" with Canada arose, Derby was receptive, if only in an unofficial capacity. He could not, as the *Times* reported, "conceive any objection on the part of the Colonial Office to a drawing closer of the ties between two parts of the Colonial Empire. So far from objecting to that, it was what the Government had always desired, and what they had always promoted as far as lay in their power."[68] To many British contemporaries, the Caribbean had experienced its economic heyday in the seventeenth and eighteenth centuries. As Britain's imperial interests shifted during the nineteenth century to Asia and Africa, the Caribbean colonies were increasingly deemed an imperial burden. In October 1884, a cartoon in the Toronto satirical magazine *Grip*, published by J.W. Bengough, played on this sentiment to suggest that Britain would be more than happy to relinquish Jamaica to Canada. Offering up a barefoot Jamaican in tattered clothing to Miss Canada, John Bull says, "You may annex him, and welcome, Miss Canada. I'm only too glad to get rid of him" (figure 1.1).[69] Just as the British government supported the federations of 1867–1873 as a means to curb colonial expenditure, a union of Canada and the Caribbean colonies promised to reduce the burden on British taxpayers.

While Derby's supportive response was unofficial, Solomon proceeded to Ottawa and assured Macdonald that the colonial secretary had endorsed the union idea. The prime minister nonetheless waited to hear directly from the imperial government.[70] Following Solomon's departure for Jamaica, Macdonald consulted his former minister of finance, Sir Francis Hincks. Having once served as governor of Barbados and the Windward Islands and later British Guiana, Hincks often advised Macdonald on Caribbean matters. Hincks strenuously objected to the federation proposal, and the idea of annexing

THE JAMAICA QUESTION.

John Bull.—You may annex him, and welcome, Miss Canada. I'm only too glad to get rid of him.

Fig. 1.1 "The Jamaica Question," *Grip*, 18 October 1884

Jamaica in particular. He had been posted in British Guiana during the Morant Bay uprising, which seemed to have left an indelible impression on him. "Canada would most assuredly be seriously embarrassed," he told Macdonald. "If you adopted federation, you would have to govern a very troublesome mixed population ... it would in my opinion be better to unite with almost any other colony than Jamaica." He also thought union was unnecessary and "impracticable" from a commercial point of view. "At present Canada has nothing to complain of in regard to Imperial trade. All the sugar colonies British & foreign are on the same footing and the refiners are satisfied. All our products are admitted at a low revenue." As for union's impact on the Caribbean, white planters would be the chief beneficiaries, while the bulk of the population would be subject to Canada's high tariff on (non-Canadian) imports. Moreover, Hincks thought the imperial government would never consent to the extension of Canada's protective tariff – already a point of contention to British free traders – to the Caribbean.[71]

Macdonald nonetheless remained open to exploring the union proposal. His interest was probably informed by his ongoing efforts to strengthen Canada's commercial relations with the Caribbean and by his second wife's Jamaican roots. Born near Spanish Town in 1836, Agnes Bernard (Macdonald) came from a long line of sugar and coffee plantation owners who built their livelihoods on the backs of enslaved labour. In the 1820s, her father, Thomas, was a member of the island's Assembly and a lawyer in Spanish Town who owned several properties in the parishes of St James, Westmoreland, and St Catherine. Emancipation and the subsequent failure to secure apprenticed or free plantation labour left Agnes's father, like many planters, in dire economic straits. When he died of cholera in 1850, the family was nearly penniless. Agnes and her mother moved to England in 1851 and then on to Canada a few years later. Following Agnes's marriage to Macdonald in 1867, the prime minister took a special interest in developing Canada's trade relations with the Caribbean. The couple spent eight months living in Jamaica while Macdonald was in opposition in the 1870s, and when they travelled west by rail following the completion of the Canadian Pacific Railway in 1885, they named their private railcar "The Jamaican." In the late 1880s, Macdonald visited British Guiana and the islands in his continuing efforts to expand Canada's trade in the region. Upon his return, he lectured about the possibilities of this trade, later publishing the speech as "Canada, the West Indies and British Guiana," in 1889.[72]

Following Solomon's visit, Macdonald met with his cabinet, which concluded that while the union question was "surrounded with difficulties," they might not be "insuperable." Lacking sufficient details to make an informed opinion on the subject, they agreed to revisit the discussion at a later date. Macdonald followed up with Solomon, encouraging him to send information about Jamaica, especially copies of the colony's tariff, customs, and excise laws. Pending the imperial government's consent, Macdonald wrote, "The Government of Canada will be quite ready to enter upon the consideration of the two important questions, first of a political Union, and failing that, of a Commercial arrangement."[73]

During the late summer and early fall of 1884, the solicitor general of the Leeward Islands, Henry Berkeley, urged the inclusion of the Leeward Islands in any Canada-Caribbean union arrangement. He was motivated primarily by the dire state of the sugar industry. The industry, "which employs and supports more than nine-tenths of the entire population, is," he maintained, "in its competition with the bounty-fed beet sugar of Europe, threatened with destruction in the immediate future ... Should this happen, unutterable misery and destitution will be entailed upon more than a million and a half of Her Majesty's subjects than whom there are none more loyal and law-abiding." Recognizing that free-trade Britain would never impose a countervailing duty on beet sugar – a commodity whose production and export was subsidized ("bounty-fed") by European governments – union with

Canada offered these islands their best chance of salvation. Berkeley appealed first to the British subcommittee of absentee proprietors and merchants who had recently passed a resolution in favour of a Canada-Jamaica union. The subcommittee subsequently passed another resolution including the Leeward Islands, and added Berkeley's name alongside Solomon's as a representative to the Canadian government.[74]

In his appeal to Ottawa, Berkeley emphasized the keen interest in both the British Caribbean and the United States for a reciprocal trade agreement. A "movement is on foot, strongly supported," he wrote, "to attain the permission of the Colonial Office for the West Indian Colonies to make reciprocal treaty arrangements with the United States ... Should such arrangements be made Canada would be practically excluded from West Indian markets either as buyer or seller" and would "be driven to the distant Brazilian market." Berkeley amended the subcommittee's original memorandum to include "the Leeward Islands and Jamaica as Provinces into the Dominion of Canada," which he forwarded to Ottawa. The new document included several additional points for consideration, including the unlikelihood of a successful beet-sugar industry in Canada, the strategic value of Antigua and Jamaica – the "Malta and Gibraltar of the West" – and the addition of three-quarter of a million consumers to the dominion's population.[75]

Access to the Caribbean market beyond Jamaica no doubt appealed to union advocates in Canada. But the prospect also gave further weight to a central criticism of the union campaign in the Caribbean: the Canadian market was not large enough to absorb the majority of British Caribbean products. To Charles Levy, a prominent white planter and merchant from Jamaica's St Thomas Parish who joined the union campaign in September 1884, Jamaicans would never join Canada if the terms of union included additional Caribbean colonies. Since the proposal had originated in Canada in 1882, he maintained, there "never has existed any intention of applying the measure generally to all West India Islands." The prospect of "throw[ing] 300,000 Tons of Sugar on the Canadian market" – more than three times as much as the dominion could consume – was impracticable and foolish. If Canadians wished to "tack on" the Leewards or any other islands to the union arrangement, they should know that Jamaica would withdraw.[76]

The negotiations for a British Caribbean–United States trade agreement, ongoing in the late fall of 1884, reminded union proponents that Canada had a formidable rival in the Caribbean. But the commercial agreement was only one aspect (and indicator) of a larger fear about America's growing influence in the region. Britain's long disengagement from its Caribbean colonies might ultimately push these colonies into the arms of the republic. And this prospect was not without supporters in the Caribbean. Solomon himself had advocated Jamaica's annexation to the US before he was introduced to Spencer Jones's proposal.[77] Loyalty to Britain was important, but at what cost? As Caribbean colonist and planter Albert P. Marryat observed, "Stand alone we cannot, and hanging on to your skirts means destruction. Give us, then, leave to apply, or, if you prefer it, hand us over to our big brother who 'bosses' the Western Hemisphere, to take us under his protection. Sentiment, though it plays a part in practical politics, never yet filled empty stomachs, and ours, stepmother dear, are getting painfully empty, and let us go." Marryat thought that union with Canada would be ideal if Caribbean circumstances did not demand such urgent attention. The Caribbean could not "afford to wait for half-a-century" for Canada to develop its "consuming powers."[78] It was clear, agreed fellow Trinidad planter P.N. Barnard, that the imperial government could not be counted on for assistance. "In effect," Whitehall was saying, "perish the colonies so long as the English people can obtain for however a short a time, and no matter by what means, sugar at an unnaturally cheap price."[79] Annexation to the United States was perhaps inevitable.

Britain's staunch commitment to free trade, which depended on unfettered access to colonial markets, dampened the prospect of a Caribbean union with either the US or Canada. While the colonial secretary had initially responded favourably to the latter prospect in August 1884, he was considerably less enthusiastic in the months that followed. After meeting with Solomon's subcommittee, Derby conferred with members of the Colonial Office as well as British civil servant George Baden-Powell, who had served on a royal commission to investigate Caribbean affairs in 1882–84.[80] In a lengthy report to the Colonial Office in October, Baden-Powell emphasized the commercial disadvantages for Britain.[81] Just as Francis Hincks anticipated, imperial authorities were concerned that union would envelop Jamaica (and possibly the other Caribbean colonies) in Canada's protective tariff and consequently deprive British exports of free (or at least equal) access to Caribbean markets.[82]

In Jamaica, the prospect of gaining access to the much larger American market went a long way in defeating Solomon's first motion in the Legislative Council at the end of October. Council members did not desire annexation to the United States but rather some form of commercial agreement. They

thought the Canada-Caribbean union scheme had not been considered carefully. It was thus unwise to initiate official discussion of the question. The
commercial advantages were unclear, while the political ramifications seemed
impractical. Would federation entail a rise in taxes? How would small-scale
farmers be affected? Would the small number of Jamaican representatives sent
to Ottawa possess adequate influence to promote Jamaican interests? When
the vote was called to negotiate and conclude "arrangements for political and
commercial confederation with the Dominion of Canada" in October 1884,
Solomon was the only member to vote in favour.[83]

"Enough Irons in the Fire"

The Canadian market's small size and slow rate of growth were directly related
to unfulfilled plans in the Northwest. At the same time, the proposal to further
expand the dominion in the Caribbean placed these plans and the current state
of the Canadian federation under scrutiny. With an undeveloped Northwest
and mounting regional and cultural animosities, union was perhaps neither
wise nor feasible. These doubts reverberated in the Caribbean, Canada, and
Britain. "The great question of the future," Jamaican merchant F.A. Autey
contended in March 1884, "is what powerful nation will control the islands
in the western hemisphere?" At least one thing was certain: Canada was not a
contender. "At present, looking at the young dominion of Canada ... we see
the seeds of dissolution in the province of Manitoba, wishful to be annexed
to the United States of America, considering after thirteen years' experience
the confederation has proven burdensome and one-sided." Nova Scotia was
"anxious to withdraw" from the federation and "become an independent
colony like her elder sister Newfoundland, who, with greater prescience
would not allow herself to be absorbed into a confederation of opposing and
dissimilar elements and interests."[84] An editorial in Jamaica's *Daily Gleaner* in
September 1884 was even more pessimistic. "If that country, which is noted
for having 'nine months winter and three months bad weather out of every
twelve,' had anything to offer us in exchange for confederation, it would be a
different matter, but they positively have scarcely anything with which to help
themselves, let alone assist Jamaica." *Gleaner* readers were advised to peruse the
headlines in recent Canadian newspapers and "then say whether they would
consent to be affiliated with a country that cries out about bankruptcies,
dull trade, closed factories, lack of employment, poor wages, high taxation,
railroad grabs and swindles, and other commercial luxuries too numerous to

mention." Jamaicans were always willing to expand their trade with Canada, but they were emphatically against union, at least until Canadians "reduced their indebtedness and showed some enterprise."[85]

While somewhat exaggerated, these observations captured the growing discontent in both eastern and western Canada in the mid-1880s. In the West, declining rates of settlement and the dramatic collapse of land prices in Winnipeg beset dreams of national expansion. These events, well underway by 1884, marked the beginning of an economic downturn that plagued the Northwest until the mid-1890s. As the West "continued to prove an expensive and undeveloped burden," Easterners increasingly criticized the costs of expansion. More vitriolically, Westerners condemned the Conservative government's tariff as a product of Eastern (and especially Ontarian) self-interest.[86] As the Edmonton *Bulletin* counselled in November 1884, "The idea that the North-West is to eastern Canada as India is to Great Britain is one that will, if not abandoned, lead to the rupture of confederation at no distant date."[87] The conviction that westward expansion would benefit both regions and strengthen the Canadian federation appeared more and more dubious.

The economic downturn similarly undermined Maritime Canada's staple industries. The tariff stimulated Maritime industry in the 1880s, but growth remained "piecemeal and haphazard," and Maritime enterprises were generally unable to compete with Montreal and Toronto. Moreover, the region experienced the highest rate of out-migration in Canada. Dissatisfaction with the federal government was particularly marked in Nova Scotia, where Liberal William S. Fielding won the provincial election of 1886 on a secessionist platform.[88]

This waning confidence in Canada's future checked union enthusiasm in the 1880s, especially in Nova Scotia. To Halifax merchant Daniel Cronan, the state of affairs in Canada made the union proposal nothing short of preposterous. Ottawa "might as well set to work and annex South America." Canada already had "enough irons in the fire," and the Fathers of Confederation should have set a fixed limit on the dominion's boundaries in 1867.[89] The "increased unwieldiness of the Dominion," as Nova Scotia's *Presbyterian Witness* put it, was already cause for concern: "We are already large enough in all reason: why should we try expansion in a region so far away?"[90] Halifax's *Morning Chronicle* – edited, significantly, by William Fielding – was more dismissive: "Nova Scotia was dragged into confederation to help the Upper Provinces out of their difficulties. She has suffered enough already. The latest proposition to help another colony out of a scrape will be about the last straw. The burdens of the present union bear hardly enough upon our shoulders. Any addition to them, such as the annexation of Jamaica would surely bring, would about break the camel's back."[91]

Some of these same concerns shaped British opposition to the union scheme. The difficulties facing Britain's Caribbean colonies, according to the *Manchester Guardian*, would not be solved by simply annexing them to Canada, which had difficulties of its own. With Nova Scotia threatening secession and the other provinces "constantly conflicting," annexing an "entirely alien and isolated province" would only cause further tension.[92] Baden-Powell similarly pointed to the current state of the Canadian federation as evidence that union was a bad idea. Union would "be a drain on the men and the money of the Dominion, and at the present the enormous fertile territories still lying undeveloped in the north and north-west and west of the Dominion itself are crying aloud for all the men and the capital, not only that Canada can spare, but can attract from other countries."[93] With the object of continental expansion far from complete, he thought Ottawa was ill prepared to annex external territories.

For Baden-Powell and others who weighed in on the union question, the "undeveloped" state of Canada's Northwest was not the only indicator that the dominion was not ready to take on the Caribbean colonies. Was the dominion prepared to govern large Black populations? What would governance look like under union? Would Caribbean peoples' political rights expand or retract? There was some consensus that Canada was neither ready nor willing to assume such "responsibility." As federal and provincial governments grappled with how to incorporate non-white subjects into Canadian society and figure out how they should be governed, the union question receded from the realm of possibilities.[94] Canada, constituted more by exclusion than inclusion, was not just unamenable to the incorporation of African Caribbeans. The prospect was antithetical.

Race and Governance

The racial mandate of Canadian nation building intensified in the 1880s, providing a critical backdrop for unionism. The federal government pushed the Indigenous peoples of the Northwest onto reserves, knowingly starved them into submission, and forced their children into residential schools.[95] When the Northwest Métis took up arms against Canadian authority in 1885, Macdonald did not negotiate as he had in 1870. Using similar tactics to the British in their various colonial wars, he dispatched the Canadian army to crush the resistance with artillery and machine guns.[96] Ottawa imposed a head tax on Chinese immigrants in an attempt to curb their migration to Canada, the expanding trade union movement excluded Blacks routinely and Asians roundly, and Nova Scotia reconfirmed its commitment to segregated schools for Black and white children.

These developments informed the union debate in different ways. In Baden-Powell's assessment of the union question in October 1884, he suggested that the dominion government's experience with Indigenous peoples scarcely qualified Canada to govern African Caribbeans. To his mind, these groups posed different challenges to Canada in the short and long term. Writing five months before hostilities broke out in the Northwest, and apparently unaware of the merciless, inhumane dispossession tactics that Macdonald's government was currently using against Plains Indigenous peoples to make way for the railroad, he wrote, "It is almost unnecessary to state that the Dominion Government, in its admirable treatment of the Red Indians within its boundaries, has conclusively shown itself to be as thoroughly imbued with true and wise philanthropy as the Home Government itself. But the Red Indians are a doomed race – a relic of the past, and no active factor in the future. At best they form but an insignificant part of the total population." The "negro and coloured races," on the other hand, made up nearly 80 per cent of the British Caribbean's total population and, most significantly, "supply all the manual labor."[97]

Baden-Powell's statements elided the continuing importance of Indigenous labour to regional economies in the 1880s,[98] and the fact that the exploitation of Black labour, though significant, was less instrumental to economic development in Canada than it was in the US and the Caribbean. Black Canadians nonetheless encountered white resistance to their labour, which was invariably cheaper than white labour. But in the 1880s, a decade marked by the rise of labour radicalism in Canada, this resistance did not reverberate in national political discourse as it did in the United States. Canadian trade union leaders, especially those in British Columbia, were more concerned with the Chinese "menace" and its implications for white labour. Chinese migrants – comprised largely of mobile, single males – tended to work as industrial labourers, while Black families more often settled in rural areas. At a "safe distance" from the industrial labour market, Black peoples were less threatening to white labour.[99] But if they trespassed on this space, white attitudes could change quickly. Labour leaders were generally sceptical of immigration policies or other federal initiatives that might precipitate an influx of Black labour, such as union with Jamaica. In the midst of the union debate in the fall of 1884, Toronto's *Daily News*, edited by the Knights of Labor radical E.E. Sheppard, argued that "a confederation in which a population of ignorant and half-civilized Negroes [are] to be placed on a level with the intelligent and self-governing white communities, is about the wildest scheme ever broached even in these days of amateur constitution making."[100] Constructs of the "half-civilized negro" functioned to discourage union and keep Blacks out of white industrial space.

To some extent, then, Baden-Powell's reservations about union were warranted. But his central objection, fuelled by the common assumption that British imperialism was "uniquely benevolent among nations,"[101] was out of touch with Caribbean sentiment and the shifting concerns of Britain's humanitarian lobby in the latter half of the nineteenth century. He argued that "the English people emancipated these negroes, and the same spirit which led them to do this still lives in the fixed determination of English public opinion to safeguard the interests of the 'subject races.' The negroes themselves appreciate the care that is taken of them by the Imperial Government, inspired as it always is by the very strong philanthropic feelings of the nation." It was "extremely doubtful," he concluded, that British humanitarians would support a change of administration in the Caribbean.[102] The absence of correspondence from humanitarian groups on the subject in the Colonial Office records (a customary forum for protest), perhaps a telling silence in itself, and the diversity of humanitarian interest and sentiment in Britain make it difficult to generalize or even speculate about humanitarian opinion. It is fair to suggest, however, that during the second half of the nineteenth century, Britain's Caribbean colonies no longer captivated British humanitarians as they once did.

There were several reasons for this shift, most notably British emancipation in the 1830s, which directed the anti-slavery cause (the central thrust of humanitarian activity) elsewhere. The humanitarians' position was additionally weakened by "material decline in the West Indies, the small numbers of missionary converts, the unwillingness of indigenous communities to absorb British ideas or commercial habits, and by what observers interpreted as the violent rejection of British ways evident in the Indian Mutiny, the Maori Wars, and the Morant Bay Rebellion."[103] The response to these events was mixed in Britain, but they nonetheless engendered a critical shift in thinking about racialized subjects and how they should be governed. While many humanitarians and especially missionaries maintained their commitment to "enlighten" subject populations – conceding, in many cases, that this process would take much longer than originally anticipated – others saw humanitarian goals as impractical or even irrelevant.[104]

Crystallized notions of racial difference replaced the early Victorian commitment to "civilizing" colonial peoples – a commitment premised on the assumption that the empire's varied peoples could progress from barbarity to civilization, albeit at different paces.[105] This emerging ethos buttressed anti-union arguments in the 1880s. African-Caribbean peoples were thought backward, idle, and unfit for self-government, with little hope for improvement. The conventional trope that rendered colonial subjects "children" who grow to adulthood (as autonomous, self-governing entities in a wider imperial family) was no longer an appropriate metaphor for non-white colonial dependencies. African Caribbeans, moreover, deemed susceptible to agitation, demanded austere governance. As Francis Hincks warned Macdonald in September 1884, "If you adopted federation, you would have to govern a very troublesome mixed population."[106] Many thought taking on such responsibility foolish and ultimately detrimental to the dominion.

In step with this hardening of racial ideas, New Brunswick writer Colville Malton's *Reminiscences of a Tour through the West Indies*, published in the mid-1880s, presented a colonial fantasy for white Canadian readers that delineated a starkly uncivilized imperial space. While Malton's stated purpose was to educate Canadians about the Caribbean and stimulate their interest in annexing the islands, his travelogue unwittingly called the advisability of union into question by widening the imperial divide.[107] Navigating colonial space in what Mary Louise Pratt has called a "contact zone," Malton narrated his engagement with Caribbean landscapes and peoples through "highly asymmetrical relations of domination and subordination."[108] In contrast to the subject position of Malton's white Canadian readers, Caribbean peoples came to life as remote, exotic, and foreign. Commonalities across the imperial divide – British institutions and ideas – were conspicuously muted.[109]

Even the language was foreign. Visiting an absentee-owned coffee plantation outside Bridgetown, Barbados, Malton described his difficulty communicating with his Black guide. One morning the guide knocked on his door to alert him that he had arrived and was waiting outside with a mule. "Jumping up I intended asking the slave to be a little more explicit, as to me it sounded like so much jargon." As Malton recounted in *Reminiscences*, it was not until he went outside that it became "clear enough of what Sambo tried to make me aware, for there was he at the foot of the steps grinning and showing his white teeth, whilst holding the mule I was to have possession of during my stay in this delightful spot."[110] Consistent with nineteenth-century travel writing, Malton employed stereotypes and hyperbole liberally. Such narrative strategies functioned to differentiate tourist from native, insider from other, Black from white, colonizer from colonized, "Massa" from "slave."[111] The "Sambo" stereotype of Black "ignorance, irrationality, and idleness ... childish irresponsibility and inept misspeaking" was a familiar one in the late nineteenth century.[112] Malton's use of the slave/"Massa" binary was more striking. Under slavery, "Massa's" rationalization of the system was, as historian and Trinidadian politician Eric Williams observed, "that the workers, both African and Indian, were inferior beings, unfit for self-government, unequal to their superior masters, permanently destined to a status of perpetual subordination, unable to achieve equality with Massa."[113] An inappropriate rhetorical strategy in the humanitarian climate of the post-emancipation decades, "Massa" and "slave" resurfaced in the final decades of the nineteenth century – in step with hardened ideas about the immutability of race – with renewed cultural and rhetorical purchase.

A cartoon of the union question, published in *Grip* in August 1884, cast John A. Macdonald in the role of "Massa" (figure 1.2). Jamaica is personified as a barefoot, underfed Black child with exaggerated features. The child holds a bottle of rum and asks Macdonald, "Massa, don' you want to 'dopt a culled chile?" Several of the Canadian provinces – represented as white, well-dressed, and well-nourished children – stand at Macdonald's feet. One rides on his back while another hides behind him. Both cling tightly to the prime minister as they gaze fearfully at the Jamaican child. An elderly woman with cross in hand looks on, presumably there to facilitate the adoption. The child's dialect is a hyperbolic rendering of a homogenized "Black English," a racialized linguistic strategy that infantilized and disparaged African-descended peoples to entertain white readers.[114] *Grip* used this strategy in more elaborate form the following month. A fictitious letter from an imaginary Virginia-born Black Jamaican was written in a crude, overwrought representation of Black vernacular English, rife with stereotypes of Black ignorance and childishness. Particularly egregious was the suggestion that Harry Piper, founder of Toronto's Zoological Gardens, would serve as the agent for prospective Jamaican migrants to Canada following union.[115] The letter not only racialized Black Jamaicans as uncivilized: it dehumanized them.

Malton conveyed the uncivilized character of Caribbean life most vividly in his description of the living conditions and spirituality of urban Jamaicans. The "huts of the natives [in Kingston] are of a very rude and primitive nature,

Fig. 1.2 "Massa," *Grip*, 30 August 1884

chiefly composed of 4 or 5 posts and a few sticks to support the bundles of straw of which the roof is comprised … there are exceptions, where is to be seen a house of a shade higher class, but the exception is rare." The crucial point on which difference was constructed (for white readers) was not that Caribbean peoples resided in crude dwellings but that they aspired to nothing more. "Quashie is not disposed" to welcome housing schemes, Malton wrote; "so long accustomed to his mud hut and the surroundings, he would feel miserable and out of his element in more refined quarters."[116] Malton similarly deployed the image of the credulous, ignorant African Caribbean to explain the continuing prevalence of Obeah in Jamaica: "Until very late years superstitions reigned rampant on this Island, having willing subjects in the negro."[117] An African-based spiritual practice imported to the Caribbean by enslaved peoples during the seventeenth century, Obeah was based on the belief that practitioners could summon supernatural forces for personal and often malevolent purposes. As spiritual leaders, practitioners might harness their popularity for political ends. They were consequently feared by whites for their power to incite resistance against white dominance. Local authorities enacted several laws against the practice of Obeah in the latter half of the nineteenth century.[118] The practice nevertheless persisted. "Though the laws are … rigid," Malton wrote, "the evil still predominates." Black Jamaicans' "blind ignorance," he warned, made them vulnerable to Obeah.[119]

Malton was optimistic that the increased emphasis on schooling in Jamaica would help eradicate Obeah and generate "a healthy moral tone and religious sentiment" on the island.[120] Schooling became increasingly important after the rebellion at Morant Bay. Before the introduction of crown colony government in 1866, the churches assumed sole charge of educating formerly enslaved people. The rebellion prompted the colonial state to intervene, establishing new elementary schools and providing financial assistance to existing church schools. The "barbarism" of the rebellion convinced colonial authorities that the safety of the upper classes and the prosperity of the island hinged on the "enlightenment" and "moral elevation" of the masses. But state assistance was limited, and compulsory elementary education was not implemented until 1912. Prior to the First World War, just over 25 per cent of school-aged Jamaican children attended elementary school.[121] Malton's emphasis on the elevating power of education reflected, in part, the growing preoccupation with moral reform in Canada during the 1880s. Industrialization and the growth of an urban working class prompted concerns about moral and racial degeneracy. The "correlate" to this growth, as Mariana Valverde has shown, was the development of an urban middle-class that initiated philanthropic schemes to "reform or 'regenerate' Canadian society,"[122] a racialized project defined by an Anglo-Saxon norm. Racial taxonomies identified "the Negro" and "the East Asian" as inassimilable "alien" races. Their moral regulation purportedly demanded rigid and coercive measures.[123]

Educational authorities in Canada may have touted the value of schooling across racial lines, but certainly not on an equal basis. In 1884, union was discussed against the backdrop of a contentious debate in Nova Scotia over the maintenance of racially segregated schools. In March, a delegation of Black and white members urged the provincial government for reform. Reverend Henry H. Johnson, a Black delegate, argued that the segregation of Black and white children was a shameful relic of slavery that did not serve the interests of the wider community.[124] Robert Hockin, a white delegate and Conservative member of Parliament for Pictou, renounced segregation as a "blot" on British justice and fair play. He put forward a motion to strike out any reference to children "of different colours" in the Education Act, but it was defeated in the Assembly.[125]

During the debate, there was a clear overlap between support for segregated schools and doubts about the union scheme. In the Assembly, Liberal member for Halifax William Fielding argued that segregated schools served the "greater good" of the public: "It might be admitted that men should be regarded for what they were worth, regardless of color or creed; but even in the neighboring republic – where if anywhere all men were supposed to be created equal – the prejudice existed, and, although all men were equal in the eyes of the law, they were not equal in matters of social life."[126] All the while, Fielding's *Morning Chronicle* remained a consistent critic of the union proposal. In November 1884, the daily concluded that "Jamaica has got itself in a tight place. Its trade languishes. Bad government, an idle population, lack of business shrewdness, lack of industry and improvidence have reduced it to that position which requires help." Why should Canada save them from the consequences of "their own want of ability to look after affairs[?]"[127] When Reverend William Murray of Jamaica extolled the benefits of union during his visit to Nova Scotia in October of that year, the *Chronicle* roundly dismissed him. "It would be a foolish speculation to abolish the present reciprocal fish trade with fifty millions of people for the sake of gaining a free fish trade with a half million of darkies." Perhaps still reeling from the schools controversy, the editor took particular issue with Murray's observation that Blacks in Jamaica were "as intelligent and well educated as the average population of Nova Scotia" before the introduction of free schools. There was not, the *Chronicle* rebutted, "'even sweet reasonableness', let alone truth, in the statement." To suggest that a society "of 600,000 souls, mostly negroes, and degraded specimens at that," would "progress" at the same rate as one with a predominantly white population was preposterous.[128] Because Jamaicans had been "found incapable of governing themselves," the *Chronicle* expressed amusement that they "were now anxious to have a share in governing Canadians."[129]

That Black Jamaicans were "uncivilized" was not the central issue for Canadian opponents of union. More important was their apparent disinterest in advancing to a civilized state – or worse, their incapacity to do so. Black Jamaicans, according to "A Gentleman" interviewed by the Halifax *Morning Chronicle*, were "the laziest creatures to be found on the face of the globe – they were of a poor, shirtless class, without any work in them and trying to live from hand to mouth."[130] It was for this reason, argued Halifax merchant James Butler, that they lost representative government in 1866 and "now ... had to be governed in the most rigid manner."[131] Jamaica's wretched conditions were not the result of Britain's ongoing neglect (not to mention a legacy of slavery). Nor were they a product of white planter and merchant efforts to maintain political and economic control. Blame for the debased state of Jamaica's affairs was placed squarely at the door of Black Jamaicans.

Claims of Blacks' idleness and an inability to withstand Canada's climate were similarly constructed to challenge the idea that Black Jamaicans would make productive citizens. E.C. Da Costa, a white Barbadian merchant who owned a commercial house that shipped sugar and other products to Canada, argued that union would be a mistake because Black Jamaicans were not good labourers. Accustomed to living "hand to mouth," they "work for a shilling a day and can get a good meal for eight cents."[132] The "idea of getting cheap labor from Jamaica," as Halifax merchant Daniel Cronan contended, "is all nonsense." Content with their simple existence, he continued, Black Jamaicans would not provide Canadian industries with productive labour, particularly given the northern climate. To Cronan, the Black "nuisance" was not a distant spectre threatening Canada's national horizon but very much a reality. Citing the large migration of enslaved and free Blacks to British North America during the middle decades of the nineteenth century, Cronan concluded that Canadians "had enough of that kind of thing when we got the extensive importations of them from the south years ago."[133] That the majority of these migrants returned to the United States during and after Reconstruction was apparently lost on him.[134]

Canadian critics of the union scheme also feared the spectre of Black resistance. Halifax alderman W.B. McSweeney, who had visited Jamaica and was apparently well acquainted with political and social conditions on the island, was strongly averse to union. With Jamaica's approximate ratio of 14,000 whites to 550,000 Blacks, union would only prove a "confounded nuisance." Black Jamaicans, "the same kind who had created so much trouble on Hayti" during the Revolution of 1791–1804, were "impossible to satisfactorily govern." There was no good reason, he concluded, that Canada should desire "looking after these very valueless colored citizens" who were prone to agitation and lacked the capacity to govern themselves.[135]

More receptive to the union proposal, Halifax's *Morning Herald* did not identify race as a serious obstacle. "Twenty years ago the Imperial government, it is true, decided that the Jamaicans were unfit for self-government. But twenty years affords time enough for considerable improvement in the educational and moral status of a country; and there is reason to believe that the Jamaica of today is far in advance of the Jamaica of 1865." Absolute self-government, moreover, should be distinguished from self-government within a federal system: "It is possible that a country may not be fit to govern itself in all things, and still be a useful member of a federation." In this way, the American case was instructive. While there were states that "would cut a sorry figure as independent nationalities," they were nonetheless productive members of the republic. The terms of union would determine the extent to which Jamaicans would "share in governing Canadians." With only ten or fifteen representatives in Ottawa, there was no fear that Jamaicans would direct Canadian affairs in any significant measure.[136]

Support for Jamaica assuming provincial status in the Canadian federation was otherwise scarce. In Nova Scotia and especially Halifax, notions of African-descended peoples as backward and idle triumphed over belief in their progressive capacities. In short, Black Jamaicans would not make good citizens. "The great bulk of the population," the Halifax *Evening Mail* warned, "know nothing about political duties. They have never had anything to do with the choice of their law makers, and do not know what voting means." It would be consequently "unsafe" to take Jamaica into the federation on the same terms as the provinces. Territorial status was a possibility, or perhaps a form of provincial government with a highly restrictive franchise to shut out the large majority of Black Jamaicans. "We believe," the *Mail* continued, "that the whole adult male population of Canada should enjoy the rights of citizenship, and may be safely trusted to elect members of the Canadian House of Commons. But we do not regard the natives of the West India islands in the same light."[137] Montreal-based writer Watson Griffin was even more direct about the main dilemma union presented: "We don't want any black men in the Canadian parliament." While union would be advantageous from a commercial point of view, it could potentially "endanger" Canadian institutions.[138]

Even the campaign's chief proponents did not support a union arrangement that presupposed the political equality of white Canadians and African Caribbeans. Responding to the Halifax *Morning Chronicle's* condemnation of union on racial grounds, Charles Levy wrote, "Speaking with all respect to the reasonable aspirations of my fellow-colonists, I think you over-rate their legal claim to representation in the Canadian Parliament." While Jamaica's population was nearly 600,000, Levy concluded that one or two seats would be adequate representation for Jamaica's white planter and merchant interests, at least to start.[139] In less diplomatic language, Spencer Jones concurred. Such equality, he maintained, would hinder national growth. In this way, the US example was again instructive. The republic, "hampered by universal suffrage, and by visionary doctrines of equality, is already encumbered with nearly two million negro voters, and consequently dare not risk the swamping of her constitution by adding the semi-barbarous Mexicans or the emancipated slaves of Cuba to her list of voters." Canada, fortunately, had never "professed her belief in such dogmas," and could thus, under a restrictive franchise (based on property and education requirements), freely admit Black people.[140] "Democratic ideals of equality are abhorrent to the white man," but whites need not worry because the small number of enfranchised African Caribbeans would support the status quo. "The negro, always imitative," would follow the white man's lead at the polls.[141] Jones's vision of union reflected a national vision that was acutely inscribed by racial thinking. To his mind, Canada's well-being depended on a racially exclusive (white) franchise.

Jones's vision ultimately came to nothing. Toward the end of the year, the negotiations for a US–Caribbean trade agreement broke down. Britain's Board of Trade and, consequently, the British Parliament were unwilling to accept an arrangement that placed British manufacturers at a disadvantage in the Caribbean market.[142] Early in 1885, in the wake of the failed negotiations, Levy, Solomon, and Jones once again pressed their governments to consider a Jamaica-Canada union or, at the very least, a commercial agreement. On 26 March, Solomon introduced another resolution in Jamaica's Legislative Council. Emphasizing the failed trade negotiations with the United States, he resolved that a Jamaican commission be sent to Ottawa to ascertain what arrangements could be made with the Canadian government on the basis of "either Confederation or Reciprocity."[143] The resolution passed, but the majority of Legislative Council members preferred reciprocity to union, and the Colonial Office refused to sanction a commission to explore anything beyond a strictly commercial agreement.[144]

In Canada, the Jamaican resolution went largely unnoticed, and the union question disappeared from public discourse soon after. The same day that Solomon introduced his resolution, armed conflict broke out at Duck Lake between Louis Riel's Métis militia and the Northwest Mounted Police. This confrontation marked the beginning of a six-week resistance against the Canadian government in what is now Saskatchewan and Alberta. For the Plains Métis and First Nations, the disappearance of the buffalo had undermined their livelihoods and means of subsistence. Many were anxious to secure title to the land they occupied and representation on the North-West Council. Disheartened by Ottawa's protracted failure to address their grievances adequately, they took up arms at Duck Lake. The Canadian government mobilized a force of five thousand and ultimately quashed the resistance at Batoche in mid-May. Much like the imperial government's response in the aftermath of Jamaica's Morant Bay rebellion, the Canadian government ramped up its agenda to rigidly control Indigenous populations.[145]

Baden-Powell's contention in October 1884 that Canada's treatment of Indigenous peoples was "thoroughly imbued with true and wise philanthropy" was a difficult case to make by the latter half of 1885. The government's heavy-handed suppression of the Northwest resistance and the coercive policies it enacted to control Indigenous lives reflected Ottawa's heightened determination to shore up Anglo-Saxon sovereignty in Canada. To many commentators in Britain and Canada, it was neither practical nor desirable for the Canadian nation-state to administer the Caribbean colonies, particularly under the austere form of government purportedly required. Macdonald had entertained the idea since 1883 and had in fact paid Spencer Jones for his efforts, but was always non-committal.[146] If union was, in the prime minister's words, "scarcely practicable" toward the end of 1884, it was inconceivable by June 1885.[147]

Conclusion

Unionism in the post-Confederation decades was a broadly bourgeois project fuelled by dreams of commercial, territorial, and national aggrandizement. Its Canadian advocates were neither powerful elites nor ordinary folk. They were intellectuals, prominent businessmen, and self-styled imperial-nationalists who saw union as a means to secure and accelerate Canada's development in the wake of US trade rivalries and Britain's retreat from the Caribbean. On Haliburton's initiative, the union idea circulated in commercial circles in the cities of Ontario, Nova Scotia, and New Brunswick, among colonial administrators in the Leeward Islands, and later in the Toronto-based political party, the Canadian National Association. In the 1880s, it resurfaced in Montreal's business class and, with Spencer Jones's fervent promulgation, generated interest in Ottawa, Jamaica, Antigua, and Britain. Jones managed to get the attention and consideration of powerful figures, most notably the Canadian prime minister, the colonial secretary, wealthy Jamaican planters, and members of the West India Committee.

A number of challenges beset unionism in these years. Most significantly, the annexation of Jamaica and the Leeward Islands clashed irreconcilably with the racially homogenous Canada that white settlers envisioned. Union proponents struggled to define terms of incorporation that would keep African-Caribbean subjects at a geographic and political distance. This struggle amplified in the face of racial strife in the United States, stringent notions of racial difference in the British Empire, and, ultimately, the violent confrontation between the Canadian state and the Northwest Métis in 1885. As settler nation building and its disappointments intensified in the 1880s, so too did efforts to fortify the racial order. These efforts, in combination with Jamaican reservations about Canada's market size and the imperial government's steadfast embrace of free trade, made union untenable.

Unionism would reappear at the turn of the century under much more favourable circumstances. Extraordinary economic development, exponential population growth, and Western settlement generated – with the help of the transcontinental railway, completed in 1885 – unprecedented optimism about Canada's national potential. Well on the way to fulfilling their much-anticipated Western destiny, many settler Canadians believed it was now possible for them to conceive – and pursue – a southern destiny.

VISIONS OF CENTURIAL GRANDEUR, 1898–1914

The union idea returned to public discourse a few weeks after the United States seized Cuba and Puerto Rico in the Spanish-American War. On 24 August 1898, Canada's first Dominion statistician, George Johnson, proposed union in a letter to the *Ottawa Citizen*. Published the following day under the heading "Canada's Opportunity," the letter initiated a transatlantic debate about union that persisted intermittently to the outbreak of war in 1914. "Why should not Canada undertake to look after the British West Indian possessions," Johnson asked. It would "give Canada what she needs – a tropical annex." Trade would flourish and the imperial government would be relieved of its generations-long burden in the Caribbean.[1] In the midst of lingering uncertainty about the empire's future, Johnson thought it was time for Canada to step up its imperial responsibilities. Canadian investment would flow into the region, stimulate development, and raise African-Caribbean subjects "up to a high plane of civilization."[2] In light of Canada's "tried capacity for self-government, love of individual freedom, and development in population [and] wealth," Johnson reckoned Canada was "entitled," so far as British possessions were concerned, "to hegemony on this continent." These claims were rooted in pretensions of white racial superiority and national destiny. Why should Canada hesitate to "assume her true place?"[3] As Johnson's timing suggested, the Spanish-American War spurred his union overture. The war provoked white Canadian anxiety about the loss of Caribbean markets and envy of the perceived economic rewards of US imperialism. The US example in Florida, California, and Hawaii purportedly demonstrated that unrestrained access to tropical (or sub-tropical) territory was crucial to national development.

Talk of Canadian entitlement and destiny proliferated in the wake of Canada's tremendous economic and population growth after 1896. Canada had the world's fastest-growing economy in the first decade of the twentieth

century, and the population increased from 5,371,000 to 7,879,000 in the
period between 1901 and 1914.[4] Foreign investment poured in, chiefly from
Britain and the United States. Mining, coal, and other mineral extraction
industries and the pulp and paper, iron and steel, and hydroelectric industries
flourished. Cities grew across the country, and two new western provinces,
Alberta and Saskatchewan, were created in 1905.[5] This growth and optimism
spilled over into Canada's relations with the Caribbean. Canadian banks and
life-insurance companies continued to expand throughout the region in the
first decade of the twentieth century; the Royal Bank alone had eighteen Caribbean branches by 1911. Canadian businessmen and petroleum engineers played
an instrumental role in the development of Trinidad's petroleum industry at
the turn of the century. Canadian-owned or part-owned street railway and
lighting companies cropped up in Trinidad, Jamaica, and British Guiana, as
well as Cuba, Puerto Rico, Mexico, and Brazil.[6]

Canadian historians have long characterized these years as a boom period,
a time of unbridled optimism, and, for British-descended Canadians, peak
enthusiasm for the empire. White settler wisdom held that the country would
ultimately assume its place among the greatest, most prosperous nations in
the world. Prime Minister Wilfrid Laurier's oft-cited declaration that the
twentieth century would be "Canada's century" was not fanciful rhetoric.[7] In
language typical of the time, the celebrated Canadian humourist and political
scientist Stephen Leacock summed up this mood in 1907: Canada's "inevitable
greatness," he wrote, was "not a vain-glorious boast … It is simple fact. Here
stand we, six million people, heirs to the greatest legacy in the history of
mankind, owners of a half a continent, trustees, under God Almighty, for the
fertile solitudes of the west."[8] In light of the high-flown rhetoric of Leacock or
like-minded writers of the time, it is unsurprising that many settler Canadians
entertained expansionist designs on the Caribbean. Hindsight has obscured
these designs and obstructed an adequate reckoning with the context that
produced them.[9]

Imperial aggrandizement was a constituent part of Canadian nation building in the early twentieth century. It was an imperial impulse related to, yet
different from, the imperialism associated with British Empire loyalties and
movements for closer unity. It was an imperialism characterized by efforts to
situate Canada in a world system in which nation-states sought external bases
of power in the form of territory, resources, or labour. Historians have long
established that nation-state formation in the nineteenth and early twentieth
centuries was a thoroughly imperial enterprise.[10] The competitive system of

the old European states – dominated from the seventeenth century by the Dutch, Portuguese, Spanish, French, and British – was challenged in the late nineteenth and early twentieth century by newer territorial states that included, most notably, the United States, Germany, and Japan but also Belgium, Italy, Canada, and Australia. As settlement colonies within Britain's empire, Canada and Australia may at first glance seem out of place on this list. Yet the absence of full sovereignty did not preclude imperial exploits at home or abroad. The impulses that animated Canadian ambitions in the Caribbean had much in common with the impulses that incited the expansionist agendas of these other new territorial states. Unlike the old countries of Europe, whose global competitiveness arose from their success in first acquiring and controlling resources outside the continent, the new states first mobilized resources within continental boundaries before looking outward. While the interests driving these expansionist projects varied widely in different political, geographic, and temporal contexts, they were all implicated in nationalist agendas.[11] The evolution of the nation-state, in turn, was very much an imperial process, in which competition for colonial acquisitions was thought indispensable to national development.

The chapter first outlines the general contours of unionism and explores, in particular, two interrelated developments that preoccupied unionists: US expansion in the Caribbean and the growing import of the "tropics" in the early twentieth century. It then shifts to the imperial context in which the union debates took place. Arguments for union emerged in a climate of acute imperial anxiety. They were based on an understanding of Canada's future role in the empire, but there was little consensus about what this should entail. The final section explores the racialized thinking and practices that doomed unionism. The twentieth century would be Canada's century not only for the dominion's British heritage, abundant resources, expansive geography, and soon-to-be mushrooming population but also its ostensible whiteness.

Trade and Tropicality

On 29 August 1898, not long after hostilities ceased in the Spanish-American War, the Charlottetown *Guardian* expressed concern over the *New York Sun*'s haughty appraisal of the war's probable impact on Canada and the British Caribbean.[12] "According to the *Sun*, Uncle Sam's Spanish victories have resulted in a victory over Canada. That is to say, [by] holding Cuba and Porto Rico, the markets for Canadian fish, the United States can now close out the Canadian fishermen." The *Sun* predicted a more ruinous outcome for British Caribbean sugar producers. Soon to be shut out of the American market, their only salvation was annexation to the United States.[13] These predictions, while somewhat arrogant, were not far off the mark. The Spanish-American War nullified a commercial agreement Spain and Britain signed in 1886, which granted a large preference to Maritime exports of fish to Puerto Rico and Canadian timber and foodstuffs to Cuba. It provoked Canadian and especially Maritime anxiety and sent producers scrambling for new markets. For British Caribbeans and sugar producers in particular, the war threatened access to the American market. It promised to worsen the already dire state of the British Caribbean sugar industry. Producers were unable to compete with the bounty-fed beet sugar of Europe, nor the cane sugar of Fiji, Natal, Brazil, Java, Cuba, and the Dominican Republic, where the introduction of modern machinery enabled large-scale production. Between 1881 and 1896, sugar prices dropped by one half, wages followed, and unemployment soared.[14]

Not surprisingly, given the region's heavy reliance on trade with the Spanish Caribbean, the union idea found the most favour in the Maritime provinces. The North Sydney fisherman and harbour commissioner George Dobson warned that the extension of the American tariff and coasting laws around these islands would be "a considerable loss to Canadian commerce and shipping, particularly that of the maritime provinces." If the British Caribbean entered a reciprocity agreement with the United States, the Maritimes might be elbowed out of the British Caribbean trade too. "Would not federation with Canada," he asked, "solve this trouble?"[15] As a Saint John resident put it in a letter to the *Montreal Weekly Witness* in June 1899, the annexation idea "has been warmly commended in the maritime provinces" because they "have much to gain and little to lose were it carried out."[16]

The significance of union transcended the need to secure markets. "Now that the great Republic has acquired some tropical insular possessions," proclaimed the Charlottetown *Guardian* in September 1898, "why shall not Canada do the same?" Unionists saw Canada's absorption of the Caribbean colonies as a logical response to Canada's lack of tropical territory and the related imperative to set the dominion on the same path to "material greatness" already trodden by the United States. Union would give Canada its "much needed complement of a southern section producing many things that we need but cannot produce. It would give us a southern market exclusively our own, and go far to compensate for the advantage gained in that regard by the United

States in Cuba and Porto Rico."[17] American expansion in the Caribbean and the Pacific, as well as Europe's ongoing exploits in Africa and Southeast Asia, spurred a proliferation of articles and books about the importance of the tropics to national economies in temperate regions.[18] Steamship technologies collapsed geographic space and increased the circulation of commodities, ideas, and people. The development of tropical medicine after 1890 prompted a preoccupation with tropical disease and a proliferation of colonial patholo-gies.[19] These developments engendered a global discourse of "tropicality" that provided a potent imaginative foundation for a range of scientific, commercial, and political pursuits.[20]

Union might also be a way to pre-empt America's expanding influence in the British Caribbean. Renewed US interest in annexing Jamaica in 1899–1902 was a troubling reminder of this threat. Jamaican sugar producers watched with considerable despair as US investment poured into Puerto Rico and Cuba, increasing their sugar production exponentially. In the United States, support for the annexation of Jamaica was never difficult to find. Not only were American investments in the island substantial but Jamaica's position was also strategically valuable. While the Spanish-American War elicited a mixed response in the United States, in some quarters it enlivened the rhetoric of US supremacy in the greater Caribbean as inevitable, rightful, and necessary. But popular support for annexation was not forthcoming in the US nor Jamaica. In the US, anti-imperial sentiment, the opposition of sugar producers, and the desire to maintain good Anglo-American relations kept the annexation idea from the realm of serious discussion. In Jamaica, the idea's appeal foundered on British loyalties and rampant US racism.[21]

The threat of US dominion in the British Caribbean lingered in the minds of unionists nonetheless. "The laws of political gravity," warned colonial trade agent Alex W. Murdoch in June 1899, were drawing the Caribbean colonies closer to the United States with each passing year. The American acquisition of Cuba, Puerto Rico, and the other Spanish possessions, he argued, was a development of considerable significance to Canada and the empire. Murdoch spent most of the 1890s promoting trade with South Africa, Australia, and the Caribbean. In 1889, he was instrumental in securing Canadian government subsidies for a new steamship line between Saint John and Demerara. He believed that unless closer relations were established between the Caribbean colonies and Britain or Canada, the agitation in these colonies for annexation to the United States would grow to alarming proportions.[22]

Murdoch combined the logic of temperate peoples' entitlement to tropical regions with an envy-inspired pronouncement of (white) fair play in the tropics. "Canada has much more reason for annexing these possessions than had the U.S. for acquiring Porto Rico and Cuba. The United States has tropical zones of its own. Canada has no tropical territory whatever."[23] George Johnson made similar arguments in the fall of 1898, adapting Joseph Chamberlain's imperialist truism that "every temperate zone country needs as its complement a tropical region."[24] Because "Canada lies altogether in the temperate zone, while part of the United States is within the tropics," Canada had a stronger justification for expansion in the Caribbean than the United States.[25]

Union attracted some interest in the Caribbean in 1898–99, for varied reasons. The expression of this interest was limited, as in Canada, to editorials, letters to the editor, and other newspaper content. Jamaican rum merchant and city councillor George E. Burke was the region's most enthusiastic proponent. Burke had long served as the island's commercial agent for Canada. A loyal British subject, he was indignant about any talk of Jamaica's annexation to the United States. He favoured union with Canada because he believed it would bring relief to Jamaica's sugar industry without severing the British connection. Burke's direct stake in the industry, by way of his rum enterprise, likely had much to do with his union advocacy.[26] Other Caribbeans who entertained union did so for the most part as a last resort. Anticipating the deleterious impact of the Spanish-American War on their trade with the United States, British Caribbean delegates convened in Barbados in September 1898 to draft resolutions urging the imperial government to do more to counteract or abolish the beet-sugar bounty system in Europe. When these efforts came to nothing, negotiations for a reciprocity agreement with the United States renewed hope. But the negotiations broke down in mid-November. Lawyer-politician Samuel C. Burke's changed response to union in the weeks before and after the negotiations collapsed underlines the desperation with which some Jamaicans contemplated union with Canada. A Jamaican of African-European descent, Burke responded to the union question in October with an emphatic *no*: "No question of affiliation, annexation, incorporation or any other 'ation' is of any value at the present time!"[27] On 18 November, a few days after the US trade negotiations failed, Burke saw few other options than union with Canada. "If the West Indies cannot obtain American reciprocity, or countervailing duties in the home markets as the only alternative to ruin, what is left us?" In the months that followed, several Caribbean newspapers, often with similar hints of desperation, deemed union worthy of consideration.[28]

The perceived value of the tropics to the industrial development of temperate countries bolstered arguments for commercial independence. Gaining "a valuable tropical island" as the *Monetary Times* put it, "would do much to round out the Dominion as an all-sufficing, self-producing country." For *Ottawa Citizen* editor Edward Morrison, this pursuit of self-sufficiency was grounded in a logic of international behaviour that, in theory, went beyond trade rivalries. Canada was more entitled than the United States to annex Jamaica, not only for their shared membership in the empire but because Canadian and Jamaican exports were more complementary. In his view, Canada's absorption of Jamaica was imperative to the dominion's industrial development and ability to compete in international markets. "Every country in the temperate zone is seeking tropical annexes so as to be able to supply within itself the most varied wants," he argued. The trend would only increase in the years to come, "now that the struggle between nations for commercial supremacy has resolved itself into determination to control by state action the course of industrial development so as to secure a predominant position and a monopoly in the international market for those industries which are best suited for expansion within the national boundaries."[29] Morrison believed that Canada needed a broader, more varied base of production to meet the changing conditions of industry.

In this context, union offered a solution to some of the trade obstacles between Canada and the British Caribbean. While this trade increased in the early twentieth century, Canada's market remained small relative to that of the United States, and many British Caribbeans feared American retaliation in the event of a reciprocity agreement with Canada. The communication and steamship services between Canada and the Caribbean were inadequate, and the main distribution points for Canada-bound goods were Boston and New York rather than Halifax and Saint John. Freight rates between Montreal, Canada's Maritime ports, and the Caribbean were not competitive, and Montreal was inaccessible in the winter months. Canadian flour, butter, and lard were more expensive and were considered – in the way of their ingredients and packaging – unsuitable for a tropical climate.[30]

Nova Scotia newspaperman W.D. Taunton became a union enthusiast during a trip to the region in 1902. The Halifax-based steamship company Pickford & Black enlisted him to visit the region and write a travelogue to promote tours on their line. Taunton and about thirty other passengers boarded the *Dahome* on the morning of 24 February to embark on a forty-two-day voyage to Bermuda, the Leeward Islands, and British Guiana.[31] While in Georgetown, British Guiana, Taunton found in the mercantile community quite a bit of interest in political union, and he returned to Canada with the idea on his mind. He gained an ally in Pictou MP Adam Bell, who had brought the union proposal before the House of Commons in March 1901. Bell argued that Canada should take in the Caribbean colonies "to give it all those diversities of climate, soil and product which will make it a self-supporting and practically independent part of the world."[32] His pitch stimulated little interest in Ottawa. When Bell lost his seat in the federal election of 1904, he joined forces with Taunton to drum up support through the Maritime Board of Trade. The union idea probably appealed to many board members because it promised to address two of the board's central concerns in 1904–05: the need for improved steamship services between Canada and the Caribbean, and the absorption of Newfoundland in the Canadian federation. If the British Caribbean formed part of Canada, the federal government would be compelled to subsidize a more frequent steamship service between Maritime Canada and the Caribbean. To avoid the risk of being shut out of the North-South trade and to take advantage of the newly inaugurated steamship service, Newfoundland would have to enter Confederation. At the annual meeting in Yarmouth in August, Taunton, Bell, and other board members representing each of the three Maritime provinces spoke in favour of union.[33] The board subsequently resolved in unanimity to urge the Canadian government "to take steps to secure the confederation" of Canada and the British Caribbean.[34]

Larger commercial interests soon followed suit. At its annual meeting on 20 September 1905, the Canadian Manufacturing Association (CMA) passed a resolution in favour of union. The association looked "with favour upon the proposition to secure the admission of the British West India Islands and Newfoundland into the Canadian Confederation and would respectfully ask the Federal Government to give the matter early consideration." Citing the "lack of proper transportation services" and a desire for broader markets, William S. Fisher argued that the Caribbean colonies "require our manufactured goods, they require our lumber and fish and many things of that kind. We in turn produce none of the goods they produce. We have for them a constantly growing market for the tropical productions of those islands."[35] As a member of both the Maritime Board of Trade and the CMA, Fisher was no doubt instrumental in bringing the proposal before the latter organization.

Union did attract brief attention in Ottawa in 1905–06. In parliamentary discussions about steamship services in June 1905, Toronto MP George Foster entertained the possibility of union in the future.[36] An "ardent advocate of imperial development through imperial tariff preferences" Foster had long promoted closer commercial relations with the Caribbean.[37] He had visited the islands in 1890 and had tried, unsuccessfully, to negotiate a reciprocity agreement. He and Opposition leader Robert Borden urged the importance of Canadian investment in the British Caribbean trade to pre-empt its further diversion to the United States. Doing so would also safeguard the possibility of union in the future. "Those islands, or some of them, may be brought within this Canadian confederation," Borden told the house. Whether this "be a dream or not," it was crucial that Canada not "take any retrograde step," nor compromise any policy designed to preserve the British Caribbean trade.[38] Liberal Prime Minister Wilfrid Laurier was more dubious. While his government was always willing to discuss the incorporation of Newfoundland, he told Parliament in March 1906, they were "not prepared at this time to invite or encourage political union" with the British Caribbean.[39] Laurier's opposition was based primarily on two concerns: the racial composition of the Caribbean and the proposal's resemblance to an imperial consolidation scheme. While Laurier appreciated the British connection, he and his government were generally sceptical of initiatives that aimed (or appeared to aim) to centralize the empire.

In the years that followed, interest grew in Canada and the Caribbean for a reciprocity agreement, and the union idea loomed up in these discussions from time to time. The Canadian government appointed its first trade commissioner to the British Caribbean in 1907, with headquarters in Barbados. That same year, the boards of trade of Toronto, Saint John, and Halifax sent a delegation to the Caribbean to investigate trade conditions in the region. The delegation subsequently released a report recommending trade reciprocity, improved cable and mail communications, and a more efficient and regular steamship service. Two years later, the imperial government appointed a royal commission to investigate trade relations between Canada and the British Caribbean. Montreal businessman H.K.S. Hemming hoped the Canadian representatives on the royal commission, Finance Minister W.S. Fielding and Minister of Customs William Paterson, would realize "the great opportunity that is offered to make up our one deficiency – a hot climate where cotton, sugar, rice, and tropical fruits can be grown." Hemming was confident that union would boost Canada's prestige and power, particularly in relation to the United States. With Bermuda and the British Caribbean part of Canada, "we should at once become a rival in importance of the United States, and gradually become independent of the Southern section of that Republic." Canada would become one of the world's leading nations.[40]

In a letter to Laurier in July 1909, Montreal stockbroker and president of the West India Electric Company James Hutchison proposed union with Jamaica, which he hoped would be the first of several British Caribbean colonies to join Canada. Laurier was aware, he told Hutchison, there was "in some quarters a strong opinion that [these colonies] should be taken in by Canada." But there was "a good deal of objection" to the idea, too. It might be possible, he ventured, to take Jamaica in "on some such tenure as the United States are now holding Porto Rico." In other words, Jamaican products would be protected behind Canada's tariff wall, but Jamaicans would have no political voice in Ottawa.[41] While Laurier indulged Hutchison, supported closer commercial relations with the British Caribbean, and may have been genuinely interested in the union question, in the coming months his attention shifted to reciprocity with the United States.

Not long after Laurier's finance minister released a draft of a Canada-US reciprocity agreement in January 1911, a new contingent of unionists set their sights on the Bahamas. The principal movers this time were Archibald de Léry Macdonald, the mayor of Rigaud, Quebec, and Conservative hopeful for Vaudreuil in the federal election of 1911, and Thomas Bassett Macaulay, the managing director of the Montreal-based Sun Life Assurance Company of Canada. Both men had ties to the Bahamas. Macaulay wintered and conducted business on the islands. Under the direction of Macaulay's father, Sun Life had opened several Caribbean branches in the 1880s, including one in Nassau.[42] Macdonald was less familiar with the islands, but when he visited the Bahamas for the first time in late January 1911, he "was struck with astonishment," he told *La Presse*, by their "immense untapped resources" and desperate need for capital.[43] Transfixed with the prospect of union, Macdonald returned to Canada and began drumming up support.

Macdonald was an interesting personality. A French-speaking Quebec politician of Scottish descent, he was (in Macaulay's description) an imperialist with "strong Bourassa leanings."[44] Henri Bourassa was a francophone politician and an outspoken critic of imperialism who had founded the Nationalist League in 1903 to foster a nationalist spirit in Quebec. He opposed the creation of a Canadian navy in 1911 and would later protest Canada's participation in the First World War.[45] Macdonald at once sympathized with Bourassa's National-istes and revered the British Empire. In step with his Conservative colleagues, he supported the formation of a Canadian navy. Macdonald also shared the general concern among Conservatives that reciprocity with the United States would precipitate Canada's annexation to the republic. He thought union with the Bahamas would lessen Canada's reliance on the US and ultimately place the dominion "on an equal footing" with its southern neighbour.[46]

Hoping to stir up interest in the idea, Macdonald and Macaulay travelled to the Bahamas in February. They organized a public meeting at Nassau's Kirk Hall on 20 February, where merchants and planters, politicians and labourers came to learn more about becoming the "Florida of Canada."[47] Macdonald's address at the meeting focused on the practical implications of union. The Canadian Pacific Railway Company's recent announcement of new steamship lines to Bermuda and Jamaica and new hotels on the islands was a testament to Canada's growing interest in strengthening ties with the region. If the Bahamas joined the Canadian federation, they too would be included in these plans. Under the tutelage of Ottawa, the Bahamas would "rapidly develop" into a "sister province" worthy of the Canadian federation. The Bahamian government would continue to exercise autonomy in local affairs, while the Canadian government would take control of federal works such as customs and post office revenues.[48] Moreover, Canada was "the most rapidly growing country on the face of the globe" and had an ever-expanding market to consume Caribbean products. When the Caribbean colonies developed sufficiently under Canada's protective wing, it would then be possible to contemplate free trade within the empire.[49]

Macaulay shared Macdonald's imperial sentiment, but he was more willing to leverage the proposed US-Canada reciprocity agreement to gain Bahamian support. One of the conditions of the proposed agreement, he told the audience at Kirk Hall, was that "fruit, and agricultural products of almost every kind in their natural, unmanufactured forms, shall be exchanged with absolute freedom between the two countries." The Bahamas would have to compete with agricultural products from Florida and California, but access to the US market was nonetheless certain to reap considerable economic returns for the islands.[50] Macaulay's promise of "absolutely free access" to the American market probably inspired many Bahamians to consider the proposed union seriously. From the 1870s, the Bahamian people had endured varying degrees of depression and economic instability. Unlike other British colonies in the Caribbean, the soil and climate of the Bahamas were not suitable for farming or the cultivation of sugar cane. In the nineteenth and early twentieth centuries, a number of products were developed for commercial purposes, including pineapples, sisal, and sponges. But transportation problems, outmoded agricultural technology, hurricanes, a lack of capital, competition with other islands, and an insufficient labour supply caused many Bahamian exports to decline or become obsolete.[51]

Several Bahamians spoke in favour of union at the meeting. Nassau pharmacist George M. Cole tabled a resolution to place the proposal before the island's legislature, and newspaper editor Charles S. Rae seconded the resolution. Five members of the Legislative Assembly were subsequently appointed to a Ways and Means Committee for this purpose.[52] A few weeks later, on 9 March, the Legislative Assembly adopted a resolution to seek Colonial Office approval to initiate union talks with the Canadian government. Six days later, the Legislative Council followed suit and unanimously endorsed the resolution. White Bahamian William Johnson thought the resolution reflected "the wish of the people." Since the meeting on 20 February, Johnson reported being "approached from all sides and by all classes" of Bahamians who were enthusiastic about union. Public meetings had been held on the Out Islands, and resolutions were adopted to urge Out Island representatives to support the resolution.[53] Bahamians were split, but the resolution passed the Assembly by a vote of 21 to 6.[54]

Encouraged by this result, Macdonald and Macaulay returned home to continue their campaign. They discussed the proposal with friends and business associates, wrote letters to the press and the Canadian government, and founded the Canada-West Indies League. Macaulay also publicized the proposal in the pages of *Sunshine*, a magazine for Sun Life policyholders, with a monthly circulation of 22,000 to 25,000.[55] The May 1911 issue featured the Bahamas exclusively, with editorials, photographs, and a cartoon promoting union with Canada. The cartoon depicts a young, white "Miss Bahamas" asking big white "Brother Canada" to take her "into partnership" with him, while Uncle Sam looks on enviously (figure 2.1). The Canada-West Indies League pushed the proposal more aggressively, often in the pages of its organ, *Canada-West Indies Magazine*.[56] By August, the league boasted a rapidly growing membership that included proprietors and associates of Canadian banks, life-insurance agencies, railroad companies, tourist associations, sugar-refining companies, and steamship agencies. The league actively sought members outside Canada too; its members included merchants, bankers, lawyers, hotel proprietors and civil servants from the Bahamas, Barbados, British Guiana, Jamaica, Cuba, Puerto Rico, the Dominican Republic, Britain, and the United States.[57]

Unionists also sought the support of prominent Canadians, including Winnipeg millionaire Elisha Hutchings, Canadian Pacific Railway president Thomas Shaughnessy, and University of Toronto president Robert Falconer. Hutchings was a member of the Commercial Travelers Club and visited the Caribbean in March 1911. He found a keen desire for annexation in the

IN THE BAHAMAS.

MISS BAHAMAS (TO HER BROTHER CANADA) "I WISH YOU WOULD TAKE ME INTO PARTNERSHIP WITH YOU."

Fig. 2.1   "I Wish She'd Ask Me," Sun Life publication *Sunshine*, May 1911

Bahamas, and consequently became a proponent of union.[58] Shaughnessey, hoping to further develop Canadian Pacific's steamer service to the Caribbean, thought union might secure government subsidies for the service and encourage greater commodity and tourist traffic between the two regions. At Macaulay's invitation, Shaughnessy accepted the honorary presidency of the Canada-West Indies League and pledged to do all he could "to help the [union] movement on."[59] Falconer was born in Charlottetown but had spent much of his youth in Trinidad because his father, a Presbyterian minister, had been posted there in the 1870s. It is possible that Falconer's interest in union was initially sparked while he was in Trinidad.[60] After completing secondary school at Trinidad's Queen's Royal College, he pursued university studies in London, Edinburgh, and Germany. In 1892, he was ordained a Presbyterian minister and shortly after took up a position at Halifax's Pine Hill College. He was appointed president of the University of Toronto in 1907, a position he held until 1932.[61] Falconer often emphasized the importance of the British Caribbean to Canada. "You cannot estimate the value of the West Indies to Canada and the Empire by what they are today," he told the Canadian Club of Toronto in February 1911. "They stand at the gateway of the greatest undeveloped country in the world, South America ... When you think of what the Americans are doing in cutting the Panama Canal, and of what it will mean when [it] is opened, the Islands assume great potential importance." Falconer urged Canadians to "wake up" from their fixation on the Northwest and appreciate the potential of the Caribbean and South American frontier.[62]

Macaulay wrote several letters to Laurier in April and May expounding the merits of union. This time the prime minister expressed more interest. Macaulay's emphasis on the "strategic position Canada would enjoy vis-à-vis the new Panama Canal" was particularly persuasive.[63] "The project in many ways would appeal to me," Laurier told Lord Grey, Canada's governor general, "but it requires a great deal of investigating and thinking over."[64] The reorienting of trade through the canal might undermine the All Red Route, which linked Europe to Australia and New Zealand through Canada.[65] Transporting freight by steamship was cheaper than rail. Having possessions along the canal route would offset the losses incurred by the reduction of traffic along the All Red Route (see figure 2.2). Laurier asked Macaulay to send him more information on the Bahamas' trade, revenue, expenditure, and resources.[66]

Macaulay was subsequently eager to tell anyone who would listen that he had the prime minister's support. But Laurier's interest was ultimately inconsequential because he lost the election in September. De Léry Macdonald

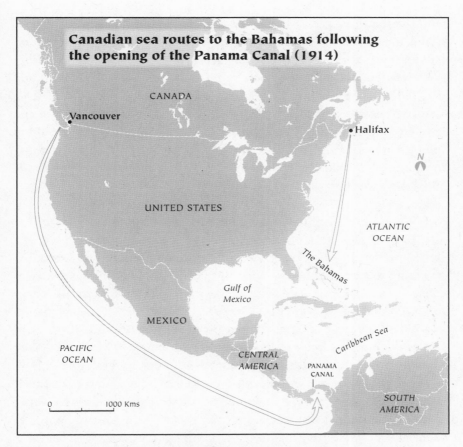

Fig. 2.2   Map of routes from Halifax and Vancouver to the Bahamas. Copyright
Robert Cronan

lost as well, to the Liberal incumbent at Vaudreuil. When the Liberals departed, so too did the possibility of a reciprocity agreement with the United States. Yet most unionists did not see the election results as much of a setback. Unionists were, in the main, Conservative imperialists who opposed the reciprocity agreement and saw in union a means to counter American influence. They continued their campaign in Canada and the Bahamas, lecturing, networking, and writing letters to politicians and the press.

When unionists outlined their respective visions, assertions of a higher purpose – sometimes national, sometimes continental or imperial – often eclipsed the commercial, pragmatic dimensions of the question. Their rhetoric was flush with presumptions of destiny, mission, and aggrandizement. Union with the Bahamas, the first of many Canadian acquisitions in the region, would, in Macdonald's words, launch the "second epoch" of Canadian nation building. Just as the Fathers of Confederation worked tirelessly to finalize the federation of 1867, so too would the "patriots at Nassau."[67] Union would consolidate and strengthen the empire, while at the same time enhancing Canada's international profile. "We have passed the old colonial days, and have now attained young manhood," Macaulay opined. It was time to stop thinking "provincially" and start thinking "imperially."[68] Canada's evolving imperial outlook might ultimately involve, perhaps precipitate, a shift in the empire's centre of gravity.

A Shifting Centre of Gravity?

Robert Borden and the Conservatives came to power in 1911 on the promise of a more robust naval policy. What this policy should entail – a monetary contribution to the British Admiralty, the development of a Canadian navy to be coordinated with the Royal Navy in times of war, or a combination of both – was a topic of bitter debate throughout 1912. In April of that year, James Aikins, newly elected MP (Conservative) for Brandon, Manitoba, shared his thoughts on the naval crisis in an address at Brandon's St Matthew's Hall. It was all very well for Canadians to sing "Rule Britannia" and talk of their loyalty to the empire, but if they wanted Britain to continue ruling the waves, they must be ready to pay their share. Why should the mother country have to foot the bill for a navy that stood in defence of the empire as a whole? It was imperative that Canadians understand the pressures and demands of the empire, he told the crowd, because they would ultimately be at its centre. Canada, and more specifically, Manitoba, were destined to be the "head and heart of the British Empire." Aikins anticipated this shift at some point in the future, and he would come to see Canada's absorption of the British Caribbean as a crucial step in this process.[69]

The rise to greatness via the Caribbean that unionists anticipated was fuelled by trade rivalry and tropical envy, but it was also based on an understanding of the empire's future, one in which Canada would take on a greater if not central role. Several developments at the turn of the century seemed to suggest that Canada was better positioned than Britain to administer the Caribbean. As amateur naturalist Benjamin Kidd argued in his widely popular *Control of the Tropics* (1898), temperate regions undergoing rapid economic development – marked most importantly by industrial and population growth – played (or would play) a particularly instrumental role in the administration and development of the tropics.[70] In the first decade of the twentieth century, Canada's industrial production came nowhere near that of Britain or the US, but optimists – encouraged by Canada's remarkable economic and population growth – expected the dominion to catch up. "Canada has not hitherto been considered a factor in the New World," Scottish writer William Pringle Livingstone enthused in 1906. "She has been looked upon as a dependency of Great Britain … With the steady growth of her political autonomy, her increasing population, the rapid progress of her manufacturing industries, and an ambition that is almost Imperial, she is becoming a force to be reckoned with."[71] In stark contrast, the British economy remained in relative decline. During the 1890s, British steel production fell behind that of the US and Germany, and in the three decades before the war, Britain's share of international trade in manufactured goods decreased 11.7 per cent.[72] The early twentieth century was also a period of domestic turmoil in Britain. Industrial unrest and the rise of trade unionism, suffragette militancy, a constitutional crisis and consequent push for House of Lords reform, Irish nationalism, and the resurgent Home Rule question all exposed deep fissures within British society.[73]

Geopolitical developments compounded insecurities about imperial decline and prompted a wider discussion about the role of Canada and the other dominions in mitigating them. The South African War (1899–1902) proved a surprisingly protracted and embarrassing conflict for Britain. It undermined confidence in Britain's military capabilities, challenged the racialized notion that "the Englishman was the born ruler of the world," and bolstered nationalist movements in Ireland and India.[74] The Yihetuan (Boxer) uprising against Western imperialism in China in 1900, violently suppressed by a British-led alliance, underscored the instability of Britain's vast empire. Japan's emergence as a major imperial power in the wake of the Russo-Japanese war in 1905 compromised British interests in China, created new naval vulnerabilities in the Pacific, and undermined the Eurocentric world order.[75] Just as Canada sought to broaden its presence in the western hemisphere in the wake of US expansion and British retraction, Japan's rise suggested that Australia and New Zealand would take on an increasingly important role in the Pacific. "A century ago Europe was virtually the whole world," the *Toronto Star* observed in 1909, "and its ideas dominated the world. Since that time we have witnessed the rise of the United States, of Japan, of Canada, of Australia, and the awakening of China. European domination is passing away. The Monroe doctrine means the end of European domination in America. The rise of Japan means the end of the hope of European domination in Asia."[76] Speculation abounded that the soon-to-be-completed Panama Canal would further undermine Europe's global dominance. In connecting the Atlantic and Pacific Oceans across the Isthmus of Panama, the canal promised to reorient the world's trade routes through the Americas and enhance the strategic and commercial value of the Caribbean and Central America.[77]

America's application of the Monroe doctrine in 1895–97 to intervene in the British Guiana–Venezuela boundary dispute was a momentous rebuff of European power that confirmed US hegemony in the hemisphere. Britain's ultimately conciliatory response to US intervention in the dispute marked the beginning of a long period of Anglo-American amity.[78] British anxiety about Germany's growing naval capacity underscored the importance of American friendship. Britain (and by extension Canada) remained neutral in the Spanish-American War, conceded US control over the construction and operation of the Panama Canal in the Hay-Pauncefort Treaty of 1901, and, much to Canada's chagrin, sided with the US in the Alaska boundary dispute in 1903.[79] Britain's influence in the western hemisphere eroded further with the reduction of British garrisons and naval squadrons in Canada and the Caribbean in 1905–06.

The imperial government's decision to withdraw British troops from the Caribbean generated considerable protest.[80] To many in the Caribbean, this withdrawal was a blatant indication of Britain's disinterest in the region. "To reverse this policy now," stated a petition from the Barbados House of Assembly, "after it has been consistently pursued for so many years, is liable to be interpreted as indicating the cessation of England's interest in the welfare of this colony."[81] Forster Alleyne, who tabled the resolution in the House, thought the withdrawal of troops was particularly alarming in the context of America's recent (and continuing) expansion in the region. Who would have thought that the "islands for which Nelson fought and Rodney fell were to be denuded of the support of the Mother Country, and were to be dependent in the time of danger on the assistance of a single cruiser, summoned by telegraph ... from heaven knows where. Could there be a greater humiliation than this?"[82] Others in London expressed similar concerns about the implications of Britain's retreat from the Caribbean. Edward Davson, who held significant commercial interests in British Guiana, was much alarmed by Britain's "tacit acquiescence" to America's growing intervention in the region. "The balance of power in the Caribbean is undergoing a subtle change, which, it must be admitted, is not altogether in favour of England."[83] America's strategic interests suggested that Jamaica was particularly vulnerable. As the West India Committee Circular warned in March 1905, the United States was rapidly acquiring a foothold in all those positions that American naval captain Alfred Mahan identified as strategically valuable, and Jamaica was among them.[84] When the Panama Canal opened, Jamaica would be, in Mahan's estimation, the "key to the Caribbean."[85]

These developments generated considerable concern about the empire's future.[86] To many imperialists, the solution to Britain's waning power was the consolidation of the empire. There was little clarity or consensus about the best route to this outcome, nor the desired outcome itself. It generally implied a change in the empire's structure that involved greater imperial responsibilities for Canada and the other dominions. On one end of the spectrum, there were imperial federationists who favoured a centralized empire with an imperial council to coordinate defence, foreign policy, and commerce for the whole, although the question of representation was much contested. With Britain's population larger than that of all the dominions combined, representation by population was unacceptable to the dominions because it threatened to undermine their autonomy. An arrangement in which Britain and the dominions were partners with an equal voice in the conduct of the empire was preferable, but it too was objectionable on the basis that it might commit the dominions to imperial pursuits contrary to their national interests. On the other end of the spectrum, advocates of a more unified or consolidated empire sought nothing more than closer commercial ties (imperial preferences, free trade within the empire, or an imperial customs union).

The idea that the empire's centre would eventually shift to Canada, as James Aikens predicted in 1912, was a popular forecast in early twentieth-century speculation about the empire's future. In *Canada and the Empire* (1911), British journalist and economist William R. Lawson observed that, forty years earlier, the central question facing imperial Britain was whether the colonies were worth keeping. Now the tables were turned, and the dominions were asking whether, and for how long, it was worth their while to hang on to the Mother Country. "No young country ever had such a call on the future as Canada has to-day." Canadians had proven themselves "to be men of action, and their opportunity is rapidly coming to them. A few more years of their present phenomenal progress will give them ... much weight in the councils of the Empire." Empire building was not for "overcrowded, overcivilised, and overburdened communities" like Britain. It was the "business of a young, hopeful, and progressive people, with a profound belief in [their] destiny." It was the business of Canada.[87] Lawson thought imperial federation was no longer an academic concern: it was a commercial and military necessity. The empire was in crisis, and an imperial council should be formed at once. As Canada's population and wealth continued to increase, Canadians would become a commanding presence and possibly the deciding voice in that council.[88] Other Britons who anticipated a shift in the empire's centre of gravity to Canada included prominent and not-so-prominent personalities: geographer Halford Mackinder, newspaper magnate Alfred Harmsworth, writer Frederick Young, and historian J. Ellis Barker. Most of these men were unabashed imperialists and conservative in political orientation. Young was an imperial federationist, Barker a Tariff Reformer and Chamberlainite imperialist, and Mackinder a Liberal Unionist; Harmsworth's newspapers supported Conservative views, including staunch opposition to Irish Home Rule.[89]

Canada's absorption of the British Caribbean related to these varied visions of the empire's future in different ways. Proponents of union framed it as a means to imperial ends, something that would consolidate the empire and possibly lay the groundwork for imperial free trade or even federation. Most unionists favoured the language of imperial consolidation over federation, although these terms were ill-defined. Montreal writer Watson Griffin, who had opposed union in the 1880s on racial grounds, conceived union as a step toward a broader "imperial alliance." Griffin was principally a journalist, but he served as the Canadian Manufacturers Association's publicist from 1902 to 1906, and in 1912 George Foster recruited him into the Department of Trade and Commerce. In 1902, Griffin defined the imperial alliance as an arrangement wherein Britain, Canada, Australia, New Zealand, and eventually South Africa shared responsibility and enjoyed equal representation in the empire. The Canadian federations of 1867–73 and the Australian federation in 1901 were early steps toward this goal. Canada's absorption of Newfoundland as a province, and Bermuda, British Guiana, British Honduras, and the Caribbean islands as territories, were the logical next steps.[90] Like imperial federationists, Griffin conceived the alliance as a racially exclusive federation constitutive of Britain and the self-governing dominions. The racialized assumption that non-white subjects were unfit for self-government precluded the Caribbean colonies.[91] In annexing British colonies proximate to them – and ascribing them territorial status – the dominions would further the work of imperial consolidation while simultaneously excluding racialized colonial subjects from imperial and national governance.

Macdonald and Macaulay conceived the implications of union for the empire differently. Macdonald saw union as means to imperial consolidation, but he never harnessed the language of imperial federation, perhaps due to his French-Canadian sensibilities. For him, the imperial goal was free trade within the empire. Macaulay often emphasized the need for a more cohesive empire. The Caribbean islands were akin to "little detached sticks lying loosely around." Any one stick could be broken easily; "Join one of these little sticks to the larger Canadian one," however, and "the little one not only shares in the strength of the large one, but even adds something to the combined strength."[92] This cohesion would further the larger goal of an imperial "federation or partnership of five great nations": Britain, Canada, Australia (presumably including New Zealand), South Africa, and India. Macaulay's inclusion of India was uncommon. India was rarely included in federation schemes before the First World War, and always on different terms from the self-governing dominions.[93] Indians were not considered fit for self-government, and their potential participation in federation clashed with notions of Anglo-Saxon kinship and superiority. Nor were imperial federationists' commercial and military arguments particularly applicable to India, which funded and maintained a large British army that could be summoned for imperial purposes elsewhere, and was a free-trade country whose imports came overwhelmingly from Britain.[94]

A few imperialists in the Caribbean similarly held that union would strengthen the empire. In 1898, Jamaican lawyer Richard Augustus Walcott, described as a "hearty supporter of imperial federation," told the *Daily Gleaner* that while he had more to learn about what union might entail, he was in favour of anything that would consolidate the constituent parts of the empire.[95] William Thorp, who identified himself as a resident of Jamaica in a letter to the *Canadian Magazine* in 1899, argued that Canada's "annexation" of the British Caribbean would "give an immense impetus to Imperial Federation." The Canadian federation was a "splendid success," and the federations to come in Australia and South Africa would be equally so. Why not extend these federations to "groups of colonies competent to offer reciprocal advantages?"[96] Bahamian George Cole argued in 1911 that union with Canada would be an important step toward a united British Empire.[97]

Imperialists in Britain offered a range of opinion on the question. Some believed union would strengthen the empire by way of consolidation or federation. Others thought it was in the best interests of neither Britain nor the empire. Would union expedite Canada's independence? Would it shift the centre of imperial power to Canada too soon? Would it injure British trade? Richard Jebb, an English journalist and imperial affairs expert, addressed the union question during an address to the Canadian Club of Winnipeg in 1905.

The time would soon come, he told the audience, when the self-governing dominions would need – for the good of the empire – to take on greater imperial responsibilities. Canada's incorporation of the British Caribbean was a "step in the right direction" in that respect.[98] Jebb was a Conservative who supported tariff reform and stronger economic ties within the empire. But he was not an imperial federationist. As he argued in *Studies in Colonial Nationalism* (1905), dominion nationalities called for a reorganization of imperial relations based on a "perpetual alliance of equal states."[99]

Many imperial federationists spoke favourably about union. Albert Grey, Canada's governor general from 1904 to 1911 and cousin of the Bahamian governor William Grey-Wilson, pressed the Canadian government to adopt policies aimed to consolidate the empire. His dreams of imperial federation came to nothing, but he did play an important role in persuading the government to establish a Canadian navy in 1910 and thus contribute to imperial defence.[100] Grey had lofty aspirations for Canada, which included speculation about Canada's future position at the head of the empire. "No other country awaits a greater destiny than Canada," he told a Calgary audience in 1909. "Nothing prevents Canada from acquiring, in the course of time, the controlling interests in the government of the empire." Canada's union with the British Caribbean would set this process in motion.[101] Hereditary peer Charles Spencer-Churchill (Duke of Marlborough and Winston Churchill's first cousin) thought the union of dominions and dependencies would facilitate a more cooperative approach to a long-neglected imperial problem, "the administration of the native races." He figured that discussions of imperial federation gave too little consideration to how the "civilizing mission" might be carried out in coordinated fashion throughout the empire. Australia possessed Papua New Guinea, "which she administers on her own lines. In ten years' time South Africa will take over the Kaffir and Zulu Protectorate, and some day or other Canada is likely to have the handling of the negro problem in the West Indies. To Great Britain will be left India, tropical Africa, and some hundreds of islands in the Pacific." Spencer-Churchill thought a coordinated effort on "native policy" would help facilitate "the ultimate union of the white States" by establishing a common imperial mandate in Britain and the dominions.[102]

Not every imperialist supported union. Alfred Milner, a member of the short-lived Imperial Federation League in the 1880s and a colonial administrator in Britain's South African colonies from 1897 to 1905, was deeply committed to imperial unity – he co-founded the Round Table movement in 1909. He expected the self-governing dominions would, in step with their economic and population development, grow closer to "those portions of the British tropics" nearest them. But he did not anticipate a time when the Caribbean colonies, the islands of the South Pacific, or South Africa's "hinterland" would be "handed over" to the dominions.[103] He favoured an arrangement that strengthened imperial bonds without disrupting the empire's existing power structure.[104] With the union of dominions and dependencies, Britain would lose control over the latter's markets, resources, and trade policies.[105]

Trade was not the only consideration that generated concern. Herbert Musgrave, an officer in the British Army, a decorated veteran of the South African War, and the Australian-born son of Sir Anthony Musgrave (late governor of South Australia), queried the implications of union for Caribbean defence. In a letter published in the Royal Colonial Institute's organ, *United Empire*, Musgrave warned that Laurier's naval policy spelled disaster for the Caribbean colonies and the empire. In his view, the prime minister's insistence that the Canadian navy would not automatically be put in the service of the British Admiralty in times of war was a disgraceful affront to the empire, an attitude of "Canada first, Canada last and Canada all the time." He saw Canada's naval policy as dangerously incompatible with the empire's interests. Until the Canadian government repudiated its anti-imperial doctrine and "unreservedly accepted the principle of Imperial solidarity," for Britain to give up the Caribbean colonies "would be the height of folly." Britain should work out a binding naval agreement with Canada before doing so.[106]

Officials in the British Colonial Office were also uneasy with the military and especially the commercial implications of union. When Governor Grey-Wilson brought the union question to their attention in April 1911, the Colonial Office had adopted an oppositional stance even before they saw the Bahamian Assembly's resolution. As Principal Clerk Gilbert Grindle remarked in an internal correspondence, "His Majesty's Government propose to await the arrival of the text of the resolution," but "when it does come we shall endeavour to find an excuse for not complying." They were concerned, first and foremost, that under union it "would become necessary for [the Caribbean colonies] to adopt the whole of the Canadian customs tariff in detail against the world in general. This adoption would involve a disturbance of the existing channels of trade, the results of which it is impossible to foresee."[107] The Colonial Office also feared that union might upset the existing structure of imperial relations and shift the seat of imperial power from London to Ottawa. As one official remarked in May 1911, "the center of gravity of the Empire will leave England for Canada in less than a quarter of a century; but we do not wish to accelerate the process at our expense."[108] Many colonies owed debts to the Imperial Exchequer but remained valuable to Britain in the way of commerce and investment. That value would "undoubtedly be diminished by a transfer of the administration to Canada, while if we keep [the Bahamas] we shall benefit by the great development which is going on and by the opening of the Panama Canal."[109] Some officials feared that Britain's loss of the Bahamas to Canada might be "the thin end of the wedge as regards the [Caribbean]," and precipitate the loss of more Caribbean colonies.[110] These observations inspired a somewhat competitive, and occasionally disdainful, attitude toward Canada. As one official asserted, "Canada has an abundance of resources already; why should we let her have any of ours?"[111]

Officials in the Colonial Office nonetheless anticipated some form of future Canada-Caribbean union. "It appears almost certain," Colonial Secretary Lewis Harcourt predicted, "that in a future not very remote the Dominions in temperate zones will desire to acquire for themselves 'hothouses' for consumable luxuries and other purposes. It is not unreasonable to contemplate the ultimate absorption of the West Indies by Canada; of the Pacific Islands by Australia and New Zealand; of Rhodesia and the native Protectorates (even of Nyassaland [sic]) by South Africa."[112] The Colonial Office's object was to elude and delay the union question rather than repudiate it outright. Opposition remained covert. As Grindle wrote in the minutes, "There are arguments which, strong as they are, can hardly be used publicly."[113] In this sense, presumptions of British benevolence provided a convenient discourse for the Colonial Office to discourage union and maintain Britain's continued interests in the region. Canadian control of the Bahamas, they warned, would threaten the well-being of the islands' Black populations, so it was the responsibility of the Colonial Office to safeguard their interests by maintaining the status quo. The imperial government, Grindle wrote, had "always looked on themselves as specially bound to look after the coloured population." With "signs of the rise of a colour question in Canada," it would be "a betrayal of trust for H[is] M[ajesty's] G[overnment] to hand over" the islands to Canada.[114] While the principle of trusteeship provided a humanitarian explanation for Britain's imperial designs, the Colonial Office's argument was nonetheless based on legitimate considerations.[115] The concern for Black Bahamians may have been overstated, but the assessment of white Canadian racism was not. The "colour question" was indeed rising, much to the detriment of unionism.

The (White Man's) Canadian Century

When white settlers spoke of Canada's greatness to come in the twentieth century, geography was a crucial determinant. The country's geographical value derived not only from its boundless resources but also from its "health-ful" climate. "Northern" symbolized "energy, strength, self-reliance, health, and purity," while its opposite, "southern," was often associated with "decay and effeminacy, even libertinism and disease." Of all the British dominions, Canada was the only one situated entirely above the forty-fifth parallel, giving weight to the argument that Canada was "pre-destined" to fulfil an important role in the world.[116] Even Britain's northern climate, described by one contemporary as "warm [and] moisture-laden," could not match the "tonic properties" of Canada's crisp, clear air.[117] These constructs abetted the fabrication of racial geographies that advanced two white settler prerogatives: maintaining (the myth of) a white Canada and justifying white encroachments in the Caribbean. In the first instance, settler Canadians mobilized the rhetoric of climatic suitability to keep racialized peoples out. In the second, they relied on well-worn constructs of Black indolence and backwardness to assert white intervention in the Caribbean. At the time, tropicality was a powerful discourse of empire across the globe. As Benjamin Kidd argued in *Control of the Tropics*, tropical regions possessed enormous potential, but this potential could only be realized through white intervention; the "natural" inhabitants of the tropics, backward and uncivilized, were incapable of either initiating or consummating development. "If we look to the native social systems of the tropical East, to the primitive savagery of Central Africa, to the West Indian Islands in the past in process of being assisted into the position of modern States by Great Britain, to the Black Republic of Hayti in the present, or to modern Liberia in the future, the lesson seems everywhere the same; it is that there will be no development of the resources of the tropics under native government."[118]

In Canada, tropicality was refracted through the pervasive myth of racelessness.[119] With or without the help of climatic constructs, the claim that Canada lacked a "colour problem" was central to settler prophecies about Canada's future greatness. This claim was usually based on an ignorance, denial, minimization, or misrepresentation of racialized peoples' histories and their continuing presence in Canada. As Ontario's deputy minister of education wrote in 1899, Canada had an auspicious future because "no crowds of half-civilized immigrants have interfered with the growth of our institutions. The duty of assimilating a variety of races has not taxed the Canadian people.

The curse of slavery has left us no negro problem to be solved."[120] For the white settler intellectuals George Parkin and W.L. Grant, Canada's harsh climate meant that such a "problem" would likely never materialize. "From the national point of view," Grant stated in an address to the Royal Geographical Society in 1911, "our climate kills out the unfit with grim efficiency. We are not likely ever to have a negro problem … Canada is not without the tramp and the wastrel; but the unemployed can never remain in sufficient numbers to become a national problem. The English climate chills but does not kill; in Canada the waster, as a class, must work, emigrate, or die."[121] Parkin leveraged climatic pseudo-science in an even more blunt and brutal attempt to dismiss Black lives. He told a Montreal reporter in 1908 that Canada's frigid winter temperature was the country's best asset because "it gets rid of the black problem altogether."[122]

Settler Canadians had mobilized these racial geographies since at least the late 1860s, following the publication of Robert Grant Haliburton's *Men of the North*. They were a fiction, of course, contingent on the violent erasure of Indigenous peoples and a denial of what were already racially heterogeneous populations. Nonetheless, they gained currency in the early twentieth century as white Canadians became increasingly anxious about the growing number of Black Caribbeans and Black Americans immigrating to Canada. While census returns from this period are imprecise, the decennial census indicates that Canada's Black population in fact declined slightly between 1901 and 1911 (from 17,437 to 16,994, according to federal census returns).[123] Yet other sources, including newspapers, company data, and Department of Immigration records, nonetheless confirm that hundreds of Black Caribbeans and thousands of Black Americans entered (or attempted to enter) Canada in the years leading up to and including 1911. They took up work as industrial labourers in Toronto, Montreal, and Sydney, as railway porters, farmers and agricultural labourers on the prairies, and domestic workers in rural and urban households across the country.[124]

White settler assumptions about African-descended peoples shaped the union discourse in different ways. Goldwin Smith thought the fifteen hundred miles of sea separating Canada from the Caribbean was "less estranging than would be the moral, social and political gulf between the negro population and ours."[125] William Ogden, a prominent Toronto doctor who vacationed in the Bahamas in November 1911, found the Bahamian people "loyal, sober, and law-abiding." But, he continued, the "colored folks, who outnumbered the whites by four to one, are ignorant and inclined to be lazy. They do not seem to possess either the incentive or the initiative to get out of their present rut of hard poverty."[126] Others tried to define blackness as something that was exterior to Canada and under union would remain so.[127] George Johnson encouraged Canadians to consider the Dutch, who managed diverse and far-distant peoples scattered across two oceans without anyone hearing "of revolt, of risings and discontent."[128] They supplied their "wards" with railways, telephones, and savings banks and won "the gratitude of the natives" in doing so. The Dutch example emphasized the peripheral positioning of racialized colonial subjects. Canada would similarly provide capital for Caribbean development and all the "paraphernalia of modern civilization," and Caribbean peoples would have no reason to migrate north.[129] "Over 2,000 miles of salt sea separate [them] from Canada," W.D. Taunton reminded *Canadian Magazine* readers in 1912. White Canadians should rest assured that African-Caribbeans "could never over-run Canada."[130]

Unionists also emphasized the British aspects of Caribbean societies and differentiated Black peoples in the British Caribbean from those in the American South. According to Taunton, the deplorable conduct of Blacks in the South was responsible for white Canadians' aversion to people of African descent. Under the protection and tutelage of the British crown, however, Black Caribbeans were "loyal, peaceful, [and] god-fearing."[131] When Governor Grey-Wilson addressed a Canadian audience at the Empire Club in Toronto, he contrasted "the horrors of the situation" in the US South with the apparently cordial state of race relations in the Bahamas. His trope of choice was the "Black brute," a Reconstruction-era construct of the "savage" Black man that whites brandished to undermine Black political power.[132] "A white woman in the Bahamas, in the most isolated position," Grey-Wilson claimed, "is as secure today as if she were in this room now. I defy anyone to say that about the Southern States of America."[133] When Thomas Macaulay of Sun Life lectured on union with the Bahamas at the Canada Club in April 1911, he assured the audience that Bahamians of all colours were "in thorough sympathy with British ideals and British standards." They were long familiar with representative institutions, having had an elected legislative assembly since 1729. On average, he concluded, "the coloured people [were] much superior to those of the Southern States." Canadian ignorance of the Bahamas probably allowed Macaulay's assurance that the colony's "races live in perfect harmony" to pass without question.[134]

The question of governance, of the political rights that Blacks would or would not exercise under union, was the most significant issue for both

Canadians and Caribbeans. That Johnson envisioned union as a colonial relationship was unambiguous. His racial and paternalistic assumptions about African Caribbeans and his claims that Canada was "entitled" to "control" and "secure hegemony" over the British Caribbean spoke for themselves. To unionists, one thing was clear: managing Caribbean peoples meant reaping the rewards of their resources, labour, and consumption while circumscribing their mobility and political rights.

Few Canadian unionists seriously considered admitting the Caribbean colonies as a province. Some suggested territorial status, but more often ideas of governance revolved around Black exclusion. In 1899, a union enthusiast writing under the pseudonym Publicola outlined a muddled plan to annex Jamaica and British Honduras to Nova Scotia while denying them representation in the House of Commons. To "prevent the white element [from] being swamped by the black," Prince Edward Island and New Brunswick would join Nova Scotia too, forming a new province styled "Acadia." Jamaica and British Honduras would somehow be "dependencies" within Nova Scotia, electing representatives to Halifax only. The two Caribbean "colonies" would, however, have senate seats in Ottawa: three for Jamaica and two for British Honduras.[135] Another model that unionists often referenced was the US relationship with Puerto Rico. Just as US Congress had done under the Foraker Act of 1900, Canada's constitution might be "perverted" to accommodate the administration of overseas colonial possessions.[136] In this configuration the federal government would be neither representative nor accountable to Caribbean peoples.[137]

Unfortunately for unionists, there was a discernible deterioration of interest in the twelve months after the Nassau meeting in February 1911. When Macaulay and Macdonald launched their campaign at that time, they generated significant enthusiasm in the islands. The *Nassau Guardian* described the meeting at Kirk Hall as "one of the largest and most representative audiences ever seen in th[e] City."[138] A year later, the mood had shifted. Macaulay posted placards in Nassau inviting Bahamians to a meeting on 13 February, but the turnout was disappointing, except for a trickle of curious American visitors.[139] The reasons for the shift were many. Macaulay's early union promises had been replete with misrepresentations. He told Bahamians that their fruit would enter the US market free of duty under Canada-US reciprocity. He exaggerated the extent of interest in Ottawa. He assured Black Bahamians that they need not fear race prejudice in Canada, that they could expect "absolutely fair and equal treatment" at all times. In a related claim, he insisted that the Bahamas would enter the Canadian federation not as a dependency or colony but as a partner. It would be a partnership "on absolutely equal terms ... in which you would be a province on precisely the same terms as Ontario, Quebec, or any other province." Bahamians, he said, would have complete control over their local affairs and representation in Ottawa in proportion to their population.[140]

None of these claims held up. The terms of the Canada-US reciprocity agreement dashed any hopes that the Bahamas would benefit. Prime Minister Laurier had expressed interest in union, but it was hardly keen. Bahamian confidence in the latter three assurances collapsed under the weight of Canadian racism. Bahamians had good reason to be sceptical of Macaulay's promises of equality. In his correspondence with Laurier, Macaulay outlined a plan of governance in the Bahamas akin to crown colony rule. The "present happy relations between the two races" in the Bahamas, he assured the prime minister, "are in no small degree due to the fact that the Islands are to a certain extent a Crown colony." The Bahamas possessed an elected Assembly, which technically negated crown colony status. But with a governor appointed from London and an Upper House appointed by the governor, Macaulay thought there were sufficient "safeguards against unwise legislation." The point of comparison here – the example to be avoided – was the United States. "It is the fear of the colored vote that makes the whites of the Southern States use such measures to keep the negro under; and it is the knowledge of their power as voters, and resentment of the oppressive attitude of the whites, that cause the colored population to become discontented and aggressive." America lacked safeguards, he continued, to protect both races. Under union, "we must devise some plan, under which it will be impossible for a condition of affairs to develop similar to that existing in the Southern States." Macaulay recommended a "rather severe" franchise qualification at the federal level. To avoid offending Bahamians, however, the qualification should refer to "tropical conditions" rather than colour. "Allusion could be made to the case with which a bare living can be obtained in the tropics, people of all colours, even including Coolies from India, being able to live there on an income which in the North would be quite inadequate." People who "live hand to mouth" and who have "little financial stake in the country" could hardly expect to be granted the vote.[141]

White Canadian racism was nothing new, but in 1911 white supremacy was on the defensive in a particularly public way. In March, April, and May, white settler animosity toward Black American immigrants on the prairies – who were, like settlers of European descent, answering the federal government's call to "settle" the west – reached a crescendo.[142] Multiple boards of trade, farmer's organizations, municipal and city councils, and women's groups across Alberta and Saskatchewan sent petitions and letters of protest to the Department of the Interior (then charged with immigration), the prime minister, and the press. Several presumptions abound in the letters: white entitlement to the land, the expectation and urgency of a white country, the absence of racial enmity therein and, consequently, a superior moral climate to the United States.[143] The hostility was so intense that the Canadian state – no stranger to racialized hostility itself – intervened to deny Black immigrants entry. In August, the government introduced an Order-in-Council prohibiting any person of African descent from entering Canada. The order never became law for fear it would cost the Liberals Black votes in the September election. But other government tactics had curbed Black immigration by the final months of 1911. Ottawa enlisted two agents (one of them a Black medical doctor) to go to Oklahoma, where the recent migrants had come from, to dissuade prospective Black migrants from moving north. The government also instructed immigration agents to use their discretionary powers to reject Black immigrants as "unsuitable to the climate and requirements of Canada," as codified in the Immigration Act of 1910.[144]

Around the same time that white racial animosity toward Black settlers escalated on the prairies, the Canadian government was scrambling to curb the migration of Black domestic workers from Guadeloupe. A first group of sixteen women arrived in September 1910 and were placed in Quebec homes with little notice. When immigration officials in Ottawa learned that two larger groups would soon arrive, they instructed their agents at Montreal and New York to examine the women with particular scrutiny to determine their suitability for domestic work. Fifty-eight women arrived in Montreal on 7 April. They were described by immigration agents as healthy, intelligent, and likely to succeed as domestic workers. The superintendent of immigration, William D. Scott, was nonetheless uneasy with the prospect of "too much" Black immigration. Perhaps hoping to find grounds to ban the scheme, he wrote to all the households that had received a Guadeloupean domestic worker to inquire whether they were satisfied with the women. Despite receiving an overwhelmingly positive response, Scott concluded that the scheme should be terminated because the women were "not all of good moral character." When ten Quebec-bound domestics arrived in New York in July, all were rejected. The scheme was officially discontinued thereafter.[145]

These events and similar episodes of white Canadian racism were reported in the British Caribbean press with greater frequency in the spring and summer of

1911.[146] "We were told that Canada would receive us, 'with open arms,'" Robert Bailey observed at the end of March, "that there was no colour prejudice in Canada. That coloured American citizens were taking up large tracts of land in the Northwest." Soon after, these assurances were "decidedly checkmated" when news reached Nassau that a party of Black Americans was refused entry at the Canadian border on the basis that they were "undesirable citizens." Originally from Barbados, Bailey was a tailor by trade and a political activist. He was an outspoken critic of racial prejudice at home and abroad and became active in Marcus Garvey's United Negro Improvement Association after its formation in 1914. He chastised the members of the Bahamian legislature for supporting the resolution for union with Canada without familiarizing themselves with racial attitudes in Canada. Given that the great majority of the colony's citizens were Black, it was shocking that the government had failed to make such inquiries "before trying to pitch us, baseball like, at Canada."[147] Did they not realize the extent of Canada's "colour prejudice"? They would certainly experience a rude awakening on their first visit to Ottawa. "Picture our House journeying to Ottawa … Canada [ready] with smiling countenance, and open arms, waiting to receive them, when suddenly she espies Messrs. Anderson, Evans, Bowen and Roxborough. The smile vanishes, her arms are slowly folded: 'No, no they are undesirable get rid of them, and [don't] come again.'"[148]

A letter to the *Nassau Guardian* the same month was similarly critical of the Bahamian government for its credulous consumption of Macaulay's promises. The legislature's "sublime confidence" that Canada would take a "community of 60,000 souls, mostly of the negro race, into the dignity of a Province and straightway [sic] proceed to spend millions on us" was a disgrace. It was "time to protest and to attempt to save some vestige of our rudely disturbed dignity as a Colony." The letter's most caustic criticism, however, was reserved for the audacious Canadians who presumed to know what was best for the Bahamas. They were nothing more than "two or three peripatetic Canadians sprung from Heaven knows where, whose personal motives are not far to seek and who are doubtless quite pleased with the notoriety which they have incidentally achieved." Macdonald was "a sort of Pied Piper of Hamelin, piping away for a lot of rats who are ready to desert their native ship because they believe they discern signs of sinking." The anonymous critic, who signed the letter "A Bahamian – and proud of it," was quite certain that union with Canada would only degrade the colony's status in the empire.[149] Even Governor Grey-Wilson, who had allied himself with the union campaign early on, conceded that the colony's non-white populations were concerned that their well-being might be compromised under Canadian rule. While British-appointed governors "have hitherto been credited with sympathy, with consideration for, and impartiality towards the coloured race," he pointed out that "doubts are felt in regard to the Governors who might be sent from Ottawa." Bahamians feared, in other words, that their treatment under the Canadian administration would "prove more American than British."[150]

As stories of white Canadian racism circulated, people across the Caribbean questioned the union idea. D.A. Corinaldi, a Jamaican of mixed descent and a long-time member of the island's Legislative Council, could confidently say from his experience working among Jamaicans of all walks of life that annexation to Canada was almost universally "abhorrent and would not be countenanced." No influx of Canadian capital would make up for the immeasurable benefits "derived from being an integral part of the British nation." Yes, Canada was part of the empire, but in the minds of Jamaicans, Corinaldi argued, there was little distinction between the Canadian and the American. There were "some things money can't buy," and being part of Great Britain was one of them.[151] Jamaican-born dentist Louis Meikle rejected annexation to either the United States or Canada on racial grounds. In his book *Confederation of the British West Indies versus Annexation to the United States of America*, published in 1912, Meikle observed that the "white people of the Dominion are no less drastic on the race problem than their American neighbours." The only distinction was that in Canada Blacks had legal status and recourse in the courts, but they encountered white animosity and discrimination in all aspects of Canadian society. White Canadian racism sounded the death knell of union for Canadians and Caribbeans alike. A Caribbean nationalist, Meikle favoured a union of all the British Caribbean territories, modelled on the Canadian federation.[152] Walter Reece, an Englishman representing the Bank of England in Jamaica, argued that Canadians lacked the experience and aptitude for judicious colonial governance. What guarantees, he wondered, could Canada give "that she would for all times treat the black and coloured people of these Islands with the same equity and protection as they have been accustomed to enjoy under the rule of the King and the government of Great Britain?"[153]

There was little evidence to suggest that Caribbean peoples could expect fair play. White Canadian racism, on display in Ottawa and the Canadian prairies from March 1911, was accentuated further by the divisive issue of inter-imperial immigration. Debates over Indian mobility in the empire had been ongoing since the late nineteenth century. Imperial citizenship, which sought to establish uniformity of British subjecthood across the empire, clashed with the racial nationalisms of the white dominions.[154] As a self-governing dominion, Canada controlled its domestic affairs, so it could exclude imperial (non-white) subjects from other parts of the empire. As British subjects, however, Indian immigrants posed particular challenges for the settler state. Ottawa's strategies to restrict the entry of other Asian groups – through a head tax on Chinese immigrants and a quota on Japanese immigrants by way of a "Gentleman's Agreement" with Japan – were unacceptable in the Indian case. White anxiety grew markedly in 1906 with the arrival of about two thousand Indians in Vancouver. In 1907 British Columbia's premier disenfranchised Indian residents, and an "Asiatic Exclusion League" formed in Vancouver and tore through the city's Asian district. The following year, the federal government introduced an Order-in-Council to curb Indian immigration. Ostensibly neutral, it required immigrants to travel to Canada by continuous journey from their country of birth or citizenship, effectively bringing Indian immigration to a halt.[155] Canada also joined the other dominions to vigorously resist imperial citizenship at the Imperial Conference in 1911, compelling the imperial government to "accept the principle that each of the Dominions must be allowed to decide for itself which elements it desires to accept in its population."[156] This rejection of imperial citizenship, which drew criticism from India and elsewhere in the colonial empire, brought white Canadian racism once more into sharp relief.

The anti-Asian sentiment that erupted in British Columbia had much to do with white working-class fears of Asian labour, but it was also part of a broader, transnational resolve to defend white supremacy. As historians Henry Reynolds and Marilyn Lake have shown, the United States and the settler dominions developed policies to formalize their existence as white men's countries. They shared knowledge in the production of passports, education and literacy tests, and other technologies designed to obstruct this immigration. The fear generated by Japan's unexpected victory over Russia in 1905 was a crucial impetus for these racialized policies, particularly in Australia.[157] In 1908, the US president Theodore Roosevelt entreated the governments of Canada, Britain, and Australia for "unity of action" to ensure white supremacy in the Pacific. Blocking Asian immigration to North America and Australia was crucial to this objective. As Roosevelt exhorted, "There should be no mass of Orientals to the countries where the English speaking peoples now form and will form the population of the future." A show of US military strength in the Pacific was apparently also in order, which the US navy carried out with its sixteen-battleship tour from December 1907 to February 1909.[158] Canada was neither equipped for nor inclined to such military bravado, but the anxiety about Japanese power was nonetheless palpable. The "grave" question of the future, Goldwin Smith warned in the years before his death in 1910, was: "Whose will British Columbia be?" Could America and Britain hold the Pacific? Would Japan's military power eventually eclipse their naval capacities? Might Japan ally with China and India against the West?[159]

These events made the prospect of union even more remote. "Annexation to Canada would mean the denial of all political rights to the mass of the population of this colony," the *Daily Gleaner* editor Herbert George DeLisser concluded at the end of June. Meikle agreed that white Canadian racism toward Asian immigrants was yet more evidence that union would be insufferable for the vast majority of Caribbeans. "It is a common occurrence for East Indian and Japanese immigrants to be mobbed in Canada, and at times the situation has become so critical that military force has had to be summoned to quell the disturbances."[160] British governance was hardly first rate, but the Caribbean colonies would undoubtedly be worse off under Canadian rule: "Would it not be a case of 'stepping out of the frying-pan into the fire?'"[161] At the end of June 1911, the *Daily Gleaner* solicited opinions from "a good many people" in Jamaica on the union question. Only two thought it was a good idea, on the basis that it would curb government expenditure. The remainder believed that Jamaica stood to gain nothing from union and in fact thought that politically it would be "a step backward" for Jamaica.[162]

Canada's rejection of imperial citizenship was not the only development at the Imperial Conference that damaged the union campaign. While in London, Laurier consulted the colonial secretary about union, as he told Macaulay he would. Harcourt cautioned the prime minister against the idea, and later told his colleagues in the Colonial Office, "The proportion of coloured to white when I mentioned it was sufficient to 'put [Laurier] off.'"[163] Of course, a few months after Laurier returned to Ottawa, he was unseated by Borden's Conservatives. For some unionists, the installation of a more imperial-minded government was reason for optimism. But Borden did not think union was opportune in light of the intense and very public display of white racial enmity in the preceding months. When Governor Grey-Wilson met with the new prime minister in Ottawa in October, Borden did not offer much encouragement. He and his new minister of trade and commerce, George Foster, were intent on working out a strictly commercial agreement with the British Caribbean.[164]

Although Grey-Wilson was in Canada on holiday rather than official business, he managed to further undermine the union campaign during an address to the Empire Club of Toronto. He too proposed a racially exclusive form of governance. Manhood suffrage was inadvisable, but "naturally, no reference should be made to colour." A satisfactory result could be produced "by putting the qualifications of an elector so high that they would automatically shut out the ignorant blacks." This arrangement would exclude some of the whites, Grey-Wilson noted, but this was not likely to "be a serious grievance." Perhaps sensitive to the depths of white Canadian racism, the governor provided additional assurances. While the Bahamas' population was only one-quarter white, "the black man almost invariably elects a white man to represent him" – not because the whites treated him as an equal but rather because the Black man "admits himself that he is the white man's inferior."[165] The address infuriated officials in the Colonial Office. "The man is an ass," Harcourt told his colleagues – who swiftly reprimanded Grey-Wilson.[166] Caribbean activists were equally livid. Robert Bailey declared that suffrage was "the birthright of every Bahamian," and legislation on racial grounds – with or without reference to it – would not be countenanced. "We will not stand this glaring suggestion to sacrifice our inherent right, the right of our manhood ... for prospective Canadian loaves and fishes." Grey-Wilson had "woken up" Black Bahamians and "produced a very bitter feeling of resentment" among them.[167]

It was perhaps not surprising, then, that few Bahamians turned out to the Nassau meeting that Macaulay organized in February 1912. In contrast to the previous year's meeting, reported the *Nassau Guardian*, working-class Black Bahamians were nowhere to be found. Union sentiment on the islands was not, of course, divided neatly along racial lines. Black tailor Ernest Bowen attended the second meeting and supported a resolution to initiate discussions with Ottawa, by way of the Colonial Office, about what union might involve. Like the others who voted for the resolution, Bowen was not endorsing union but rather expressing his desire to continue the conversation.[168] Alfred Dillet, a Bahamian of mixed descent, voted for the resolution as well. Born into a family of political activists, Dillet was adamant that Bahamians' political rights must remain intact under any future union arrangement. His Haitian-born father was the first person of African descent elected to the islands' Legislative Assembly, on the heels of Emancipation in 1834. Dillet saw union with Canada as a last resort. If annexation to either Canada or the United States was inevitable, he thought the former was the lesser of "two evils."[169] *Nassau Tribune* proprietor Leon Dupuch, a Bahamian of mixed descent, wrote favourably about the union proposal in the final months of 1911. Yet he may have done so in an effort to, in his words, "arouse the attention of the Britisher" rather than out of a burning desire for union.[170] It was not uncommon for Bahamians to support union discussions for no other reason than to draw Britain's attention to the value of the islands, or to attract tourist interest.

Several white Bahamians supported the resolution in 1911 and in 1912,[171] while some opposed it.[172] Opponents of the resolution (and union) may have feared that Canada's more inclusive franchise would undermine the islands' white oligarchy. As Grey-Wilson told the colonial secretary in May 1911, "There is a well-defined fear among the whites that unscrupulous Canadian professional politicians might, for political purposes, seek to disturb the existing harmony as regards representation, and by playing upon the impressionable minds of the Negroes, overthrow the white domination."[173] Many middle-class Bahamians of mixed descent, including Charles Anderson, chief clerk of the post office, shared this concern. As he remarked at the February 1911 meeting, "We have a mixed population and, in my opinion, we are not ripe for the form of government which would be conferred on us as a province of the Dominion of Canada. It would mean a larger measure of local self-government to which I am opposed as our people are not alive to their interests."[174] To many white and mixed-descent Bahamians, the prospect of enfranchising Blacks was anathema.[175]

The resolution was ultimately inconsequential. It was not taken up by the Bahamian government, while opposition in London and insufficient interest in Ottawa made union impractical. In April, most of the British Caribbean colonies finalized the details of a reciprocity agreement with Canada. Neither Jamaica nor the Bahamas entered the agreement, mainly for fear that the United States would raise its tariffs in retaliation.[176] Some unionists interpreted the Bahamian rejection of reciprocity as a sign of their preference for union. During the trade conference, the *Montreal Star* published a cartoon suggesting as much. Under the title "Friendly Signals," a Caribbean merchant approaches Canada's coast in a boat laden with Caribbean products (figure 2.3). The merchant is white, probably because the illustrator recognized that a Black man approaching Canadian soil would elicit alarm. He has two harbours to choose from, "Confederation Harbour" and "Reciprocal Trade Harbour." The caption says, "It must be into one of these harbors, or he may be driven to a treaty with foreigners. The Bahama Islands prefer Confederation Harbor." The merchant waves to a man at Confederation Harbour, an indication of his preference.

FRIENDLY SIGNALS

It must be into one of these harbors, or he may be driven to a treaty with foreigners.—*Montreal Star.*
The Bahama Islands prefer Confederation Harbor.

Fig. 2.3   "Friendly Signals," *Montreal Star*, 8 April 1912

Nassau Guardian's editor, Mary Moseley, was not amused by the cartoon. She saw it as one more example of the Canadian tendency to misrepresent Bahamian opinion. To the statement that Bahamians favoured federation over reciprocity, she retorted, "Who knows that? And on what authority is publicity given to such a statement which is to say the least not founded on truth?" She enumerated numerous examples of similar misstatements in the Canadian press over the previous twelve months, reports with headlines such as "Bahamas Have Petitioned the British Government for Annexation to Canada," "Bahamas Are Satisfied to Join Canada," and "A Union Has Been Approved by the Resolution of Both Branches of the Bahama Legislature." It was offensive to Bahamians, insisted Moseley, who knew there had been "absolutely and positively no pronouncement on this question by the Colony."[177] Moseley was no proponent of union, but her critiques had merit. Reports of the Nassau meeting in February 1911 were exaggerated to ridiculous proportions. Montreal's *Gazette* described outright hysteria. The Bahamian legislature "suspended its sittings" and "workmen dropped their tools on the streets ... to talk over the question of asking Canada to take them under her wing." There were reportedly twenty thousand people in attendance (one-third of the Bahamian population), a considerable deviation from the estimated four hundred to five hundred reported in Bahamian newspapers.[178] These embellished reports were no doubt encouraged by Canadian unionists themselves. The editor of the *Canada-West Indies Magazine*, A.M. Mackay, thought it was "only for Canada to say 'yes' and presto! 'tis done!"[179] The assumption that union was in Canada's (and Britain's) hands, that unanimous support in the Bahamas was a given, was common, but it was born of white Canadian arrogance and paternalism rather than knowledge of opinion on the ground.

The union proposal had all but disappeared by the summer of 1912. In September of that year, the Colonial Office refused Macaulay's request to meet with Harcourt. Macaulay was, according to Grindle, a "gas bag with infinite possibilities of explosive mischief" whose efforts should not be encouraged.[180] George Haddon-Smith, the new Bahamian governor, assured the Colonial Office in April 1913 that the issue had not been raised recently in the Assembly, no meetings on the subject had been held, and no "accredited representatives" of the Canadian government had expressed any interest in discussing the matter with him. When De Léry MacDonald travelled to Nassau in March 1913 to revive interest in the proposal, Haddon-Smith informed him he was not at liberty to discuss the matter. MacDonald had intended to stay in Nassau for a month but left the island within ten days.[181]

Conclusion

In the late nineteenth and early twentieth centuries, the union idea loomed up in response to anxieties about America's expanding empire and British imperial decline. The Spanish-American War generated anxiety about the loss of markets in the face of US protectionism and envy of the perceived benefits of US imperialism. Union would pre-empt US influence in the region and secure Canadian access to Caribbean markets. The vicissitudes of US trade policy galvanized unionists again in 1911, though for different reasons. The proposed Canada-US reciprocity agreement provoked concerns about

Canadian sovereignty. Unionists, most of whom were protectionists, saw union as a way to offset American influence in Canada by making the dominion less reliant on US trade. Fewer leveraged the prospect of free trade with the United States to win Caribbean support. But whether they were protectionists or free traders, for unionists the salient point was that a permanent association with the British Caribbean would make Canada less vulnerable to the changing trade policies of future governments.

At the same time, the union idea was part of a broader discussion about the empire's future, generated in the wake of Britain's industrial decline and geopolitical challenges within and outside the empire. Various proposals for imperial unity, federation, or alliance maintained their currency among a persistent if shrinking group of imperial-minded Canadians. Union was often considered in relation to these proposals, most notably a restructured empire in which Britain and the self-governing dominions conducted the empire's work as partners. Yet what this might entail was much contested in the dominions. There was also a good deal of speculation that the empire's centre of gravity might eventually shift from London to Ottawa. Union was seen as an early stage in this process.

The principal dilemma for unionists was that union was irreconcilable with Canada's presumed whiteness. Maintaining the fiction of white homogeneity depended upon a virulent anti-blackness that derailed unionism again and again. Unionists tried unsuccessfully, mainly by peddling a union vision that exteriorized blackness, to convince white Canadians that union would not compromise the country's whiteness. The racial heterogeneity or blackness of the Caribbean was acceptable because it was, and would remain – with restrictive migration policies and investment in Caribbean industries – outside Canada.[182] These arguments came under strain when American and Caribbean Blacks moved north to take advantage of the employment opportunities offered by Canada's expanding economy. The white racism that flared up in the midst of this migration in 1911 elicited indignation in the Caribbean and scuttled the union dream.

Unionism suffered also from a lack of official support in Ottawa, London, and the colonial governments in the Caribbean. Laurier and Borden briefly entertained the idea, but they too had difficulty squaring white Canadian racism with the incorporation of territories with large Black populations. Borden and members of the imperial government, though largely outside the Colonial Office, would take a very different stance in only a few years' time.

3

SOVEREIGNTY AND THE
SPOILS OF WAR

The Allied occupation of German colonies in Africa and the Pacific during the early years of the Great War inspired a flurry of discussion about territorial changes after the war, and in August 1916, Britain's Committee of Imperial Defence appointed an interdepartmental Committee on Territorial Changes. Concerned primarily with the future administration of former German territories, the committee did not report on the Caribbean.[1] Its work nonetheless aroused Canadian interest, most notably that of Prime Minister Robert Borden, in the prospect of territorial gains. Australia, New Zealand, and South Africa had either laid claim to or anticipated the acquisition of proximate German territories, so Borden thought the time was opportune to annex the British Caribbean. The absence of German colonies in the Americas – which no doubt relieved Canadians at the outbreak of war – placed Canada at a distinct disadvantage in the scramble for postwar accessions. As a confidential report from Canada's Department of State read, "It behooves Canada to consider in what measure she can best secure an equivalent to those territorial advantages which she will be glad to see her sister Dominions acquire."[2] Many of the advantages were now familiar: free access to tropical products, a large, secure market for Canadian exports, the development of Canadian sea power – a vital prerequisite to administer, trade with, and protect geographically isolated islands and a long-term goal of Borden's government – and the national prestige associated with governing "subject races."[3]

Historians have long identified the First World War as "one of the great turning points in the evolution of the Empire."[4] For India and the dominions, the war prompted increased participation in imperial affairs and incited, in many cases, a heightened national consciousness. Canadian, New Zealander, and Australian soldiers "blooded" a new nationality at the

Front, while dominion statesmen fought for a greater voice in the conduct of war and the constitutional reorganization of the empire.[5] In the popular anthropomorphizing of the constituent parts of the empire, Canada and the other dominions matured from "children" to "sisters" of Britain. Borden introduced Resolution IX at the Imperial War Conference in 1917, calling for the postwar recognition of the dominions "as autonomous nations of an Imperial Commonwealth" with a "right ... to an adequate voice in foreign policy." With the help of Australian prime minister W.M. Hughes, Borden also secured separate representation for the dominions at the Peace Conference and separate signatures on the Treaty of Versailles.[6]

The wartime campaign for union was part of this push for greater autonomy. Borden and other union enthusiasts held that administering external territories and "developing" the "subject races" that inhabited them would boost Canada's imperial stature. While the commercial dimension remained important, unionists saw Canada's annexation of the British Caribbean colonies as a means to greater sovereignty and status in the world. Yet the central dilemma that ultimately scuttled union once again was white settler racism and the attendant refusal to consider a union arrangement approaching provincial status.

This refusal was strikingly at odds with the parallel struggles for self-determination in the Caribbean. Like millions of other colonial subjects, Caribbean peoples contributed to the Allied cause in France, northern Africa, and the Middle East, and they did so with the expectation of greater political representation and autonomy after the war.[7] Racialized communities in self-governing societies were similarly eager to do their part in the war and were equally invested in postwar change. "The present war is another epoch period in history," reported one of Canada's Black newspapers in April 1917. "The war cry is Justice and Freedom. May it be obtained and be maintained after the war, by all the combatant nations in its fullest sense, and thus the darker races will have their reward for the blood that is, and will be, spilled, and lives sacrificed upon the battlefields."[8] Yet their contributions were often made in the face of considerable adversity and racial animosity. Black soldiers and seamen, as well as labourers and students at home, encountered ongoing and sometimes violent bigotry during the war.

According to historian P.J. Wigley, in an excellent study of the wartime campaign for a Canadian-Caribbean union, the general chaos of the postwar period and the fading enthusiasm of formerly keen advocates blunted the

union momentum.[9] Records in Ottawa and London confirm that by the fall
of 1919, the considerable interest in union in the latter years of the war had
dissipated. But the explanation for this demise is more complex. A product
of the historiographical tradition that conceptualizes Canada's imperial roles
and responsibilities in the context of Canada's relationships with Britain and
the other "white dominions," Wigley's study does not seriously consider the
import of the Caribbean, and especially white Canadians' racialization of
African Caribbeans, to the wartime negotiation of Canada's position in the
empire and the world. Nor does it take adequate account of the role played by
Caribbean peoples in shaping the outcome of the union question. In assessing
the significance of the Caribbean to the wartime discourse about Canadian
autonomy, this chapter demonstrates that wartime unionism and, by extension,
the struggle for Canadian autonomy, were racially inscribed projects whose
outcomes were contingent on the increasingly fraught relations between white
Canadians and African Caribbeans.

The chapter begins by introducing the chief advocates of union in Canada
and Britain. In the halls of government, Borden found several notable allies for
the cause, including British prime minister David Lloyd George and several
Canadian and imperial officials. A confidential report on the question drafted
by the Department of External Affairs in 1917 served as the basis for Borden to
advance the proposal formally at the Imperial War Cabinet meetings, generating further interest in Canada, Britain, and the Caribbean.[10] The hemispheric
context, especially America's growing influence, was equally instrumental in
unionism's wartime return. Unionists identified formal Canadian control of
the British Caribbean as a means to temper American expansion in the region
and secure commercial relationships during the war. They were less assured
about the form of governance under union. While Canadian proponents might
articulate slightly different ideas about political representation and the franchise, they agreed on "annexation" rather than "confederation," a distinction
rooted in a mistaken understanding of the diverse political circumstances and
social relations in the region and in the assumption that governing racialized
subjects – in a paternalistic system marked by unequal power relations –
was a compelling indicator of national status. Yet for Black Canadians and
Black Caribbeans, the maintenance of this system was an insult to colonial
peoples' wartime sacrifices and their ongoing battles for racial justice. In part
of a broader pattern of colonial resistance during the war, Black peoples in
Canada mobilized against white racism at recruiting stations and on university
campuses, ultimately quashing the possibility of union.

Negotiating Territorial Desiderata
in Ottawa and London

Harry J. Crowe was the most vocal and influential advocate of annexation in the commercial sphere during the war. Born in Halifax in 1868, he worked in his father's wholesale grocery firm before entering Nova Scotia's lumber trade. He established sawmills in different parts of the province in the late 1890s but soon sold these operations to exploit the much vaster timber resources of Newfoundland. In 1903, with three partners, he founded the Newfoundland Timber Estates Company, purchasing several timber operations and establishing two pulp and paper mills in the dominion.[11] After a first trip to the Caribbean in 1915, Crowe became an ardent promoter of some form of union with the British Caribbean, hoping in part to compel Newfoundland to enter the federation. Newfoundland conducted considerable trade with the Caribbean, and the prospect of gaining free access to the region's markets and resources under confederation, Crowe argued, would be too enticing to refuse.[12] The 1914 completion of the Panama Canal made annexation all the more appealing and urgent. "What is of paramount importance in this Confederation," Crowe opined, "is the strategical position of these British West Indies, lying as they do in the pathway of trade routes between North and South America, with Jamaica at the entrance to the Panama Canal, upon which the future development of British Columbia will, to a considerable extent, depend." As earlier unionists argued, Crowe believed union would give Canada free access to tropical agriculture, a crucial impetus to national development.[13]

Crowe was a regular correspondent with Borden between 1916 and 1919, and his vigorous pursuit of union no doubt influenced the prime minister. Not long after Crowe's initial letter in April 1916, which cited broad support for union within Jamaica's business community,[14] Borden wired Canada's high commissioner to Britain, Sir George Perley, and asked him to assess the British government's opinion on the question. The colonial secretary, Andrew Bonar Law, informed Perley that he did not think the British government would object to the scheme. In the midst of war, however, he thought the timing inopportune, a view shared by British prime minister H.H. Asquith.[15] Undeterred by this lukewarm response, Borden enlisted the undersecretary of state for external affairs, Joseph Pope, to draft a report on the viability of union. Released to the cabinet in February 1917, the nine-page report was titled "Confidential Memorandum upon the Subject of the Annexation of the West India Islands to the Dominion of Canada" (figure 3.1). It included a brief history of the question, the advantages and disadvantages of annexation for Canada, and an appendix of British Caribbean trade statistics, furnished by the Department of Trade and Commerce. Consistent with the paternalistic, sanctimonious pronouncements of earlier Canadian unionists, the report erroneously located the origins of the union question in nineteenth-century Jamaica rather than in Canada. Moved by the depressed state of the sugar industry, as the story was often told, Jamaicans clamoured for salvation under Canada's "protective wing." While union had not, Pope observed, been previously propitious and was roundly "mooted" in Ottawa and London, much had changed since then. The dominion's extensive contribution to the Allied war effort supported this outlook. These experiences foregrounded Canada's maturity, underlined Ottawa's readiness for extraterritorial governance, and seemed to bolster Canada's case in London.[16] The advantages were mostly familiar, reiterated since the 1860s by successive generations of Canadian expansionists: free access to tropical products would allow Canada to be more economically self-sufficient, and the Caribbean would provide a ready market for Canadian flour, fish, lumber, and manufactured goods while Canada would take in much of the sugar and tropical fruit produced in the Caribbean.[17]

The report also identified some more ambiguous results of a possible union. Appreciating trade advantages would take patience. The free admission of Caribbean products would mean a loss of revenue for Canada in the short term, but this "diminution would eventually be more than made up by the great development of trade" that would follow union.[18] Pope's report also suggested that political union would spur the development of Canadian sea power, but warned of potentially uncomfortable entanglements. Administering, trading with, and protecting geographically isolated islands, particularly in a region whose value had increased considerably in 1914 with the opening of the Panama Canal, required an expanded Canadian navy.[19] To many English-speaking Conservatives, including Prime Minister Borden, this was likely an advantage of – or at the very least a perk to be gained from – union.[20] At the same time, the report identified the defence issue as a disadvantage. Annexing the islands "might excite the jealousy" of other countries and "multiply sources of friction" between Canada and those other countries. The "isolated and exposed" position of the islands "would render the Dominion vulnerable to attack, and would thus necessitate a permanent expenditure for both naval and military defense on a considerably larger scale than hitherto contemplated" by the Canadian government. Finally, the question of distance received careful examination in the report. While not as distant as London, "many leagues

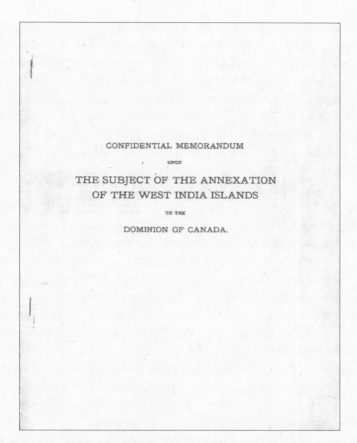

CONFIDENTIAL MEMORANDUM

UPON

THE SUBJECT OF THE ANNEXATION
OF THE WEST INDIA ISLANDS

TO THE

DOMINION OF CANADA.

Fig. 3.1 "Confidential Memorandum," Department of External
Affairs, 1917

of ocean" lay between the islands and the seat of government in Ottawa. Yet
advances in travel and communications technologies meant that steamships
were cheaper than railroads. Relative to the vast distances separating Eastern
and Western Canada, the Caribbean was not particularly remote. "A swift line
of steamers would bring Jamaica nearer to Halifax in point of time than is
Winnipeg to-day, with much cheaper freight rates. At present it costs less to
ship from Montreal or Toronto to Trinidad, than to points west of Winnipeg."[21]

The report contained one novel argument: the urgency and timeliness
of the union question in the context of war. As the Allied powers discussed
the ground rules of peace, it was important that the Canadian government

forcefully articulate its own interest in territorial gains. In his correspondence with Borden, Crowe had made this argument too, citing Canada's tremendous contribution to the war. As Crowe had done, the 1917 report noted that German territory in southern Africa and the South Pacific had made Australia, New Zealand, and South Africa likely benefactors of territorial spoils. "It was fitting that this should be so," but by "what means then is Canada to be territorially recompensed in the day of triumph for the blood and treasure she has poured out to preserve and augment the integrity and greatness of the British Empire?" The annexation of the Caribbean colonies to Canada, the report concluded, "would seem to supply the answer."[22]

While in London during the spring of 1917 to attend the Imperial War Cabinet meetings, Borden and the other Canadian delegates used the report as a basis to discuss the question with the imperial government. In the war's early years, Borden had been frustrated by the government's failure to consult – or even update – Canada and the other dominions about the war's progress.[23] He was thus pleased when David Lloyd George replaced Asquith in December 1916 and (wanting to ensure the dominions' continued contributions to the Allied cause) created the Imperial War Cabinet. The cabinet meetings were a forum to brief the dominions on the war and discuss, if only in a preliminary sense, the terms of peace. Under the leadership of Lord Curzon, a subcommittee assembled in April 1917 to consider territorial readjustments. With no German colonies in the Americas, the Canadian delegates expressed interest in the islands of St Pierre and Miquelon, a portion of the Alaska panhandle, Greenland, and the British Caribbean.[24] While these territories were under the sovereignty of four different states and each offered different strategic and material advantages, Canada was interested in them for at least one common reason: America's growing influence in the hemisphere. A strip of the Alaska panhandle, lost to Canada in the settlement of 1903, remained a sore point for many Canadians, so discussions of territorial shuffling provided opportunities to request an amendment to the 1903 boundary.[25] St Pierre and Miquelon's reduced importance to the French fishing industry inspired Canadian and Newfoundland interest. Not wanting them to fall into American hands, each dominion encouraged the imperial government to negotiate a transfer on its behalf. While officials in the Colonial Office were sympathetic, and even contemplated exchanging territory in British Africa for the islands, they did not wish to choose sides and subsequently informed the dominions that the matter would only be taken up if France initiated negotiations (which it never did).[26]

Canadian interest in Greenland arose in large part from the US acquisition of the Danish Caribbean on 31 March 1917. Anxious that Greenland might also be sold, the Canadian government urged the British to secure a first right of purchase in the event that Denmark decided to sell. These concerns were not unfounded. American Admiral Robert Peary's claim to have reached the North Pole in 1909, alongside African-American explorer Matthew Henson and Inuit guides Ootah, Seegloo, Egingwah, and Ooqueah, had raised questions about US sovereignty in the region.[27] Peary and other American explorers had also claimed rights of discovery along Greenland's northern coast, reviving Canadian anxieties about the possibility of a northern Monroe Doctrine. At the Imperial War Conference in 1917, the Canadian delegates subsequently urged Curzon to initiate an inquiry with the Foreign Office.[28] The Danish government's reply that it had no plans to place Greenland on the market only temporarily relieved Canadian officials, who raised the question again in 1919 during the Peace Conference. Denmark reiterated its earlier position and went a step further, submitting a request that the Great Powers acknowledge Danish sovereignty over the whole of Greenland. To the satisfaction of the Canadian government, the American, French, and British representatives acquiesced.[29] When the American secretary of state, Robert Lansing, signed the Convention Respecting the Cession of the Danish West Indian Islands to the United States on 4 August 1916, he issued a declaration on behalf of his government that the US would not object if Denmark extended its political and economic presence over the whole of Greenland.[30] In light of this declaration, it seemed to the British Foreign Office somewhat puzzling that the Canadian government raised concerns about Greenland three years later in Paris.[31]

Borden's claim to the Caribbean colonies nonetheless garnered considerable support in the imperial government. Curzon dismissed discussion of the Caribbean on the grounds that it did not involve foreign territory and was thus outside the purview of the cabinet,[32] but Leo Amery (assistant secretary in the War Cabinet), Alfred Milner (member of the British Cabinet), and Philip Kerr (Lloyd George's private secretary) expressed interest. All three were members of the Round Table group, an organization whose central object was imperial union.[33] In a change of heart from his pre-war aversion to Canadian rule in the Caribbean, Milner, alongside Amery and Kerr, identified a Canada-Caribbean union as a step toward the larger goal of imperial union. While Borden appreciated this imperial angle, he eschewed larger schemes to federate or centralize the empire on a constitutional basis, favouring an increasingly autonomous role for Canada in the empire. Consistent with this vision, the "Confidential Memorandum" of 1917 included not a single reference to Britain, focusing exclusively on Canada. Amery, Milner, and Kerr nonetheless provided Borden with influential allies in the imperial government. By the summer of 1918, the British prime minister himself actively supported union. As Borden observed in August, "[Lloyd George] suggested that we should take over the West Indies, and I acquiesced."[34] Amery was Borden's strongest ally. He wrote to Borden regularly on the subject in the summer and fall of 1918. "The United Kingdom obviously cannot do it all," he argued, echoing an earlier statement by Lloyd George, "and the Dominions would naturally throw themselves into the work with greater zest if the connection were a direct one, at any rate as regards certain parts of the dependent Empire." Canada would have more reason, in other words, to invest capital and energy in the development of the Caribbean under a federal arrangement. "My project," he continued, "would be the expansion of Canada into what would in fact be a Greater Dominion of British America" that included Newfoundland, Bermuda, the Caribbean territories and, "if you liked to have them thrown in," the Falkland Islands.[35]

Ever mindful of the necessity of good Anglo-American relations, Amery was nonetheless confident that such an arrangement would not offend the United States. In fact, Amery thought the US government would respond favourably to his scheme for a "Greater Dominion of British America" because it furthered the tenets of the Monroe Doctrine: Europe's retreat from the Western Hemisphere. If Britain relinquished control of the Caribbean colonies to Canada, moreover, it would "make Americans realize that we are not simply out at the United Kingdom end to grab all the territory in the world we can from mere lust of domination."[36] Canada's annexation of these colonies did not constitute an expansion of the British Empire's territory, but rather a transfer in the administration of existing territory from London to Ottawa. This transfer was important for two reasons. First, in demonstrating that Britain was not power hungry, it might temper the US response to British claims in East Africa and the Middle East. Second, it would allow the Canadian government to circumvent the charge of having imperial ambitions. Borden, like US president Woodrow Wilson, was eager to avoid the appearance of wanton expansion. Taking up a share of the "imperial burden" – or, in what became the preferred language in the months following the cession of war, holding the Caribbean colonies "in trust" – allowed the Canadian government to take the moral high ground and effectively disguise its expansionist aspirations.[37]

The United States and the Necessity
of Formal Canadian Imperialism

Outside the halls of government, unionists cared less about the appearance of unrestrained, self-aggrandizing expansion. In language almost indistinguishable from Benjamin's Kidd's unabashed pronouncements in *The Control of the Tropics* twenty years earlier, Crowe predicted that the "great rivalry of the future will be for control of the tropics."[38] There was no more compelling indicator of this trend, he maintained, than in America's recent expansion in the Caribbean and Latin America.[39]

In the years leading up to 1917, the United States purchased the Danish islands and intervened in Nicaragua, Mexico, Haiti, and the Dominican Republic. Wartime circumstances and the completion of the Panama Canal in 1914 intensified American interest in the region. As Secretary of State Robert Lansing observed in January 1917, the "Caribbean is within the peculiar sphere of influence of the United States, especially since the completion of the Panama Canal and the possibility of a change of sovereignty of any of the islands now under foreign jurisdiction, is of grave concern to the United States."[40] The Dutch Caribbean, comprising Surinam on the South American continent and a few islands off Venezuela, fell within this purview. Dutch neutrality in the war was increasingly uncertain. Britain's blockade had cut off crucial imports, and the situation worsened after April 1917 when the US entered the war and enacted its own embargo. As New York's *Independent* warned in July 1917, Holland "lies between the belligerents, and has been steering a difficult course of neutrality for the last three years. It is doubtful if this neutrality can be preserved much longer." Of negligible worth to Holland, the article continued, the Dutch Caribbean would be of great strategic and commercial value to the United States. The French (Berbice) and British (Demerara) Guianas "could not expect to prosper so long as they remain under European control. But if transferred to the United States their prospects would be bright." American capital and enterprise would flow into the region, and before too long a railroad would connect the rich Amazon interior to the coast.[41]

American interest in Britain's colonies provoked concern among many people in the Caribbean, as well as Canadians with commercial interests (or aspirations) in the region. Four days before the US declared war on Germany, an article appeared in the *New York Evening Mail* titled "We Need the Bahamas Islands." Forming a semicircle from the north coast of Cuba to the south coast of Florida, the Bahamas were thought crucial to the defence of both the United States and the route to the Panama Canal. Possession of these islands by any foreign power was a threat to American security. Britain "ought to be willing to sell [the islands] to America" because their strategic and commercial value to Britain was apparently negligible. Trade between the Bahamas and the US exceeded that between the Bahamas and Britain, and the islands had long experienced economic stagnation under British rule. It was only "natural" that America should absorb the Bahamas. "The manifest destiny of the people of the Bahamas, geographically and commercially, tends toward a union with the United States." Such a union would ensure Bahamian prosperity while protecting America's strategic and commercial interests.[42]

The idea that the United States might annex the Bahamas met sharp rebuke in the Bahamian press. In June 1917, the *Nassau Tribune* responded to rumours that Britain might relinquish the Bahamas to the US in partial payment of the latter country's war loans. According to the *Tribune*, many white Bahamians supported annexation to the US, while Black Bahamians wished to remain under the British flag. The *Tribune*'s frequent reports of episodes of racial discrimination and conflict in the US no doubt generated anti-American sentiment among Black Bahamians.[43] The *Nassau Guardian* was more hostile to the suggestion of American annexation. Responding to an October 1917 declaration in the *New York Evening Mail* that America would "like to get the Bahamas,"[44] several Bahamians (all writing under pseudonyms) wrote letters of protest to Daniel Moseley, the *Nassau Guardian*'s editor during the war. A writer using the pseudonym Bahamian levelled the sharpest criticism. Citing the US's poor record of race relations and its recent imperial exploits in the Caribbean basin, the author concluded that "the United States (on the whole) cannot be considered a civilized country."[45]

American aspirations in the Bahamas (or any other Caribbean colony) were also of ongoing interest to many Canadians. Not surprisingly, the proprietors and readers of the *Canada-West Indies Magazine* watched the issue closely. The magazine frequently covered American commercial and military initiatives in the Caribbean and reproduced articles from the American press – like those in the *Evening Mail* – that urged US expansion in the region. Many of the magazine's long-term subscribers enjoyed strong commercial ties to the Caribbean and were thus keenly interested in any developments that might affect these ties. The Royal Bank of Canada, for example, which had established branches throughout the Caribbean in the late nineteenth and early twentieth century, maintained an institutional membership in the Canada-West Indies League from its inception in 1911 to its demise in 1934. The *Canada-West*

Indies Magazine, originally founded as the league's official organ, continued publication for two more decades, and Royal Bank executives remained on its subscription roll for the duration.[46] Wartime speculation about American designs on the Bahamas was of particular import to the bank, whose executives had expansionist aspirations of their own. The Royal established its first Bahamian branch in 1908 and then in June 1917 purchased the Bank of Nassau, effectively producing a banking monopoly in the islands that ran until 1947. America's growing presence in the region sparked a lively spirit of competition that was often chronicled in (and no doubt fuelled by) the popular press. When six Royal Bank executives toured the Caribbean in the winter of 1916, the trip was reported with much interest in the United States.[47] For Royal Bank's inspector of foreign branches, Solomon Randolph Noble, who negotiated the Bank of Nassau purchase, and for managing director Edson Loy Pease, the driving force behind Royal Bank's original foray and subsequent expansion in the Caribbean, the economic potential of the British Caribbean and, correspondingly, Royal Bank's prosperity, might be more fully realized under a Canada-Caribbean union.[48]

Political union was certainly not a prerequisite for the introduction, growth, or prosperity of Canadian banking overseas. In the late nineteenth and early twentieth century, Canadian banks – particularly the Bank of Nova Scotia and the Royal Bank – thrived in Newfoundland and St Pierre, Bermuda and the Caribbean, Europe, and Central and South America, as well as in the United States. When and where convenient, they benefited from the resources and reputation of countries with political, economic, or sentimental influence in these regions – British imperial territory, for example, or French-speaking jurisdictions like France, Guadeloupe, and Martinique. US intervention in Cuba and Puerto Rico during the Spanish-American War, and later in the Dominican Republic, provided further opportunities for the expansion of Canadian banking. Royal Bank's first Caribbean branch (then named the Halifax Merchants' Bank) was in fact established in Cuba. In financial ruin after the war, Cuba needed reliable banks to furnish capital and a stable currency. Pease seized the opportunity, successfully convincing the bank's board of directors to open a Havana branch (the first of what would amount to sixty-five branches by the early 1920s) in March 1899. The bank's early success was in large part the result of American legislation that effectively minimized competition. Not until the Federal Reserve Act of 1913 could American banks (with federal charters) set up foreign branches. Even more advantageous was the Platt Amendment of 1901, which granted the US government authority to intervene in Cuba's political and commercial affairs to protect life, property, and individual liberty. In prohibiting new commercial agreements that would increase Cuba's debt to foreign parties, and threatening military intervention in times of political instability, the amendment safeguarded Royal Bank's operations. Canadian banks in Puerto Rico, and later the Dominican Republic, were likewise protected.[49]

Other Canadian enterprises in the Caribbean benefited from similar circumstances and relationships. Often riding on the coattails of British or American imperialism in the region, these enterprises did not require formal political or military support from Ottawa. Nor did their success depend upon a system of informal Canadian imperialism, whereby Canadian entrepreneurs forged contracts with local Caribbean governments that placed these governments in a state of long-term debt and thus vulnerable to continued exploitation.[50] As H.V. Nelles and Christopher Armstrong conclude in their pioneering study of Canadian-initiated public utilities companies in Latin America and the Caribbean from 1896 to 1930, relations between these companies and Caribbean authorities were complex and ever changing.[51] They were "characterized by continuous negotiations, in which alterations in the flow of information and capital, not to mention upheavals in international affairs, dramatically changed the bargaining power of negotiators over time." To suggest that capitalists who invested in these utilities companies "bought their way into positions of power and dictated terms to local authorities thereafter, creating conditions of permanent dependency," would be misleading.[52]

To be sure, myriad impulses directed Canadian enterprise and investment in the Caribbean and Latin America. While Canadian businessmen were no doubt driven by the promise of gain, their means to this end should be generally differentiated from the methods of commercial intervention that drove much American enterprise in the region. Canadian commercial and financial ventures were often characterized by uneven and exploitative relationships between entrepreneurs and local authorities, capital and labour,[53] but they were a far cry from "dollar diplomacy" in which American investors – with support from the US State Department – established control over a particular region's public finances, creating conditions conducive to political control. As Yale professor Edwin M. Borchard described it in 1917, "It is only a short step from private investment in a railroad or in a large concession for the exploitation of a weak country's important resources to the exercise of a sphere of influence by the home government of the investor; and the sphere of influence easily merges into political control. Hence the adoption by the United States of its

Caribbean and particularly its Central American diplomacy of encouraging American enterprises, which would promote our political interests."[54]

While Ottawa encouraged Canadian enterprise in the Caribbean and Latin America, especially endeavours aimed to strengthen north-south trade, it was neither inclined nor in a position to use military or diplomatic intervention. Autonomous in all matters save external affairs and defence, the Canadian government lacked the constitutional authority to conduct diplomatic negotiations directly with foreign or British colonial governments. This status placed Canadian commercial interests at a disadvantage and subsequently underlined the benefits of formal imperialism in the region. Economic expansion, as John Gallagher and Ronald Robinson argued, "will tend to flow into the regions of maximum opportunity, but maximum opportunity depends as much upon political considerations of security as upon questions of profit. Consequently, in any particular region, if economic opportunity seems large but political security small, then full absorption into the extending economy tends to be frustrated until power is exerted upon the state in question."[55]

Canada's status in the British Empire hampered the ability of Canadian entrepreneurs and investors to take full advantage of economic opportunities in other ways as well. Britain's long disengagement from the region impeded commercial endeavours in the British Caribbean in particular. The dwindled flow of British capital into these colonies, combined with Britain's ongoing commitment to free trade, had devastated regional economies. As Pease observed in 1916, the "trade of the West Indies has been almost criminally neglected in the past. The sugar industry, which at one time was the main industry, nearly suffered extinction." These colonies possessed "the elements that would tend to cheap production – namely, a rich soil and cheap labor" but lacked the modern machinery and infrastructure to maximize this production. Trade agreements with the US and Canada helped to some extent to revive select sectors of Caribbean economies, such as the American preference for Jamaican bananas and Canada's preference for British Caribbean sugar. But the absence of modern equipment, particularly in the sugar industry, limited output and kept prices uncompetitive. Britain's Caribbean colonies produced about 200,000 tons of sugar in 1915, the bulk of which Canada absorbed, but they were capable, according to Pease, of producing three million tons per year.[56]

Under formal Canadian control, the British Caribbean would realize this potential. The *Canada-West Indies Magazine* reported in January 1917, "A union confined to commerce would be subject to change by the future governments of all countries concerned;" it would consequently lack the "permanence necessary to inspire confidence in Canadian capital and enterprise for the development of these islands." Under a strictly commercial agreement with Canada, the Caribbean colonies would also be vulnerable to demands for trade concessions and possibly retaliation from the US.[57] Jamaica and the Bahamas declined to enter the Canada-West Indies trade agreement of 1912, for example, partly because they feared American retaliation.[58] Political union would shield the Caribbean colonies from these deleterious possibilities and strengthen the trade output of both regions. The colonies would diversify Canada's industries and exports, and Canada would secure political recognition and commercial preference for the Caribbean in the markets of the world. The permanence of political union would inspire confidence in the future stability of the region, and Canadian-directed capital would flow readily into the development of modern infrastructures and agricultural technologies.[59]

Union rather than trade reciprocity was also attractive to Canadians because it promised to secure trade relationships during the war. The war had cut off European trade with central and South America, which presented opportunities for the expansion of trade between North and South America. "The after-war struggle for foreign trade will be the sharpest and keenest the world has yet seen," remarked an American contemporary in 1917. "With a thoroughly awakened England made efficient as never before, a Germany hungry for the trade she has lost, and a France sharpened by her recent great trials, we shall need all that we have of money, ships and brains."[60] With such stiff competition on the horizon, Canadian control of the British Caribbean offered some degree of commercial certainty in a very uncertain global environment.

Annexation, Not Confederation

This heightened interest in union inspired a more comprehensive discussion of what governance would look like. As in the past, in 1917 the confidential report identified the "negro question" as the greatest obstacle to union. Caribbean history, characterized by "insurrection and disorder," foretold a future under union in which "negroes" might not acquiesce quietly to the paternalistic assumptions and policies of the Canadian government. Black Caribbean peoples might expect – and perhaps even demand – greater political concessions. "It is not unlikely," the report stated, "that under confederation the negroes would clamour for larger political privileges than they at present possess." Admitting the Caribbean colonies under the same terms as Canada's provinces and, in particular, granting them self-government, was simply "out of the question."[61] For this reason, "confederation" was not appropriate: "There can be no confederation of the British West Indies with Canada at the start in the sense in which that word was used in the case of Nova Scotia and New Brunswick half a century ago. There can be no equality of status at the outset ... 'Annexation' or 'incorporation' would more closely describe the initial process of admission into the union, under which they would become, as it were, 'Territories' of the Dominion." Consistent with the paternalistic and, for the most part, mistaken assumption of other unionists, the report suggested that equality at the outset was neither expected nor desired by Caribbean peoples themselves.[62]

Guided by notions of white racial superiority and the principle of trustee-ship, these recommendations outlined a form of crown colony government similar to that already practised in many of the islands. The central change, of course, was rule from Ottawa rather than London. The report neither took account of, nor even recognized, the diversity of governance in the region, ranging from austere crown colony rule to varying degrees of legislative auton-omy and representative government. Barbados and the Bahamas, for example, had long operated under the old representative system, which included a legis-lative assembly as well as a council. For the most part, Trinidad and Tobago, Jamaica, and British Guiana remained crown colonies until the interwar period, with varying concessions in the intervening years. While a federation of the Caribbean colonies was not a prerequisite to union with Canada,[63] unionists expected it would follow. Because union entailed some measure of uniformity in governance, the more prosperous islands (and particularly the prosperous islanders) and those with greater legislative autonomy (particularly the islanders who dominated the legislature) were no doubt apprehensive about the scheme.[64]

In the end, Canadian politicians and officials came to different conclusions. Largely ignorant of Caribbean opinion, the confidential report concluded that "the advantages of union of the British West Indies to Canada outweigh the disadvantages." While the report outlined challenges, none – "with the possible exception of the negro problem" – were insurmountable. The best way of addressing this "problem" – territorial rather than provincial status and a restrictive franchise – was consistent with Borden's vision of union.[65] Other Canadian politicians differed in their recommendations. The minister of trade and commerce, George Foster, proposed few changes beyond a transfer of administration from Ottawa to London. Foster thought it appropriate to govern the colonies under the same terms as Britain, but to avoid the appearance of exploitation, the Caribbean should initiate the discussion.[66] As in the past, the former minister of finance W.S. Fielding was reluctant to endorse union: "The whole mass of the inhabitants ... are not of the white race. A handful of white men from the Old Country have been remarkably successful in guiding and directing West Indian affairs and in enlisting the sympathy and co-operation of the native races, who are given as large a share in the business of government as circumstances permit." While he was willing to entertain political union, he favoured a commercial union of the two regions.[67] The Canadian high commissioner to the UK, George Perley, expressed more serious reservations. Responding to a letter from Borden in June 1916, Perley wrote, "while I see many things in favour of it ... I see serious difficulties in connection with the franchise ... I feel that [Caribbean peoples] would probably expect a good many more concessions from Canada in the way of political rights than they get from the Mother Country."[68]

These concerns were not unfounded. The idea that Caribbean peoples could expect greater political rights in the Canadian federation was liberally propagated throughout the Caribbean by Harry Crowe. During his many visits to the Caribbean, he assured its peoples that union would bring about a provincial government of the islands, with elected representatives in Ottawa.[69] This assurance was visualized in an illustration printed alongside Crowe's letter to Jamaica's *Daily Gleaner* in August 1919 (figure 3.2). The illustration depicts a thoroughly paternalistic relationship between "Big White Brother" Canada and the Black Caribbean labourer to whom he is extolling the benefits of union. Brother Canada has two placards beside him outlining the political and commercial advantages of union. From the "Political Advantages" placard, we learn that "Provincial governments would handle local affairs as at present," the Caribbean would have "representation in the federal government at Ottawa," and there would be "no race prejudice."[70]

While Crowe's assurances were usually ambiguous, carefully excluding details that might alienate any segment of the region's diverse populations, they went some way in convincing Caribbean peoples that union meant increased political rights. In a letter to the *Daily Gleaner* under the pseudonym Patriot, one Jamaican argued, "We would take a big step in advance politically ... No longer a little quasi Crown colony ... [we would] rank as an integral part of the Dominion with full representation and local powers to settle our matters locally, under the lead of young virile Canadian leadership, shaping our destiny on more progressive lines than is possible from ultra-conservative Downing Street."[71]

In Political Union There is Commercial Strength

BIG WHITE BROTHER:—Come on brother, Together we will Broaden and Build up Your Avenues of Trade, and Consolidate British Possessions in North America.

Fig. 3.2   "Big White Brother," *Daily Gleaner* (Jamaica), 29 August 1919

A rich debate turned on the distinction between confederation and annexation. In an address to the Manchester branch of the Jamaica League, W.E. Harrison similarly extolled the political benefits of union. Harrison, the headmaster of the Munro and Dickinson School in St Elizabeth's Parish, spoke in place of Crowe, who was unable to attend. Pope had insisted that the term "annexation" was more appropriate than "confederation" because the latter implied an equality of status, but Harrison argued the reverse: "There are others who talk about confederation as annexation. The essential principle of confederation is union of Sovereign States with independent rights, and it is as a colony of independent position under the Crown that we approach this question, and it is in that light that Canada also views it." Both men emphasized a distinction, but for entirely different reasons.[72] Others thought that this was a distinction without a difference. Inspired by Crowe's vision of a revitalized Jamaica under Canadian rule, Reverend J.W. Graham of the Church of England in Guy's Hill, St Ann Parish, urged the formation of a

"Canada Annexation Association." Graham hoped to gather the support of prominent men in Jamaica's major towns and cities and enlist them to form branch associations. A few delegates from each branch would then attend a central meeting to formalize the aims of the association. While it is unclear whether the association ever materialized, J. Kissock Braham, a Wesleyan pastor in Port Antonio, Portland Parish, enthusiastically endorsed Graham's proposal. "I am quite sure," he asserted, "that every man in the island who has the welfare of the island at heart, views with favour the proposal." In an increasingly exasperated tone, he concluded, "Oh let us wake up out of our lethargic state, and do something for the benefit of our much beloved island."[73]

Crowe's speeches to Canadian audiences, his articles in British and Canadian newspapers, and his correspondence with members of the Canadian government reveal a very different vision of union than the one he peddled in the Caribbean. According to Crowe, there was little possibility of common citizenship or increased migration of African Caribbeans to Canada. Like Foster, he proposed a simple transfer of administration from London to Ottawa. Existing structures of local governance would remain unchanged. Canada would assume control over foreign affairs, tariffs, the post office, the marine and fisheries departments, and public works, allowing "limited but adequate" Caribbean representation in these areas.[74] More importantly, the restrictive Caribbean and liberal Canadian franchises would not be synchronized: "There is no demand for extending the vote there, and there is no reason why there should be in the future, unless the development of the people justified it." Caribbean peoples would be similarly disinclined, Crowe argued, to migrate to Canada. "Because of climatic conditions prevailing in Canada, the coloured population of the B.W.I. would never invade our Dominion." Many African Americans who migrated to Canada during the American Civil War had, after all, returned to the southern United States when peace was restored. In Crowe's logic, this was compelling evidence that "darker races" were unsuited to "temperate and frigid zones."[75] Caribbean peoples would be less likely to leave the region, moreover, because union would stimulate the agricultural and industrial development of the region and consequently increase the demand for labour.[76]

Crowe's contention that there was no demand for an expanded franchise in the Caribbean was misleading and self-serving. It was based on the misguided yet common assumption that African Caribbeans were content with white-dominated colonial governance. In the midst of war, Crowe and others perhaps found it difficult to recognize how profoundly the war had accentuated inequalities in the region, or to predict the mass protest and political organization that would follow.[77] After the war, many Canadians continued to identify the paternal model as both necessary and even popular. John R. Reid, past president of the Ottawa Board of Trade, argued in January 1919 that a paternal (white) administration was not only appropriate but desired by African Caribbeans. While visiting Barbados and Bermuda, Reid discussed with several islanders the racially disproportionate composition of the legislative bodies. In Bermuda, where approximately two-thirds of the population was of African or African-European descent, all but two of the twenty-nine members of the island's Assembly were white. Yet Reid insisted that Black Bermudians "were contented with the political condition, and informed me that while they were proud of the representatives of their race in the Chamber, they would be quite satisfied if the entire body was white." Britain's paternal administration had been "so wise and beneficent" for so long that African Caribbeans apparently did not desire greater political rights. For this reason, Reid objected to any change of administration that might upset this arrangement, including annexation to Canada.[78]

In Jamaica, Crowe's conclusions about public sentiment were based on the interests and inclinations of the island's "leading men," many of whom were enfranchised and did not wish to disrupt the status quo. Not surprisingly, during his visits Crowe concentrated his efforts on winning the support of the island's middle and upper classes. He forged connections with members of the middle-class Jamaica League and the more elite Jamaica Imperial Association, but gave scant consideration to the island's majority population, the Black labouring classes, since they were thought unfit to vote. Yet African Caribbeans did assume an important role in Crowe's vision of a "Greater Canada." It was their very "unfitness" that demanded paternal guidance from white Canadians. This guidance, in turn, was thought crucial to the development of Canada's national outlook and hemispheric prominence. "Do not let us be 'Little Canadians,' but rather Expansionists in the broadest sense of the word," he urged. "Let us do what lies in our power to bring about the confederation of Canada and the B.W.I. Let us assist in the developments of our brothers of a darker race, and add to our borders what is an almost tropical dominion." Doing so would place Canada "on an equal footing" with the United States and "[raise] up on this Continent a magnificent nation." To dispel white Canadian fears of a "race problem," Crowe later distinguished Black Caribbeans from Blacks in the US and Canada, the former being "receptive to enlightenment" and eager to "grasp the hand of their more highly favoured brothers of the same Imperial family." The implications of annexation thus went far beyond commercial questions. Broadening Canada's national outlook and prestige, according to Crowe, required the dominion to take responsibility for both the economic development of the Caribbean and the cultural development or "enlightenment" of its diverse populations.[79]

The Department of External Affairs report on annexation similarly outlined the connection between national prestige and governing "darker races." Assuming responsibility for the development of the hundreds of thousands of dark-skinned and thus – by the logic of early twentieth-century Anglo-Saxon racial pretention – socially and intellectually challenged Caribbean peoples would add "considerably to the importance and influence of the Dominion."[80] As the histories of the European powers were alleged to demonstrate, acquiring and administering colonial territories were more than prerequisites to domestic economic growth. "The responsibilities of governing subject races," Robert Borden remarked in June 1916, "would probably exercise a broadening influence upon our people as the Dominion thus constituted would closely resemble in its problems and its duties the Empire as a whole."[81] Administering "a territory largely inhabited by backward races," he wrote in a subsequent correspondence, would provide Canada's public service with invaluable training.[82] The Department of Trade and Commerce's Watson Griffin, who had furnished the trade statistics for the report, was more explicit in modelling Canada's imperial trajectory on that of Britain's. Invoking the British Raj, Griffin hinted that British Guiana could become for Canada what India was to Britain.[83]

Despite Crowe's claim that "climatic conditions" would deter Caribbean peoples from leaving home, many did journey north to join the Canadian Expeditionary Forces or meet the labour shortage created by wartime economic expansion. Companies such as Sydney's Dominion Steel and Coal Company and the Canadian Pacific Railway ignored the informal strictures against recruiting Black workers, while Canadian universities expanded their recruitment efforts in the Caribbean to offset the loss of enlisted students.[84] Resistance to the formation of a Black Caribbean regiment for overseas service in the British War Office and the Colonial Office prompted eager African Caribbeans to make their own way to England or Canada to enlist. By the time a British West Indies Regiment was approved in May 1915, many young Caribbean men had already enlisted elsewhere.[85] Several joined fighting battalions with white Canadian soldiers, while discrimination forced others to wait, once again, for the formation of an all-Black labour battalion in the summer of 1916.

While this migration may have proved inconvenient for white unionists like Crowe, it alone did not threaten to derail the union proposal. More detrimental was the resistance of these new migrants to the racism they encountered in Canada. Unwilling to abide this discrimination, particularly amidst the egalitarian rhetoric bantered about during the war, African Caribbeans established periodicals to articulate their claims for equality, formed protective associations, and appealed to their imperial and colonial governments for redress. In the process, they made plain to white Canadians and especially the government at Ottawa that racial discrimination would not be tolerated.

Organizing for Racial Justice across the Global Colour Line

In the months following the outbreak of war in August 1914, tens of thousands of men flocked to Canadian recruiting stations. Hundreds of Black Canadians and Caribbeans were among them.[86] There were no formal racial restrictions, but military officials across Canada advised against integrated regiments,[87] and recruiting officers routinely sent Black volunteers away, claiming the conflict was "a white man's war."[88] Across the British dominions, officials feared that combatant service would entitle racialized peoples to political rights and thus destabilize white hegemony.[89]

Rejected recruits and their supporters did not sit idly by in the face of this discrimination. They appealed directly to their members of Parliament, the Department of Militia and Defence, and the governor general.[90] The Black Canadian newspaper *Canadian Observer*, run by Canadian-born J.R.B. Whitney, launched a vigorous protest campaign that went a long way in pressuring Ottawa to approve a segregated Black construction battalion in July 1916. Sarah-Jane Mathieu argues persuasively that these protests gave rise to a transnational "infrastructure" of organized resistance that laid a critical foundation for racial justice struggles after the war.[91]

Caribbean migrants in Canada were no less active. Halifax-based African-Caribbeans founded the *Atlantic Advocate* in April 1915, a monthly journal "devoted to the interests of colored people in the Dominion generally," but especially to those in the Maritimes (figure 3.3).[92] Wilfred Alleyne DeCosta, a Jamaican-born gardener and collection agent who immigrated to Nova Scotia around 1908, was the *Advocate*'s president and associate editor, and his wife, Miriam, served as secretary. Ethelbert L. Cross, originally of San Fernando, Trinidad, served as editor in 1916, and Dr Clement C. Ligoure, also from San

Fig. 3.3   Cover, *Atlantic Advocate*, May 1917

Fernando and a recent graduate of Queen's University's medical school, took the position the following year.[93]

Like the *Canadian Observer*, the *Atlantic Advocate* spent several months recruiting for the Black construction battalion and was always quick to speak out against racial discrimination. When the No. 2 Construction Battalion was denied the customary patriotic farewell from friends and family on its departure for Europe in March 1917, the *Advocate* admonished the military officials responsible. "Why," Ligoure asked, "should our Race be huddled together in one mass, like cattle, marched from the Barracks to the train at Truro, then on arriving at Halifax, driven ... on board the outgoing transport without the last long good-bye to those near and dear to them?" Mothers, sisters, wives, and daughters, many of whom had travelled hundreds of miles to bid farewell to their loved ones, were refused the same privilege extended to white families. This unceremonious farewell, Ligoure continued, combined with a series of other discriminatory episodes since the outbreak of war, had fuelled considerable dissatisfaction among Canada's populations of African descent. "There is without doubt a whirlwind of discontentment sweeping over the Dominion among the Colored population which would have been averted had they been given justice," he warned.[94]

Discontent spread in the late summer and early fall of 1917 when conscription came into force under the Military Service Act. Canadian prime minister Robert Borden had travelled to Europe in the spring of 1917 and witnessed the devastation at the front first-hand, returning home determined to enact conscription for overseas service. He introduced the proposition to Parliament on 18 May 1917, and the Military Service Act became law on 29 August.[95] Many Black Canadians were outraged to learn that they would be drafted into military service after being turned away – sometimes multiple times – from recruiting stations in the preceding months. Voluntary enlistment was widely understood as a patriotic and honourable duty. Turning away Black Canadians and then forcing them to enlist was considered a shameful betrayal of British justice and fair play.[96]

The West Indian Trading Association of Canada (WITA) took a lead role in the protest. Founded in Toronto in 1916 as an auxiliary organization of Marcus Garvey's Universal Negro Improvement Association, WITA was a cooperative grocery and trading association with shareholders in Quebec, Ontario, and Nova Scotia.[97] Its membership was not confined to Caribbean peoples and, like the Universal Negro Improvement Association, its overarching object-ive was the "advancement of colored people." WITA established a produce trade with the Caribbean, opened at least one grocery store in Toronto, and purchased residential properties for rental to Black men and women.[98] The association believed that the "organization and commercialization of the race" would ultimately provide the necessary leverage to effect social and political change. "By becoming commercialized," E. Millington argued during a WITA meeting in December 1916, "we can make larger demands, can fight the immigration question, and all other questions along Race lines."[99] In the fall of 1917, Toronto members discussed alternatives to conscription at monthly meetings, sent delegates to gather support from WITA shareholders in Montreal, and presented their grievances to the federal government.[100]

The Department of Militia and Defence largely ignored the protests against compulsory enlistment. The Canadian Expeditionary Force suffered enormous losses in 1917, at Vimy Ridge in the spring and then at Passchendaele in the fall.[101] In Ottawa, concerns about the limited – or worse, dangerous – fighting capabilities of Blacks and the "mingling" of Black and white soldiers were blunted by an acute need for reinforcements. Like others who evaded the draft, Black Canadians who failed to present exemption documents when questioned by military officials were apprehended and forced into service.[102]

Concerns about interracial "mingling" prompted the enactment of exclusionary policies in a range of social and institutional contexts, including restaurants, social clubs, and universities. During the war, the medical schools at Queen's and McGill universities placed restrictions on Black students. Clinical instruction, usually conducted at nearby hospitals, presented a problem because white patients – many of them returned soldiers – refused treatment from Black physicians and medical students. In 1916, with the support of Queen's University Senate, the dean of medicine, J.C. Connell, prohibited the admission of prospective Black students and expelled all fifteen Black students in residence, most of whom were Caribbean. In a community where "a great deal of prejudice against the colored race survives," Connell explained, "the Faculty decided some months ago that it would not be possible to continue the education of these men." Those expelled included students in their early years of study who were not yet in the clinical phase of the program.[103]

McGill admitted Black medical students, but they were required to undergo their obstetrical training elsewhere, usually at a medical training facility in New York or Boston. The Montreal Maternity Hospital had closed its doors to Black students a few years earlier, and McGill was thereafter unable to offer incoming Black students the clinical course in obstetrics. McGill's Faculty of Medicine was represented on the Medical Board of the Maternity Hospital, but, according to the registrar, J.W. Scane, the faculty "had no voice at all in the management of the institution."[104] The "problem," in other words, "was taken out of [McGill's] hands" by the Hospital's restriction.[105]

Not long after McGill barred its first Black students from obstetrical training courses in September 1916, a group of Caribbean medical students formed the Gamma Medical League. Aimed at "bringing together the men from various parts of the Empire for their professional, social and mutual benefit," the league persistently contested McGill's discriminatory policies.[106] Following the unsatisfactory results of their discussions with medical faculty and the registrar, the league sent a petition to McGill's board of governors on 21 October, "setting forth [their] position and praying for redress."[107] University principal William Peterson acknowledged receipt of their petition at the end of October but informed them that it would be "quite some time" before the body that considered student petitions, the university corporation, reconvened.[108] When the petitioners received no response in the following weeks, they confronted Peterson in person to "enquire as to the fate of their attempt to get justice." Peterson informed them that the petition had been referred to the medical faculty.[109] The students then met with Registrar Scane in January 1917, who assured them that arrangements would be made to facilitate obstetrics and gynecology courses for Black students.[110]

When the league had not yet received confirmation in June 1917 that such arrangements would be made, they broadened their forum of protest to the Caribbean. They sent letters to several prominent newspapers, including Jamaica's *Daily Gleaner*, the *Jamaica Times*, Demerara's *Daily Argosy*, and the *Barbados Advocate*.[111] Emphasizing the importance of protest and perseverance in effecting change, the league called Caribbeans to action. Change "will depend upon the interest you display in the matter to decide whether your children and your children's children will be debarred from the education so indispensable to civilization … [We] earnestly ask whether [you] can afford to remain indifferent and see the shrines of knowledge gradually closing their doors on the faces of [your] children." Caribbean peoples resident in Canada were "on the spot" and could see more readily than those at home that the discrimination at McGill was merely "the thin edge of the wedge."[112]

The *Jamaica Times* was particularly vitriolic in its condemnation of McGill. Dr Scane's statement that the Montreal Maternity Hospital had tied McGill's hands was a poor excuse. Rather than "tamely yielding" to the hospital's restriction, the university should have sought – "at all costs" – vindication for its Black students, even if this required the university to build and run its own hospital. The newspaper entreated Caribbean governments to register their disapproval with the proper authorities at McGill. They should highlight, in particular, how antithetical the university's practices were to British principles of justice and fair play. Doing so would make McGill and "all the other Canadian centers that are inclined to follow the broad and easy road of prejudice" realize that "their native island and their fellow countrymen have no intention of looking on apathetically." United action on the part of the colonial governments would, moreover, demonstrate Caribbean solidarity against racial prejudice.[113]

J.A.G. Smith, a Black lawyer and member of the Jamaican Legislative Council, brought the issue before the council as early as April 1918. The council subsequently sent an inquiry, by way of the island's colonial secretary, to Registrar Scane.[114] In Scane's reply, he assured the council that arrangements had been made with an institution in New York City where Black students could undergo obstetrical training in the summer between their fourth and fifth years. Scane also emphasized the small minority of Black students in the Faculty of Medicine, which, at present, met their "quota" of eight to ten.[115] The implication was, of course, that it was unrealistic to expect McGill to go to great lengths to accommodate so few students. McGill's arrangement, he added, was much more accommodating than the policy at Queen's University, which barred Black students entirely from the medical school.[116]

Queen's discriminatory policy was met with similar disapprobation. The *Canadian Observer* once again took a lead role in the protest. "Those of our Government that stand for freedom, justice and fair play, should not overlook vital instances in the life of a struggling race of people seeking to obtain higher education, [so] that they may be of greater service to that people." It was disappointing that an influential, distinguished university had submitted so easily to prejudice. That an institution of higher learning – comprised of and supported by individuals who claim to be highly cultured – practised racial discrimination was nothing short of hypocrisy.[117] As Toronto resident W.E. Benfield wrote in a letter to the editor in February 1918, are Black students "not human beings just the same?" Was Canada's government not conscripting Black students as well as white to squash militarism and autocracy in Europe? Canada was fighting for freedom and justice throughout the world while betraying these same principles at home.[118]

Just as McGill's Gamma Medical League had sent a petition to all the British Caribbean governments, so too did the West Indian Club at Queen's. The club's president, E.W. Reece, similarly emphasized the hypocrisy of enlisting

Black soldiers to fight the cause of freedom overseas while simultaneously discriminating against them at home. That several Caribbean colonies had recently contributed funds "rather liberally" to alleviate the suffering caused by the Halifax explosion in December 1917 made such discrimination all the more offensive. Reece and the other petitioners also underlined the incongruity of this discrimination and Canada's interest in strengthening ties with the Caribbean. After the war, they wrote, Canada "is contemplating not only extensive trade relations with the West Indian islands, but [a] Governmental relationship as well, and it would appear inconsistent in policy that a Government which desires such intimate commercial and political relationships with another people should through its institutions of learning set up barriers against those living in their midst." The West Indian Club urged Caribbean governments to intervene on their behalf by sending an appeal to either the Canadian government or the appropriate governing body at Queen's.[119]

The colonial governors of Bermuda and Barbados went a step further and forwarded the petition directly to the Colonial Office in London. Bermuda Governor James Willcocks indicated that there were not, to his knowledge, any Bermudian students at Queen's Medical School. He nevertheless thought it advisable to forward the letter to the Colonial Office for their information.[120] The acting governor of Barbados, T.E. Fell, did more than forward the petition; he outlined the implications of Queen's discriminatory policy in a supplementary letter. Because there were no universities in the Caribbean, it was crucial that Caribbean students continue to have access to universities overseas. The education boards in several Caribbean colonies granted their students scholarships to pursue university degrees in Britain, Canada, and the United States. If Canadian universities continued to bar Caribbean students from particular courses of study, the Education Acts of the various Caribbean colonies would require amendment. Section 57 of Barbados' Education Act of 1890, for example, stipulated that the Barbados scholarship was tenable, with the approval of the Education Board, "at any university in Europe or Canada." Amending the act to exclude Canada would draw attention to Canada's discriminatory practices and surely engender bitter feelings. If Canadian universities continued to bar (or place restrictions on) Caribbean students, Fell argued, it was "liable to provoke keen resentment amongst the coloured people of Barbados" and ultimately "induce a feeling of estrangement" toward Canada.[121]

The Colonial Office agreed that discrimination against Caribbean students at Canadian universities was sure to provoke resentment. It was, as one colonial official remarked, a particularly "unfortunate time for embittering the colour feeling," given that thousands of Caribbean soldiers were fighting (or had fought) for the Allied cause in France, northern Africa and the Middle East.[122] At the same time, the Colonial Office recognized there was little it could do to check racial discrimination in Canada. As a self-governing dominion, Canada controlled its domestic affairs, which included the discretion to exclude imperial (non-white) subjects from other parts of the empire. Debates over imperial migration and citizenship at the Imperial Conference of 1911 had (re)confirmed this autonomy (see chapter 2).[123] If the imperial government conceded autonomy in immigration, it was certainly not in a position to influence Canadian universities' admission policies – at least formally.

The imperial and Caribbean governments were unable to intervene on behalf of the student petitioners to eradicate the discriminatory policies at McGill and Queen's universities. The petitioners' protests were nonetheless significant because they laid bare the increasingly organized quality and transnational scope of Black resistance in Canada. They exposed the alarming persistence of racial discrimination in Canada while simultaneously making it plain that this discrimination would not be tolerated. In doing so, their protests prompted many in Canada and the Caribbean to explicitly question the desirability of union.

"Imperial Brotherhood" Denied, Union Denied

"The McGill incident has dealt a terrible blow to the idea of closer union between these two different parts of the British world," Jamaica's *Daily Gleaner* bluntly reported in June 1917. If Canadian universities continued to close the doors of their medical colleges to Black people, it "would put an end once [and] for all to any possibility of closer political unity between the Dominion and the British West Indies." McGill had "beyond doubt" wounded "the susceptibilities of millions of people" and would in the future "inflict hardships on scores of intelligent, well-mannered and entirely respectable men." Until Canadian universities repudiated their narrow-minded policies and practices, Caribbean peoples would regard union proposals with "strong aversion."[124] A writer under the pseudonym "ITALEAN" shared these sentiments in a letter to the editor: "It appears very strange to me that Canada should be wanting political union with the British Caribbean, and at the same time raise the colour bar against the majority of the inhabitants of these islands." Such a step was "sufficient to damn the scheme" for political union with Canada.[125] It laid bare, moreover, that institutional racism was still thriving in Canada.

The protests of Caribbean migrants in Canada were also taken under consideration at meetings of the Associated West Indian Chamber of Commerce, the Georgetown Chamber of Commerce in British Guiana, London's West India Committee, and Canada's Department of Trade and Commerce. Once again, the tension between race and commerce was explicit. As early as August 1916, Demerara's *Daily Chronicle* argued that "in Canadian eyes we possess a certain commercial value," but if Canada attempts to "exclude from her land a great majority of the people of these colonies, she has been guilty of chicanery … which will make the creation of that Imperial brotherhood which we expect to arise as one of the outcomes of the great War, very much more difficult to attain."[126] In response to discrimination against African Caribbeans at the Canadian border, the executive committee of the Georgetown Chamber decided "this is not an opportune time to press the [union] question but it is one we will not lose sight of."[127] In June 1917, the *Barbados Advocate* admonished the Canadian government's racist immigration practices: "The illegal discrimination now being practiced by the Canadian Authorities against coloured passengers from the West Indies to Canada is sowing the seeds of discontent which will be certain to ultimately develop into strong protest against closer connexion with Canada whether in the form of Trade or otherwise."[128] Canada's trade commissioner at Barbados forwarded the article to Canada's superintendent of immigration, William D. Scott, requesting an explanation. "It is true," Scott replied in a form letter sent to countless trade agents and boards, steamship company proprietors, and prospective Caribbean migrants, "that our Immigration Act contains a provision that the Governor in Council may prohibit the entry of immigrants of any race, etc., deemed unsuited to the climate or requirements of Canada."[129] Immigration inspectors possessed the discretionary power to prohibit the entry of Black migrants, in other words, without explicitly restricting immigration on racial grounds.

London's West India Committee (wic) was likewise concerned that Canadian attitudes toward Black people were detrimental to closer commercial and political relations between the two regions. wic members had expressed interest in the possibility of union during the war. But like the Georgetown Chamber of Commerce, the committee now supported the deferral of negotiations until Canada resolved its race question.[130] Members of the Royal Colonial Institute, another London-based organization with a wider, more diverse membership and broader purview of imperial interest, concurred. In October 1917, the institute's organ, *United Empire*, argued that while the scheme for union was sound commercially, it was "on less sure ground" from a political standpoint. The Caribbean possessed the tropical produce necessary to fuel both Canada's population and its growing industries, while Canada could offer the Caribbean the much needed capital that Britain consistently failed to provide. But Canada's "racial difficulties" were "not likely to be helped toward a solution by the addition of two millions of the West Indian population." The idea that African Caribbeans should be given a decisive voice in Canada's future, and vice versa, was questionable.[131]

African Caribbeans resident in Canada were understandably more interested, and to varying degrees uneasy, about union. While Canadian annexationists assured Caribbean peoples that Canada would welcome them with open arms and give them a voice in Ottawa, they simultaneously reassured white Canadians that restrictions would be placed on Caribbean representation and northward migration. When Judge S. Rowan-Hamilton of the Supreme Court of the Leeward Islands advocated union during his visit to Halifax in March 1918, the *Canadian Observer* highlighted the "stir among the natives of the West Indies who are in Canada as to the advisability of this move."[132] As residents of Canada, they were all too familiar with white Canadian racism. The promise of Canadian capital – leading to agricultural and industrial development, higher wages, and the ultimate prosperity and improved well-being of Caribbean peoples – was no doubt appealing. But their own experiences in Canada foretold a different outcome.

In the twelve months following the Armistice, African Caribbeans inter-preted and responded to these experiences – and white Canadian racism more generally – with much less patience. November 1918 marked the cession of war, but it did not witness an immediate ideological, constitutional, or political break with the past. History is much messier than such a break implies; there was change as well as continuity in the immediate postwar period. Colonial peoples and other subaltern groups remained hopeful that change would still come in the form of increased representation, autonomy, and self-determination. In March 1919, Black Torontonian and WITA president Arthur King still identified a Canada-Caribbean union as the best means for Caribbean peoples to obtain these concessions. He placed some faith in Harry Crowe's promise that the Caribbean would have proportional representation under union. Black Canadians had equal access to the franchise as white Canadians, so it was natural to assume that Black Caribbeans would too.[133] While it would be an oversimplification to assume race unity across class, colour, and regional differences, the prospect of two million newly enfranchised Canadians of African descent probably appealed to some Black Canadian advocates of race equality. Canada's Black population comprised less than 2 per cent of the population in 1919,[134] and the federal legislature was not, consequently, an efficacious forum in which to pursue race reform.

The Pan-African Congress, which – not coincidentally – convened in Paris at the same time as the Paris Peace Conference, provided a crucial forum for Black peoples worldwide to discuss racism, colonialism, and proposals for reform. As an international delegation representing Black populations in Africa, the Caribbean, and the US, the Congress hoped to influence discussions about racial equality and colonial self-government at the peace talks. The Congress was "an opportunity that we should grasp," Black Canadian George F. Bon asserted in March 1919, "so that we may be able to press our demands with greater energy and influence." To Bon, the social and political conditions prevailing in the Caribbean exemplified the contradictions and injustices of colonial rule. They were "a group of islands, rich in resources, and possessing men with educational qualifications equal to the best that Europe or America can produce, yet they are ... undeveloped and divided, and with few exceptions the inhabitants suffer the burdens of taxation without representation." With "representatives of the race" assembled in Paris, Bon concluded, now was the time for change: "How can we be denied the right to rule ourselves in our own lands when the 'slogan' of the Allies ... is 'democracy' and 'self-determination.' It is inconceivable that the Allies will ignore their own avowed pronunciamento."[135]

Bon soon learned that the white Allied powers convened in Paris would do just that. The Pan-African Congress was ignored and in some cases obstructed. The US government refused passports to Paris-bound Black activists, and the Congress's manifesto, which entreated the League of Nations to acknowledge the right of all "civilized citizens" to take part in the political and cultural life of their respective states, was disregarded.[136] The outcome of the Peace Conference, especially the defeat of the racial equality clause in the League of Nations covenant, incited worldwide disillusionment.[137] The clause, put forward by the Japanese delegates, stated that because the "equality of nations" was a basic principle of the League of Nations, League members should "agree that concerning the treatment and rights to be accorded to aliens in their territories, they will not discriminate, either in law or in fact, against any person or persons on account of his or their race or nationality."[138] Japanese delegate Makino Nobuaki echoed the aspirations of non-white peoples worldwide when he stated that "different races have fought together on the battlefield, in the trenches, on the high seas, and they have helped each other and brought succour to the disabled, and have saved the lives of their fellow men irrespective of racial differences." These unprecedented experiences, he concluded, had set the tone for a transformative world order based on racial equality.[139] But the clause was defeated on 13 April. As Marilyn Lake and Henry Reynolds point out, the dominions – Canada, New Zealand, South Africa, and especially Australia – played a significant role in crushing Japan's campaign. Granted separate representation at Versailles (as part of the British delegation), the dominions staunchly opposed the clause for fear that it might encourage Asian immigration to their respective countries.[140]

The riots, strikes, and general unrest that characterized demobilization and the return home of hundreds of thousands of servicemen compounded the disillusionment generated by the Paris disappointments. White skilled workers were in most cases granted priority in the demobilization timeline. The Black West Indies Regiment, Canada's No. 2 Construction Battalion, and working-class white servicemen waited in overcrowded European camps for several months before returning home. As Sarah-Jane Mathieu observes, race riots broke out throughout the winter, spring, and early summer, exposing Canada's "preoccupation with race and class to the Empire and the world." These riots made clear that the war "had done little to equalize Canadian society."[141]

This mass unrest and general lawlessness continued when servicemen returned home. White Canadian veterans were livid to find their jobs had been (or might be) filled by "coloured" labour, while Black Caribbeans, still smarting from their experiences in Europe, returned home to mass unemployment and dire living conditions.[142] The war had produced uneven degrees of economic prosperity and devastation within and across different colonial (and metropolitan) contexts. In the British Caribbean, the price of foodstuffs and clothing had risen dramatically between 1914 and 1919, while wages remained largely the same. White planters and large-scale merchants, on the other hand, earned substantial profits from increased production and prices. Representatives of the labouring and professional classes had certainly condemned planters and merchants in the pre-war decades, but this condemnation became more vigorous and vitriolic after the war. In the British Caribbean, argues Glenford Howe, the significance of the war "lay not so much in the novelty of its impact as in the unprecedented way it exacerbated underlying tensions and contradictions implicit" in Caribbean societies.[143] Manifest in the strikes, lootings, riots, and other violent disturbances throughout the spring, summer, and fall, these tensions undermined existing structures of colonial rule and, by extension, the prospect of a Canada-Caribbean union.

Dr Robert M. Stimpson, a Black Jamaican who graduated from Quebec's Bishop's University in 1898 with a medical degree, had a very different opinion of Canada in May 1919 from that of two years earlier. In May 1917, Stimpson had dismissed Caribbean concerns about racial discrimination at McGill University on the basis that Montreal's population was, relative to other Canadian cities, "un-British."[144] By May 1919, however, Stimpson was more aware of the broad scope of Canada's "colour bar." This scope was particularly alarming in the context of Canada's loyalist history. Anyone with knowledge of the Underground Railway or Harriet Beecher Stowe's *Uncle Tom's Cabin* would hardly imagine that Canada had "become such a degenerate as to close the doors of its seats of learning" to peoples of African descent. Highlighting the contradictions inherent in Enlightenment notions of progress (more acute in the postwar climate), he continued, "But such it is in this twentieth century of our boasted civilization!"[145] A closer relationship between Canada and the Caribbean could only be forged if the dominion reformed its racist outlook: "Canada must be prepared to come with clean hands, and ample and sufficient guarantees that it has mended its ways." Jamaicans, he elaborated, were sensitive to any sign of racial discrimination. As a people of integrity and honour, they expected the same courtesies that any civilized community would expect from another, and even more so from imperial peers. Having "failed to comply with these simple observances," Canadians should not be surprised if they "are taken at a discount" in the Caribbean.[146]

The principle of self-determination, liberally propagated by US president Woodrow Wilson in the spring and summer of 1919, left a lasting impression on colonial subjects worldwide. Erez Manela argues persuasively that colonial peoples in Egypt, India, China, and Korea shrewdly appropriated Wilson's rhetoric in ways that "would help them gain the right to self-determination."[147] Middle-class Caribbeans deployed this rhetoric as well. When Harold Harmsworth, a former minister in Lloyd George's wartime government, suggested that Britain relinquish several Caribbean colonies to the United States to help settle Britain's war debt, Trinidadian Kathleen I. Liddelow was livid: "Whatever the reason may be, one may well express astonishment that the ink of the Peace Treaty has hardly dried before the principle of self-determination of which we have heard so much lately is apparently forgotten."[148] In the wake of what Manela calls the "Wilsonian moment," Liddelow was understandably outraged at the suggestion that Britain might cavalierly barter its Caribbean colonies without even consulting the peoples inhabiting them.

Harmsworth's suggestion was thoroughly out of touch with the emerging political and social milieu in the Caribbean. So too was the idea of union. Many commentators who were previously sceptical of union for commercial reasons, were, by the latter half of 1919, even more firmly opposed on racial grounds. These opponents included the West India Committee, the Jamaica Imperial Association, president of the Associated West Indian Chambers of Commerce Edward Davson, and Gideon Murray, British member of Parliament and former administrator of St Vincent and St Lucia.[149] Even those who during the war were keenly interested in union, most notably Leo Amery and Robert Borden, were now dubious. Amery's earlier contention that the Caribbean colonies were Canada's "birthright" proved no longer politically or constitutionally appropriate, though in the 1920s he would continue to press the dominions to take on a more active role in the colonial dependencies proximate to them. Borden had supported the union proposal as late as March 1919, and he had encouraged his parliamentary undersecretary of state, Francis Keefer, to advance the proposal in Canada and the Caribbean while he was in Paris.[150] By May, however, Borden was no longer interested. Earlier that year, the prime minister had expressed the concern that Black Caribbeans might "desire and perhaps insist upon representation in Parliament," especially because Canadian Blacks were enfranchised.[151] He had also been in Paris at the same time as the Pan-African Congress, had witnessed the controversy over (and actively opposed) the racial equality clause, and had come home in May to heightened labour unrest, anti-immigrant campaigns, and racial violence.[152] Moreover, Keefer's tour of the British Caribbean had been disappointing. When he returned to Ottawa in the summer of 1919, he regretfully informed Borden that he had "found practically no sentiment in favour" of union.[153]

The most remarkable about-face in 1919 was that of Jamaica's *Daily Gleaner* editor, Herbert George DeLisser. During the union debates of 1911–12 (see chapter 2), DeLisser staunchly opposed union on the basis of white Canadian racism. By 1916, his opinion had changed considerably. He thought the increased flow of Jamaican migrants to Canada in the early years of the war was a testament to Canada's connection to Jamaica – a connection that, in his assessment, might soon transform into some form of political and commercial union. Even after the war, he wrote in April 1916, "Canada will make a bid for tropical provinces on lines that will do no violence to the feelings of West Indians and no injury to their material interests."[154] But by the fall of 1919, his opinion had swung back to opposition with a vengeance. "The West Indies would be for Canada," he remarked in October, "but Canada would not be for the West Indies." That the dominions were interested in forming closer relationships with nearby dependencies was clear enough, "But why? Not because they want to benefit the people of those colonies. What has Australia done with her natives? Slaughtered them off the face of the earth. What is South Africa doing with hers? Making them slaves – for the position of these unfortunate people is not far removed from that of slaves." DeLisser admonished Milner and Borden for assuming Caribbean willingness to be an appendage of Canada: "The falsehood is being steadily propagated that the British West Indies would view such a transference with favour." Delisser was sure the colonial secretary would "drop the Canadian federation idea as though it were blazing hot" when he realized that the Caribbean colonies were not far off from claiming the right to self-determination.[155]

Conclusion

Those who debated the problems and possibilities of the union question during the war were not simply responding to the geopolitical and economic pressures of a specific historical moment. They were negotiating the terms on which their particular national or imperial formations would take shape. War contributions were expected to reap postwar dividends for the empire's peoples in the form of increased political representation and autonomy. For Canada's union proponents, acquiring territorial spoils and administering the peoples who inhabited them were a means to greater national autonomy in the empire and the world. The war provided unionists with an unprecedented opportunity to stake Canada's claim to the Caribbean. With territorial reshuffling underway elsewhere in the empire and support at the highest echelons of government in Ottawa and London, union came closer to realization than ever before.

The terms of union that Canadians envisioned for the Caribbean during the war – territorial rather than provincial status, a limited franchise, and migration restrictions – were an affront to Caribbean peoples. The travails of African Caribbeans in Canada had exposed white Canadian attitudes toward Black people and had offered them a rude glimpse of life under union. Their struggles during and immediately following the war birthed a collective consciousness that was increasingly difficult to reconcile with colonial rule – whether from Port of Spain, Ottawa, or London.[156] In 1919, the ideal of self-determination did not mobilize Caribbean peoples to seek immediate independence, but it did mobilize expectations for an autonomous future. They consequently rejected union with Canada and other schemes that threatened to derail this trajectory.

More broadly, the war dealt a serious blow to the civilizing mission ideology, and the protracted process was underway by which colonialism eventually became a dirty word.[157] The postwar rhetoric of equality and greater autonomy for all the constituent parts of the British Empire – however conflicted this rhetoric may have been – was incompatible with new colonial acquisitions. Yet these developments were not sufficient to stamp out the union dream. The war boosted Canadian autonomy and put the dominion on track for a constitutional milestone during the interwar decades that would enhance Canada's sovereignty and status in the Empire-Commonwealth. For some Canadians, these developments induced an inflated sense of hemispheric and imperial purpose in the Caribbean. Moreover, racial entitlement and paternalism were too deeply ingrained in white Canadians' worldviews for them to earnestly contemplate Caribbean self-determination.

4

A "NEW AMERICAN EMPIRE HEADED BY CANADA"

Interwar Overtures

In January 1928, the Pan-American Conference at Havana was abuzz with rumours that Britain would soon transfer its Caribbean colonies to "Canadian guardianship." As reported in the *Chicago Tribune* on 26 January, under the heading "New American Empire Headed by Canada Seen," a "circumstantial report" of unclear origin had circulated at the conference, claiming that negotiations were well underway in London and Ottawa. The report generated much speculation about such a transfer in light of the remarkable expansion of Canadian industry and trade in recent years, the "successive steps in the rise of the Dominion to the rank of a world power and the growth of a vigorous nationalistic sentiment among its people." Significant, too, was Canada's new status in the British Commonwealth. "Canada," the *Tribune* reported, "is seeking to place herself at the head of a federation of British States in the new world, as a further step in the development of her status as an independent [nation] in the British Empire." Many of the Latin American delegates at the conference apparently looked favourably on the idea, seeing in it the potential to check American influence in the hemisphere, while the US delegates pondered the implications of a Canadian Caribbean for their own country's strategic priorities.[1] Canada was not a member of the Pan-American Union and so was not in attendance to refute the report's baseless claims about official negotiations in Ottawa.[2] The informal discussion it generated nonetheless captured the main contours of union advocacy in the interwar period.

This chapter explores unionism's interwar return in relation to three central dynamics: Canada's new status in the Empire-Commonwealth, the threat of America's ever-expanding presence in the Caribbean, and the unprecedented rise of Black activism and anti-colonialism across the Atlantic World. The constitutional trajectories of Canada and the British Caribbean colonies continued to diverge in the interwar decades. In 1931, the Statute of Westminster recognized the dominions and Britain as "autonomous communities within the British Empire, equal in status, in no way subordinate one to another in any aspect of their domestic or external affairs,"[3] which established Canada as an independent actor on the world stage. By contrast, wartime service did not elevate the stature of the Caribbean colonies nor advance their position along the path to self-determination. Constitutional concessions were denied, colonial governments remained unrepresentative and self-serving, and the imperial government refused to formally acknowledge the need for reform until the late 1930s.[4] As in the past, these divergent histories generated incompatible responses to union in Canada and the Caribbean.

Canada's newfound status in the Empire-Commonwealth also had hemispheric consequences. Interwar calls for the transfer of Britain's Caribbean colonies to the United States in payment of Britain's substantial war debt worried unionists. If Canada did not seize the opportunity to strengthen its ties with the Caribbean colonies, unionists argued, they would soon drift permanently into America's ambit, "beyond the range of Canadian intercourse or influence."[5] Yet the transnational proliferation of Black activism in these decades ultimately rendered the prospect of union ludicrous. Colonial and other racialized people were increasingly unwilling to countenance the imperial thinking that sustained the status quo of colonialism and white supremacy before the war.

These dynamics and the durability of the union idea complicate our understanding of Canada's role in the world in the interwar years. The well-known story of isolationism – the conviction that Canada was far removed from Britain's ongoing quarrels in Asia and Africa and had no business being "dragged" into them, and that international engagements that divided Canadians along linguistic and class lines were best avoided[6] – underplays Canada's connections to the "dependent empire" in these decades. Union enthusiasts believed that Canada's increased autonomy signalled a new era in imperial and hemispheric relations. They sought a greater presence for Canada in the Caribbean, one guided, as they saw it, by a sense of imperial responsibility and partnership. They were also animated, once again, by envy of the United States. Unionists argued that Canada's new status validated Canadian intervention in the hemisphere as a North American actor rather than a European one.

This chapter first explores the logic of imperial partnership, which saw Canada's growing involvement in the dependent empire and in the Caribbean in particular. The discussion then turns to Canadian thinking about the hemisphere, particularly anxiety and jealousy around US expansion in the region. In light of Canada's enhanced autonomy, unionists believed there should be new ground rules for this expansion. After briefly outlining the racialized thinking that guided unionists, the chapter shifts to the interwar wave of Black activism and the Caribbean rebuke of union.

As Caribbean peoples grew more critical of the racialized logic that ordered imperial relations, they re-evaluated their relationship with Canada. Their critiques of white Canadian racism, especially with regard to immigration, rose to a level that challenged some of the core assumptions that had long guided the relationship. White settler notions of imperial brotherhood and sentiment, British justice and fair play, and pretensions of Canada's moral superiority to the United States frequently accompanied arguments for a stronger Canada-Caribbean relationship, whether commercial or political. They were a go-to rationale to persuade Caribbean peoples of the desirability of forging closer relations with Canada over the US. But for Black peoples in the Caribbean and Canada, who persistently confronted white racism, these arguments were insulting hypocrisies.

In an atmosphere of heightened Black consciousness, this response to union is not surprising. But it begs the question of why many Canadians continued to see union as a viable arrangement in the midst of these critiques of white racism specifically and flourishing Black activism and anti-colonialism more generally. The answer lies in the enduring preponderance of racialized thinking about colonial peoples and the conditions under which they should be governed. The civilizing mission rhetoric might have lost its currency after the war, but white paternalism prevailed. White Britons and Canadians cast themselves as the guardians of Caribbean well-being; they purportedly knew better than Caribbean peoples what was best for the region. According to this reasoning, Black activism that served political or anti-colonial ends was not only illegitimate but dangerous. It challenged white supremacy and should be contained.

Imperial Partnership

During a luncheon at Toronto's Royal York Hotel in March 1930, Canada's governor general, Lord Willingdon, spoke of his recent goodwill tour to the British Caribbean. The people of these colonies, he told the audience, looked to Canada more than Britain for encouragement and support. Long neglected by Downing Street, the Caribbean was the Cinderella of the empire. He noted that the Canada-West Indies trade agreement of 1925 and the recent inauguration of a regular steamship service between Canadian and Caribbean ports had done much to restore confidence in the region's future. But developments in the British Empire since the Great War gestured toward an even closer association.[7] In Willingdon's interpretation, the dominions were now "equal partners in working out the Empire's destiny." To this end, Canada should play its part in easing Britain's colonial burden and assume control of the Caribbean colonies.[8] Willingdon's speech was widely criticized in Canada, not principally for his suggestion of union but because he had, ironically, betrayed the Canadian autonomy he had so eloquently lauded.[9] The constitutional crisis of 1926, which pitted the powers of the prime minister against those of the governor general, had made these duties perspicuous. The governor general was merely the crown's representative in Canada and should not meddle in Canadian affairs. Pressed to explain his indiscretion, Willingdon stated he was only expressing his personal viewpoint and not acting in any official capacity.[10]

In speaking out of turn, Willingdon may have offended political sensibilities in Canada, but the substance of his proposal reflected unionist thinking in the interwar decades. For union enthusiasts on both sides of the Atlantic, the war redefined power relations within the empire. This redefinition involved several interrelated processes: a recognition of equality and partnership among Britain and the self-governing dominions, greater dominion responsibilities in the dependent empire, the rise of the Commonwealth idea and the concept of trusteeship, and the piecemeal reorganization of empire around national rather than imperial lines. The League of Nations legitimized this new world order and recast the relationship between dominions and dependencies. Australia, New Zealand, and South Africa took on League mandates in former German territories in the South Pacific and southwest Africa, and Canada was encouraged to cultivate a similarly paternalistic relationship with the Caribbean colonies. The British Empire was now the Empire and Commonwealth.

In what John Darwin calls the "Third British Empire," Britain's power on the world stage "came to depend more and more upon partnership with the White Dominions" during the twentieth century.[11] Contrasted with the nineteenth-century characterization of the dominions as imperial liabilities, in the twentieth century Downing Street viewed them as crucial imperial assets. Wartime demands for manpower and economic resources had much to do with this shifting perspective. But other important developments also inspired uncertainty and anxiety about the empire's future and prompted greater reliance on the dominions. In the two decades after 1917, British India's political and economic infrastructure transformed, Britain acquired a new empire in the Middle East, revolution in Ireland led to the creation of the Irish Free State as a self-governing dominion, the world sank into a debilitating, decade-long economic depression, the British government abandoned the gold standard and its long-held commitment to free trade, and labour unrest and anti-colonial nationalist movements proliferated. The anxieties produced by these developments were compounded in Britain by widespread unemployment, a widened franchise, a massive war debt, and stringent economic policies.[12]

Pressed to defend their interests under these circumstances, imperialists in Britain often looked to the dominions to shoulder a share of imperial responsibilities. Alfred Milner and Leo Amery, former members of the Round Table movement (largely defunct by 1921), argued that responsibility for the dependent empire was not Britain's alone but the dominions' as well.[13] In the 1920s Amery entreated Canadians to help the imperial government address the "immense problem of development" facing the empire. "With the wider responsibility of a worldwide Empire," he told a Toronto audience in June 1920, "your outlook will increasingly be an Empire outlook."[14] Amery identified the Canada-Caribbean trade conference, which he had recently attended in Ottawa, as a step in this direction. He predicted that the empire's balance of power would ultimately shift to North America, with Canada at the imperial centre.[15] Taking up similar themes in a *United Empire* article in 1922, British colonial official Charles Prestwood Lucas argued that the empire's balance of power was inextricably linked to the evolution of self-government in the dominions. As the autonomy of Canada, Australia, New Zealand, and South Africa increased incrementally in the nineteenth and early twentieth centuries, power shifted gradually from Britain to the dominions, while the war completed their national status. Now they stood beside Britain, ready to take up their share of responsibility for the dependent empire. South Africa, Australia, and New Zealand had already done so in taking on League of Nations mandates.[16] Lucas expressed dismay that Canada had not been "so geographically situated as to have had new territory allotted to her." He thought the balance of power within the empire would be more equitably distributed if all the dominions took up, on a smaller scale, "the same kind of work and exert[ed] the same kind of power as the Mother Country." To this end, Lucas hoped the Caribbean colonies would elect to "throw in their lot" with Canada.[17]

The mandates system was only one example of British efforts to refashion the dominions as imperial partners after the war. These efforts were also conspicuous at the interwar imperial conferences. Discussion of the dependent empire at these conferences – starting with the first postwar conference in 1921, was a departure from earlier conference proceedings. "Until recently," the former Colonial Office undersecretary George Fiddes remarked in 1926, "the Colonies might have been non-existent so far as [Imperial] Conference discussions were concerned; but there are signs of a change in the outlook of Dominion representatives." Fiddes understood this changed outlook as a product of the dominions' elevated status in the postwar empire.[18] In 1921, the colonial secretary, Winston Churchill, made a general statement on the economic and constitutional development of the colonies and their importance to the dominions. Churchill pointed out that although responsibility was presently confined to the Colonial Office, these colonies were arousing more interest in the dominions. He thought the trade agreement in which Canada had recently entered with the Caribbean colonies was a case in point. Addressing the Canadian prime minister, Churchill stated, "I hope Mr. Meighen and the Canadian government will advance with increasing confidence on this path, because it seems to me that for all the greatness of Canada and its tremendous producing potentialities, it is not a complete entity without connexion with these semi-tropical islands." Compared to the United States, he continued, Canada lay entirely in the North and produced a limited variety of products, while America with its diverse geography produced a variety of temperate and semi-tropical products. With a view to making Canada "a far more complete entity" economically, he looked "forward to everything which tends to promote closer association between these West Indian Islands and the Dominion."[19] British, Canadian, and American newspapers reproduced Churchill's statement, giving special attention to his remark that Canada was incomplete without a tropical connection.[20]

At the Imperial Conference of 1923, the new colonial secretary, Victor Cavendish (Duke of Devonshire), delivered a more comprehensive report on the empire's various colonies, protectorates, and mandated territories. Cavendish, who earlier served as Canada's governor general (1916–21), reiterated Churchill's plea for greater dominion engagement with the colonies. Developments in the Caribbean were discussed, including the desire and prospects for constitutional reform in many of the colonies – a subject addressed in the recently published report of former parliamentary undersecretary Edward Wood, the improvement of telegraphic communications between Canada and the Caribbean, the dire state of the region's sugar and cocoa industries, the expanding scope of Trinidad's newly named Imperial College of Tropical

Agriculture, and the demand for immigration to British Guiana. The Colonial Office, he told the conference delegates, welcomed advice or counsel from the dominions on any of the many challenges facing the colonies.[21]

In the years between the Imperial Conferences of 1923 and 1926, Amery was appointed colonial secretary, and under his direction a Dominions Office was created with its own secretary of state (although Amery held both posts from 1925 to 1929). Calls for change in the machinery of empire administration dated back to the nineteenth century.[22] Settler governments wanted a clear distinction between crown colonies and self-governing dominions, an even more powerful argument once the empire became a commonwealth of "partner nations."[23] When the British prime minister, Stanley Baldwin, announced the creation of the Dominions Office in June 1925, he noted that the Colonial Office was no longer "in correspondence with the actual constitutional position in the Empire."[24] In explaining the rationale behind the change to the House of Commons a few weeks later, Amery described Britain's function in the colonies as "administrative and directive," while relations with the dominions were "political, consultative, [and] quasi-diplomatic."[25] The Dominions Office, as another member of Parliament put it, was "a Foreign Office with a family feeling."[26]

To Amery, the creation of the Dominions Office was a necessary prelude to the productive development of diplomatic relations between Britain, the dominions, and the Commonwealth more generally.[27] There had been some long-standing concern that imperial reorganization would make it more difficult for the dominions to assert their influence – whether commercial, financial, or political – in the colonial empire. Former colonial secretary Lewis Harcourt had expressed misgivings about the complete bifurcation of the Colonial Office in 1911 on these grounds: it would sever the dominions from their most accurate stream of knowledge about the colonies.[28]

Amery insisted on the colonial secretary's permanent inclusion at the Imperial Conference. At the conference of 1926, Amery (in the role of both colonial and dominions secretary) followed the precedent by briefing the delegates on the colonial empire and stressing the importance of dominion involvement.[29] Statements by dominion leaders followed, reviewing the mandates and territories within their spheres of influence. Australia's Stanley Bruce outlined the possibilities for economic development in New Guinea and the great importance of the island to Australia; Gordon Coates of New Zealand discussed the economic and constitutional initiatives underway in Western Samoa; South Africa's J.B.M. Hertzog shared the recent constitutional

and administrative developments introduced in Southwest Africa; Mackenzie King discussed the Canada-West Indies trade agreement of 1925.[30] From
King's remarks, it appears he did not want to be too outdone by the other
dominions' (ostensibly) benevolent interventions in the dependent empire and
was sensitive to Amery's commitment to imperial unity and cooperation. He
pointed out that Canada had entered the agreement "in no haggling spirit,"
but "with a full appreciation of the desirability of rendering still closer the ties
between these two North American units of the British Empire."[31]

Amery also used the conference to promote the recruitment of dominion
candidates for the colonial service. While visiting Canada in 1920, Amery
learned that many Canadians were interested in enlisting, so he encouraged
Colonial Office staffer Ralph Furse to set up a recruitment program.[32] Furse
shared Amery's conviction that the dominions had an important role to play in
the postwar empire. In a memo on the creation of the Canadian recruitment
scheme, he noted that Canadian participation in the colonial service would
broaden the dominion's knowledge of and interest in the colonial empire and
provide crucial administrative training.[33] Under Furse, a recruiting board was
set up under the Dominion Selection Scheme in Canada in 1923, in New
Zealand in 1928, and in Australia in 1929. Amery heartily endorsed the scheme
as a means to take Canada "into partnership in 'The White Man's Burden.'"[34]

Administering the colonies, Amery told the dominion premiers at the 1926
conference, was "the most direct and practical contribution that we, the
white peoples of the Empire, can make to the general welfare of mankind."
In every part of the empire, he continued, the colonial service was engaged in
important work, "lifting people from the more elementary to the higher stages
of civilisation, preparing them for a better kind of life as ordinary citizens,
preparing them also, by slow degrees, even for the opportunities of a greater
measure of self-government."[35] The scheme was somewhat successful. By the
early 1940s, there were around three hundred personnel in the service from
Canada, Australia, and New Zealand combined.[36]

To ardent imperialists who held fast to pre-war visions of empire based
on integrated foreign, defence, and economic policies, the interwar imperial
conferences were disappointing.[37] The colonial empire did not even appear
on the 1930 agenda – it returned at the final Imperial Conference in 1937 –
and the topic never managed to go beyond speechmaking and discussion.[38]
The *Round Table*, for example, dismissed the conference of 1923 as a waste of
time, consisting of nothing more than fruitless chit-chat. If prime ministers
were to be "dragged from the ends of the earth for little more than a friendly

talk," the Imperial Conference would soon "perish for want of practical usefulness."[39] This response was no doubt inspired by the emphatic push-back of Mackenzie King to any suggestion at the conference of an imperial foreign policy.[40] The *Round Table* found the dominions' Commonwealth membership and their aversion to entanglements in world affairs a flagrant contradiction. The "real battle of opinion in the Empire today," it continued, "is between those who see in nationhood responsibility and labour for world ends and those who see in it the road to escape from these things." The journal framed this responsibility as a moral issue on which their national futures – and the very future of civilization – hinged. If the dominions adopted a hermit policy, they would stunt the progress of civilization and become lesser, morally enfeebled nations.[41]

Many Canadians who supported union with the Caribbean colonies similarly argued that the dominion's new status came with greater responsibilities in the world, and that discharging them would enhance Canada's national outlook. Harry Crowe, for example, the prominent wartime unionist who continued campaigning for the cause until his death in 1928, often argued that Canada should annex the Caribbean colonies in fulfilment of the country's new duties on the world stage.[42] Australia, New Zealand, and South Africa had taken on this responsibility through the imperial mandates system; Canada should do so through a political union – or, failing that, a customs union – with the Caribbean. Conversely, if Canadians shirked their imperial duties, could they in good conscience claim equality with Britain and the other dominions? Was it hypocritical to make this claim and allow Britain to continue shouldering the weight of responsibility in the colonies? In the wake of Willingdon's controversial statements at the Royal York Hotel, the Toronto *Globe* urged its readers to consider these questions: "It would seem that if a status of equality is established it calls automatically for a division of responsibility within the Empire."[43]

Unionist James Aikins, president of the Canadian Bar Association and former lieutenant governor of Manitoba, agreed that Canada should assume the "correlative duties" that accompanied its new status. Aikins believed that a young, growing nation like Canada needed this kind of "outside interest" to ensure the country's continued development.[44] Addressing the Young Men's Canadian Club of Montreal in 1928, he echoed the sentiments of Amery and the *Round Table* in associating Canada's paternalism in the Caribbean with the march of civilization. "Bringing light and leading to other nations of the world," he claimed, would be "a benediction to ourselves, and a blessing to everyone." Geographically, Canada was better positioned than Britain to carry out this work. Establishing a stronger, direct link between Canada and the Caribbean, moreover, was a logical step if the empire's centre of influence was eventually going to shift to Canada. Aikins had anticipated this future shift in 1912, as discussed in chapter 2. By the late 1920s, he still believed it was not beyond the realm of possibilities.[45]

This kind of future thinking found a willing audience among Canada's political elites, but not much practical action followed. Calvin Reid, a Canadian-born educational advisor at Columbia University, joined the union cause in the early 1930s. He brought the idea to Prime Minister R.B. Bennett's attention during a reception at Calgary's Palliser Hotel in 1932 and was pleased to learn that Bennett had already given it considerable thought. The prime minister encouraged Reid to write or visit him at Ottawa to discuss the matter in greater detail. Reid eventually did so in 1934. In a letter dated 24 March, he outlined the benefits of union, laying emphasis on union's crucial role in facilitating Canada's "maximum greatness." Apparently unencumbered by his work at Columbia, Reid offered Bennett the next few years of his life in pursuance of the union scheme.[46]

The prime minister's response to Reid's letter, sent by way of A.E. Miller, secretary of the Prime Minister's Office, was not encouraging. In his brief reply, Miller noted that the time was inopportune to consider enlarging Canada's borders.[47] In fact, there is little evidence to suggest that Bennett would have seriously entertained the union idea. The interest he expressed during his conversation with Reid at the Palliser Hotel was probably nothing more than political politeness. Bennett zealously respected the empire, but he was rarely receptive to imperial schemes that failed to prioritize Canadian interests. Before coming to power, he raised more than a few eyebrows when he suggested that Canada-US trade should be encouraged over empire trade if it made better economic sense. "If a dollar goes to the West Indies that should go to a Canadian," he remarked in May 1930, "it is no better than if the money went to the United States."[48] Two years later, he raised alarm at the Imperial Economic Conference in Ottawa with his aggressive bargaining tactics. A series of trade agreements were signed, but the conference was hardly a win for imperial cooperation.[49] Even Mackenzie King criticized Bennett's brash statements about the empire.[50]

During the 1920s, King had approached the Canada-Caribbean union idea with an open mind. He was a staunch Canadian nationalist who balked at coordinated imperial foreign and defence policies, but he valued the empire and considered any scheme that served imperial ends if Canada stood to benefit. He met with Harry Crowe in 1923 to discuss the union idea, later noting in his diary that it "had much to commend it." King was apprehensive about what he identified as potential obstacles to union: the "colour problem" and the increased naval expenditure required to secure the islands. But he agreed with Crowe that the exchange of products between northern and southern countries was "nature's intention."[51] A few years later, King encouraged Henry Thornton, president of the Canadian National Railway, to write to Amery about the federation of the Caribbean colonies, noting the inevitability of an even wider British North American union: "I told him by all means to do so," he wrote in his diary, "that eventually all would be blended with N[ew] F[oundland] & Canada in a British North America."[52]

King, however, was less receptive to union proposals emanating from Britain. In 1928, he discouraged Lord Willingdon's proposed tour of the Caribbean for fear it would become "an imperial mission for annexation of [the] West Indies" and disrupt a Canadian trade mission that same year.[53] After discussing the issue with Britain's ambassador to the United States in January 1930, King wrote in his diary that he was "hesitant about any kind of political annexation of the W.I. & Canada which is clearly what Britain would like to see."[54] A combination of factors may have inspired his hesitancy – Canada's worsening economic circumstances and concerns about naval expenditure and the "colour problem" – but King was notoriously sensitive to British intrusion on Canadian affairs. Whatever the prime minister may have felt about union, he probably did not think British officials should lead the discussion.

King's cautious approach to imperial affairs was a response to Canada's growing autonomy since the war. This autonomy was not incompatible with union but rather provided its rationale. Steeped in the rhetoric of imperial equality, partnership, and duty, it was a logic more commonly cited by British politicians. For statesmen like Milner and Amery, meeting the postwar challenge of administering and developing an expanded, unwieldy empire in the face of significant economic constraints was inconceivable without dominion support. While Canadian unionists appreciated the wider imperial implications of union, they were more concerned with developments in the hemisphere. American appeals to transfer the British Caribbean colonies to the US in settlement of Britain's war debt, in particular, intensified Canadian anxieties. At the same time, Canadian unionists admired and sought to replicate many aspects of American imperialism elsewhere in the Caribbean.

Hemispheric Rivalry and Entitlement

In May 1925, University of Toronto president Robert Falconer delivered a lecture at Oxford University on the subject of Canadian-American relations, later expanding his speech into a book, *The United States as a Neighbour from a Canadian Point of View*.[55] In it, Falconer, a long-time unionist, considered Canada's role in the western hemisphere in light of the dominion's new status in the British Commonwealth. Since 1823 the Monroe Doctrine – which delineated Europe and the Americas as separate spheres of interest – had long set the parameters of acceptable behaviour in the hemisphere. Throughout the doctrine's various reinterpretations over the years, the United States assumed a role in the hemisphere that was authoritative and often interventionist. The doctrine's implications were keenly felt by Britain and Canada in 1895 when the United States intervened in a boundary dispute with a settlement that favoured Venezuela over British Guiana. Now times had changed, Falconer argued. If a dispute arose in the Caribbean "of such proportions as to demand the intervention of Britain as the head of the Commonwealth of Nations, would the United States step in and assert her sole right to settle it?"[56] In view of Canada's new status, American unilateralism in hemispheric affairs was no longer appropriate. British imperial policy was not the domain of Britain alone but the British Commonwealth. Perhaps Americans had not yet grasped the meaning of "autonomy within the empire," but Falconer was optimistic that they were beginning to appreciate Canada's interests and future role in the hemisphere.[57]

By the end of the decade, some Americans did appreciate this role. In the trade agreement of 1925, the Canadian government committed to provide a more regular steamship service between Canada's eastern ports and various destinations in the British Caribbean. Canadian National (West Indies) Steamship Limited was incorporated in 1927, and five new freight and passenger vessels went into operation by early 1929. The *New York Times* regarded these developments as an indication of Canada's maturity. While maintaining that the Caribbean territories should, from a geographical perspective, belong to the United States, the *Times* noted that Canada "is now getting big enough to swing the enterprise of saving the West Indian colonies by her own efforts."[58] Chicago's *Daily Tribune* seemed to appreciate, as Falconer had hoped, the meaning of autonomy in the empire. Canada was not simply an appendage of Britain but a nation in its own right. The Monroe Doctrine continued to apply: the British, French, and Dutch possessions in the Americas were "holdovers from the days of discovery, conquection [*sic*], and exploitation," and they "ought to be out." But Canada was an American nation with American interests. A "transfer of British islands to Canadian administration" would consequently "be welcomed as a change in the right direction. The islands then would be in the jurisdiction of a western people similar in most respects to the people of the United States."[59]

American support for Canadian interests in the Caribbean was not particularly reassuring to Canadians, in large part because the voices asserting rights to the remaining European possessions in the hemisphere were much louder. As discussed in chapter 3, in 1919 the former British Air Council president Harold Harmsworth suggested the transfer of Caribbean colonies to the US in partial payment of Britain's war debt. The proposal aroused concern in both Canada and the Caribbean. In British Guiana, for example, a large meeting of legislators, teachers, clergymen, soldiers, and other citizens drafted a resolution, "affirming fervent loyalty to the King's throne" and expressing "grave alarm" that such a transaction might take place without their consent. They emphasized their right to self-determination, a right betrayed by any talk of bartering their homeland to a foreign power.[60] The resolution travelled widely; its authors even sent copies to the leaders of Canada's political parties. A transfer of the Caribbean colonies from British to American hands, the resolution stated, had significant implications for Canada. The Canada-Caribbean trade relationship was at stake, as were the strength and unity of the British Empire. With these implications in mind, surely Canada could be counted on to join their protest and quash further discussion of Harmsworth's proposal.[61] The proposal received fleeting attention in the Canadian press in the fall of 1919, and the Guianese resolution circulated in Canada's Department of External Affairs and Department of Trade and Commerce in January 1920.[62]

Ambivalence turned to concern the following month when American interest in acquiring the British Caribbean gained momentum. At the end of February, politician and former US treasury secretary William Gibbs McAdoo promoted the acquisition publicly, and US senator William S. Kenyon introduced a resolution to undertake negotiations with Britain to acquire the Bermuda Islands.[63] In an interview with the *St Louis Globe-Democrat*, McAdoo pointed out that, beyond the matter of alleviating Britain's war debt, transferring the British Caribbean to the US made sense from a geopolitical perspective. Over time, the United States had become the leading economic power in the world, developed a navy and a merchant marine of stupendous strength, and most importantly, had revolutionized the world's shipping routes with the opening of the Panama Canal. America's strategic and commercial interests in the Caribbean region were heightened like never before.[64] American Senator Joseph McCormick echoed these sentiments in November 1920 in an interview with the London *Times*. Whereas America did not have the same interest as France and Britain in the Mediterranean or the Balkans, it did have an "overwhelming interest" in the Caribbean, and, McCormick maintained, assumed responsibility for the region "to the exclusion of France and Britain."[65] Senator James A. Reed of Missouri followed the efforts of McAdoo and Kenyon with Senate resolutions of his own in 1921 and 1923.[66] Neither resolution was acted upon due to insufficient interest, although the latter resolution was supported by Vice-President Calvin Coolidge and a number of senators.[67] Regardless, American support for the resolutions was ultimately inconsequential, because the British government dismissed them outright.[68]

The prospect of America annexing the British Caribbean, however remote, was nonetheless alarming to many Canadians. It underscored the urgency of strengthening the Canada-Caribbean relationship, whether commercially or politically. "It is time for us to wake up," W.K. Baldwin thundered in the House of Commons in May 1920. If the United States annexed the British Caribbean territories, "where would Canada be?" A Liberal MP and prominent Quebec lumber merchant, Baldwin used his parliamentary seat to promote union throughout the 1920s. He believed that Canada's future prosperity was inextricably tied to the Caribbean. With the elimination of tariffs and the inauguration of a regular steamship service, Canada would no longer be at the mercy of the US for the provision of tropical products (much of which relied on American steam and rail services). Baldwin estimated that under these conditions Canada could accelerate the growth of its manufacturing sector – perhaps becoming one of the "greatest workshops of the world" – and ultimately sustain a population of "hundreds of millions." Canada should seize the moment. In a little over two decades, the United States had absorbed Hawaii and Puerto Rico, established a protectorate over Cuba, gained control of the Panama Canal, purchased the Danish islands, and intervened militarily in the Dominican Republic, Mexico, Nicaragua, and Haiti.[69] This expanding presence concerned Baldwin, but he also thought it commendable. The Americans had acquired territories capable of producing a diverse range of tropical and semi-tropical products. Canada, on the other hand, covered one-half of the North American continent but lacked the capability to produce one ounce of either tropical or semi-tropical products. To Baldwin the message was clear: if Canada's full potential was to be realized, the country needed a stronger foothold in the Caribbean.[70]

Fellow lumber baron Harry Crowe was equally concerned about the American "quest for supremacy" in the Caribbean. He made several trips to Jamaica in the early 1920s, railing against American designs on the island. Crowe was amazed at Senator McAdoo's brazen remark that the United States assumed responsibility in the Caribbean "to the exclusion" of Britain and France. Among the many implications for Canada of making the Caribbean an "American lake" was British Columbia's trade with Europe, the bulk of which now travelled through the Panama Canal.[71] The loss of British coaling stations in the Caribbean would not bode well for this trade. Crowe was also alarmed at the growing influence in Jamaica of the Boston-based United Fruit Company, which monopolized the island's banana trade. In depriving Jamaican producers of the market value of their bananas in the world economy, Crowe argued, the company had brought the island to the "verge of economic slavery." Union with Canada, he assured Jamaicans, would release the island from the tentacles of the United Fruit Company octopus.[72]

Crowe found an ally in William T. Graham, a white member of Jamaica's Legislative Council. Graham shared Crowe's concerns about American influence on the island and the United Fruit Company in particular. The recent election of a company employee to Jamaica's legislative council, coupled with public support in the US for the expansionist agendas of McAdoo, Kenyon, and Reed, were cause for action.[73] In August 1921, Graham tabled a motion in the Legislative Council to ascertain whether there was any interest in Canada, the Colonial Office, and the other Caribbean colonies in federating all the British territories in the hemisphere. The motion received little support in the council and was quickly defeated. Some members expressed uncertainty about what federation actually meant, while others supported a federation of the Caribbean colonies only, without yet another white overseer offshore.[74]

Undeterred by this setback, Crowe and his fellow unionists redoubled their efforts in promoting their cause. With each American overture for hemispheric supremacy, they found themselves on the defensive. Unionist Thomas Bassett Macaulay's defensive strategy was multifaceted. First, make Americans feel guilty for their insistence that war-ravaged Britain and France repay their war debts (no war debt, no transference of colonies to the US in payment for said war debt). Second, highlight the inconsistency between America's anti-imperial stance after the war – their refusal to take on any League of Nations mandates – and their current designs on the Caribbean.

Third, cultivate American sympathy for Canada's geographical disadvantages: "Surely our American friends who are themselves so fortunately situated, do not grudge Canada this small tropical connection?" Fourth, point out the implications for the British Empire; surely Americans would not want to be responsible for its dismemberment. And finally, draw attention to the historic and strengthening ties between Canada and the Caribbean, ties that suggested that "if there is to be any transferring," Canada should have "first claim."[75]

Macaulay was a long-standing advocate for political union, but he was a pragmatic thinker who shifted positions in the face of Caribbean criticism of Canada's "colour bar." By 1919, he was promoting a customs union as an "intermediate arrangement" that he hoped would lead to political union in the future. His plan was first to incorporate the Caribbean colonies into Canada's tariff system, starting with British Guiana. The South American colony was of particular interest to Macaulay because it was much less developed than the islands and had tremendous potential. Its resources were rich and diverse: sugar, rice, balata timber, bauxite, gold, diamonds, and thousands of square miles in the southwest to raise cattle.[76]

Under the proposed union, there would be no tariff between Canada and British Guiana, a 50 per cent preference to Britain, and the full Canadian tariff against the United States and other foreign countries. For commercial purposes, the people of British Guiana would "be practically Canadians." Their development would increase their purchasing power for Canadian products, which would in turn strengthen the Canadian economy. Macaulay estimated that approximately 350 miles of railroad would be needed to facilitate this development, at a cost of about £2 million. He thought it reasonable for Canada to contribute half of this sum and guarantee the interest on half of the bonds necessary to build the railway. This arrangement would be conditional on British Guiana agreeing to purchase all the rails and equipment from Canada.[77]

Macaulay informed Prime Minister Robert Borden that British Guiana's Chamber of Commerce was enthusiastic about a customs union, as was the colony's controller of customs. But he expected the people of British Guiana to gradually realize that political union was a much better arrangement. Canada would pay the full cost of the railway under a political union, a precedent set when Canada's eastern and western provinces entered Confederation. Macaulay hoped this prospect would be too enticing for the Guianese to refuse: "Is it worth their while to incur a debt of half the cost of the railway merely to continue under the Colonial Office rather than under Ottawa?" He was willing to be patient, resting assured that political union would naturally evolve from commercial union. He was also confident that many of the other Caribbean colonies would follow British Guiana's lead. Colonies that produced the same products as British Guiana and did not want to accept lower prices in the Canadian market would be particularly eager to enter the union.[78]

Macaulay and other unionists often drew examples from America's expansionist playbook. Many of the territories under American control, influence, or "protection" made appearances in their arguments. Macaulay thought the US–Puerto Rico relationship – widely regarded as a success story in unionist circles – was the example to follow. As he explained to Borden, there was free trade between Puerto Rico and the US, and the full American tariff applied to everything imported into the island from other countries. Rather than grant Puerto Rico a subsidy to make up for the loss of revenue under the union (a practice exercised in Canada through a system of provincial subventions), customs collected on the island were retained by the local government.[79]

Canadian unionists found these examples instructive because many of them demonstrated the benefits of a customs union over a system of preferences. Puerto Rico–US trade had increased tremendously, but Canada-Caribbean trade agreements – based on mutual preferences – were disappointing.[80] In the years following the 1920 agreement, the value of Canadian exports to the British Caribbean dropped, from $24.1 million in 1921 to $13.2 million in 1923. British Caribbean exports to Canada were similarly discouraging, dropping from $24.1 million in 1921 to $14.5 million in 1922.[81] In 1924, the value of British Caribbean imports was $90 million, of which the Canadian share was only $18 million.[82] The postwar recession was partly responsible, as was the Canadian government's failure to improve steamship services.[83] But the 1925 agreement had similarly disappointing results.[84] In Harry Crowe's opinion, trade agreements were futile.[85] Montreal lawyer and politician Charles H. Cahan agreed, arguing in 1929 that the dominion "must assume control of the administration, placing in charge competent men who will see to it that the productivity of those people is rapidly increased and that they assume a higher standard of living than they have ever enjoyed up to the present time."[86]

In fact, the reciprocal advantages of union – whether political or commercial – were not borne out by the US–Puerto Rico example. The Foraker Act (1900–17) outlined the political and economic dimensions of the new relationship between Puerto Rico and the US. The act extended to Puerto Rico the structure of North American tariffs, US currency, and commercial relations mandated by Congress. The island was unable to create its own tariff structure or negotiate trade agreements with foreign nations; all the products shipped between Puerto Rico and the US had to be transported in American vessels; and the Spanish peso was devalued by 60 per cent. These policies influenced prices, wages, accumulated wealth, and availability of goods. Coupled with North American capital investment, the policies transformed Puerto Rico's economy from one based on subsistence agriculture to a cash-based framework dependent on American markets. In 1938, around 92 per cent of Puerto Rican imports came from the US, while 98 per cent of Puerto Rican exports went to the United States. By incorporating Puerto Rico in the American economy in this way, the act provided, as Blanca Silvestrini has argued, "the legal framework for economic dependency."[87]

Of course a Canada-Caribbean union would have its own distinctive characteristics and consequences. Political, legal, economic, and social differences in and across Canada and the British Caribbean, compared to the United States and Puerto Rico, would give rise to unique relationships. Yet many of the features of the US–Puerto Rico arrangement were championed by Canadian unionists: extending the Canadian tariff to the Caribbean, negotiating commercial treaties on behalf of the Caribbean territories, requiring Canadian vessels to transport the trade goods travelling between them, and requiring the Caribbean territories to purchase Canadian manufactures in colonial development projects (such as the British Guiana railway proposed by Macaulay). These initiatives would be realized, as they had been in Puerto Rico under the Foraker Act, under a form of government controlled from abroad.[88]

Paternalism Prevails

For interwar unionists, the Caribbean colonies would be administered as colonial dependencies and developed under Canada's purported protective wing. A greater measure of representative government was conceivable, but any talk of self-government was imagined in a distant future. In the early 1920s, University of Toronto historian Hume Wrong published *Government of the West Indies*, a constitutional history of the region.[89] Of particular interest to students familiar with the history of the white dominions, Hume noted, was the remarkably different course of constitutional change in the Caribbean. The evolution of representative and eventually responsible government in the dominions played out in reverse in most of the Caribbean colonies, with the elimination of elected assemblies after 1865.[90] As Canadian and British statesmen worked out the federal structure in the British North America

Act in 1866, the crown asserted greater control over its Caribbean colonies. For Hume and his white contemporaries, these divergent histories were a product of racial difference. The task of working out the constitutional futures of the Caribbean colonies was similarly dependent on racialized reasoning. The central "condition" to be considered in any discussion of constitutional development in the region, Hume maintained, was the "fitness of the negro to play his part in a self-governing community." In the well-worn, racialized logic of development, Caribbean peoples had made much progress under Britain's guiding hand and could hardly be compared to the "transplanted African savage" who had arrived on America's shores in the days of slavery.[91] Although he thought this progress warranted greater concessions in the way of representative government – a conclusion supported by the recently published Wood Report on political conditions in the British Caribbean – complete self-government was out of the question. "Public opinion in the West Indies is temperamental rather than rational," he wrote, and thus "a good Governor is of far higher value than a good constitution." The Caribbean colonies should, in Hume's assessment, remain under the direction of the Colonial Office for many years to come.[92]

Union enthusiasts made the same racialized assumptions about Caribbean development. The most significant concern – and the overriding explanation for the dismissal of provincial status – remained Black Caribbean access to the franchise. With the Dominion Elections Act of 1920, Canadian residents twenty-one years of age and older (with the exception of Asian and Indigenous peoples) were entitled to vote. Extending the vote to two million subjects in the Caribbean was an alarming prospect to white Canadians. As Montreal financier Andrew Drummond warned in 1919, "If the British West Indies entered Canada two millions of coloured population in these Crown colonies would be entitled to claim the franchise on equal terms with the eight millions of Canada's population." The notion that Caribbean members of Parliament – whose constituents did not yet possess the requisite "qualities" to participate in government – might take up one-fifth of Canada's parliamentary seats was inconceivable to unionists and anti-unionists alike.[93]

The possibility that union might spur Caribbean migration to Canada proved deeply disconcerting as well. Unionists attempted to allay these concerns with familiar arguments: Black Caribbeans would not migrate to Canada because the country's temperate climate was unsuitable for "tropical races," and the development and diversification of Caribbean economies under union would produce abundant employment opportunities and thus eliminate the main catalyst of out-migration. To Harry Crowe, union might actually improve race relations in Canada by providing a solution to the South Asian migrant "problem" in British Columbia, while at the same time addressing British Guiana's labour demand. With the end of the Indian indenture system in 1917 and the failure of British Guiana's government to secure a continued supply of labour, Crowe thought Canada might have the solution. If British Guiana was part of Canada, the Canadian government might convince India to "divert" some of its surplus labourers "to the southern portion" of the dominion, "to a more suitable climate than British Columbia, where they now attempt to enter, much to the embarrassment of all Governments concerned."[94]

Advocates and opponents of union both relied on common constructs of Black Caribbeans as indolent and simple-minded. If they were enfranchised in the Canadian federation, the Canadian public affairs magazine *Willison's Monthly* warned in 1929, they could be easily manipulated by unscrupulous Canadian politicians. In Grenada, St Lucia, and St Vincent, less than 5 per cent of the population were "pure whites," the magazine cautioned. "So great is the majority of those described as coloured people that if the franchise were given as in Canada a few demagogues, playing upon ignorance and prejudice, could make chaos where peace now reigns."[95] According to a report in Toronto's *Daily Star* in May 1930, there was "little public opinion among the colored citizens on any political question, let alone the matter of federation with Canada."[96] Responding to the suggestion that a plebiscite be held in the Caribbean to gauge public opinion on the union question in the late 1930s, unionist and Ontario doctor Ezra Stafford disparaged the idea, claiming that Black Caribbeans were "too ignorant of the world scene" to understand what union would mean.[97]

The *Canada West Indies Magazine* reinforced racialized representations of the Black Caribbean as an apolitical subject. According to an article published in February 1932, when Blacks in the Caribbean took up positions of consequence in business, political, or religious life, the responsibilities proved too great, and they abandoned them. A "smiling carelessness," a feeling of "easy inconsequence," and a "persistent tendency to religious emotionalism" characterized this "junior race."[98] References to this "religious emotionalism" often appeared in articles on the continued practice of Obeah in the Caribbean. It was surprising, the editor observed in September 1934, that this "practice of evil magic" exercised such a powerful influence "even in this enlightened day."[99] The cover of the March 1936 issue, which featured a photograph of an elderly Caribbean man smiling while relaxing with his pipe, conveyed the familiar image of the complacent African Caribbean with little ambition and few wants. The man represented, according to the caption, "Coloured Contentment."[100]

Unionists had deployed such images of African Caribbean peoples for decades, but during the interwar period they borrowed from the increasingly popular rhetoric of trusteeship.[101] As the "big British brother of the north," Canada was obliged to take the Caribbean colonies under its "guiding wing."[102] The claim that Canada was bound to protect the region's Black subjects harkened backed to the narrative of Canada-as-saviour to Blacks seeking refuge from American slavery in the mid-nineteenth century. The concept of trusteeship, articulated in Frederick Lugard's influential *The Dual Mandate in British Tropical Africa* in 1922, outlined the twin duties of the mandate system: to the colonies, to advance their "moral and educational progress," and to the world, "to exploit and develop the abundant resources of the colonies under their trust."[103] As writer Robert Stokes argued eight years later in *New Imperial Ideals: A Plea for the Association of the Dominions in the Government of the Dependent Empire*, it was important for the dominions to appreciate that the exploitation of a "backward land" went "hand in hand" with the guardianship of its peoples.[104] During the course of the interwar period, this paternalism was at odds with the increasingly tenacious push for self-determination in the Caribbean.

Black Activism and Anti-Colonialism in Canada and the British Caribbean

The activism that emerged from the oppressive political and economic circumstances in the British Caribbean in the 1920s and '30s found expression in a multitude of transnational, regional, and local organizations. Marcus Garvey's Universal Negro Improvement Association (UNIA), founded in New York, was the most successful pan-Caribbean political movement in the 1920s, with branches throughout the Caribbean, Latin America, the United States, and Canada. Garvey promoted Black pride, African nationalism, and anti-colonialism, and he founded the People's Political Party in Jamaica in 1929 to advocate constitutional change and workers' rights. Labour organizations of varying influence emerged elsewhere in the region, providing a space to educate workers, critique employers and the government, and turn worker discontent into political action.[105] In the 1930s, deteriorating economic and social conditions wrought by the Great Depression heightened labour unrest. Strikes and riots broke out across the region, thrusting the question of self-government to the fore. In 1938, British Caribbean labour leaders established the British Guiana and West Indies Labour Congress to strengthen regional solidarity among workers (and their associated unions and political parties). The congress outlined a program of economic and political reform, which included a call for self-government based on adult suffrage and wholly elected legislatures.[106] The same year, at the height of labour unrest, the British government appointed a royal commission chaired by former Conservative politician Lord Moyne to investigate conditions in the region.[107] The commission's report, released in 1945, was significant because it was the first time the imperial government officially acknowledged the dire need for reform.[108]

The 1930s were also a decade of increased labour radicalism and race activism in Canada. Mass unemployment and federal conservatism fed many forms of radical politics, but since employers prioritized white male employment, and most mainstream labour unions excluded racialized minorities, African Canadians looked to Black labour unions to represent their interests, with Caribbean peoples playing a central role.[109] John Arthur Robinson, the St Kitts–born founder of Canada's Order of Sleeping Car Porters (1917), was a prominent activist from the First World War to the 1940s. In 1931, Robinson's nephew, Arthur Blanchette, joined him in Winnipeg, and they spent the final years of the decade promoting Black radicalism among the city's workers. Robinson and Blanchette blended traditional workplace activism with social justice and community-building initiatives, in a manner not unlike that of Caribbean unions, broadening "the scope of workers' demands from the railway station to full-scale desegregation, shifting African Canadians' requests from the workplace to the courts, the press, and other areas of racialized conflict."[110] Overall, it was a fruitful period of Black organization.

The Dawn of Tomorrow, founded in London in 1923 and the official organ of the Canadian League for the Advancement of Colored People (CLACP) from 1927, was a forum of unrelenting Black activism.[111] Throughout the 1920s and '30s, the newspaper's activism was multi-levelled, addressing racial and colonial injustices in Canada and the world. The *Dawn* protested racism in Canadian restaurants, hotels, schools, city pools, factories, and government, at amusement parks, concert halls, and sports venues, and on national railways. Its editors and contributors initiated petitions, organized meetings, and mobilized communities into action. In its international coverage, the *Dawn* drew attention to racial and colonial injustices within and outside the British Empire. It levelled acerbic criticisms at South Africa's racist policies, British imperialism in China, America's intervention in Haiti, and Italian aggression in Abyssinia. It encouraged anti-colonial nationalist movements: "China has awakened, as have Japan, India and Egypt. They are tired of being treated as inferior peoples although their skin is dark. It only remains now for Africa, the giant of them all, to cast off her slumber."[112]

The assault on colonialism was also waged by a growing community of transnational Black activists. During the interwar decades, African and Caribbean intellectuals, students, and political activists coalesced in London, Paris, Berlin, Montreal, New York City, and Moscow.[113] The Harlem Renaissance involved several expatriate Black Caribbeans, such as Claude McKay, Marcus Garvey, and Richard B. Moore, who created a literary culture that advanced their political agenda for the Caribbean.[114] The African-American scholar and intellectual W.E.B. DuBois convened Pan-African congresses in several European capitals in 1919, 1921, 1923, and 1927, where African Caribbeans sometimes comprised the majority of attendees. The Jamaica-born doctor and activist Harold Moody founded the League for Colored Peoples (LCP) in London in 1931, and in 1937 George Padmore and C.L.R. James, both Trinidad-born activists, founded the London-based International African Service Bureau (IASB) with other Pan-Africanists.[115] Both organizations publicized colonial conditions in Britain and lobbied the British government to initiate reforms.

A combination of circumstances shaped the varied contours and concerns of Black activism in Canada and the Caribbean. Yet despite their differences, in each case the source of grievance – whether paltry wages and long working hours, employment, housing, and social discrimination, or disenfranchisement and the right to self-determination – was a product, wholly or partly, of colonialism. Reckoning with this reality in the interwar years involved an expansive, organized challenge to European colonialism's most faithful collaborator, white supremacy. As African Caribbeans and Black Canadians confronted white Canadian racism, they exposed the hypocritical logic that had given rise to and sustained the Canada-Caribbean relationship over time.

Spurning the Would-Be Canadian "Overlord"

In familiar fashion, Canadian unionists often contrasted America's "race problem" with the purportedly cordial state of race relations in Canada. Union was a benevolent proposition, they claimed, and British justice and fair play would continue under Canadian rule. As Winnipeg unionist Jules Preudhomme argued in January 1926, Black Canadians "receive the fairest treatment in Canada and enjoy the rights of citizenship without any of the

friction which similar conditions produce in the United States of America."[116]
This line of reasoning derived in large part from the British liberal tradition – especially notions of British tolerance, justice, and fair play – and the
legacy of abolitionism in Upper Canada. In fact, while the Upper Canadian
legislature introduced legislation for the gradual abolition of slavery in 1793,
decades before the United States did so in 1865, several northeastern states
had introduced legislation for the gradual abolition of slavery well before
1793, and Massachusetts outlawed slavery outright in 1783. Accuracy, however,
was less important than myth; inconvenient details could be forgotten in the
nationalist narrative of moral superiority to the US. White Canadians missed
no opportunity to juxtapose British justice with American lawlessness.[117]

Canada's abolitionist history resonated differently with Blacks in Canada
and the Caribbean. Persistent racial discrimination in all aspects of social
life confirmed that Canada's proud abolitionist legacy was a sham and that
"British justice" did not prevail on Canadian soil. Black Canadians frequently
challenged the white narrative of this legacy. When a watchmaker from Kitch-
ener, Ontario, F.V. Franklin, was refused service at a London café in July 1923
and subsequently initiated court proceedings against the café owner, *Dawn
of Tomorrow* urged its readers to rally in support of Franklin. "Prejudice is on
trial," the editor wrote, and it would "soon be decided if Canada is the Proud
Lady of the Snows, or the mere tail of the American kite."[118] In its editorial
"Ontario or Mississippi?" on 1 August 1925, the newspaper recounted the
experience of Dr George Wendell Morrison, a Toronto physician who was
refused service at Hamilton's Connaught Hotel. Morrison's lawyer was on a
mission, the *Dawn* reported, to determine when "the customs of Alabama or
Mississippi [have] been in vogue in this country."[119] And when a London hotel
fired its Black employees and replaced them with white ex-servicemen in 1934,
the *Dawn* called on the Canadian Department of Labour and the courts to
intervene. Failing such intervention, the editor remarked, "We are compelled
to think Canada is trying to go one step ahead of the United States of America
in its race relations."[120] White Canadian declarations of moral superiority to
the US were not easily reconciled with Black Canadian experiences.

Canada's discriminatory immigration policy in the interwar decades was
an even more distasteful hypocrisy. Immigration authorities routinely rejected
Caribbean immigrants on the premise that Blacks did not make good farmers.
Despite the advertised demand for domestic workers, Caribbean domestics
were routinely refused entry to Canada. According to the deputy minister of
immigration, F.C. Blair, Caribbean immigrants were not welcome in Canada,

regardless of whether they met the immigration regulations. As he wrote to Canada's trade agent in Jamaica in April 1925, "It makes no difference whether the intending immigrant is a farmer, farm labourer, or domestic servant or anything else, so far as encouragement goes we do not offer it." In response to the agent's query about the case of a "near white" Jamaican woman who met all the immigration requirements – she was a British subject, possessed the funds necessary to purchase her ticket and to land, and planned to take up work in a field advertised as in demand in Canada – Blair was unequivocal: "The class that may be described as 'Near White' is really no more wanted than the class that has more colour. The really white people of European origin are treated with more consideration, but the number of these coming to Canada from the West Indies is very small indeed." While Canada desired closer commercial relations, immigration was another entirely matter. "If you were compelled frankly to state the facts to Jamaicans," Blair concluded, "you would have to say to them that though Canada is seeking closer trade relations she is not seeking immigration and that Jamaicans are really not wanted in Canada."[121]

In Canada and the Caribbean, the Black press regularly reported incidences of racial discrimination against would-be Caribbean immigrants. Were they not British subjects? Were they not loyal? Why were they judged on their colour rather than their skills and work experience? Why were they refused entry "when hordes of the trash and scum of Central Europe and thousands of bums even from England are entering each year?" asked the *Dawn* in 1929. Blacks in Canada and the Caribbean called on the Canadian government to explain its hypocritical and offensive immigration policies.[122] In the fall of 1925, the Jamaican press gave much attention to the case of Mercy Ann Holness, a sixteen-year-old Jamaican girl who was detained at Montreal's immigration quarters for five days without reasonable cause. With her mother recently deceased and her father ill, Mercy Ann had travelled to Canada to take up residence with her older sister in Toronto. The cause for her detainment, according to her sister, was her colour: immigration officials at Montreal interrogated her about her parentage and "demanded to know whether she was not black."[123] The editor of Jamaica's *Daily Gleaner*, Herbert DeLisser, in his many articles condemning the Holness incident, often highlighted the implications of such discrimination for Canada's trade relationship with the Caribbean. He pointed to the hypocrisy of Canadian efforts to strengthen trade under the banner of imperial friendship while denying Caribbean immigrants entry to Canada.[124]

Black Canadians similarly drew attention to the contradiction of promoting trade relations while discriminating against African Caribbean peoples. When the University of Western Ontario banned the enrolment of Black medical students in 1931, London's Black community rallied. With the assistance of B.J. Spencer Pitt, a Grenada-born, Dalhousie-educated lawyer, they sent letters of protest to Western, the Canadian government, and the Black press in Canada, the US, and the Caribbean.[125]

By linking domestic racism to Canadian-Caribbean relations, Black activists attacked the basic premise of the unionist cause. In the wake of the Holness incident, Black Grenadian politician and journalist T.A. Marryshow published a caustic editorial on the union question in his newspaper, the *West Indian*. Union with Canada, he argued, was the last thing any of the British Caribbean colonies would contemplate. He counselled Canadian unionists to take a hard look at conditions within their own country, where "equality of men" had yet to be realized. Marryshow valued the British connection and supported the creation of a federated Caribbean dominion within the empire. But Canada was not Britain. Caribbean people, he argued, "have grown to think of the Canadians as more akin to his lynching brother to his south than to the justice-loving men of Britain." Trade was fine, but any talk of political association must be deferred until Canadians divested themselves of the "American conception of the darker races of mankind."[126]

In the late 1920s, white prejudice against Black Caribbeans on the Canadian National Railway (CNR) and its newly minted steamship service gave Marryshow and other Caribbean people additional grounds to question their relationship with Canada. Many African-Caribbean travellers encountered difficulties purchasing tickets, some holding first-class tickets were bumped to second-class, while others were harassed on board or removed from the ship without cause.[127] The steamers were, according to Marryshow, "floating Alabamas" on which "Jim Crowism" prevailed openly and unabashedly.[128] This discrimination was particularly infuriating to Caribbean peoples given that the much-publicized purpose of CNR's new West Indies line was to strengthen the imperial bond between Canada and the British Caribbean. When the formation of the line was authorized in the Canadian National Steamships Act in 1927, *Daily Gleaner* editor DeLisser recalled the "frothy ebullitions of sentiment" that frequently accompanied efforts to characterize Canada's relationship with the region. There was much talk of Canada's ardent desire – as a "big brother" – to "help" the Caribbean colonies develop and prosper, but few in the Caribbean, according to DeLisser, were buying this rhetoric.[129]

Besides, Canadian trade was not about to transform "heaven and earth" or usher in an unprecedented period of prosperity in the British Caribbean.[130] This lack of enthusiasm was born of the long-held understanding that the Canadian market was no substitute for the US market. DeLisser and Marryshow were fully aware that the United States was their most important customer, and would remain so for some time.[131] Trade with the US was more straightforward; unlike Canadian trade, it was not accompanied by sentimental nonsense and sanctimonious pronouncements of paternal guidance. Moreover, the US did not feign racial harmony within its borders. It was, according to DeLisser, the "better and more honest" country.[132] Reinforcing this view, the Canadian government's response to claims of racial prejudice on the Canadian National Steamships (cns) was often dismissive and unapologetic.[133] Unless Ottawa aimed to make Canadians "intensely disliked," DeLisser warned, it should intervene immediately and put an end to racial discrimination on the steamship line.[134]

cns was embroiled in controversy once again in the late 1930s when the labour disturbances in the British Caribbean made their way onto the ships. The company employed African Caribbeans on their Eastern and Western Caribbean routes. Indeed, on some ships – the *Lady Somers* and the *Lady Rodney*, for example – the majority of crew members were Caribbean. cns first reported labour trouble in the summer and fall of 1938, especially on ships employing Jamaican crew.[135] In June of that year, the influential Jamaican labour leader Alexander Bustamante had formed the Maritime Trade Union, which represented longshoremen, banana carriers, and stowers, dock and ship workers, and shipping clerks.[136] When the *Lady Somers* docked in Jamaica in November, Bustamante went aboard to protest the Saturday working hours of the ship's Jamaican firemen. W.B. Armit, the ship's master, informed Bustamante that the *Lady Somers* was a Canadian ship whose workers must abide by Canadian labour laws and regulations.[137] Of course, Canadian law reflected the interests of shipping companies rather than workers. cns managed to keep Canada's trade unions at bay, at least on ocean-going vessels, until the mid-1940s.[138] And even then, Canada's Maritime Labour Relations Board excluded Caribbean personnel working on cns and Merchant Marine ships from union contracts.[139]

For Jamaican workers, abiding by Canadian laws and regulations meant tolerating racialized inequalities: lower wages, longer working hours, and more gruelling working conditions. Aboard the *Lady Somers*, Armit frankly informed Bustamante, Jamaican seamen were dispensable. Unhappy workers were free to seek employment elsewhere,[140] and there was "plenty of white help in Canada" to fill these positions.[141] Bustamante reportedly threatened to tie up the ship and, if the CNS replaced Jamaican crew with Canadians, "drive all Canadians from Jamaica." When Armit retorted that all Jamaicans in Canada could return to Jamaica, Bustamante threatened – or so Armit told CNS General Manager R.B. Teakle – "to bend and break" him. After leaving the ship for a brief time, Bustamante announced that he would not tie up the ship, and the *Lady Somers* left the harbour without further incident.[142]

A few months later, the *Lady Rodney* was delayed in Kingston when the captain dismissed seven Jamaican stewards, owing to a light load of passengers on the return voyage to Halifax. The remaining Jamaican stewards walked off the ship and refused to sign back on for fear they would be required to take on the work of their dismissed colleagues.[143] Bustamante, the ship's captain, and a CNS executive mediated the dispute and proposed a resolution: the stewards (excepting the dismissed seven) would return to work and certain cabins would be unattended and cordoned off until the number of stewards returned to full force. As the *Lady Rodney* approached Halifax, however, the stewards were ordered to prepare the empty rooms for southbound passengers. When three stewards challenged the order for breaching the agreement signed at Kingston, the captain docked their pay. The stewards' union delegate intervened and was charged with insubordination and dismissed.[144] Upon the *Lady Rodney*'s return to Kingston, Bustamante boarded the ship to discuss the stewards' grievances with the captain, who reportedly "refused to be advised as to how to maintain discipline on his ship." Bustamante consequently called an all-out strike against Canadian National Steamships, and the *Lady Rodney* left Kingston harbour without unloading its cargo. The strike was short-lived, however. Shortly after the ship's departure, the colonial secretary and privy councillor agreed to appoint an arbitration board to settle the dispute, and Bustamante called off the strike.[145] His opinion of Canada, though, had been irreparably damaged. In subsequent years, he was an acerbic critic of Canadian racism (which he too concluded was more pernicious than the American variety), pledging "to resist with all influence at my command any attempt by Canada for Jamaica to become part of its dominion."[146]

Trinidad labour leader W. Howard Bishop was even more pessimistic about the future of the Canada-British Caribbean relationship. Bishop was an active Garveyite, the secretary of the Trinidad Workingmen's Association, and editor of its official organ, the *Labour Leader*.[147] In his opinion, Caribbean peoples were fed up with all the "propaganda" about Canada's charity and goodwill.

The reciprocity agreement of 1925, wherein Canada was "taking much and giving nothing in return," underscored the speciousness of this role. While the effects of the 1925 agreement were mixed in both Canada and the Caribbean, Bishop's characterization had merit in the Trinidadian context. Like Jamaica and some of the Windward islands, Trinidad was not wholly reliant on the production and export of sugar but rather produced a wide variety of primary export commodities. Because British Caribbean sugar was shut out of the US market for most of the twentieth century in favour of Cuban sugar, colonial economies based on sugar production relied heavily on other markets. But for those with more diverse economies, trade with the US market made better commercial sense. In addition to its significantly larger market than Canada, the US was geographically closer and generally offered superior transport facilities and rates.[148] Bishop's pessimism about the value of Canada-Caribbean trade was shared by other prominent Black Caribbeans, including DeLisser and the Jamaican community leader U. Theo McKay.[149] During trade negotiations at Ottawa during the summer of 1925, McKay warned Jamaicans not to allow Canada's sentimental "brothers under the flag" rhetoric to beguile them into entering an agreement they would later regret.[150]

Bishop's response to the entire union idea was scathing. In an editorial in the *Labour Leader* in March 1929, he decried the comments of Canadian media mogul Horace Hunter, who had addressed the union question in the *Financial Post*. Hunter, who had recently visited the islands, echoed the hackneyed concerns of other white Canadian unionists, particularly potential Caribbean access to the franchise. If Canada annexed territory in which "90 percent of the 2,000,000 population are black," he cautioned, Canada might become entangled in the same difficulties currently facing the United States. This statement, Bishop retorted, "gives ample indication of the mentality of the Canadian overlord who evidently would start out on a propaganda having as its great objective the keeping of the heel of the white man firmly planted upon the necks of the coloured subjects of His Majesty the King in this corner of the Empire." Canada, he continued, had "shown enough of the open teeth of the boar in the cunningly devised colour bar on board the National Steamship line and in respect of banging and bolting the door of immigration toward peoples of Negro blood. We have seen all of this in daylight and we are not prepared to support any suggestion bearing upon a Confederacy with such a Dominion."[151]

Bishop dismissed Hunter's statements about widespread illiteracy in the Caribbean as if this was a characteristic unique to Blacks. If literacy was a marker of a progressive civilization, Euro-Canadians should perhaps be more concerned with the myriad illiterate and half-literate persons to be found among the "advanced white races."[152] Bishop was equally infuriated with Hunter's assumption (common among white Canadian unionists) that Caribbean peoples were clamouring for union. This assumption played into the white unionist narrative that cast Canada as the saviour of the hapless, ignorant Black Caribbean. In the midst of forceful assertions of white suprem-acy throughout the British Empire and the US (and the corresponding assault on racial equality)[153] Bishop and other Black activists had little patience for this kind of posturing.

Containing Anti-colonialism, Conserving White Supremacy

Whatever white Canadians may have thought about union, they were generally uneasy with the rise of Black activism and anti-colonialism. These develop-ments challenged the social, economic, and political infrastructure of white supremacy and British-Canadian self-identity. Their unease was discernible in a series of episodes during the interwar years. A few examples are instructive. The first centres on the Canadian government's response to Garvey's UNIA, which attracted Ottawa's concern on more than one occasion. In the early 1920s, the Department of Immigration instructed its agents to interrogate Canada-bound migrants of African descent from the United States, the Caribbean, and the Panama Canal zone[154] to ascertain whether they were affiliated with the UNIA. Migrants who were members of the UNIA, subscribed to the *Negro World* (the UNIA's official organ), or held stock in Garvey's Black Star Line were subject to increased scrutiny. The UNIA was anti-British and anti-white, Canadian immigration commissioner W.R. Little informed his agent at Ellis Island, and was "engaged in pernicious propaganda to create disturbances between white and coloured people" in the empire.[155] In 1921 Garvey wrote to Robert Borden (recently retired from political life) to solicit a Christmas message for the *Negro World*.[156] Unfamiliar with the UNIA, Borden asked his former private secretary to obtain information from the British ambassador at Washington.[157] An embassy secretary reported that Garvey was a man of "socialistic tendencies," a political agitator who supported African, Indian, and Irish self-determination. He advised Borden to disregard Garvey's request. Borden heeded the advice.[158]

For the Canadian Department of Immigration, the category of "agitator" became a powerful tool of exclusion. During the war, government officials systematized the deportation of enemy aliens and other suspected "agitators": labour activists, foreign radicals, and especially Bolsheviks. After the war, the category continued to provide grounds to suppress and deport migrants for their political activities.[159] Surveillance was transatlantic: authorities in Britain and the United States often monitored Black activists and, when relevant, shared intelligence with Canadian authorities.[160] When Garvey arrived in Montreal in late October 1928, immigration authorities arrested him, deemed him a political agitator, and ordered his deportation.[161] Soon after his arrival, Garvey had made public remarks that caused offence in Britain and the US. He described London, which he had recently visited, as a city unfriendly to Black subjects, and later declared his intention to "swing 5 million votes" to US Democratic presidential candidate Alfred E. Smith in the upcoming election. Garvey was known for his bombast, and it is unclear that he could deliver on his threat, but his promise raised hackles in Montreal and Washington. The American consul at Montreal complained to Canadian authorities, and Garvey was arrested shortly thereafter.[162]

In 1934, political and racial anxieties were in evidence once again when the West Indian Federation of America (WIFA), founded in New York in 1933, requested a message from the Bennett government to mark the centenary of British slave emancipation on 1 August 1934. The federation's objectives were to encourage solidarity among Blacks in the British Caribbean and elsewhere in North America, generate interest in their political and civic well-being, promote the development of their homelands through trade and commerce, and "advocate the early federation of, and self-government for, the British West Indies, British Guiana, British Honduras, Bermuda and the Bahamas within the British Commonwealth of Nations." Bennett's message, WIFA secretary A.M. Wendell Malliet wrote, would be "a welcome gesture of goodwill," and its influence "would be incalculable in strengthening the bond of friendship existing between British West Indians and Canadians." Malliet outlined the various linkages between Canada and the Caribbean colonies over the years: the expansion of Canadian trade and investment, the education of Caribbean students at Canadian universities, and the employment of Caribbean peoples on Canada's railroads. These linkages, Malliet predicted, were sure to become even stronger in the future.[163]

Malliet sent his request to W.D. Herridge of the Canadian Legation at Washington, who forwarded it to Canada's undersecretary of state for external affairs, O.D. Skelton. Herridge joked – rather contemptuously – that Bennett should send WIFA a message that underscored Canada's disinterest in continuing to trade with the Caribbean on a preferential basis, the benefits of which he understood to be one-sided: "The Canadian government, now having reached a state of relative sobriety, and realizing that it takes a little more than unrequited love to make the Empire go round, has decided and hereby declares that on and after August 1st, 1934, the unwarranted preferences granted at various times to the West Indies shall cease ... God save the King."[164] It was a flippant joke about a serious subject – the end of an institution that wrought centuries of human suffering to satiate European avarice. Skelton was more compassionate, noting that emancipation was an event worth commemorating. But he worried about the diplomatic consequences of sending a message to WIFA, which might be construed as Canadian support for the organization's most controversial object: self-government in the Caribbean.[165]

Beyond diplomatic considerations, white Canadian reluctance to encourage self-government in the region was a product of racialized thinking about Black Caribbeans' fitness for such responsibility and a corresponding commitment to the status quo. The newly formed *Globe and Mail* (born from the 1936 merger of the *Globe* and Toronto's *Mail and Empire*) regularly reported the labour unrest that swept the Caribbean in the latter half of the 1930s, but showed little support for self-government, empathy for the paltry wages and dire living conditions that prompted the unrest, or antipathy for colonial governments' heavy-handed responses to the rioting.[166] Caribbean peoples were not presenting their grievances in a civilized fashion but were "running amok in an attempt to force more wages from their white employers."[167] Jamaican colonial authorities' violent suppression of the strikes and riots that tore through the island in May-June 1938 were, in the *Globe and Mail's* assessment, appropriate.[168] The newspaper commended colonial military and police forces for establishing "effective control" in the colony.[169] It conceded that the "hordes of natives" were somewhat justified in protesting low wages, but its greater sympathy was reserved for the Caribbean planter. With the declining value of sugar in the world economy, the planter could hardly expect to increase wages and make a profit. The possibility that the labour disturbances might "sweep the white man from the islands" was, in short, a "grim prediction."[170]

Prime Minister Mackenzie King, back in power from October 1935, was more sympathetic to the circumstances animating Black protest in the British Caribbean, but his racialized worldview nonetheless framed his assessment of the political situation in the region. He witnessed the labour and political unrest first-hand during a holiday to the islands in November 1938. While in Jamaica, he found the rioting "quite menacing," but concluded that the islands' labourers were only trying to improve their standard of living and "assert their rights to enjoyment of a country which is essentially their own." King's diarized musings on the subject, however, fell short of identifying self-determination as the necessary condition to realize these rights. His conversations with imperial and colonial authorities in the Caribbean confirmed his impression that the prospect of union with Canada (which he readily dismissed) was even less remote than the formation of an autonomous Caribbean dominion.[171]

Conclusion

Perhaps King's dismissive attitude formed a fitting end to interwar unionism. From one perspective, the idea was anything but marginal: it reached the lofty heights of the prime minister's office more than once, and its advocates adeptly merged unionism with Canada's shifting status in the Empire-Commonwealth and, by extension, the Americas. This shift raised unionist hopes and animated their arguments in the interwar years. Still, the persistence of unionism was remarkable in light of broader developments. Colonial reform movements, anti-colonial nationalism, and Pan-Africanism proliferated. The League of Nations, formed in 1920, provided the apparatus (at least in theory) to hold member nations accountable for their conduct on the world stage, which included the colonies and mandates under their administration. The British Caribbean colonies were not, of course, a League of Nations mandate. Yet the ethos that produced the League of Nations and its mandate system, given expression in 1918 by US president Woodrow Wilson in his "Fourteen Points," generated a broader expectation that empires and nations should act in the best interests of the colonial subjects under their charge or within their geographic realm. For many colonial peoples, this included supporting initiatives that facilitated self-determination and eventual independence.[172]

To a large degree, white supremacy, not disinterest, doomed the union cause. Safeguarding racial supremacy required the robust enforcement of the global colour line,[173] which in turn shaped white Canadians' uneasy encounter with Black activism and anti-colonialism, and their reluctance to envision Caribbean self-determination in anything less than an undefined, remote future. Anti-colonial activism was problematic because it compromised the logic that sustained this racialized geography and threatened the status quo of imperial relations. Despite white Canadians' paternalistic rhetoric, the struggle to contain anti-colonialism was rooted in Canadian interests rather than a genuine concern for Caribbean well-being. The prospect of an autonomous Caribbean dominion raised uncomfortable questions. What were the implications of Caribbean home rule for Canada? In dealing directly with Caribbean governments, would Canada secure favourable commercial agreements? Would a self-governing Caribbean be the death knell of union with Canada? Would the new nation leverage its elevated stature in the world to exert pressure on Canada to reform its immigration policies? As the lines blurred between dominions and colonies, what would become of the empire and Commonwealth? Canadians would confront the issues raised by these questions in the decades to come.

A SHIFTING GLOBAL ORDER

Anxieties and Opportunities, 1945–1966

In April 1946, Jean-François Pouliot rose in the Canadian House of Commons and asked his parliamentary colleagues, "Why should we not have Bermuda? Why should we not have Jamaica, with its rum, its sugar, its molasses? Why should we not have the bananas of Trinidad?" An Independent Liberal MP representing Témiscouata, Quebec, Pouliot believed Canada was entitled to "something territorial" in return for the country's tremendous contributions to the war effort and its generous postwar loan to the UK of $1.25 billion.[1] Two years later, Pouliot addressed the House again, this time with a greater sense of urgency. The British Empire was dissolving rapidly. India and the newly created Pakistan, Ceylon (Sri Lanka), and Burma (Myanmar) were now independent, the former three joining the Commonwealth soon after. Britain's withdrawal from Palestine was near complete, and it looked like Egypt, Malaya, and Israel might be next. "Let us at least save the West Indies for Canada," he exhorted.[2] Critical of what he understood as Canada's subservience to the UK and the United States, Pouliot thought it was time for Canadians to cast off their "inferiority complex" and follow the lead of the "English bulldog who tries to get all he can for his country." For Pouliot, an avowed anti-communist, "saving" the Caribbean colonies was also a geopolitical imperative.[3] When a sterling crisis exacerbated Britain's economic problems in 1949, he pitched union one last time: Canada should move swiftly in the Caribbean before Britain went bankrupt and the US scooped up the colonies in a fire sale.[4]

This chapter explores the union question in relation to the shifting geopolitics of the postwar decades. In his various speeches, Pouliot flagged the key issues that shaped unionist discourse: growing English-Canadian nationalism, the deepening Cold War, decolonization, and the expanding Commonwealth. Yet Pouliot surely knew that there was no clear path for Canada through these complex dynamics. Unionism was a means to navigate the new global order and Canada's place within it. It also evinced the country's conflicted embrace of the new Commonwealth and American hegemony in the hemisphere. In the interests of global stability and economic growth, Canadians appreciated that an expanded Commonwealth encouraged trade relationships, provided a bulwark against communism, fostered opportunities for international dialogue independent of the United States and US-led organizations, and symbolized "the pursuit of peace, liberty and progress."[5] Yet many Canadians were less inclined to accept the ethos of racial equality that came to define the new Commonwealth.[6] At the same time, while the country's relations with the United States were in the main cooperative, unionists had mixed feelings about American involvement in the Caribbean. Most supported Washington's anti-communist agenda, but they worried that this agenda made the British Caribbean more vulnerable to US economic and political domination. In this sense, Canada's absorption of one or more Caribbean colonies would check both communism and American influence.

There was, finally, an additional complication. The union debates in these years corresponded with a number of key events in Canada's evolving rights culture and the cultivation of Canada's international image as a champion of equality, human rights, and liberal democratic principles. These developments were not easily reconciled with the continued practice of racial discrimination in Canada. As Caribbean peoples made clear, this discrimination tarnished the country's international image and compromised Canada's anti-communist agenda. Moreover, it underscored white Canadians' failure to engage the new Commonwealth on a basis of racial and national equality, a failure particularly pronounced during the short-lived West Indies Federation (WIF), 1958–1962. These hypocrisies, coupled with a fierce desire for independence in the Caribbean, made the idea of union during the Cold War's early decades nothing short of preposterous. The chapter first explores the motivations and tensions that characterized the union debate in the decade following the cession of war in 1945 and then traces the debate during and immediately following the WIF, concluding with the Canada-Caribbean Conference in 1966.

Postwar Unionism

While intertwined in so many ways with weighty geopolitical developments, the union idea emerged in the immediate postwar years in more traditional ways. Unionists were, as usual, dissatisfied with Canadian and British trade policies and fixated on the question of territorial expansion, made all the more topical by Newfoundland's entry into Confederation in March 1949. In contemplating Newfoundland's future in the latter years of the war, Prime Minister King had, in an about-face from his lukewarm attitude in 1938, expressed interest in a broader federation that included the British Caribbean. "It might be worth considering some way of bringing Bermuda and the West Indies also into Confederation," he wrote in his diary in September 1943, "but what would really be best would be to have all of these and the three Maritime provinces made into one provincial entity."[7] This interest, much like so many of King's musings, proved fleeting. While he continued to support Newfoundland's entry into Confederation at war's end, he was considerably less enthused about the prospect of a Caribbean province. Convinced that union remained on Britain's wish list, he worried that Newfoundland's entry might generate unwanted pressure from London to annex the Caribbean colonies as well. The "problem of annexation," he told his cabinet in December 1946, would not end with Newfoundland: "The British government would wish us later to take in the West Indies and others as a sun-room for the Dom[inion] in the South." To King's relief, there was general consensus among his ministers that the federal government was already overextended in the way of financial commitments, and that any initiatives involving large expenditures, such as the annexation of Caribbean colonies, were best avoided.[8]

Neil McLean, senator for the Southern New Brunswick Division and a Newfoundland confederate, was more optimistic about the possibility of a Caribbean province for Canada. McLean chaired the Senate Committee on Canadian Trade Relations and owned one of the country's largest fish-processing firms in Blacks Harbour, New Brunswick. After his dream of incorporating Newfoundland as Canada's tenth province came to fruition, he turned his sights on the Caribbean. Newfoundland Premier Joseph Smallwood and his closest pro-Confederate advisor, Gregory Power, publicly supported McLean's new union crusade, much to the embarrassment of Ottawa.[9] When Smallwood and Power vacationed in Jamaica in July 1949, Power reportedly encouraged Jamaicans – and British Caribbean peoples more generally – to "take steps to explore becoming Canada's 11th province," while Smallwood told them to "come on in [to Confederation], the water's fine" (figure 5.1).[10] But this welcoming attitude was shared by neither the majority of Canadians nor King's successor, Louis St Laurent. The racialized worldview that distinguished Newfoundlanders from African Caribbeans blunted the expansionist momentum generated by Newfoundland's entry.[11] The Newfoundland example was of limited utility to unionists.

Fig. 5.1   "Confederation Swimming Hole," *Evening Telegram*, 9 August 1949

Where unionists could not or would not address racial concerns, they focused instead on the economic benefits. In his bid for union in 1948, Jean-François Pouliot groused that Canada's Caribbean trade suffered from the Canadian government's monopoly on bulk cane-sugar purchasing under the Transitional Measures Act. During the war, Ottawa had agreed to purchase a portion of the empire's surplus cane sugar from Britain. The Wartime Prices and Trade Board appointed a sugar administrator, who controlled Canada's bulk sugar purchasing. At war's end, Ottawa agreed, with Britain's encouragement, to extend this arrangement to 1949, with the proviso that Canada could opt out at the end of any given year. The agreement was unsatisfactory to Canada's sugar refiners, who had to purchase their raw sugar from the corporation rather than on the free market. It was a subject of ongoing parliamentary debate in the late 1940s, in particular drawing Pouliot's ire. The Témiscouata MP saw it as one more embarrassing example of Canada's subservience to Britain. Annexing the Caribbean colonies would allow Canadian refiners to buy sugar directly from the colonies and, with new responsibilities in world affairs, boost Canada's international profile in the process.[12]

Commercial circumstances of another kind galvanized unionists the following year. In the wake of a postwar convertibility crisis and the devaluation of sterling, Britain enacted restrictions on dollar purchases, which damaged Canada's trade with Britain and the Caribbean region. These restrictions diverted a large portion of Canadian trade to the United States. Before the war, Canadian exports to Britain and the US were roughly balanced, but by 1949, Britain received 23 per cent of Canadian exports, the US 50 per cent. One year later, these figures diverged more significantly, to 15 and 60 per cent, respectively. By 1950, Canadian-American trade represented two-thirds of Canada's total trade volume.[13] With the import-export controls that Britain applied to the Caribbean colonies to centre the region's trade in the sterling area, Canadian exports to the British Caribbean plummeted by 50 per cent between 1947 and 1949. In Neil McLean's assessment, the Caribbean colonies were obliged to follow "dictatorial instructions from England as to what nations they [c]ould trade with." On these instructions, trade had been diverted away from Canada, making a mockery of the Commonwealth and the dominion's trading prowess.[14]

In the early 1950s, McLean's efforts resonated with the managing editor of the *Fredericton Gleaner*, John Sancton, and three federal MPs: Alfred Brooks, a teacher and lawyer from Royal, New Brunswick; Harry White, a farmer from Middlesex, Ontario; and George Fulford, the owner of a successful patented medicine company in Brockville, Ontario. In addressing their parliamentary colleagues in Ottawa, McLean, Brooks, and Fulford noted the deleterious impact of Britain's colonial economic policies on Canada's trade with the British Caribbean. Union, they opined, would remove Britain from the equation and grant Canada unfettered access to British Caribbean markets

and resources. It would "round out" Canada's northern economy with a steady
supply of sugar, rum, molasses, copra, coffee, hardwood, citrus fruit, bananas,
aluminum ore, and asphalt and provide Canada with a "three-hundred million
dollar market" for its fish, lumber, manufactured goods, and processed farm
products.[15] After lamenting Britain's "deliberate refusal" to allow Canada to
trade with the British Caribbean directly and on an equitable basis, Fulford
underscored the benefits of union in a more roundabout way. He recounted
the histories of Australian, New Zealand, and South African expansionism
in the South Pacific and southwest Africa – and the important lessons to
be learned from them. Sensitive, perhaps, to colonialism's sullied postwar
reputation, he observed that while "no one could conceive of Canada having
any ambitions of colonial expansion," it was clear enough that the other
dominions of the old Commonwealth had "all been ceded territory which
virtually amount to colonial possessions and from which they derive no
uncertain trade advantages."[16]

In the weeks after Brooks promoted union in Ottawa, he received letters
from across Canada, in equal parts agreeable and averse to the idea. Opinion
varied by region, with letter writers from the Maritimes and Quebec largely
in favour, those from Ontario split down the middle, and those in western
Canada largely opposed. The main objections recurred: union would precipitate the "free entry of colored 'new Canadians' attracted by tales of high
wages, but not adapted to living and working in this country," burdening
Canadian taxpayers with the addition of a "poorhouse population" entitled
to the country's welfare benefits. As one indignant businessman told *Maclean's*
in 1953, "If we accept the West Indies their population would rank equally
with all other Canadians for old-age pensions, baby bonuses, unemployment
insurance, mothers' allowance and all other handouts of the 'welfare state,'
including socialized medicine at some future date." The costs of extending
these services to a rapidly increasing Caribbean population, he continued,
would far exceed their value as citizens or other contributions to Canada.[17]
Financial Post editor Ted Ertl expressed similar concerns: "Are we going to plan
a big boondoggle, to enlarge confederation ... and then ... spread bonuses
and subsistence payments and aid plans all over the Caribbean as if we were a
country of seventy five million taxpayers out to remake the world in spite of
itself?" There might be some "glory in adding real estate," he conceded, but
fourteen million Canadians "could hardly be expected to bestow the benefits
of their economy, in the modern spirit of equalitarianism, to the millions
whose chief value, from the political point of view, would lie in their numbers

and in the pressure groups that could be formed among them ... There are a lot of things Canada can afford. To start collecting an empire is not one of them."[18] In Canada's booming postwar economy, the central issue was not, of course, the expenditure per se but its beneficiaries. One need look no further than Halifax's Africville or the country's Indigenous reserves to get a sense of Canada's aversion to spending resources on racialized communities.

During a visit to the British Caribbean in 1953, *Maclean's* writer Eric Hutton interviewed Caribbean peoples "from all walks of life" to assess the validity of the claim that union would prompt a Caribbean exodus to Canada. The owner of a sizable coconut plantation in Tobago told Hutton he did not fear an exodus of his labourers given Canada's cold climate, the $200 necessary to purchase a passage to Canada, and his labourers' apparent disinterest in chasing higher wages. He explained to Hutton that his labourers generally preferred to work a three-hour day on the plantation, followed by a few more hours' work in their own gardens, and then spend the remainder of the day at leisure, fishing, napping, or popping into the rum shop for "a few drinks and a gossip." They could increase their wages by working additional hours on the plantation, but few availed themselves of this opportunity, seemingly content with small ambitions.[19]

Hutton had difficulty making sense of this response. "A competent economist or sociologist would probably knock wide holes in the West Indian employer's appraisal of his workers," he speculated. In Hutton's racialized rendering, a "man who is content with low earnings is possibly undernourished, or suffering from a mild chronic parasitical disease like hookworm or malaria, or he requires education to enlighten him on the joys of radio, packaged breakfast food, mortgages and other rewards of ambition."[20] Hutton found these aspirations present to some extent in subsequent interviews elsewhere in the region, but he was ultimately convinced that white Canadians had nothing to fear. Gobbling up the Caribbean, he assured *Maclean's* readers, was unlikely to prompt an exodus of "indigent" and "indigestible colored folk" to Canada.[21]

In the early 1950s, unionists rarely viewed British Caribbean sovereignty as viable. McLean and John Sancton thought that the colonies would be absorbed soon enough by either Canada or the United States.[22] In Brooks's assessment, Britain's weakened position had left the islands desperately "looking for some country to join," and he and Harry White urged fellow MPs to act before it was too late. "The United States has her eyes on the West Indies," warned Brooks in December 1952.[23] "Unless we take them over," White cautioned two months later, the United States would surely do so.[24] These concerns were not unfounded. US influence in the Caribbean had expanded in recent years with the destroyers-for-bases deal in 1940, the work of the Anglo-American Caribbean Commission (established in 1942 to coordinate cooperation between Britain and the US in promoting development in the British Caribbean), and other ongoing military and economic initiatives to maintain stability in the region and contain the spread of communism.[25]

Unionists familiar with the exploitative and racist dimensions of US intervention in the Caribbean were more confident about Canada's odds. Racial discrimination, segregation, and racialized violence on the US bases set up in the British Caribbean under the destroyers-for-bases deal were oft-cited examples. Despite President Franklin Roosevelt's directive to establish a policy of racial accommodation on the bases, the United States deployed (at the insistence of British and local authorities) mostly white officers, soldiers, and civilian workers who brought with them Jim Crow practices and set about entrenching them into policy.[26] Together with America's decades of exploitative – and often violent – imperial actions in the Caribbean, chiefly in Haiti, Puerto Rico, Nicaragua, and Panama, many in the British Caribbean looked on the United States with deep reservations. That civil rights activists met with violent repression in the South added to African Caribbeans' misgivings about drawing closer to so racist a country. In light of this behaviour, it was, in Hutton's assessment, "extremely unlikely" that the Caribbean colonies would voluntarily join the United States. Many Caribbeans agreed. As an article in Georgetown's *Daily Argosy* put it, "Since local people have had an opportunity of judging the United States' conception of colonial administration, they have learned their lesson and, if anything, more than ever realize and appreciate the privileges which are theirs because of birth and residence under the British flag."[27] The racist behaviour of US service personnel on and off the bases, observed one Trinidadian historian, "was a great shock to people who were pretty high up in government and the professions, but who did not happen to be Anglo-Saxons." In the opinion of Trinidad lawyer and legislator Ralph Vignale, this offensive behaviour had made the prospect of union with the US exceedingly "distasteful" to the majority of Caribbean peoples.[28]

Vignale was one of a few Caribbeans of African descent who were open to the possibility of union with Canada in the early 1950s.[29] His interest was rooted in his reverence for British institutions and traditions and a wish to remain under the Union Jack. He reportedly told *Maclean's* in 1953 that he had "thought for a long time that our salvation lies with Canada. If we can prove that we can get together among ourselves – and I think federation of the colonies will soon take place – then we should approach Canada."[30] Vignale thought a Caribbean federation was a prerequisite to union with Canada, as did Donald Sangster, Jamaica's minister for social welfare and the deputy leader of the island's Labour Party. Sangster and W.H. Courtney, a member of British Honduras's Executive Council and chairman of the West Indies Economic Committee, attended the Commonwealth Parliamentary Association (CPA) conference in Ottawa in 1952 and returned home with favourable impressions of Canada. The CPA's mandate was to foster dialogue and consultation on different aspects of parliamentary governance, and as the Commonwealth expanded after the war, so too did the diversity of representation at the conference. Attendees included representatives from established and newly independent members of the Commonwealth, as well as observers from territories in the process of constitutional and parliamentary transition.

Although Courtenay valued the Commonwealth's role in world affairs, he remained sceptical of Britain's leadership role in the association. In his opinion, Britain had "become decadent" and was "living in the past." It was "time that a younger nation like Canada [should] take the lead in this Commonwealth."[31] Such optimism about Canada's evolving relationship with the Caribbean was based on the assumption of equal status for the Caribbean territories within the Commonwealth realm – a status that Sangster, Vignale, and Courtenay anticipated in the near future. This optimism was increasingly scarce in the 1950s as white Canadians' interpretation of the Commonwealth – an interpretation that varied according to context – became apparent. In matters of trade and investment, the Commonwealth family included all British domains, regardless of their racial composition or constitutional status, but in matters of immigration, it was much more narrowly defined.

Commonwealth Contradictions

If commercial dreams and financial worries were long-standing in the union movement, postwar geopolitics introduced fundamentally new dynamics. America's growing presence in the Caribbean continued to rouse unionists after the war. But union arguments based on Canada's superior status in the Empire-Commonwealth began to unravel. The war accelerated the long process of decolonization in the European empires and initiated the British Commonwealth's transition from an association of privileged "white men's countries"[32] to a multi-ethnic one based – in theory – on racial equality. By the end of 1966, more than twenty African, Asian, and Caribbean states had joined the organization. Yet the imminence and implications of this expansion were not wholly apparent to Canadians in the two years between the cession of war in 1945 and India's independence in 1947. In 1946, King's government introduced the Canadian Citizenship Act, a nationalist initiative that prioritized Canadian citizenship over British subjecthood. The act also recognized the special status of Commonwealth members in Canada: "A person, who has acquired the status of a British subject by birth or naturalization under the laws of any country of the British Commonwealth other than Canada to which he was subject at the time of his birth or naturalization, shall be recognised in Canada as a British subject."[33] These countries, as defined in the first schedule of the act, included the UK, Australia, New Zealand, South Africa, Newfoundland, and Ireland. British subjects from these countries gained the privileges of Canadian citizenship after a short period of residence in Canada. They could vote after one year and could apply for a certificate of Canadian citizenship after five years.[34]

The Canadian government introduced its citizenship legislation before India, Pakistan, and Ceylon had gained independence. As new nations in the Commonwealth realm, they commanded international recognition and respect, while their citizens were now entitled, in theory, to the privileges of "full British subjecthood." These developments presented a conundrum for the Canadian government, which had long equated whiteness with *full* British subjecthood.[35] Before 1947, white Canadians had deflected accusations of racial prejudice by cloaking their racialized engagement with the Empire-Commonwealth in constitutional distinctions between dominions and dependencies. This work of obfuscation was not foolproof, of course, because the dominions were not wholly – or, as in South Africa, mostly – white. Moreover, the key ingredient of dominion status after the Statute of Westminster in 1931 – sovereignty in internal and external affairs – was hardly universal among the "white dominions." Newfoundland gave up responsible government in 1934, and Australia and New Zealand did not ratify the Statute of Westminster until 1942 and 1947, respectively.

Nonetheless, as the Commonwealth expanded beyond the old dominions, Canada devised new strategies to keep itself white. Lest there be any confusion over what constituted a British subject for the purposes of immigration, the government defined the term in an order-in-council in 1950 as "a person born or naturalized in the United Kingdom of Great Britain and Northern Ireland, Australia, New Zealand or the Union of South Africa, or a citizen of Ireland who has become a citizen of the United Kingdom by registration under the British Nationality Act, 1948."[36] By this order in council, the Jewish Labour Committee observed in one of its publications, Canada "abridges" or "shortens the size of the Commonwealth to far less proportions than for any other purposes."[37] Charges of racial discrimination soon followed from new Commonwealth countries, prompting the Canadian government to implement a quota system in 1951, admitting 150 Indians, one hundred Pakistanis, and fifty Ceylonese annually.[38]

A new Canadian immigration act came into law in June 1952 that continued to prioritize white immigration from Britain, the United States, and the Commonwealth.[39] However, as more Canadian women worked outside the home in the postwar decades, demand for domestic help grew, and with a diminishing supply of European applicants, the Canadian government looked to the Caribbean. In 1955, the first year of what became known as the West Indian Domestic Scheme, seventy-five Jamaican and twenty-five Barbadian women were admitted.[40] But the scheme was a last resort rather than an expression of goodwill toward the Caribbean.[41] Racially discriminatory policies and attitudes prevailed in Ottawa throughout the 1950s. As a Department of Trade and Commerce memorandum noted only a few months before the government approved the Domestic Scheme, "Coloured people in the present state of the white man's thinking are not a tangible community asset ... They do not assimilate readily and pretty much vegetate to a low standard of living." Increasing immigration from the Caribbean would be "an act of misguided generosity" because it would not bring about "a worthwhile solution to the problem of coloured people" and would only intensify Canada's existing social and economic problems.[42]

The Immigration Act of 1952 drew sharp criticism from Black Caribbeans. The Barbadian premier (and future prime minister of the West Indies Federation) Grantley Adams thought the act was particularly contemptible in light of America's McCarran-Walter Act, under which one hundred nationals from each colony in the British Caribbean could enter the US annually.[43] Adams censured Ottawa for treating prospective Caribbean immigrants as aliens rather than fellow British subjects.[44] The premier experienced this discrimination first-hand in October 1954 when he stopped over in Montreal on his way home from Britain. Trans-Canada Airlines had made a reservation for Adams at the city's Windsor Hotel, but when the premier arrived, the hotel clerk refused him a room. When the airline called the hotel manager for an explanation, he was unapologetic. He claimed the hotel had not received sufficient notice of Adams's arrival, nor had they known he was the premier of Barbados.[45]

Lester Pearson, then Canadian secretary of state for external affairs, who knew Adams personally from United Nations activities, was more apologetic, but his response reflected an effort to minimize the incident. "The Canadian people as a whole," he wrote to Adams, "share the concern of the government at the occasional example of discriminatory treatment by private individuals which still unfortunately occurs."[46] Pearson's claim that incidents of racial discrimination were isolated and perpetrated by private individuals rather than systemic and state driven was no doubt a dubious one to Adams.

The continuing reality of anti-Black discrimination in the immediate post-war years, particularly in the context of an expanding Commonwealth, did not help the union cause. When Ranjit Kumar, an influential member of Trinidad and Tobago's Legislative Council, raised the union idea in 1948, it was not well received. Kumar expressed the common concern that the Caribbean colonies were too small, economically underdeveloped, and geographically scattered to stand on their own. Without taking a firm position one way or another, he urged the government to carefully consider a number of options, including a union of all the European colonies in the region as well as union with Canada. Albert Gomes, a prominent Trinidadian of Portuguese descent and a fellow member of the council, had little patience for Kumar's suggestions, which to his mind delved "into the realms of the fantastic." Gomes was acquainted with white Canadian racism, having introduced a motion in council a year earlier protesting the Toronto Bridge Club's refusal to allow a Black Trinidadian student to participate in one of their tournaments.[47] Yet Kumar and the few African Caribbeans willing to entertain the prospect of union with Canada in the early 1950s were very clear on one point: union would have to be entered on a basis of equality with the other Canadian provinces. "Union under any other line," as one Caribbean newspaper put it, "would be indignantly turned down as an insult."[48]

Gomes's dismissal of union as an absurd proposition reflected a pessimistic, albeit realistic, assessment of the continuing durability of white Canadian racism. It was "inconceivable" to many Caribbean peoples, as Jamaica's *Daily Gleaner* put it in 1952, "that Canada would undertake terms of political merger with the British West Indies on any conditions approaching citizen equality." Canada, like Australia and New Zealand, had long pledged to "work for a future in which their territories would develop exclusively Caucasian." Canada's immigration policy of 1952 was "more ruthlesslessly discriminatory" than the American policy.[49] The Barbadian newspaper editor and radio personality George Hunte similarly pointed to the 1952 act as sufficient evidence to demonstrate that union was "completely impossible."[50] Another Barbadian politician, Theodore Brancker, was under no illusion about what union with Canada would mean for African Caribbeans. A prominent personality in the island's push for franchise reform and Black rights since the late 1930s, Brancker reasoned that joining Canada would only perpetuate Caribbeans' colonial status and was incompatible with their political and national aspirations.[51]

The West Indies Federation

In the postwar period, important reforms were underway in the British Caribbean that would also raise new challenges for union. In the wake of the Moyne Commission, appointed in 1938 to investigate social and economic conditions in the region, the imperial government widened the franchise and introduced a greater measure of self-government in most of the territories. Universal suffrage was introduced in Jamaica in 1944, in Trinidad in 1946, in Barbados in 1950, in the Windward and Leeward Islands in 1951, and in British Guiana in 1952.[52] The idea of a West Indies federation, discussed on and off since the nineteenth century, gained momentum at a regional conference at Montego Bay in 1947. Then, at a conference in London in February 1956, Jamaica, Trinidad and Tobago, Barbados, Antigua and Barbuda, Dominica, Grenada, Montserrat, St Kitts-Nevis-Anguilla, St Lucia, and St Vincent agreed to federate. The British Parliament passed the British Caribbean Federation Act into law later that year, enabling the federation's creation; an order-in-council established its constitutional basis in 1957, and the federation came into existence on 3 January 1958. Similar to the constitutional trajectories of earlier federations in the Empire-Commonwealth, a modified form of self-government was introduced at the outset, with Britain retaining authority over defence, foreign affairs, and certain matters concerning the financial stability of the federation.[53] Full internal self-government was achieved in August 1960, and a new constitution was introduced in London in May 1961 that proposed independence the following year.

The amended constitution was never ratified. The federation was plagued with problems from the outset. These included the weakness of the federal government and disputes over its powers, the location of the capital, migration within the federation, and the timeline for independence; the concentration of resources and population in Jamaica and Trinidad, the considerable distances between the islands, and meagre popular support; competing local nationalisms; tensions between island leaders and the federal government; and a lack of confidence in Prime Minister Adams. Discontent was especially pronounced in Jamaica. The island's opposition party leader and long-time critic of federation, Alexander Bustamante, led a successful campaign for Jamaica's secession in 1961 only a few years into the federation experiment. In September of that year, Jamaican premier Norman Manley called a referendum that returned a 54 per cent majority vote in favour of Jamaica leaving the federation. Trinidad was unwilling to remain in a federation that did not include Jamaica, and, no longer viable without its two strongest units, the federation dissolved in May 1962.[54]

The West Indies Federation and its demise produced new political and diplomatic pressures in Canada. Following the London Conference in 1956, the British government requested Ottawa's help in providing financial assistance to the Caribbean colonies that would soon federate. The Canadian government subsequently conducted a multi-department study of Canada's past and current relations with the British Caribbean, ultimately offering the federation an aid program of C$10 million over a five-year period. The program included two ships to facilitate interisland trade (just over $6 million), the construction of a wharf at St Vincent ($1 million), a student residence for the new University of the West Indies in Trinidad ($750,000), technical assistance ($750,000), port handling equipment ($450,000), and the development of a broadcasting network ($350,000).[55] Canadian interest in providing development aid to the new federation was animated in no small way by concerns about global stability and the spread of communism. Underdevelopment in decolonizing Africa, Asia, and the Caribbean was a leading source of geopolitical anxiety in the industrial-capitalist nations of the West.[56] Developed countries, Prime Minister St Laurent told a Victoria audience in 1957, must help underdeveloped countries raise their standards of living and "remove one of the occasions for the spreading of this false doctrine of Communism."[57] The Commonwealth played a central role in realizing this objective. Canada was a major contributor to the Colombo Plan, an aid program launched at the Commonwealth Conference of Foreign Ministers in 1950 to fund development projects in South and Southeast Asia. Canada's aid to the West Indies Federation was similarly part of a cooperative Commonwealth initiative, as was its contribution to the Commonwealth Africa Program in 1960.[58]

Canada distributed its aid widely in the postwar decades, but the British Caribbean territories were of "special interest" given their geographical proximity and strong commercial ties to Canada.[59] Britain's withdrawal from the region sharpened this interest, as did America's expanding presence. Forging closer Commonwealth ties in the hemisphere would help counterbalance Canada's relationship with the US and provide opportunities for regional cooperation outside the US-led Organization of American States (OAS).[60] "It would seem undesirable from Canada's point of view," Lester Pearson observed in a cabinet memo in April 1957, that the "vacuum caused by the decline of the U.K.'s influence and participation in the affairs of the area should be filled by the United States alone."[61] In Pearson's view, there were "responsibilities" and "opportunities" for Canada in the region.[62] The prospect that Soviet Russia might fill the vacuum left by the UK alarmed Canada and the US alike, and certainly did not seem beyond the realm of possibilities. There were already unsettling developments in the region. British Guiana had elected the communist-leaning Cheddi Jagan and the People's Progressive Party (PPP) in its first elections under universal suffrage in 1953. The Central American republic of Guatemala – a hotbed of communist activity, in the (exaggerated) assessments of both Washington and the Boston-based United Fruit Company – bordered and had expansionist designs on British Honduras. And in the British Caribbean islands more generally, labour organizations included communist factions of varying influence.[63]

The communist threat was particularly acute for Canadian companies with investments in the region. The largest Canadian investment in the British Caribbean was that of the Aluminum Company of Canada Limited (ALCAN), which had subsidiaries in Jamaica, British Guiana, and Trinidad. At the end of 1960, foreign private investment in Jamaica totalled $300 million, of which approximately $200 million came from Canada. The bulk of this investment was in Jamaican bauxite, but there were also significant Canadian investments in the production of an increasing number of goods from paint, sports equipment, and typewriters to transistor radios, wool blankets, and footwear. As of 1960, nineteen Canadian companies were operating factories in Jamaica. Other Canadian interests on the island included four banks with a total of thirty-six branches, ten insurance companies, one investment firm, one Canadian-owned public utility, and three Canadian hotels. In British Guiana, Canadian investment totalled $70 million in 1961, similarly concentrated in the bauxite industry.[64]

Suspicious of Jagan and the PPP, the British government suspended British Guiana's constitution in October 1953, appointed an interim government, and deployed British troops to maintain order. These developments allayed Canadian concerns for a few years, until Jagan was elected in 1957 following the return of constitutional government, and then again in the election of 1961. "In view of [Jagan's] leftist leanings," Canada's external affairs minister observed, "there is a distinct possibility that if he does not obtain a sufficiently encouraging response from Western countries he will turn to the Soviet Bloc." With Canadians' substantial economic interests in British Guiana, it was "highly desirable that Dr. Jagan should be encouraged to continue to look to the Western world for support" and to keep his country in the Commonwealth.[65]

The installation of a communist government in Cuba in the wake of revolution in 1959 further heightened these anxieties. Officials in Canada's departments of trade and external affairs were increasingly concerned about the implications of a communist Cuba for the Caribbean region and the hemisphere more generally. In Jamaica in the early 1960s, Canadian concerns centred on the growth of Rastafarianism and its possible connections to, or sympathies with, communist Cuba.[66] By the late colonial period, Rastafari were no longer just "a racialist nuisance" to the island's political and business elite but "a primary threat to the security of the Jamaican state as the result of purported or potential alliances with leftist political organizations."[67] While Rastafari often repudiated these alliances, anti-communist paranoia made any expression of Black radicalism or resistance to the status quo suspect. This paranoia intensified in April 1960 when authorities raided Rastafari elder Claudius Henry's church and discovered a letter addressed to Fidel Castro outlining his sect's intention to overthrow the Jamaican government and turn it over to Castro.[68] Canada's commissioner at Port of Spain, R.G.C. Smith, characterized Rastafarians as "fanatics … bent on driving the white man out of Jamaica," a prospect he found "disturbing." In light of the escalating violence between Rastafari and British troops, Smith likened the circumstances to the protracted and bloody Mau Mau resistance to British rule in Kenya (1952–60). Analogous to British depictions of the Mau Mau as a savage, violent cult susceptible to communist influences, Smith and the Canadian press characterized Rastafari as variously "sub-human," "sub-intelligent," and "primitive Negro cultists" prone to violence and emboldened by Castro and the Cuban revolution.[69]

White Canadian racism like Smith's did not mix well with Canada's anti-communist program in the Caribbean, nor its wider Commonwealth interests. Many Caribbean peoples believed their new status in the Commonwealth realm demanded increased respect among nations. When it was not forthcoming, Caribbean criticism of Canada intensified. Nine months after the birth of the federation, a Jamaican studying in Canada, E.P.W. Guy, castigated Canadians for failing to treat African Caribbean peoples with the same respect accorded members of the old Commonwealth. The territories of the new federation had recently taken on a new "justified loftiness of dignity after the recent honor ... of being elevated, at the Queen's command, to nationhood within the British Commonwealth of Nations." For them to then come to Canada with their "increasing prestige and natural self-assurance" and be treated as "inferior beings" was certain to damage irreparably Canada's relationship with the federation.[70] In a lengthy article to the *Globe and Mail*, Guy recounted the many social, educational, and professional challenges that African Caribbeans faced in Canada. Guy's experience seeking employment in Canada illustrates vividly how white Canadians differentiated the old from the new Commonwealth. Born to an English father and a mother of mixed Spanish and African descent, he self-identified as a Jamaican "quadroon" who was "accepted as 'white'" back home. With his light skin colour and his accent, which prospective Canadian employers routinely mistook for English or Welsh, Guy recounts being at first received cordially. But at the mention of Jamaica, the employer "undergoes a shudder, and I am subjected to a sharp scrutiny."[71] While employers were ready enough to consider employing an English or Welsh subject of the Commonwealth, Guy's Jamaican-ness precluded him from reaping equal access to the cultural and professional benefits of Commonwealth association.

As Guy made abundantly clear, if Canadians did not change their ways and treat Caribbean peoples with the same dignity and respect given to white Commonwealth subjects, they should not be surprised if the West Indies Federation sought relationships outside the Commonwealth. The persistence of Canada's "color scruple, which is the traditional way of Canadians," he warned, "will offend and embitter" Caribbean peoples. "Trouble will start. They will be kindly disposed to those who are not kindly disposed to you. Trouble will draw world attention. You are the only large white Power so far at whom the Russians have not been able to point an accusing finger on a racial charge. In not one heart in the millions of dark-skinned peoples will you expect to find a thought of kindness."[72] In referencing Soviet Russia, Guy was playing on Canadian fears of communist infiltration, not only in the Caribbean but in Canada as well. The alliance of international communism with anti-racist and anti-colonial struggles worldwide – real or potential – had been an ongoing source of anxiety in countries of the global West since the interwar period.[73] Eradicating policies of racial discrimination in these countries was recognized as a means of checking communist influences. As

Diefenbaker stated at a press conference at the governor's residence in Jamaica in January 1961 when questioned about Canada's attitude toward Caribbean immigration, non-discrimination "was the only policy by which the free world could meet the challenge posed today by communism and its works."[74] While communism did not gain much traction among Black Canadian communities, the threat lingered in white Canadian minds. Like white segregationists in the United States, many white Canadians blamed "foreign agitators," especially communists, for Blacks' civil- and human-rights advocacy while dismissing the reality that this activism was not new in the 1950s and was in fact a consequence of ongoing violations of Black Canadians' citizenship rights.[75] And while communism's lure in the face of white Canadian race discrimination may have been limited, it was not universally eschewed by Black Canadians, nor Black Caribbeans. In the midst of civil-rights struggles in Dresden, Ontario, in the 1950s, Black Canadian activist Hugh Burnett observed that while there were currently "no Communists among the coloured people at Dresden ... I don't know how long we can assure that if the discrimination practised there is to continue."[76] In 1962, Grantley Adams and Trinidad premier Eric Williams, both avowedly anti-communist, warned that the racially restrictive immigration policies of the old Commonwealth countries would heighten communism's appeal in the Caribbean.[77]

Despite the communist threat, Guy was not optimistic that white Canadians' "keen color-sensitivity" would become any less so in the near future. He thus did not encourage Caribbean immigration to Canada, let alone union. In his opinion, the best way forward was for Canada to devise a generous aid program for the federation in order to facilitate economic and educational development. It was better for Canada "to play the role of an indulgent uncle" than a "wanton foster-mother," he opined.[78] But his vision of an arms-length Canada-Caribbean relationship was not a practical solution for Caribbean peoples currently living, working, and studying in Canada. Their poor treatment in Canada was the subject of ongoing discussion in the federal government of the West Indies Federation at Port of Spain.

In July 1961, the federation government resolved to investigate claims of rampant racial prejudice in Nova Scotia schools. They enlisted the assistant commissioner for students in the Commission for the West Indies, British Guiana, and British Honduras in Canada to conduct an inquiry. The assistant commissioner met with Caribbean students attending Nova Scotia Technical College, Mount St Vincent College, St Mary's, and Dalhousie universities, as well as with several white Canadian students attending these institutions. The results of his inquiry revealed widespread racial prejudice: barbers refusing to attend to Black men, landladies routinely rejecting applications from Black people, and local businesses refusing to employ them in the summer months because their "white employees may not wish to work with coloured people." There were also troubling examples of prejudice institutionally: a dean of men's residence cautioning a white student not to sign up for a vacant bed in a double room because the other student in the room was a Black man, and a dean of women's residence threatening white Canadian women with informing their parents if they were found socializing with Black men. Several white students were reportedly friendly toward Black students, but they limited their activities with these students for fear of what their parents, friends, or neighbours might say.[79]

When the minister of labour and social affairs of the West Indies Federation, Phyllis Allfrey, reviewed the report of the assistant commissioner, she brought it to the attention of Smith, Canada's commissioner at Port of Spain. Allfrey suggested that some educational work be initiated to foster more understanding between Canadians and Caribbeans, especially given that the West Indies Federation was now a fellow member of the Commonwealth.[80] Allfrey had proposed, with discouraging results, a number of labour-migration schemes to the Canadian government in previous years; she was well acquainted with white Canadian racism. Smith's response was similarly discouraging. He told Allfrey that racial discrimination was "not something a government could necessarily deal with." It was a product of "human habits" that could "not be changed overnight."[81] Much as Lester Pearson had done in his earlier response to Grantley Adams, Smith dismissed racial discrimination as a regrettable practice that had little to do with government. It was an audacious claim given that such discrimination had been the cornerstone of the federal government's immigration policy since the nineteenth century.

This discrimination was out of step with Canada's growing advocacy of human rights at home and abroad, a point seldom lost on Caribbean critics of union. When Adams and the Jamaican minister of trade and industry, Wills Issacs, visited Canada in February 1958, they expressed disappointment with Canada's immigration policies in light of Canada's moralistic posturing in the Commonwealth and at the UN. Isaacs had supported union with Canada in the early 1950s, but the nagging impact of white Canadian racism had changed his mind. In an interview with the Toronto press, he described "how sensitive and bewildered" his compatriots were at being barred from Canada because of their skin colour. It was a blatant hypocrisy, he said, for "a country that takes seriously its responsibilities in the United Nations and in respect to the declaration of Human Rights" to then use race as a criterion in the immigration selection process. Caribbean peoples expected Canada, as a respected member of the Commonwealth and a nation that touted high moral principles on the international stage, "to behave well ... not like people in Johannesburg or Little Rock."[82]

The use of South Africa as a counterpoint to Canada's supposed model behaviour in the Commonwealth and beyond took on greater significance in 1961 when the Canadian government supported – spearheaded, by some accounts – South Africa's departure from the Commonwealth because of its apartheid policies. However duplicitous and contested this stand might have been, it elevated Canada's reputation among new Commonwealth members. It prompted the Jamaica-based *West Indian Economist*, for example, to ponder the possibility of a new Commonwealth with Ottawa at the centre. With Britain contemplating entry to the European Economic Community, the Commonwealth's centre of gravity was likely to shift in any case, and South Africa's withdrawal gave Canada "a big leg-up in this respect." In taking "the lead in refusing the new Republic membership in the Commonwealth," the article continued, "Mr. Diefenbaker thus left a bridge open for the Commonwealth states of Africa and Asia to join a Commonwealth reconstructed round Ottawa. With seaboards on the Atlantic and the Pacific, Canada is well suited to be the centre of a new commercial union."[83] While such talk was probably too fanciful to elicit concern in Ottawa, Canada's stance on the South Africa question had the potential to generate expectations of a much more troubling kind. As commissioner Smith warned Department of External Affairs officials in late March 1961, since "West Indians credit Canada with having played an important role leading to [the] South African decision they will, logically or not, begin to question" the extent to which this attitude might induce the elimination of racial barriers in Canadian immigration policy.[84]

The Canadian government introduced immigration reforms soon after the South Africa decision. The domestic groups that lobbied for these reforms in the late 1950s and early '60s frequently based their appeals, as did Caribbean critics, on the hypocrisy of Canada's discriminatory policies in the face of the country's professed commitment to civil liberties, international human rights, and liberal democratic principles.[85] The prestige that Canada currently enjoyed "among the Afro-Asian nations," observed Canadian immigration critic Ray Greenidge in September 1958, "was being steadily compromised by her thinly veiled efforts to avoid a 'color question' in Canada by virtually shutting her doors to West Indians." Like other critics of Canadian immigration policy, Greenidge thought that Canada's development aid program in the Caribbean should address, at least in the short term, overpopulation in the region. Development assistance based on capital investment and technical training, with the object of increasing industrial and agricultural production, creating jobs, and raising living standards, was a long-range solution.[86] In devising Canada's aid program to the approaching West Indies Federation in 1957, officials in Canada's departments of finance and external affairs acknowledged that emigration, as "a means of alleviating economic and social difficulties," could not be "entirely disassociated" from other development initiatives designed to achieve the same ends.[87] But they were not prepared to acknowledge this association publicly, let alone include immigration reform in their development-aid recommendations.

By way of Order-in-Council PC-86, 1962, the government eliminated race, ethnicity, and national origin as admission criteria, at least officially.[88] But these reforms were more about the appearance of progressive principles than a commitment to their implementation. The main objective of the new regulations, in the words of the minister of citizenship and immigration, Ellen Fairclough, was to eliminate "any valid grounds for arguing that they contain any restrictions or controls based on racial, ethnic, or color discrimination."[89] In non-public sources, the government continued to indicate a preference for immigrants from traditional (white) source countries; they actively recruited migrants only from Europe and the United States; and the imprecise nature of the new selection criteria granted immigration agents considerable discretion to practice racial prejudice under the pretext of insufficient skills or training.[90] The Immigration Act of 1952 and the façade of reform in 1962 would hamstring unionism when it re-emerged in the early 1960s.

The Dissolution of the West Indies Federation: Insecurities and Opportunities

Few unionists had believed that Caribbean independence was feasible. They congratulated Caribbean peoples on their "political-coming-of-age" and spoke warmly of their new "Commonwealth sister," yet they continued to make paternalistic and racialized distinctions between the old Commonwealth and the new. The West Indies Federation was a sister, but a "little brown sister" whose future depended on Canada's guiding hand.[91] As the federation headed toward dissolution in 1961–62, unionism resumed swiftly and took on greater urgency in the context of heightened communist anxiety, America's deepening fixation on the Caribbean, and Commonwealth insecurities. "The diminution of British imperial responsibilities in the Caribbean," University of Toronto political economist Alexander Brady wrote in a lengthy report in the early 1960s, "alters the old Anglo-American balance of influence in the region and augments the relative weight of the U.S. The independent units [in the Caribbean] ... will increasingly look to Americans to help solve their problems." US interests in the region had heightened considerably since 1945, Brady observed, which called for Canadian assertiveness in securing and expanding its own interests. There were, after all, several developments that had "tightened the social and economic nexus" between Canada and the British Caribbean since the Second World War. Foremost among them was Canada's rapid industrial growth and prosperity, which had aroused in many Canadians "an urge to push southward to the nearby British Caribbean for trade, investment, enterprise, and merely idle pleasure in the sun." Canadian investment in bauxite was the most striking example of this push southward, but the region's tourist industry was also attracting attention. Traffic on Trans-Canada Airlines (TCA) to the Caribbean increased from 10,352 passengers in 1949 to 42,984 in 1961, with a further 22 per cent growth projected by the end of 1963. For Brady, these commercial ties provided a much-needed counterweight to America's dominating presence in the Caribbean and reduced Canada's "excessive dependence" on the United States, which (he warned in an earlier publication) had weakened economic ties with Britain and the Commonwealth, a trend he found "disturbing."[92]

For many thinkers at the time, Commonwealth identity reinforced these economic priorities. Brady thought that Canada, as the British Caribbean's closest Commonwealth neighbour, was "morally obligated" to take an interest in Caribbean affairs.[93] It fell to Canada, moreover, to energize the Commonwealth at a time when Britain's commitment to the association seemed to waver. Commonwealth politics were hardly cordial. Members' discontent with Britain's heavy-handed actions at Suez in 1956, South Africa's forced withdrawal from the association in 1961, and the UK's turn to Europe and the European Economic Community inspired uncertainty.[94] Who would take responsibility for Caribbean islands "set adrift," Canadian journalist Charles Lynch wondered. Jamaica and Trinidad gained independence in 1962, but Lynch could not imagine such an outcome for the so-called "Little Eight" (Barbados, Antigua-Barbuda, St Kitts-Nevis-Anguilla, Montserrat, Dominica, St Lucia, St Vincent, and Grenada), the smaller islands of the

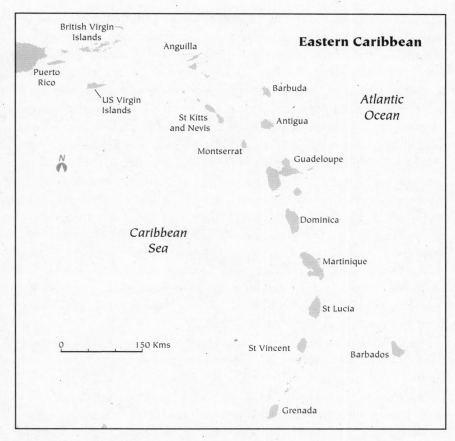

Fig. 5.2   Map showing the "Little Eight" of the Eastern Caribbean. Copyright Robert Cronan

eastern Caribbean: "Should that concern be purely something for Britain to worry about, or does Canada have a responsibility as the only Commonwealth member in the Western Hemisphere?"[95] As the international-relations scholar James Eayrs put it in *Northern Approaches* (1961), for "those colonies with small populations and feeble resources, alternatives to independence" – such as union with Canada – should be considered.[96] It was a common concern among imperial powers and colonial leaders alike. How could territories with undiversified economies, paltry resources, and weak infrastructures sustain themselves? Was it not absurd to suggest that tiny island populations should have (and could reasonably finance) premiers, cabinets, and a civil service?

Not surprisingly, Cold War priorities only amplified worries about the Little Eight. Would the small islands be politically unstable and vulnerable to sinister outside influences – namely, communism? Lynch thought Canada should invite representatives from the Little Eight to Ottawa to flesh out the possibility of union. Doing so made sense not only because union was in line with Canada's "Commonwealth pretensions" but also because of the country's historic relationship with the region and Canadian concerns about the political stability of the islands.[97] Advocating union in May 1962, Saskatoon-born writer D.G. Dainton urged Canada to step in and save Barbados and the Leeward and Windward islands for the West. Canada was in a position, he contended, to exert Western influence on the Little Eight, thereby preserving "the whole concept of democracy and all that it stands for." It was time to reopen the union discussion and consider offering the Little Eight provincial status.[98] George E. Brooks of Hamilton, Ontario, in a letter to Prime Minister Diefenbaker a few months earlier, made a similar plea. Beyond the obvious advantages – expanded opportunities for investment, trade, and tourism, Brooks maintained, Canada's political and economic foothold in the Little Eight would help keep communism at bay.[99]

While economic and defence concerns went a long way in convincing some of the small Caribbean islands to either delay their independence or opt for continued association with Britain, the salient though still controversial point by the early 1960s was that it was each island's decision to make, not Britain's nor Canada's. In December 1960, the UN General Assembly adopted Resolution 1514, a Declaration on the Granting of Independence to Colonial Countries and Peoples. Drawing from the UN's Universal Declaration of Human Rights (1948), the resolution affirmed the right of colonial peoples to determine their political status and the course of their economic, social, and cultural development free from outside interference. Canada voted in favour of Resolution 1514, but this support belied the resilience of paternalistic thinking about British Caribbean futures. Apologist statements about the ongoing need for British and/or Canadian intervention, arguments for Canada's absorption of the Little Eight, and dismissive attitudes about the prospect of independence for the small islands of the eastern Caribbean abounded, effectively betraying the principles outlined in the resolution.

For colonies that could be persuaded to abandon their national aspirations, according to Eayrs, there were two obvious alternatives: absorption by the UK, or by the Commonwealth member in closest proximity.[100] As an early example of the first option, Eayrs pointed to Malta, whose people had voted in favour of integration with the UK in 1956. While the union never came to pass (Malta gained independence in 1964), under the proposals endorsed in 1956 Malta would be internally self-governing and have representation at Westminster, with the UK retaining responsibility for foreign affairs, defence, and some matters related to taxation.[101] There were also precedents outside the British Empire-Commonwealth. In 1946, the French colonies in the Caribbean eschewed independence in favour of complete integration into the French republic as overseas *départements*, and in 1954 the Dutch government absorbed its Caribbean colonies into the Kingdom of the Netherlands.[102] Eayrs thought the second option – union with the nearest Commonwealth member – also deserved careful consideration. While recognizing that it might be premature and somewhat tactless to revive the question of union with Canada at a time when the West Indies Federation was "still struggling with the responsibilities of self-government," he nonetheless found the benefits of such a union for Canada clear and compelling. In a plea reminiscent of Robert Borden's appeal for union forty-five years earlier, Eayrs observed that by "voluntarily assuming the challenges of a multi-racial society" and "experiencing its tensions at first-hand," Canadians would "gain maturity as a people, prestige within the Commonwealth, and a surer touch in their diplomacy throughout the world."[103] In his assessment, Canada had a pivotal role to play in the Commonwealth. It was "neither fair nor desirable," he concluded, "that one member of a proprietary Commonwealth should bear both the burdens and the benefits of devolution."[104] Canada, in other words, was both responsible for and entitled to the fragments of a decolonizing empire.

Union also generated debate in official circles. In the months following Jamaica's decision to leave the federation in September 1961, the Colonial Office and the remaining federation governments convened several meetings to consider alternatives. These included a Trinidad-led federation or association of the nine remaining territories, a Barbados-led federation of the Little Eight, and smaller federations (or associations) making up two or three island groupings such as the one proposed between Grenada and Trinidad. When these discussions bore no fruit, the Colonial Office encouraged assistance from the US and Canada, particularly in the way of development aid.[105] The imminent collapse of the federation had already prompted Ottawa to contemplate taking on a larger role in the affairs of the Little Eight (or, excluding Barbados, the Little Seven), whether through development assistance or, less likely, an offer of union with Canada.[106] Given Britain's ongoing efforts to divest itself of its Caribbean territories, officials in Canada's Department of External Affairs were not surprised that the Colonial Office was looking to Canada and the United States to "share the cloak of fiscal and administrative responsibility" in the wake of the failed federation. External Affairs officials were not enthusiastic about a political relationship but nevertheless made inquiries about union in Britain and the Caribbean, and solicited information and opinions from Canadians knowledgeable about the region.[107] They were unimpressed with British presumptions of Canadian responsibility in the Caribbean, expressing unease, for example, with one British MP's estimation that Canada, rather than the UK, would ultimately become the most influential member of the Commonwealth.[108] When Sir John Mordecai, the former deputy governor general of the West Indies Federation, visited Ottawa in May 1962, External Affairs officials asked him if Caribbean peoples in the non-self-governing territories were interested in union with Canada. Mordecai did not report much enthusiasm in the region but expressed the hope that Canada would continue to provide aid. In his assessment, the future of the British Caribbean would be tied much more closely to the United States.[109]

When Dominica's chief minister, Edward O. LeBlanc, suggested union with Canada in the fall of 1962, Diefenbaker and the Department of External Affairs gave the proposal closer attention. Pessimistic about the prospects for a political and economic association of the small islands of the now-defunct West Indies Federation, LeBlanc saw union with Canada as one of Dominica's last chances for salvation.[110] External Affairs undersecretary Norman Robertson subsequently drafted recommendations for Diefenbaker's reply, as well as a five-page memorandum outlining the implications of a union of Dominica (and Britain's other remaining dependencies in the Caribbean) with Canada. Robertson concluded that if political association with Canada was ruled out, the Little Eight faced a bleak future. There were also important strategic implications for a proposed association. In the midst of mounting tensions between the US and the Soviet Union over the installation of Soviet missiles in Cuba in October, the communist menace loomed large. "The position of these Caribbean islands, poor, disappointed, frustrated, without visible political destiny, cannot be regarded with equanimity," Robertson continued. "The eventual adoption of some counsels of despair, whether Castroism or some West Indian radical and racialist doctrines, and of cynical encouragement and support by Communist countries is not beyond the realm of possibility. In this light, political association of the islands with Canada could be considered a contribution to stability and to the removal of further tension in the Caribbean between the two great power groupings of the world." But there were other options – generous aid, commercial concessions, or a customs union – that might be equally effective in containing the spread of communism in the region.[111] Robertson figured these latter options were preferable because they would serve Canada's strategic and commercial interests while avoiding the undesirable racial and economic entanglements of political union: the "introduction of a large coloured element" into the country's population and the financial strain of taking on one or more dependencies. While Dominica's population was small at sixty thousand, Robertson worried that successful federation with Canada would prompt similar applications from the other small islands.[112]

Robertson ultimately resolved that union with Dominica was impractical. Diefenbaker agreed.[113] In his response to LeBlanc, the prime minister expressed regret over the failed West Indies Federation and the chief minister's lack of confidence in a federation of the Little Eight. Drawing from Robertson's detailed memo, Diefenbaker referenced the nearly one-hundred-year history of proposals for various forms of political association between Canada and one or more of the British Caribbean territories. These proposals were a testament to the strength of the Canada-Caribbean relationship over the years, but "it was never apparent that general public support for such a union existed," at least not in Canada.[114] No doubt aware of the racialized thinking lurking behind this lack of Canadian support, Diefenbaker centred his rebuff of union on the more innocuous – if not entirely persuasive – provisions of the British North America Act.[115] He pointed out that the territorial limits of the Canadian state, as conceived in the act, extended from the Atlantic to the Pacific coasts and from the US border to the Arctic Ocean. Disregarding Robertson's notation that the act could be amended, Diefenbaker informed LeBlanc that it made "no provision for the admission of other territories" and that Canadians generally agreed that their country's "normal and proper territorial limits" had been reached.[116] Diefenbaker was sympathetic to the economic and social struggles of Caribbean peoples. He valued the Commonwealth and was ardently anti-communist, but he thought union woefully impractical, in part because it was incompatible with Caribbean peoples' own nationalist aspirations. Having vacationed in the Caribbean the previous year, he had been struck by "the desire of several islands to be free and independent." It was this desire, the prime minister concluded – particularly in Jamaica – that had doomed the West Indies Federation.[117]

LeBlanc's query nonetheless reinforced Ottawa's impression that Caribbean interest in union remained widespread, particularly in the islands comprising the Little Eight. When the Department of External Affairs learned of Barbadian premier Errol Barrow's visit to Canada in 1963, they speculated that he was planning to ask for some form of association with Canada.[118] They could not have been more mistaken. At a conference of the Canadian Institute of International Affairs held in Fredericton that October, Barrow levelled a lengthy, multi-faceted critique of Canada that rejected union unequivocally. Canadian immigration policy was duplicitous and hypocritical, he charged: "To be brutally frank, there is a feeling that in view of the large influx of unskilled Italian and other European immigrants coming into this country, there is either tacitly or explicitly some element of discrimination against the West Indian immigrant." It was hypocrisy to deny prospective Caribbean immigrants on the basis of unemployment figures in Canada while welcoming thousands of Italians and other European immigrants "who cannot even speak English or French, and who have no skill at all ... people who will probably have to spend two or three years even to begin to understand how to order a loaf of bread or to speak to a taxi driver."[119] Barrow criticized the immigration reforms of 1962 for effectively undermining Caribbean development by poaching the highly skilled, professional, and educated classes from Caribbean society, putting their labour to Canada's profit. In the premier's assessment, it was one of the paradoxes of the relationship between wealthy countries and poor countries that the former continued to deprive the latter of the means of production they so badly needed.[120] Canada's commitment to the Commonwealth and Canadian declarations of moral duty to underdeveloped countries rang hollow.[121] Canada needed to implement immigration and aid policies consistent with its international do-gooder image, or the world community would increasingly "look askance at the *bona fides* of Canadian declarations." Barrow stated bluntly, "I make no apology for saying Canada has failed as a government very miserably" to meet the Caribbean territories as equal partners in the Commonwealth.[122]

Barrow dismissed union as ludicrous. To be sure, white Canadian racism hindered unionism's appeal in the Caribbean. More importantly, he argued, union would strip Caribbean peoples of their individuality and independence. "No self-respecting West Indian wants to become a part of any body," he thundered – not the US, the UK, the Soviet Union, nor Canada. The failure of the West Indies Federation was a testament to the "rugged individuality" and fierce desire for independence across the region.[123] Barrow also quashed the "very popular heresy" that the majority of Caribbean peoples were clamouring for union: "Can you seriously suggest ... that these Islands, which have ... problems of acceptance in the European communities because of racial and ethnic differences, would voluntarily surrender the independence which some of them have only just achieved" to join a country that would "not only bring about the complete loss of their identity but their complete assimilation, culturally and otherwise?"[124] When Eric Williams, Trinidad and Tobago's first prime minister, visited Ottawa in April 1964, he too discounted outright this "popular heresy." Asked at a press conference whether Caribbean peoples desired a political association with Canada, Williams riposted a definitive no: "We didn't get political independence so as to join another political grouping." And besides, Williams quipped to one reporter, the Canadian Confederation was experiencing enough problems as it was.[125]

At the time of Williams's visit, Lester Pearson's Liberal government was focused on a stepped-up aid program in the Caribbean, not union. The country's paltry foreign aid contributions in 1962 (.14 per cent of GDP) relative to other Western nations had drawn international criticism. Canada had the second-highest per capita income, but its foreign aid contribution ranked second last worldwide. Pearson set out to restore confidence in the country's foreign aid reputation following his election victory in April 1963; he had in fact campaigned in the Maritimes on a platform that included a Colombo-style aid program for the Commonwealth Caribbean.[126] At a meeting in May 1963 in Hyannis Port, Massachusetts, Pearson and President John F. Kennedy made a joint declaration of their common interest in the political and economic stability of the Caribbean and their commitment to expand development assistance to the region. Against the background of Castroism in Cuba, the continued threat posed by Jagan's leadership in British Guiana, and signs of "restiveness" in other parts of the Caribbean at the "apparent lack of interest on the part of the wealthy countries in the hemisphere" in the region's economic problems, it was crucial that Ottawa "[do] something quickly."[127] In the spring of 1964, the Canadian government pledged $10 million to the Commonwealth Caribbean annually for the next five years.

Talk of union all but disappeared in 1965–66, re-emerging briefly in the midst of constitutional talks between Britain and the "Little Seven." When the protracted negotiations for an eastern Caribbean federation ended in failure in the spring of 1965, Whitehall began exploring alternatives to facilitate Britain's disengagement. In late December, the British government announced that St Kitts-Nevis-Anguilla, Dominica, Grenada, St Lucia, and St Vincent would soon become states in "free association" with Britain.[128] Much like the constitutional status of the old dominions before the Statute of Westminster in 1931, the associated states would be internally autonomous, with Britain retaining responsibility for external affairs and defence. In the weeks before these negotiations concluded, officials from Canada's Department of External Affairs met with British ministers in London, fully prepared to evade a possible nudging to lead the association in Britain's stead. Canada's secretary of state, Paul Martin Sr, however, was not entirely averse to the idea. While reviewing the External Affairs briefing paper (which included the notation "No consideration has been given to the possibility of Canada accepting responsibility for a 'Free Association' arrangement for e.g. the conduct of the external affairs of any of the islands") en route to their meetings in London, Martin questioned his assistant, John Hadwen, at length about the reasoning behind this position.[129] Hadwen told him that Canada's formal position was that the islands were Britain's colonial responsibility and should remain so until independence. Canada would maintain close relations with the colonies in the way of aid and trade but was "reluctant to become a Caribbean colonial power." Pressed by Martin to elaborate the grounds on which Canada might consider an association, Hadwen ventured that three general criteria would need to be met: a clear desire in the Caribbean territories to associate with Canada, Britain's unequivocal support, and terms of association acceptable to Canada. Hadwen concluded that these criteria would be difficult to establish and reiterated External Affairs' aversion to schemes with a colonial flavour. The department hoped, he told Martin, that the secretary of state would "stonewall" if such schemes came up in conversation with British ministers.[130]

Nothing came of Martin's apparent interest, however minimal, for a few reasons. If there were hopes in London for Canada formalizing its role in the Caribbean, America's heightened fear of communist infiltration in the region – palpable in the wake of the US invasion of the Dominican Republic in April 1965 – sidelined them. British officials were not fully committed to significant reserve powers in foreign affairs and defence until the colonial secretary met in October with the US secretary of state, who gently pressured Britain to work out constitutional arrangements in the eastern Caribbean that would safeguard American security. This meeting, legal scholar Raphael Cox Alomar argues, "sealed the constitutional fate" of the eastern Caribbean territories.[131] Forging a free association with these territories was not politically expedient, moreover, in light of the growing sovereignty movement in Quebec, with some sovereigntists promoting the very concept of "associate statehood."[132]

Perhaps most importantly, Pearson was not keen on the association idea. His main agenda in the Caribbean remained the stimulation of economic growth through development aid and trade, and supporting initiatives for regional integration. Not long after his election victory, he began floating the idea of a meeting with all the Commonwealth Caribbean prime ministers, which eventually came to pass in Ottawa in July 1966. During or soon after the conference, Canada boosted its aid allotment to $65 million over the next five years, provided $10 million for the development of a Caribbean broadcasting service and the Universities of the West Indies and Guyana, and contributed $10 million to the Caribbean Development Bank. Canada also entered a partnership with Air Jamaica, granted the Caribbean governments a tariff rebate on raw sugar, and waived the transshipment rules for Caribbean imports so they were no longer required to travel direct from the Caribbean to qualify for preferential duties.[133] The conference garnered considerable publicity in the weeks before it convened, with some speculating that Pearson might "unveil an ingenious plan" for a "Canada-Caribbean confederacy."[134] But this was not meant to be.

Conclusion

After the Second World War, union was a response to the new global order and a means to work out Canada's place within it. In the wake of Britain's diminished power and turn toward the European Economic Community, unionists believed Canada was obligated to take on a greater share of Commonwealth responsibility and restore confidence in the organization in a time of crisis. They saw union as something that would temper American ascendancy over the Caribbean and the Canadian economies, an opportunity for Canada to engage the Americas outside the United States and US-dominated organizations, and a strategy to contain communism. And, much as it had in the period between 1898 and 1914, the impulse to "push southward" loomed up in the midst of Canada's tremendous economic growth.

The postwar order was also marked by anti-colonial nationalism, increasingly assertive demands for self-determination, and the emergence of new post-colonial states. The persistence of unionism in light of these developments is somewhat puzzling. Unionists rarely took serious account of the shifting political climate in the Caribbean that gave rise to decolonization, focusing instead on the commercial and strategic implications of an independent Caribbean for Canada, the Cold War, Canada-US relations, and the Commonwealth. The tension between unionism and Canada's burgeoning rights culture, or between unionism and Canada's international posturing as a benevolent interlocutor unencumbered by a history of colonial exploits, demands scrutiny too. Canadian expansion in the Caribbean was presumably an affront to human rights principles, most blatantly so in its contravention of the UN Declaration on the Granting of Independence to Colonial Countries and Peoples in 1960. What accounted for these tensions and the general ignorance of Caribbean aspirations? The answers are perhaps not surprising. Much like the enduring myth that Caribbean peoples coveted union while Canadians beneficently entertained their pleas for help, the tensions were a testament to the racial arrogance and paternalism that continued to shape settler Canadian thinking about the Caribbean.

The implications of this racial worldview were considerable in the post-war decades. That worldview flew in the face of Canada's anti-communist agenda, trade relationships, and "helpful fixer" image abroad. It hindered Canada's egalitarian embrace of the new Commonwealth and consequently undermined the organization itself. The tenacity of unionism in the postwar decades confirms what is now self-evident: the racial logic of empire outlived the empire. While Canada shed its British imperial identity in these decades, Eurocentrism and presumptions of white superiority endured, enabling unionists to continue injecting themselves into Caribbean futures. The dream of a Canadian Caribbean would not only endure into the 1970s but would become a national sensation.

6

DECOLONIZATION AND DENIAL

The Persistence of the Union Dream, 1967–1974

> Deprived of a West Indian empire by imperialists older and more powerful than ourselves, we have had to make do with a neo-colonialist's role in the Caribbean.
>
> James Eayrs, *Toronto Daily Star*, 18 March 1970

Canada's relations with the Commonwealth Caribbean had reached a nadir when international relations scholar James Eayrs wrote the above words. The year before, a protest led by Black students against the alleged racism of a professor at Montreal's Sir George Williams University, and the university administration's failure to adequately investigate their complaints, erupted into violence and brought white Canadian racism into sharp relief. Five days before Eayrs's article appeared in the *Toronto Star*, an all-white Montreal jury found eight Trinidadian students guilty of conspiring to occupy university property illegally. These events inspired a wave of anti-Canadianism in the Caribbean that led to the destruction of Canadian property, protests against Canadian visitors, and strident calls for the nationalization of foreign-owned companies.[1] As tensions mounted on the Sir George Williams campus early in 1969, the Canadian Senate's Standing Committee on Foreign Affairs launched a fourteen-month review of Canada-Caribbean relations.[2]

Drawing from testimony before the committee in his *Star* piece, Eayrs outlined the magnitude of foreign investment in Trinidad alone, much of it Canadian: the country's oil and sugar industries, manufacturing plants, banks, life-insurance companies, and mass media were nearly all foreign owned. In light of the Canadian economy's parallel domination by American multinational corporations, Eayrs thought Canadians ought to sympathize with the disquiet and economic nationalism gripping the Caribbean. But he was not optimistic: "As perpetrators of neo-colonialism, distinct from its beholders, we seem to be myopic," he wrote. "We do not detect in ourselves what we so bitterly resent in others." In Eayrs's assessment, while the Senate Standing Committee acknowledged the exploitative dimensions of Canadian conduct in the Caribbean, it came to the "complacent conclusion" that, so far as Caribbean peoples were concerned, "there is good will and really a welcome for Canadian involvement with them."[3] It was probably no surprise to Eayrs, then, that the committee's final report, released in June 1970, advised the Canadian government to reconsider the possibility of a constitutional association with the not-yet-independent Commonwealth Caribbean countries – what Eayrs facetiously called a "West Indian empire."

Eayrs's article, decidedly more critical of Canada's role in the Caribbean than his sanguine appraisal in *Northern Approaches* (1961), exposed the contradictions in this latest version of the union idea. While the Senate committee report was filled with liberal and progressive phrases, its foundation remained imperial, growing from a myth of Canadian innocence that belied, even as it recognized, long-underway struggles for decolonization, civil rights, and racial justice. Indeed, these movements had intensified and multiplied in the years – and weeks – immediately preceding the Senate report. How could the committee's insistence that Canada "respect the distinct character and diverse aspirations of the countries and territories in the Commonwealth Caribbean" and take "great care" to engage them in ways "so as not to infringe upon [their] sovereignty or self-determination" be reconciled with its conclusion that the Canadian government "should be prepared to discuss proposals for closer economic and political association between Canada and countries of the area"?[4] What accounted for the psychological schism between Canadian and Caribbean anxieties about foreign capital? How could the extension of Canadian sovereignty in the Caribbean be squared with the vociferous transnational critiques of Canadian corporations in the region, with the growing separatist movement in Quebec, or with Canadian antipathy for American imperialism – whether in Canada, the Caribbean and Latin America, or further afield in Vietnam? This chapter grapples with these questions. It explores the uneasy coexistence of unionism and decolonization at a time of intensifying nationalisms, New Left activism, and Canadian disenchantment with the United States in the late 1960s and early '70s.

Unionism in these years was a bundle of contradictions. In one way, it was a response to American power in Canada and the world. As the British connection faded into the past in the 1960s, Canadians were left without a comparable counterweight to the United States. Unionists believed an association with the Little Seven of the eastern Caribbean and later the Turks and Caicos Islands would go some way in tempering the preponderance of American influence in Canada's economy and international relations. With the growing winter exodus of Canadians to American sun spots, tourism would be a particular advantage, but the benefits would be strategic as well. Union would allow Canada to fulfill its middle-power purpose and cultivate its egalitarian image abroad, in stark contrast to America's depredations in Vietnam and racial strife at home. In this sense, the union idea took on a different cast, stripped of explicit references to empire and steeped in liberal and sometimes progressive ideas. It even attracted some social democrats in the New Democratic Party (NDP), who saw union as one plank of a moderately left nationalist agenda for the country. But at a time of late decolonization, these dreams were remarkably out of sync with the ubiquity and intensity of anti-imperial sensibilities within and beyond the Caribbean. Of course, Canadian advocacy of colonial self-determination and independence was well established by 1970. Canada supported these principles at the United Nations, Commonwealth ministers conferences, and other international forums, while a growing number of activists, politicians, and intellectuals did so at home. Most unionists did not see their agenda as an affront to these principles, because their embrace of decolonization was largely superficial. Like many white Canadians, unionists supported colonial peoples' right to self-determination without earnestly confronting centuries of colonial devastation and white supremacy.

This chapter first outlines the main contours of unionism in the late 1960s, giving particular focus to the nationalist anxieties fomenting unionists' designs. It then considers the swell of anti-colonial and anti-racist activism that challenged the assumptions underlying unionism. The proliferation of anti-Canadian sentiment in the wake of the Sir George Williams affair generated a highly publicized attack on Canada's exploitative operations in the Caribbean, which the Senate Standing Committee on Foreign Affairs addressed in its 1970 report. The chapter's third section takes a closer look at this committee, both its proceedings and the reasoning behind its recommendation that a constitutional association with the Little Seven should not be ruled out. As the final section discusses, anti-American nationalism, idealistic visions of world governance, and the lingering import of racialized thinking about Caribbean peoples gave impetus to unionism's return in 1974.

"Sun Seeking" in the Late 1960s

The Commonwealth's significance to unionists dwindled in the late 1960s alongside its diminishing import to Canadians in general. With Britain's turn to Europe and pervasive scepticism about the benefits of Commonwealth trade, unionists rarely invoked the organization beyond vague platitudes. Instead, they trotted out familiar arguments about commercial rivalry with the United States, commitments to communist containment, and Canada's egalitarian approach to race relations. However, intensifying debates about Quebec's future, the elevated threat of anti-colonial activism to Canadian investment in the Caribbean, and a re-energized Canadian nationalism – spurred by heightened unease with American cultural, military, and especially economic influence in Canada – introduced new dynamics. The enduring impulse to lessen Canadian dependence on US trade shifted focus too, from commodities to tourism. Several factors inspired this shift, including the commercial interests and investments of particular unionists, the conviction that tourism was the most promising route to economic growth in the smaller islands of the eastern Caribbean, and the increase in Canadian tourists abroad. Over 90 per cent of these tourists travelled to the United States, and between 1966 and 1969, the volume of Canadians vacationing there rose more than 27 per cent, from 6.76 million to 8.61 million, figures that served to magnify unionist anxiety about American economic power.[5] Redirecting US-bound tourists to Canadian destinations in the Caribbean would help mitigate this discomfort.

The most influential proponent of union in the late 1960s was Ken Patrick. A wealthy Montreal engineer and businessman, Patrick owned Marigot Investments, a corporation with extensive holdings in the Caribbean that included ownership of Bernet Bryson in Antigua and Marigot Bay in St Lucia and controlling shares in the Trinidad stock exchange.[6] In 1966–68, he lobbied various government bodies and commercial associations in Canada and the Caribbean to have the Little Seven (which included, perhaps not coincidentally, St Lucia and Antigua) enter an association with Canada. By the late 1960s, only four Commonwealth countries in the region were independent: Jamaica (1962), Trinidad and Tobago (1962), Guyana (1966, formerly British Guiana), and Barbados (1966). British Honduras attained full internal self-government in 1964, the Bahamas in 1969. Montserrat and the British Virgin Islands took on a more limited form of self-government in 1967, while the Turks and Caicos Islands and the Cayman Islands remained crown colonies. That same year, Antigua, St Kitts-Nevis-Anguilla, Dominica, Grenada, and St Lucia became

Associated States of Britain, joined by St Vincent in 1969.[7] In Patrick's plan, the latter six territories, plus Montserrat, would become part of the Canadian currency area, trade barriers would be reduced or eliminated, and Canada would control the defence and foreign affairs of the islands.[8]

In Patrick's estimation, association with the Little Seven would raise Canada's international profile and alleviate the country's economic dependence on the United States in the way of tourism and, to a lesser extent, foodstuffs. Canada, he argued, would retain a much larger portion of the $380 million annual spending by Canadian tourists travelling south for the winter. "The unfortunate lack of planning on the part of our forefathers," he told the Senate Standing Committee on Canada-Caribbean Relations in December 1969, "dividing North America by an east west line instead of north south, has deprived us of the sun areas with which the Americans are so blessed – Florida, California, Hawaii, Puerto Rico, Virgin Islands and so on. Sun seeking is a permanent feature of the leisure industry and we in Canada need access to a place in the sun."[9] Canadian investment and technical knowhow would also expand the islands' fruit and vegetable production, saving Canada millions in foreign exchange spent on imports from the southern US. Patrick outlined the benefits for the islands in somewhat more nebulous terms, gesturing more at the anticipated boon to Canada's international image: instead of just "prancing about the world stage, preaching to the great powers about what they should do," Canada would play a constructive role in Caribbean development. Patrick assumed that association with Canada would be welcomed in the Caribbean: "We do so little down there now, yet we're treated as heroes. What an opportunity for Canada if we *really* put our backs into it."[10]

Patrick's efforts generated marginal interest in the Caribbean. With his substantial investments in Antigua and St Lucia, he was well known in government circles. His proposal reportedly intrigued Antiguan chief minister Vere Bird, who told *Maclean's* magazine in February 1967, "We like the attitude of the Canadians. We're hoping that something comes of it all."[11] No action ensued from Bird's interest, perhaps because social unrest soon gripped Antigua. St Lucia's chief minister John Compton was less enthused, citing Caribbean peoples' "profoundly degrading" encounters with white Canadian racism. He concurred with Toronto-based Barbadian writer Austin Clarke's assessment that the Caribbean islands were becoming "the brothels of Canada." As *Maclean's* reported, Clarke accused Canadian businessmen of "growing fat off the West Indies" without any concern for their economies. Compton was particularly aggrieved by Canada's paltry aid disbursement of $300,000 to

St Lucia: "So far your aid has just been a dribble, a sleight-of-hand to make the world think you're doing something."[12] Ottawa's apparent preoccupation with appearance over impact hardly inspired confidence.

Patrick's lobbying did garner interest in Ottawa among a handful of MPs. Enthusiasts ran across the political spectrum, including long-serving Progressive Conservative MP for Prince Edward Island, Heath Macquarrie, Liberal MPs Jean-Eudes Dubé (Restigouche, NB) and John Matheson (Leeds, ON), and NDP MP Arnold Peters (Timiskaming, ON). Macquarrie had introduced several private members' motions in the years following the collapse of the West Indies Federation in 1962, ranging from a strengthening of trade relations to economic and political union with the Commonwealth Caribbean.[13] On 5 February 1968, he proposed negotiations for closer commercial relations with the Little Seven, and, if their residents "so desire it, economic and political union ... with the Dominion of Canada."[14] Before entering politics in 1957, Macquarrie had taught political science and international relations at several Canadian universities. His interest in union may have been aroused by his doctoral dissertation on Robert Laird Borden, completed at McGill in 1953, and particularly by the former prime minister's interest in union during the First World War.[15] Macquarrie's arguments for union were familiar: historical ties, geographical proximity, need for assistance in the smaller Caribbean islands, and Canada's responsibility to meet that need. He thought that extending Canadian sovereignty to the Little Seven was also propitious considering Canada's already extensive involvement in the islands' tourism industry.[16]

A union organizer and former miner, Peters was sympathetic to the proposal for the same reasons as his colleagues. He saw many advantages in having "a winter wonderland where our people can enjoy the sunshine and the sea." Tourist revenue was a significant part of Canada's national income, he pointed out, but the country was consistently running trade deficits with the US, "mainly because of the climatic difference between the two countries."[17] Peters was reluctant to endorse the idea fully, however. He worried about Quebec, especially the rising sovereigntist movement and the divisive battles over language in the province. These developments, for which Peters expressed considerable disdain, made it foolish to contemplate Canadian expansion in the Caribbean.[18] Entering any arrangement with the Caribbean would only shore up Quebec's sovereigntist forces.

Drawing arguments from classic Canadian myths, Peters also worried that a "race problem" would develop in the event of an association with the Little Seven. Union might compromise Canada's "simon pure" race relations, he argued, since Canadians had apparently avoided the racial conflict so prevalent in the US simply because of its much smaller Black population. An influx of Caribbean migrants to Canada would upset this cordial state of race relations, and Canada might soon find itself experiencing problems similar to the "Puerto Rican problem of New York, the Harlem problem, or the ghetto problem of Detroit."[19] For someone like Peters, the possibility that such "problems" might materialize in Canada was perhaps stronger since the immigration reforms of 1967. In the mid-1960s, following the lead of Caribbean critics and their activist allies in Canada, an increasing number of MPs pushed for a new, liberalized act that would eliminate racial discrimination. While for Caribbean migrants the act did not represent a sea change – educational and professional barriers remained – its impact was not insignificant. In the three years following its introduction, immigration from the Commonwealth Caribbean and Bermuda more than tripled, from 4,582 in 1966 to 14,468 in 1969.[20] Peters was hopeful that the "problems" presented by an influx of Caribbean migrants, by way of the 1967 act or a constitutional association with the Little Seven, would not be insurmountable. But he did not think white Canadians were yet comfortable with this prospect.[21]

Interestingly, Matheson, a Brockville lawyer, thought Peters's concerns – race, language, and Quebec sovereignty – were reasons to embrace rather than reject the proposal. Taking on political responsibilities in the eastern Caribbean would help Canadians rise above the battle over language and other "petty differences" and make them "a bigger, prouder, more generous and more united people."[22] Moreover, resistance to union based on a fear of increased Caribbean immigration to Canada undermined efforts to brand Canada as a nation strengthened by diversity in the years since the Royal Commission on Bilingualism and Biculturalism (1963). Was Canada prepared to stop "taking a superior attitude toward others in the world who find themselves encountering racial problems and responsibilities?" In the interests of both the Commonwealth and the free world, Matheson thought Canada had a significant responsibility to support Caribbean development initiatives and thereby contain the communist threat. While rebuking the generations-worn argument that union was undesirable because it would open Canada's borders to African Caribbeans and create a race problem akin to that of the United States, Matheson reiterated the older and more pernicious trope of white racial responsibility.[23]

Dubé was a New Brunswick lawyer who first extolled the merits of union in June 1966 in the midst of ongoing discussions in Britain and the Caribbean about the futures of the smaller islands making up the Little Seven. He predicted that the constitutional arrangements arising from these discussions would mark the end of colonial rule in the eastern Caribbean and send these islands in search of a new direction in alliance with other states. The time was thus opportune for Canada to become a "senior partner" of these newly independent states, forging stronger commercial relations and assuming control of their defence and external affairs.[24] Dubé was confident that Caribbeans would welcome association with Canada in light of the Commonwealth connection and geographical propinquity, as well as what Canada could offer in the way of development aid. Perhaps uneasy with America's brazen manoeuvres in the Caribbean, most recently in the Dominican Republic, Dubé rehashed the fallacious distinction between racist America and tolerant, hospitable Canada as a final selling feature for the Little Seven.[25]

Beyond these often-cited advantages, Dubé saw in union an opportunity to train a mobile contingent of Canada's armed forces in tropical conditions, readying them for brushfire combat anywhere in the world. It was a vision shared by General Jean-Victor Allard, Canada's chief of defence staff from July 1966 to September 1969. Allard's interest in union came by way of his friendship with Patrick, a fellow veteran of the Second World War. When Allard vacationed in St Lucia in the winter of 1966, he lived on Patrick's boat for a month, allowing ample opportunity to discuss the proposal.[26] While an association with the Little Seven would never materialize, in Allard's final year as chief of defence staff, Canadian troops underwent military training exercises in Jamaica. Officially, the mission aimed to prepare Canadian forces for future United Nations' peacekeeping operations in similar environments.[27]

Despite their racialized claims of responsibility and their advocacy of an anachronistic constitutional relationship with the British Caribbean, unionists like Matheson, Macquarrie, and Dubé expressed genuine concern for the significant economic and social challenges plaguing the Little Seven. Geopolitics and self-interest aside, humanitarian and global justice impulses played an increasingly influential role in how Canadians thought about and engaged the Caribbean. The strengthening of a domestic humanitarian consciousness and the attendant surge in public support for social welfare programs reverberated beyond Canadian borders.[28] Canada's increased foreign aid disbursements – institutionalized in the Canadian International Development Agency (CIDA) in 1968, the spread of Canadian non-governmental organizations (NGOs) in Third World societies, and the liberalization of Canada's immigration policy in 1967 – emerged, in part, out of an evolving commitment to global justice.

A related, though more strident and often grassroots manifestation of this commitment proliferated within the New Left, whose activists challenged the capitalist-imperialist structures that had long ordered Canada's relations with the Third World. Of course, the meanings and implications of a more egalitarian world were neither uniform nor uncontested. For unionists, Canada's association with the Little Seven would further this goal: the steady flow of Canadian capital to the islands following association would stimulate economic growth, create jobs, and alleviate poverty.

A trio of enduring misconceptions – Canada's heroic image in the Caribbean, Caribbean peoples' unbounded affection and gratitude toward their northern sibling, and lack of racial prejudice in Canada – sustained this idealism. Those who peddled these misrepresentations were in for a rude awakening. The events at Sir George Williams in February 1969 – and the subsequent failure of the university and the federal government to conduct a proper investigation – exposed the social, institutional, and governmental depths of white Canadian racism and set off a prolonged wave of anti-Canadianism in the Caribbean. The events also mobilized and expanded Black and Caribbean activist organizations in Canada.

Sir George Williams University and the "Second Offensive" against Canadian Banks, Bauxite, and Beaches

Much of the ideological and intellectual groundwork of this activism had been laid in the years leading up to the Sir George Williams incident. In 1965, a group of Caribbean men and women formed the Caribbean Conference Committee (ccc) in Montreal, part of the swell of New Left organizations emerging worldwide. With a mandate to raise awareness about the social, economic, and political challenges facing Caribbean societies, the ccc brought several Caribbean intellectuals to the city in its first two years.[29] In 1968, a new group of activists emerged in Montreal who reoriented the ccc's focus. Inspired by the Black Power movement in the United States and concerned more with the experience of African-descended people in Canada than in the Caribbean, the Caribbean Conference Committee became the Canadian Conference Committee. Not long after the reconstructed committee held its first meeting in October 1968, Black students at McGill and Sir George Williams convened the Congress of Black Writers, whose participants included prominent Black intellectuals, civil rights activists, and Pan-Africanists from the Americas and beyond.[30] When Guyanese-born historian and Pan-Africanist Walter Rodney returned to Jamaica after the Congress to resume his teaching position at the Mona campus of the University of the West Indies (UWI), the Jamaican government refused him re-entry for his alleged involvement in subversive political discussions in Montreal.[31] His expulsion activated long-simmering antagonisms against the Jamaican government and the bourgeoisie, setting off riots against government offices and foreign property. Many of the rioters directed their fury at foreign companies operating in Jamaica, including the Canadian Imperial Bank of Commerce, the Royal Bank of Canada, and the Bank of Montreal. The rioting provided the impetus for the alliance of dissimilar groups – radical intellectuals, politically radical Rastafarians, youth activists – who came together under the umbrella of Abeng, a short-lived but influential Jamaican political organization.[32] The riots and their political aftermath are viewed by many as the beginning of the Black Power movement in the Anglophone Caribbean, while Abeng represented the first of many Caribbean New Left organizations with Canadian connections.[33]

Organizing in Canada accelerated in 1969. In late January, less than four months after the Congress of Black Writers and the Rodney riots, a group of more than two hundred demonstrators occupied the computer centre at Sir George Williams to protest the university's protracted failure to adequately address six Black students' allegations of racism on the part of a biology professor.[34] A confrontation ensued two weeks later when an armed riot squad arrived on the scene to forcibly remove the protestors, leading to more than $2 million in damage to the computer centre. Ninety-seven demonstrators were arrested, forty-two of them Black. While the majority of those arrested were white students, the media, government officials, and many bystanders focused on the Black protesters, many of whom were not Canadian citizens but Caribbeans studying in Canada.[35] Eight months later, the CCC helped found the National Black Coalition of Canada (NBCC), which subsequently opened chapters across the country. The NBCC was the first Canadian-grown national civil rights organization to challenge the social, political and economic barriers faced by Black Canadians.[36] Several locally based organizations and community newspapers were also established to promote and defend the rights of Black Canadians: in Toronto, the Black Liberation Front of Canada (BLFC) and its organ, *Black Liberation News*, in 1969, and the Black Youth Organization (BYO) the following year;[37] in Montreal, the Black Coalition of Quebec, Black Action Party, Black Study Centre, Black Theatre workshop, Quebec Board of Black Educators, and several community associations. Notable newspapers included

Uhuru (July 1969–November 1970), and the *Black Voice* (May 1972–October 1974), both based in Montreal.[38]

The events at Sir George Williams ignited considerable protest in the Caribbean. When Canada's governor general, Roland Michener, travelled to Trinidad for a state visit less than two weeks after the computer centre occupation erupted into violence, students at the University of the West Indies St Augustine blocked Michener's entry to the campus. Embarrassed, the university's academic board met with some of the protesters and demanded they make a public apology to Michener and his party. UWI student president Geddes Granger, an active participant in the protest, refused, arguing that the demonstration was a warranted response to the racial discrimination and violence at Sir George Williams.[39] Granger and fellow student radical Dave Darbeau were concerned that the Trinidad media – controlled in large part by white foreign interests – were not disseminating a full and truthful picture of what transpired in Montreal. They consequently founded the National Joint Action Committee (NJAC) on the night of the protest to disseminate information about the events at Sir George Williams specifically and the depths of white Canadian racism and imperialism more generally.[40] The following week, about one hundred students at UWI's Cave Hill campus in Barbados staged a mock funeral for the administration at Sir George Williams, during which they burned an effigy of the accused biology professor. They marched through campus with a makeshift coffin, shouting, "We Shall Overcome," the popular mantra of the late Martin Luther King Jr.[41] Several Caribbean communities also mobilized in support of the arrested Caribbean students, raising thousands of dollars for their legal defense.[42]

One month after the riots at Sir George Williams, eight hundred Canadian troops were airlifted to Jamaica for jungle warfare training, further mobilizing critics of Canadian imperialism in the Caribbean. Code-named Nimrod Caper, the exercise evolved from a military cooperation agreement between the Canadian and Jamaican governments, but these exercises had wider implications.[43] In bringing large numbers of Canadian troops to Jamaica in a matter of hours and establishing an island-wide radio communications network linked directly to Ontario, the exercises demonstrated the ease and efficiency with which a Canadian battalion could intervene in future. It was the first time a Jamaican ally had demonstrated this capacity.[44] Nimrod Caper "reflected the economic and commercial importance of the Caribbean to Canada, and the consequent political weight of [Canada's] Caribbean diplomacy."[45] In 1969, Canadian private direct investment in the Commonwealth Caribbean approached $600 million, with half that figure invested in bauxite enterprises in Guyana and Jamaica.[46] The objective of the military operations in Jamaica, historian Sean Maloney confirms, "revolved around securing and protecting the Alcan facilities from mob unrest and outright seizure or sabotage."[47] This reality was not lost on Caribbean critics of Canadian corporations in Jamaica. It was clear enough to Dominica-born McGill student and accused ringleader of the Sir George Williams riots, Roosevelt "Rosie" Douglas, who had no qualms implicating Patrick and Allard by name. With the "potential for social revolution [in Jamaica] increasing each day," he fumed in one of Montreal's Black newspapers, "the Canadian government[,] upon advice from Imperialist Ken Patrick of Marigot Investments and General Jean Allard of the Military elite, have begun a program of sending troops into the country under the sham of allowing them to acclimatize themselves with the tropical conditions for United Nations 'peace keeping' purposes."[48]

In combination with the Sir George Williams affair, these events gave rise to what the NJAC termed the "Second Offensive." The failure of the university administration and the Canadian government to conduct proper investigations into the confrontation, in the words of NJAC chairman Geddes Granger, was an example of "the lengths to which the white, racist, capitalistic Canadian people are prepared to go in order to keep [Blacks] ... in their place." It was a call to peoples in the African diaspora to reflect critically on Canada's role in perpetuating their dehumanization at home and abroad. Just as white Canadian societies, institutions, and governments collaborated in preserving the status quo of white hegemony at home, Granger said, Canadian corporations operating in the Caribbean worked in cooperation with local governments to safeguard a capitalist, exploitative system in which Blacks were still unable to reap the benefits of their labour.[49]

In the year following the violence at Sir George Williams, the activities of Black intellectuals, activists, and student radicals in Canada and the Caribbean reflected an increased commitment to publicize and critique the connections among white racism, the exploitative activities of Canada abroad, and the pernicious endurance of the colonial status quo in the post-independence Caribbean. As the *Black Liberation News* observed in August 1969, "The West Indian masses have been ... taught to believe that they have been led by black governments in independent countries. But for the thinking man, this has been a myth. Neo-colonialism has crept into the West Indian society ... they are begin[ning] to see that the same people who deny them full rights abroad are the same people who are exploiting their countries and controlling their leaders."[50] Not unlike the Canadian government in the post-1945 period, Caribbean governments exercised open-door policies to foreign investment. In competition with one another, they offered generous fiscal incentives and other concessions to foreign investors, who consequently established considerable control over Caribbean resources. This control carried over into the post-independence period, often with the assistance of Caribbean leaders who continued to value the development potential of foreign investment.[51] As a growing number of Caribbean economists argued from the late 1960s, the postwar trend of accommodating foreign capital had facilitated the exploitation of Caribbean resources and locked the region in a state of perpetual underdevelopment.[52]

Many of these economists were members of the New World Group, a collective of mostly Caribbean intellectuals formed in Georgetown in 1962 to discuss the socioeconomic challenges facing Caribbean societies. With hubs in Jamaica, Trinidad, and Montreal and a widely read organ, *New World Quarterly*, the group counted some influential thinkers among its members, including Caribbean economists Lloyd Best, George Beckford, Alister McIntyre, William Demas, Norman Girvan, and Canadian economist Kari Polanyi Levitt. Following the 1965 publication of Demas's seminal *The Economics of Development in Small Countries with Special Reference to the Caribbean*, regional integration replaced "industrialization by invitation" as the guiding development model.[53] A number of initiatives grew out of this focus, most notably the Caribbean Free Trade Association (CARIFTA) in 1968. Not long after Levitt completed an early version of her groundbreaking study of American multinational corporations in Canada (published in *New World Quarterly* in 1968, two years before the publication of her *Silent Surrender: The Multinational Corporation in Canada*), she collaborated with Best on an extensive study of Caribbean economies. They traced the region's current challenges – dependency on foreign capital, technology, and imperial preferences, a structure of production based on foreign rather than domestic consumption, and an overwhelming dependence on imports – back to the plantation economy. They found that multinational corporations operating in the Caribbean replicated many aspects of the pure plantation economy, controlling the capital, technology, entrepreneurship, and organization of their Caribbean operations. Under multinational corporations, the Caribbean continued to serve the needs of overseas metropolitan economies, primarily as a source of raw materials (bauxite ore, petroleum) and more recently as a site of product assembly (manufacturing) and services (tourism).[54]

Canadian enterprises in the Caribbean perpetuated this pattern. In the late 1960s, Canadian private direct investment in the Caribbean was higher than in any other developing region. Alcan was the largest Canadian investor, totalling over $300 million, with subsidiaries in Jamaica, Guyana, and Trinidad.[55] With the bulk of raw bauxite ore shipped to factories in Canada and the US for production, Guyana's natural resources were extracted for use in the industrialization of the North American economy, while Guyana remained underdeveloped, its people poor and economically disenfranchised.[56] The more lucrative stages of the bauxite-aluminum industry – and the greatest demand for labour – were in smelting and fabrication, processes that Alcan centred in Canada rather than the Caribbean. Guyanese and Jamaican bauxite supported two main industrial communities in Canada, Arvida, Quebec (population 14,000) and Kitimat, BC (population 8,500), and was the major industry in the Quebec towns of Shawinigan, Isle Maligne, Beauharois, and Port Alfred. By the late 1960s, Alcan's Canadian operations employed approximately 17,200 people, provided C$95 million in wages, paid Canadian federal taxes of about $14.3 million, and with exports totalling more than $227 million, was Canada's sixth-largest exporter.[57] The benefits to the Canadian economy were substantial.

The foreign-controlled tourist industry was also a growing source of Caribbean enmity. By the late 1960s, Canadian involvement in Caribbean tourism – as investors, resort owners, promoters, suppliers, and tourists – was ubiquitous. The leftist magazine *Last Post* described the Canadian presence in the Bahamas in 1970: "Driving into Nassau from Windsor Field Airport, you can see Canadian money sprinkled along the route like icing on a cake ... [Toronto business magnate] E.P. Taylor has plans to build a city of 100,000 people next door to Nassau, to include five golf courses, a millionaires' ghetto, and at least one resort hotel. His New Providence Development Co. has already generated revenues of $1.1 million without having erected a single building."[58] Taylor exerted a powerful influence on the Bahamian economy in the 1960s and '70s. He was chairman of the bank consortium RoyWest Ltd, the islands' main source of venture capital; chairman of the Trust Corporation of the Bahamas, which handled the financial affairs of approximately a thousand chartered companies; and unpaid chairman of the Bahamian economic council. Canadians, the *Financial Post* reported in 1970, "are Nassau's new colonizers and E.P. Taylor is their prophet."[59] Foreign investors and business people like Taylor drew the increased ire of local populations from the late 1960s. Pre- and post-independence Caribbean governments continued to offer generous tax incentives and other concessions to attract foreign businesses. Local control of the tourist industry was typically absent at every stage – from development, asset ownership, and revenues to management, hiring practices, and the sourcing of foodstuffs and other commodities. Foreign tourist enterprises consequently played an exploitative role in the Caribbean, perpetuating rather than alleviating underdevelopment.[60]

The tourist and bauxite industries were more recent examples of a historic pattern of Canadian economic control and exploitation in the Caribbean, one that emerged much earlier with the proliferation of Canadian banks and life-insurance companies at the turn of the twentieth century. By the early 1970s, the Canadian banking presence remained considerable, with more than two hundred branches of RBC, CIBC, and the Bank of Nova Scotia conducting over half of the region's business.[61] Throughout most of their history in the Commonwealth Caribbean, Canadian banks effectively collected and controlled savings but were generally reluctant to invest in fledgling, locally run enterprises, which were considered risky, low-return ventures. They made their capital available to large exporting firms and high-return commercial enterprises while denying small local businesses long-term, low-interest loans.[62] Rather than assist in the development of a native business class, Canadian banks worked with Caribbean governments to attract foreign capital (with generous tax incentives and profit repatriation) to exploit Caribbean resources. Scarce funds remained in the region to stimulate economic growth. Canadian life-insurance companies were similarly reluctant to support Caribbean development initiatives. Comprising about half of the life-insurance companies in the English-speaking Caribbean and carrying out about 70 per cent of the industry's business, these companies were well positioned to mobilize domestic savings for long-term investment in the region. Instead, they generally opted to reinvest these savings elsewhere.[63] Canadian banks and insurance companies, in other words, were agents of Caribbean underdevelopment.[64]

For anti-colonial activists, the connection between white corporate interests in the Caribbean and the failure of Sir George Williams University to conduct a proper investigation were painfully clear. As an article in *Uhuru* in August 1969 reported, Montreal millionaire Ken Patrick, the leading proponent of Canada's union with the Little Seven, had previously served on the university's board of governors. Allan Bronfman, a current member of the board, was senior vice-president of his family's company, Seagram's, which operated distilleries in Jamaica and elsewhere in the Caribbean.[65] Ray Edwin Powell, honorary president (and past president) of Alcan, was an advisor to the board. For these stakeholders, acknowledging the racism at Sir George Williams might have compromised their financial interests in the Caribbean.[66]

In the two weeks leading up to the Montreal trial of ten Trinidadian students for their alleged roles in the computer centre occupation, the NJAC organized a series of peaceful demonstrations in Trinidad with a dual purpose: to stand in solidarity with the students awaiting trial, and to protest Canadian imperialism in the Caribbean. On 26 February 1970, Granger led a large coalition of NJAC members to the Royal Bank of Canada's headquarters in Port of Spain to protest the grip that the bank and other foreign financial institutions held on Trinidad's economy. This protest initiated the "February Revolution," a wave of Black Power demonstrations that turned violent in April and prompted Eric Williams's government to declare a state of emergency.[67] On 2 March, eleven days before the trial of the "Trinidad 10" concluded in Montreal, Granger warned there would be serious repercussions for Canada if Ottawa did not conduct a fair investigation prior to the trial. "If one student is convicted in the courts, Canada will also be on trial in the West Indies ... I hope that the Canadian people remember that there are many Canadian businesses and interests which are exploiting our country ... we are about to embark upon our 'Second Offensive' and I hope that the Canadian government, who is reaping in the West Indies, keep that in mind."[68]

On 10 March, *Edmonton Journal* cartoonist Edd Uluschak depicted the depths to which Canada's reputation had plummeted in Trinidad. The cartoon shows a group of Trinidadian protestors chasing two American tourists from a local beach (figure 6.1). The woman scolds her companion, "You and your ideas of telling people we're Canadians because they're more welcome than us Americans!" Recent events had laid bare a central fallacy of Canadian identity – that Canadians were morally virtuous and loved around the world, unlike their depraved, imperialist American cousins.

The Canadian government ultimately declined to investigate, and on 13 March an all-white male jury found eight of the ten Trinidadian students guilty of conspiring to illegally occupy the computer centre and fined them a combined total of $33,500.[69] Many of the students who had previously stood trial for their involvement in the occupation were similarly found guilty and fined. Three Black students were sentenced to prison terms for their more active roles, including Rosie Douglas, who was sentenced to two years. (He served

"You and your ideas of telling people we're Canadians because
they're more welcome anywhere than us Americans!"

Fig. 6.1   "Welcome to Trinidad," cartoon by Edd Uluschak, *Edmonton Journal*,
10 March 1970

eighteen months.)[70] The biology professor at the centre of the controversy,
on the other hand, was reinstated soon after the occupation (he had been
suspended during the crisis), and later that year the university acquitted him
of all charges brought against him.

Following the verdict, protestors in Dominica set Canadian flags ablaze
outside the RBC branch in Roseau, and a wave of destruction against colonial
landmarks and foreign property spread to Grenada, Barbados, and elsewhere
in the Caribbean. In the final days of April, protestors firebombed RBC's
headquarters in Port of Spain and several other foreign enterprises.[71]

The Senate Report, Foreign Investment
Parallels, and the Persistence of Unionism

It would be reasonable to assume that this anti-Canadian backlash extinguished any vestiges of unionism. It did not. The Senate Standing Committee on Foreign Affairs' study of Canada-Caribbean relations, launched in the midst of the Sir George Williams upheaval in February 1969 and concluded during the Trinidad protests in April 1970, advised Ottawa to "re-appraise the possibility of constitutional links" with the Little Seven. Now was perhaps not the time to discuss association, given the "unrest and hostility" in the region, but it should be revisited in the future.[72] This recommendation was curious for a few reasons, not least because anti-colonial activism was flourishing from Montreal to Port of Spain. First, and most significantly, the committee made little effort to solicit Caribbean opinions on the question. Neither of the two Caribbean-born experts interviewed during the course of the committee's work, Trinidadian economist William Demas and Jamaican labour economist and York University professor George Eaton, was questioned about association with Canada. Demas did not broach the idea, and Eaton dismissed it as "invidious." The assumption that "once a colonial power withdraws, somebody has to dash in, because the people are incapable of mobilizing their own resources or of standing alone," Eaton told the committee in April 1970, "is a very negative approach for Canada to adopt ... in the Caribbean." He condemned the "vacuum thesis," to which Canadians and Americans frequently subscribed, as "an excuse for big powers to bully little ones and for wealthy powers to exploit poor ones."[73]

Second, the association idea's inclusion in the Senate committee's final report was somewhat out of place among its many progressive recommendations. Committee chair John B. Aird warned the Senate when he released the report on 23 June, "Many of the comfortable assumptions of the past are dangerously inappropriate in the current Caribbean context."[74] In view of the "distinct trends within the area, Canada can expect continuing, and even growing criticism and hostility from some sectors of opinion in the Caribbean." It was therefore crucial to demonstrate that Canada was "not committed to the status quo and recognizes the case for progressive change."[75] To this end, the report outlined the need for increased local control of Caribbean resources and industry, a greater sense of civic responsibility among Canadian corporations operating in the region, a reduction in the tying of government aid, the redirection of Canadian investment into Caribbean development projects, more support for initiatives designed to expand and diversify Caribbean exports, and a greater sensitivity to the diversity of aspirations in the Caribbean.[76] The committee also recommended greater consultation with Caribbean governments in major trade decisions affecting the region. The Canadian government had recently terminated, unilaterally, a sugar-tariff rebate granted in 1966, generating considerable confusion and ill will in the Caribbean. Canadians should be more sensitive to the lopsided nature of the relationship and realize that "in the eyes of the small nations of the Caribbean, Canada can appear to be a major and potentially threatening power." The committee advised that Canadian policy must take account of these sentiments and engage the region on a more cooperative and consultative basis.[77]

Finally, the Department of External Affairs discouraged association with the Little Seven. Prior to Secretary of State Mitchell Sharp's interview with the Senate committee in November 1969, the department submitted a brief on Canada-Caribbean relations for the committee's consideration, advising against establishing "constitutional links of a quasi-colonial nature." Sharp elaborated this position in his testimony. Ottawa's objective should be supporting the Commonwealth Caribbean countries in their efforts to achieve "true independence." Entering a constitutional arrangement, he warned, might "give substance to the ideas that are sometimes floating about that because we are taking an interest in the development of the Caribbean ... somehow we want to put the ... area into a position of inferiority to us or dependence upon us." Canadian initiatives that might create such an impression should be avoided at all costs.[78]

Senate committee vice-chair Allister Grosart, who pressed Sharp on the association question, disparaged External Affairs' "too careful" approach on the world stage. "We have been afraid of being called colonial. We have been afraid of going beyond the tight little realm of diplomatic protocol." In language that surely rankled someone like George Eaton, Grosart lamented Canada's ongoing failure to fill the "void" left by Britain's withdrawal from the Caribbean.[79] A trained lawyer turned journalist whom Prime Minister Diefenbaker had appointed to the Senate in 1962, Grosart had an interest in association with the Little Seven dating back to at least 1968. As a chief executive of the Commonwealth Parliamentary Association (CPA), Grosart and his CPA colleagues had accompanied fifteen Caribbean parliamentarians – including premiers Vere Bird (Antigua), Eric Gairy (Grenada), and Robert Bradshaw (St Kitts) – on a tour from Montreal to Victoria. Soon after, Grosart pushed the association idea in the Senate, while conceding, curiously, that he had not discussed it with any of the Caribbean parliamentarians during their visit. In familiar fashion, he was nonetheless confident that "an approach from Canada would be welcomed."[80] Aside from his conviction that the region's peoples were looking for something more from Canada, "something from the heart," Grosart envisioned association with the Little Seven as a way for Canada to fulfill its obligations in the world. As a leading middle power, he argued, Canada should be more assertive in international affairs, seeking to "find and assess gaps" in the smaller nations of the world in particular. "The alternative," he cautioned, was "complete domination of the world" by the United States and Soviet Russia.[81] Association was desirable given Canada's already substantial commercial presence in the Caribbean: "Canadians are the bankers of these islands. We are rapidly becoming the main tourist operators in those islands."[82]

Several senators on and off the foreign affairs committee thought association was worthy of further debate, including former secretary of state for external affairs Paul Martin Sr, law professor John Connolly, and committee chair John B. Aird, a lawyer, future lieutenant-governor of Ontario, and grandson of prominent banking executive Sir John Aird.[83] But Grosart was clearly the main proponent, and his questioning of witnesses before the committee evinced a genuine concern for the well-being of Caribbean peoples. More than any other committee member, Grosart pressed for information on the extent and consequences of foreign investment in the Caribbean. While he dismissed External Affairs' concerns about Canada "being called colonial," he was nonetheless sensitive to the exploitative potential of foreign capital. "The impression I have," he observed after reviewing material from External Affairs, CIDA, and the recently published *Canada-West Indies Economic Relations*, co-authored by economists Kari Levitt (McGill) and Alister McIntyre (UWI St Augustine), "is that [Canadian investment in the region] is mostly 'take-out' rather than 'put-in' investment ... There is very little evidence of any investment in up-grading manufacturing capability there." No witness was able to provide an accurate figure on Canadian private investment in the region, but it was clear to Grosart that this investment was draining Caribbean economies at an alarming rate.[84]

As Grosart observed, foreign investment was creating similar problems in Canada.[85] The country's dependence on foreign capital was nothing new, but the dramatic rise of foreign and especially American ownership after the Second World War worried a growing number of Canadians from the mid-1950s. Many of the concerns raised by economic nationalists in Canada mirrored those in the Caribbean: external control of resources, enterprises managed by foreign executives, shares controlled from outside Canada, branch plants sourcing materials from their home country rather than their host country, and scarce investment in local research and development. A series of government-sponsored studies recommended moderate reforms to regulate foreign investment, commencing with the Royal Commission on Canada's Economic Prospects in 1957–58, chaired by businessman and future finance minister Walter Gordon. A decade later, at Gordon's urging, Lester Pearson's Liberal government assembled a task force on foreign ownership, led by University of Toronto political economist Mel Watkins. The task force's report, released in February 1968, reiterated many of the concerns outlined by the Gordon commission. It highlighted the need for national policies to reduce the costs of foreign investment, particularly the extraterritorial application of American laws on Canadian subsidiaries.[86] Much more significant in raising public awareness about the dangers of foreign ownership was Kari Levitt's *Silent Surrender*, published in 1970. Earlier iterations had circulated widely in 1968–69, rousing the political left in Canada.[87] Her work influenced several New Democrats, including Watkins, who co-founded the Waffle in 1969, a radical left faction within the NDP that called for the nationalization of Canadian industry.[88]

While Grosart and a few other members of the Senate foreign affairs committee referenced in passing Canada's parallel experience with foreign investment, this experience had little discernable impact on the committee's deliberations and conclusions. This was somewhat surprising, because in both Canada and the Caribbean, apprehension about foreign investment reflected weightier anxieties about national sovereignty and independence. A sensitivity to these sentiments and the concomitant aversion to foreign control in the Caribbean would presumably rule out the possibility of a constitutional association with Canada. Of course, in the late 1960s and early '70s, economic nationalism and anti-Americanism were neither uniform nor ubiquitous in Canada. Grosart, for example, was not especially concerned by America's expanding presence above the 49th parallel, dismissing the current flurry of alarm as merely another "phase of the cyclical anti-Americanism which is so much a part of our history."[89] He in fact believed that the "integration" of the Canadian and American economies – on "a planned and programmed basis" – was "absolutely necessary."[90] In the midst of the new nationalist surge and the ongoing anti-colonial ferment in the Caribbean, however, he and his colleagues were sensitive to the appearance of international impropriety. The prospect of associate statehood for the Little Seven should not be quashed emphatically because it would ultimately produce neo-colonial relationships; rather, it should be put on hold, as in the present anti-Canadian tumult it "might be widely felt to have neo-colonial characteristics."[91]

In this way, the committee's recommendations were a pragmatic response to the anti-Canadian upheaval in the Caribbean rather than a frank reckoning with the past and continuing reality of Canadian imperialism. The lingering prospect of constitutional association, as outlined in the committee's report, was the most blatant expression of this failed reckoning, but it was not the only one. Among the nearly fifty formal interviews conducted with "expert witnesses on the Caribbean area," only Demas and Eaton were indigenous to the Caribbean. The rest of these "experts" were representatives of various agencies and departments of the Canadian government, NGOs operating in the Caribbean such as Canadian University Services Overseas (CUSO) and Canadian churches, and several Canadian and American economists and international relations specialists.[92] More dubiously, they included Canadian executives of companies conducting business in the Caribbean, most notably Ken Patrick of Marigot Investments and Alcan Aluminum's Nathaniel Davis. The dearth of Caribbean-born experts betrayed the commission's advocacy of a more consultative relationship and reflected the long-held bias that white Canadians knew best.[93] The report also downplayed the exploitative history of Canada's engagement with the Caribbean, whitewashed and romanticized the history of Canada-Caribbean relations – a history apparently characterized by Caribbean peoples' "unlimited goodwill"[94] toward Canada – and identified racial difference as an obstacle to improving these relations rather than a Western construct perpetuated by white Canadians to serve their Caribbean agendas over the years. Aside from the testimony of Demas and Eaton, connections were scarcely drawn between the Caribbean's long histories of colonialism and racial oppression and the ongoing social and economic challenges bedevilling much of the region.[95] While New Left activists chipped away at the white supremacist thinking that had long structured Canadian society, in 1970 it remained preponderant. This race-thinking was no doubt responsible in part for the Canadian "myopia" that James Eayrs diagnosed in March 1970[96] – the psychological disconnect between Canadian discomfort with foreign investment and its parallel in the Caribbean. The United States and Canada were wealthy Western nations governed by a white capitalist class; one's exploitation of another was not apropos. Yet it was a matter of course for a wealthy Western nation to take colonial liberties or otherwise insert itself in the developing world.

Fears of becoming a satellite of the American empire did not inspire much introspection among unionists about Caribbean peoples' ongoing confrontation with colonialism, nor did it prompt them to abandon their dreams. Unionism re-emerged in 1974 with a bang, generating more national interest than ever before. This interest reflected persisting anxieties about America's excessive influence on Canada's economy and international conduct and an acute desire to temper it. It also evinced an unfulfilled reckoning with the history and legacies of colonialism within and beyond Canadian borders.

Chasing the "Canada South" Dream in the 1970s

In January 1974, New Democrat MP Max Saltsman introduced a private members bill to explore the possibility of the Turks and Caicos Islands (TCI) becoming "an overseas maritime province or territory of Canada."[97] The chain of Caribbean islands three hundred kilometres north of Haiti and the Dominican Republic (figure 6.2), with a population of six thousand, was a British crown colony whose affairs the Bahamas governor had administered prior to Bahamian independence in 1973. When the TCI's State Council deliberated the constitutional and economic future of the islands in 1972–73 (in the wake of not only Bahamian independence but Britain's entry into the EEC), councillor Liam Maguire proposed union with Canada. Maguire, also a local land developer, hotel owner, and the only British expatriate elected to the State Council, persuaded his fellow councillors in March 1973 to explore the possibility.[98] Maguire travelled to Ottawa shortly thereafter, where he caught the ear of Progressive Conservative MP and long-time unionist Heath Macquarrie. Then, at the invitation of the TCI's Commonwealth Parliamentary Association, a delegation of the Canadian branch of the association visited the islands in August 1973 to continue the conversation. The delegation included Macquarrie (Hillsborough, PEI), Saltsman (Waterloo-Cambridge), and MPs Stanley Knowles (NDP, Winnipeg), Maurice Dupras (Liberal, Labelle), and Jacques Trudel (Liberal, Montreal-Bourassa). Saltsman returned to Canada intrigued by the possibilities of union and joined Macquarrie in promoting the idea.

Saltsman's bill generated considerable excitement across Canada. It was discussed on national and local television and radio networks and in newspapers.[99] The Canadian Broadcasting Corporation (CBC) and a commercial network sent production teams at the end of January 1974 to produce television content on the islands.[100] Canadian investors and land speculators descended

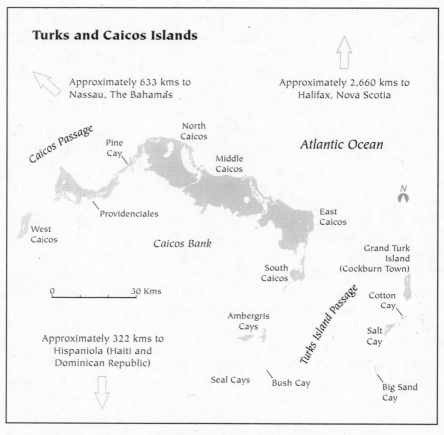

Fig. 6.2 Map of the Turks and Caicos Islands. Copyright Robert Cronan

on the TCI to scope out opportunities.[101] Saltsman gave out "Turks and Caicos – I Choose Canada" buttons, and a Toronto tailor made "I Choose Canada" badges to distribute to Canadians and islanders who signed a petition supporting union (figure 6.4).[102] A Toronto musician composed a song to commemorate the would-be union called "Living Should Be Fun for Everyone at Turks Island."[103] Elementary students drafted school petitions supporting union, secondary students conducted "feasibility studies," and university students wrote theses on the question.[104] Canadians bombarded the TCI tourist board with endless letters. "We've had about 600 letters from Canadians," the tourist board secretary told the *Gazette* (Montreal) in early February. "Every mail brings a hundred more. The letters come from everywhere in the country and they want to know everything there is to know."[105] The

Fig. 6.3   "Une partie du Canada?," *Le Quotidien*, 10 January 1974

Gazette published excerpts from some of the letters from Quebec: "'Can we camp there?' asks Jacques Limoges of Sherbrooke. 'Are our investments secure down there?' writes a man from St Lambert. Asks Conrad Leroux of Pierrefonds: 'The general population – are they friendly and good hosts?' Like dozens of other people, a man named Rene Levesque of Dorval wants to know the best way to get here and John Roch of Joliette wants to buy a business. Richard Baroni of Barclay St. in Montreal wants a vacation that 'is

Fig. 6.4   "I Choose Canada,"
advertisement, *Globe and Mail,*
6 February 1974

tranquil but not luxurious.'"[106] Thousands of Canadians weighed in on the
question by sending letters to Saltsman and other MPs, External Affairs, and
the Canadian press. The letters, overwhelmingly in favour of union, reveal
a populace enthralled by the prospect of Canada finally laying claim to "a
place in the sun."[107]

In a departure from the generally non-partisan history of unionism, in
1974 most politician-enthusiasts were New Democrats and, to a lesser extent,
Progressive Conservatives, while detractors tended to be Liberal. Saltsman
gained the support – or at least piqued the interest – of long-time social

democrat Stanley Knowles (who had accompanied Saltsman to the TCI in August 1973); former NDP leader Tommy Douglas; the previously reluctant Timiskaming MP Arnold Peters; past Cooperative Commonwealth Federation (CCF) leader-turned Liberal Senator, Hazen Argue; and Nova Scotia NDP leader Jeremy Akerman – who found the idea "appealing in the extreme."[108]

To some extent, NDP interest in union reflected the party's political priorities and especially concerns about US power. While America's imposing presence disquieted Canadians of all political stripes, this disquiet was most strident among New Democrats. There were important exceptions to this trend, most notably Walter Gordon, the father of post-1945 economic nationalism. But there were also several Liberals within the non-partisan Committee for an Independent Canada (CIC), founded in September 1970 to promote Canadian independence from the United States. In general, however, the Liberals were less perturbed than New Democrats about America's influence north of the border. This was certainly the case for Prime Minister Pierre Trudeau, in power at the height of anti-American sentiment in Canada. Decidedly federalist but not nationalist, Trudeau was mostly ambivalent about the flow of American capital into Canada. Only with significant prodding from his Liberal colleagues, and his own desire to secure parliamentary support for his minority government between 1972 and 1974, did he agree to introduce moderate nationalist reforms. Under Trudeau, the Liberals had established the Canada Development Corporation (CDC) in 1971 to increase domestic ownership of Canadian industries, announced plans to strengthen economic relations with Japan and Europe in 1972, and created the Foreign Investment Review Agency (FIRA) in 1973 to screen foreign investment.[109]

To be sure, union enthusiasts within the NDP were mainstream social democrats; their views on the United States were certainly more moderate than the radical Waffle group who broke from the party in 1972 and morphed into the Movement for an Independent Socialist Canada – a political organization largely defunct by the fall of 1974. They were nonetheless intent on establishing a greater measure of independence in Canada's economic and foreign policies than were the Liberals and PCs, and union with the TCI – for a contingent of New Democrats – was a step in that direction. Saltsman, Douglas, and many of their NDP colleagues were social democratic internationalists who "envisioned the evolution of a world federation based on peaceful cooperation and politico-economic equality among all nations, large and small."[110] This idealist vision took shape in explicit contrast to America's vulgar, capitalist-militarist approach to foreign affairs that ensnared weaker nations in a ruthless cycle of exploitation and dependency. Moreover, according to Saltsman, it was a vision in contradistinction to the atomizing tendencies of a liberalist worldview. "According to modern liberalism," he schooled Parliament in March 1974, "it is fine for [small Caribbean] islands to seek independence. We will give them a little foreign aid, pat them on the head and tell them to go on their own way, but we want no part of them. Such thinking masquerades as modern thinking. It is all right to atomize the world!"[111] While the cooperative approach of international organizations such as the United Nations and the Commonwealth aimed, in theory, to guard against the atomization that Saltsman bemoaned, their efficacy in achieving their goals – international peace and security, the protection of human rights, or the distribution of humanitarian aid – was often constrained by their function as advisory bodies. For Saltsman, the absorption of Third World societies in wealthy, proximate societies would better serve these goals: "If we want to help people, if we really want to redistribute wealth, we will take them in." Doing so might very well signal "the beginning of the end of people being pushed around" and the birth of a new, modern form of federalism.[112]

While the concept of world federalism was ill defined, several Canadians who wrote to Saltsman in the early months of 1974 envisioned a Canada-Caribbean association as a new federalist model to which other nations might aspire. Absorbing the Turks and Caicos Islands, ventured an Ottawa writer, offered exciting possibilities to restructure Canada in the form of a "multi-national state" and thereby to mitigate the country's "divisive tendencies." While it was "basically impossible to have [one] province culturally autonomous, or another economically independent," he argued, if Canada added several other provinces that similarly required internal autonomy, then Quebec would no longer be a special case. With autonomous statehood for the existing provinces, and new states in the Caribbean, the North (i.e., an Inuit state), or elsewhere, Canada would provide an inspiring model of modern federalism, an "alternative to domination by some national culture, whether the US, Russia, Chinese, or some other."[113]

The spectre of this domination, especially foreign investment anxieties in Canada and the Caribbean, informed unionist discourse in different ways. NDP enthusiasts often acknowledged the distasteful aspects of Canadian involvement in the Caribbean and urged measures to guard against them under union.[114] Commentators were more often concerned with the implications of union for Canada's dependence on the United States. Many cited the hefty trade deficit that Canada incurred annually when Canadians migrated south in wintertime.

A writer from the Niagara Region had "often wondered why Canada [hadn't] made some attempt to annex some of the British Caribbean [islands] ... as a tropical addition to our country rather than be satisfied to give the U.S.A. all of our tourist traffic revenue."[115] Others were more explicit about the need to pre-empt US influence. In a letter to *La Presse* in March 1974, Montrealer and self-identified New Democrat Réal Lalonde wholeheartedly supported a more formal role for Canada in the Caribbean as a way to fight "yankee imperialism" in the world and especially the Americas.[116] One of Saltsman's constituents urged that Canada should swiftly absorb the Turks and Caicos Islands "before the United States takes them over as they did the Hawaiian Islands, and the way they will take us over if we don't 'Smarten Up'... Let's unite together, and stand up for our rights, instead of being dominated by another country."[117] There would be obstacles to overcome, a Saskatchewan woman conceded, but the historic dream of "winning the West for Canada 100 years ago" had met with obstacles too. The men of that era, she continued, had the foresight and determination to foil American designs on the Northwest.[118] It was time once again to resist the republic's expansionist tendencies.

In typical fashion, this anti-Americanism fuelled assertions of Canada's superiority and benevolent approach to the developing world. The idea that Canada needed to save the Turks and Caicos Islands from American invasion appeared in more than a few letters. "Any place on earth is better served by the British way of life than the American," a Vancouver Island woman declared. "A place policed by the R.C.M.P. and served by the Canadian judiciary would be a happier place than one given over to the Mafia and the American style of corruption."[119] A Quebec man who travelled regularly in the Caribbean concluded that Americans were "distorting the minds of the natives with their immoral, excessive, and glutinous [*sic*] behavior. I never saw so many fat pigs (from USA) in my life. They will sink the islands with numbers (of people) + garbage + rotten behaviour." He made his recommendation plain: "Get the islands for us, then make sure that the Americans & their money don't get in, or = ruinous results."[120] Another BC writer was optimistic that Canada, unlike the "big and rarely benevolent big Brother in the South," would proceed in good will and negotiate a mutually complementary arrangement.[121]

This optimism and the wave of national excitement that Saltman's bill aroused did not echo in official circles, nor among Black Canadians and New Left activists. The Foreign and Commonwealth Office (FCO) had been suspicious of Liam Maguire's declarations of widespread support in the TCI, which their governor, Alex Mitchell, confirmed in February 1974. According to Mitchell, Maguire's campaign was one of "wilful misrepresentation." The expatriate's vague statements about the benefits of a "Canadian connection" had generated much perfunctory support, but there remained "a core of doubt among more perceptive members of the community."[122] Officials in the FCO were not opposed to a TCI-Canada association but assumed that it was a non-starter – an idea Ottawa would speedily lay to rest. Their main concern was that the union buzz was diverting attention away from the negotiation of constitutional reforms in the Turks and Caicos, ongoing in the early months of 1974.[123] The FCO thus encouraged Canada's Department of External Affairs to issue a statement that would "discourage the Islanders from chasing moonbeams" and focus their attention on the next stages of constitutional development and independence.[124]

External Affairs did not disappoint. In a statement to the House on 15 April, Secretary of State Mitchell Sharp quashed the idea, as he had five years earlier. There was little evidence, he maintained, that a constitutional association would benefit either Canada or the Turks and Caicos Islands. The complications would be extensive, reaching into several areas – taxation, tariffs, defence, immigration, and the relations of Canada and the TCI with the wider Caribbean region. Canada would ultimately introduce a "destabilizing influence" in the region by effectively "fencing off" and financially favouring one region over its neighbours. "The problem of disparities between rich countries and poorer ones," Sharp insisted, "must be solved through co-operation, within regions and among regions." It was, moreover, the appropriate approach to development in a decolonizing world. Political and constitutional arrangements were not the solution to national economic inequalities, arrangements that could, in Sharp's words, "be represented as neo-colonial."[125]

External Affairs' official statement probably did not surprise unionists, as Sharp had already disparaged the idea publicly. On 25 January, two weeks after Saltsman introduced his bill, Sharp addressed the union question on a national radio program. No matter the political, economic, or constitutional terms of the arrangement between Canada and the Turks and Caicos Islands, he insisted, Canada would inevitably be accused of neo-colonialism. His thinking was consistent with his department's scepticism about the rectitude of similar international arrangements in which imperial states, such as Portugal and formerly France, had rebranded their colonies as overseas provinces or *départements* of the nation. The international community looked askance at these kinds of arrangements and had for some time. Support for Saltsman's proposal in Ottawa would not only raise suspicions about Canadian motives, Sharp cautioned, but would compromise Canada's image as a nation untainted by colonialism: "We do not have any colonies and Canadians would not want to."[126]

Pierre Trudeau reportedly said much the same thing in early February. Canada, he told the press, was "not a colonialist country."[127] The prime minister was no doubt unmoved by (and probably disinterested in) the argument that union with the TCI would bolster Canadian nationalism. Aside from its "colonialist" concerns, Trudeau's union rebuke was probably based on two main considerations. At least three Caribbean leaders – Barbados' Errol Barrow, the Bahamas' Lynden Pindling, and Jamaica's Michael Manley – advised Trudeau against the idea, no doubt reminding him that such an arrangement would contravene the principle of self-determination and regional integration initiatives in the Caribbean.[128] More importantly, an association with the TCI might boost sovereigntist forces in Quebec. While for New Democrats and Conservatives, Canada's greatest threat was the United States, for Trudeau and many Liberals, it was Quebec sovereignty. In the late 1960s, the prime minister's aloof response to the humanitarian crisis in Nigeria in the wake of a secessionist insurrection in the province of Biafra spoke volumes about his preoccupation with the secessionist threat within Canadian borders.[129] By the time that Saltsman introduced his bill, the violence and social turmoil generated by the separatist movement's militant fringe – most notably the Front de libération du Québec (FLQ) – had long dissipated. But the Parti Québécois (PQ), a moderate channel of the sovereigntist movement, was slowly gaining ground. In the provincial election of 1973, the PQ won 30 per cent of the popular vote (up from 24 per cent) and became the official opposition in the national assembly. While its leader, Réne Lévesque, failed to win a seat, his growing popularity was unmistakable.[130] These were all worrisome developments for Trudeau, who clearly understood that entertaining the Turks and Caicos question, even cursorily, could undermine the existing federation.

Trudeau's insistence that Canada was "not a colonialist country" reflected a broader current of thought within the Liberal Party. Several parliamentarians cautioned that Canada's absorption of the TCI would undermine Canada's reputation as an impartial international interlocutor free of colonialist impulses.[131] Responding to Senator Hazen Argue's efforts to rally support for a Canada-TCI union in the upper house, Senator Jean-Paul Deschatelets stated, "I am so convinced of the importance of the image that Canada has succeeded in projecting in developing countries, the image of a disinterested Canada, free of any colonialist spirit, that I would apprehend problems that would certainly arise for us if we were to embark in this new venture put forward in Senator Argue's resolution."[132] Like many Canadians, Deschatelets understood colonialism in a particular and narrow way: as a metropolitan state's unequal, exploitative relationship with territorial dependencies that were external or non-contiguous to the state's "logical" or "natural" boundaries. Liberal MP Claude-André Lachance made this distinction plain in opposing union with the TCI. He repeated the familiar contention that Canada had "reached the logical limits of its territorial development" when Newfoundland joined Confederation in 1949, thus completing the historic vision expressed in section 146 of the BNA Act. "The time when one could take possession of non-contiguous territories, an effective way to determine what we call colonialism, even with the consent of its inhabitants, is gone once and for all."[133] To be sure, these claims of Canadian righteousness belied the historic and continuing salience of colonialism within the country's borders. They also obscured the substance of Canadian involvement in the Caribbean. Tied aid, exploitative corporations, inadequate consultation with Caribbean stakeholders, and immigration policies that poached the region's professional and educated classes perpetuated conditions of dependency and hindered economic self-sufficiency in the region.

Another version of this myth of Canadian innocence flowed from an emerging multicultural policy in Ottawa. The changing demographic of Canadian society postwar (further diversified by the immigration reforms of the 1960s), the irrelevance of Canadian biculturalism to a growing population of Canadians who were neither French nor British, the rights activism of Indigenous and other racialized Canadians, and the rise of Quebecois nationalism compelled Trudeau to declare multiculturalism official policy in 1971.[134] The government approved a Multicultural Directorate within the Department of State in 1972, created a Ministry of Multiculturalism the following year, and would introduce a new Immigration Act in 1976 that reiterated the government's commitment to multicultural principles. Some Canadians who supported union harnessed the emerging discourse of multiculturalism generated by these developments. In an age when multiculturalism was the norm, observed a York Region man, surely "we would not be making a mistake to add one more link to our democratic chain."[135] Canadians would readily accept Turks and Caicos islanders, a Saltsman constituent argued, because Canada was a mixture of many different people.[136] Their culture, stated another, would only enrich Canada's multiculturalism.[137]

References to multiculturalism and the increased diversity of Canadian society as a way to negate concerns about racial animosity or conflict under union were problematic because they did not reflect the lived reality of Black people in Canada. They were part of a broader and continuing obfuscation of anti-blackness that was (and is) facilitated by what Rinaldo Walcott aptly calls the "multicultural con-game."[138] Despite the introduction of a multicultural policy – and the incremental gains in civil and human rights between the Bill of Rights in 1960 and the Charter of Rights and Freedoms in 1982 – Blacks and other racialized Canadians continued to suffer racial discrimination in all aspects of society.[139]

In light of this discrimination and the network of transnational solidarities that brought Third World struggles for self-determination into Canada's political discourse, Black Canadian support for union was difficult to find. Canada's absorption of the TCI was, for those Black Canadians who did weigh in on the question, a bad idea. Three central concerns guided their critiques: the injustices that Black people continued to experience in Canada, the exploitative record of Canadian corporations in the Caribbean, and the violation of self-determination that the proposed union represented. "I am wondering if these people [in the islands] are aware of what Canada is [today]," ruminated a Nova Scotia man in a letter to Saltsman. "These people are seeking respect, and kindness ... do you truly feel that they will acquire what they are seeking[?] Will they be considered as just a few thousand Blacks, or be accepted as British subjects[?]" The former was more likely, he lamented, particularly under the administration of Canada's two main political parties. A Liberal or Tory government in office "could only treat the new comers as they treat the Coloured Canadians who are now in Canada, belonging to Canada. Maybe you will not see it as I do, by reason you are not coloured. I see conditions in this light ... I have served Canada in peace and war, and I have a very bitter taste in my mouth."[140] The ubiquity of this racial prejudice against Black people in Canada, warned Ryerson journalism student Ken Thomas, foreshadowed an unhappy existence for Islanders under union. They would be subject to oppression far worse than that meted out by Britain. Let the British continue to rule, he argued: it was "the lesser of two evils."[141] Union with Canada would not serve the interests of most of the TCI people, argued another critic in *Black Voice*, because it was nothing more than an exchange of one imperial master for another. The Montreal monthly found it a disturbing contradiction that an NDP member of Parliament – "who is supposed to be a socialist" – was encouraging Canadian imperialism in the Caribbean.[142]

Black Canadian critics understood too well that Canada's absorption of the TCI flew in the face of decolonization. That this bore repeating in 1974 was, for some, a source of frustration and regret. It reflected an ignorance of the historic and continuing struggles of colonial peoples and the pernicious persistence of white paternalism. As one critic writing under the name Akua outlined in February 1974, "Over the last three decades, the world has witnessed a change in the relationship between the colonists and the colonized which has led to violent revolution in some neo-colonial countries, as these populations demand and continually struggle for freedom, ultimate self determination and self reliance." The union proposal represented a failure to confront this history, to recognize and respect "the truth of a colonial people."[143] In this way, the proposal was not an aberration in Canada's otherwise progressive, enlightened approach to the world: it was one more episode in a repertoire of international misbehaviour. For Black activists, it could be counted among the many disheartening examples of Canadian conduct in 1974 alone: Ottawa's purchase of commodities farmed by enslaved Africans; its trade preferences for apartheid South Africa; its reluctance to sufficiently condemn the endemic violence white minorities perpetrated on Black Africans throughout southern Africa; its failure to take a stronger stand in NATO and demand an end to Portugal's violent grip on Angola, Mozambique, and Guinea-Bissau; and its failure to speak out against South Africa's illegal occupation of Namibia. In peeling back the veneer of Canadian benevolence abroad, Black activists also detailed the predatory and exploitative conduct of Canadian mining corporations in southern Africa, fuelled in some cases by labour practices "akin to slavery."[144] Canada's policies, *Contrast* observed, were "shot through with contradictions, and instead of winning friends, however lukewarm, the present Canadian practice of waffling and of making self righteous statements while doing no positively righteous thing" served only to lose friends.[145]

In the 1970s, many progressive white Canadians were similarly critical of instances in which Canada reaped colonialism's benefits or abetted colonialism abroad through inaction. It was thus not surprising that many union detractors were driven by a commitment to global justice and a corresponding aversion to relationships with a colonial or imperial flavour. Many doubted that the TCI would enter confederation on a basis of equality and maintain control over its resources. As an Ottawa woman lamented in a letter to Saltsman, the people of the Turks and Caicos would surely "become tenants to foreign owners in their own country."[146] One of his constituents came to the same conclusion: "Who owns and controls the sea-side developments and tourist areas of Hawaii, Jamaica, Barbados and Nassau? (The great white developer)"; meanwhile, the locals "live in ghettos."[147] Would "this not in effect be one 'colonial' administrator replacing another?" asked a student working in the

Caribbean with Canadian University Services Overseas (CUSO).[148] Turks and Caicos islanders needed only to consult the Métis, Inuit, and First Nations to "see how far their influence will go in Ottawa," warned another writer. The many powerful interests in the Caribbean would certainly not allow Canada to "upset the economic applecart."[149] Others pointed to Caribbean nationalisms and decolonization as reasons enough to reject Saltsman's proposal. As one of his constituents put it, "The time of building empires is gone."[150]

Conclusion

Nationalism and decolonization were salient forces on multiple fronts within and without Canada in the 1960s and '70s. Canadian efforts to formalize the country's presence in the Caribbean were not easily reconciled with these forces. While the economic nationalism that surged in the wake of Canadians' expanded consciousness about the extent of US foreign investment in their country inspired unionism (as an admittedly small abatement of US influence), it was difficult to square it with an initiative that would see Canadians dominate Caribbean economies. Canada's postwar nationalism, further unmoored in the 1960s and '70s from its British Empire and Commonwealth roots, was incompatible with an arrangement that would see Canada absorb one of the fragments of Britain's former empire. The threat to Confederation posed by Quebec nationalism and the rise of separatism in particular made the proposal for a new Caribbean province or territory inopportune and politically dangerous.

The persistence of unionism and the ongoing denial of Canada's colonialist proclivities into the 1970s were remarkable in the context of the increasingly organized resistance to white Canadian encroachments at home and abroad. Black Power activists mobilized a formidable resistance to white Canadians' racialized, exploitative conduct in Canada and in the Caribbean. At the same time, Canada's Indigenous peoples organized political bodies at the provincial and national level to more effectively assert Indigenous title and negotiate land claims, resist or control the course of settler development projects, establish political sovereignty, and later, in 1982, entrench their rights in the Canadian constitution. In the midst of this activism and what were often widely publicized confrontations between racialized people and the state or private corporations within and beyond Canadian borders – from the George Williams affair to the attacks on Canadian property in Trinidad to the protracted confrontation between James Bay Cree and the Quebec government – the persistent denial of Canadian colonialism, past and present, is confounding. It begs the question: What sustained and continues to sustain such ignorance for so long? The answer has long been apparent to Indigenous peoples and other racialized groups. White settler societies like Canada have been unwilling to adequately confront their histories of colonialism and racial exclusion because these histories challenge the legitimacy and supremacy of white Canadian power and the circumstances under which the nation was founded.[151]

Making the case for union in the 1970s – despite the best intentions of its proponents – signalled an inadequate reckoning with Canada's complicity in the long histories of white supremacy and colonialism that produced rampant poverty and underdevelopment in the Caribbean. Settler Canadians generally supported decolonization and the right to self-determination, yet many had not confronted the capitalist impulses and racialized worldview that enabled colonialism to endure, nor the scope and depth of the inequalities it produced. The fashioning of multicultural Canada and the steadfast embrace of the country's international image as a helpful fixer, impartial interlocutor, and benevolent benefactor of foreign aid hindered this reckoning in the 1970s. So too did the continued dominance of Eurocentric historical narratives in Canadian public schools touting the progressive virtues of British imperialism while whitewashing or silencing racialized peoples' experiences.[152] Also significant was the continued tendency in Canada and other wealthy, industrialized nations to discount colonialism's role in Third World underdevelopment. Despite a growing body of work to the contrary, most notably Walter Rodney's *How Europe Underdeveloped Africa*, published in 1972, a reluctance to implicate colonialism in this underdevelopment and the world's vastly uneven distribution of wealth endured.[153] The assumption that external (white) intervention was fundamental to Third World development persisted. In the postwar decades, the language of racial superiority shifted – *uncivilized* became *underdeveloped; backward peoples* became *the Third World* – and the thinking that sustained it unravelled.[154] Notions of global justice were no longer linked to the idea of a civilizing British Empire, but they could not be wholly disentangled from this inheritance, from the understanding that capitalism, human rights and other progressive values were Western concepts to be conveyed to the decolonizing world.[155] There was a heartfelt distaste of racial thinking and a genuine commitment to equality, but a deeply rooted paternalism and a stubborn empire apologism survived.

Conclusion

A DREAM UNFULFILLED

True to form, the union idea did not expire in the 1970s. It was a subject of parliamentary and public debate in 1981 amidst renewed discussions about Turks and Caicos' independence in London and Cockburn Town.[1] Five years later, a delegation from Oshawa's Conservative Association again promoted union at the Progressive Conservative National Convention in Montreal. Led by insurance broker and former Oshawa city councillor John Dehart, the delegates distributed an "annexation manifesto" at the convention and presented a union resolution at a foreign policy workshop chaired by External Affairs Minister Joe Clark.[2] The Department of External Affairs validated Dehart's efforts in May 1986 when it conducted a brief study of the union question. Its conclusions, however, were discouraging, for familiar reasons. Union would be too expensive, thwart ongoing regional integration initiatives in the Caribbean, compromise Canada's bilateral relations with other Caribbean nations, possibly lead to racial tension on the islands as well-to-do white Canadians "flocked south to be served by the new, but still poor, black Canadians," and open Canada to charges of neo-imperialism.[3]

In 1987, the Conservative MP for Winnipeg, Dan McKenzie, generated sufficient interest among Tory MPs to establish a five-member parliamentary committee to study the pros and cons of a constitutional association with the Turks and Caicos Islands. Senators Hazen Argue and Heath Macquarrie, union stalwarts in the 1970s, revived the proposal in the upper chamber.[4] Journalists, politicians, and intellectuals weighed in, and constituent letters poured into MP offices. A small, Toronto-based group founded the Turks and Caicos Islands Research and Development Corporation to promote both Canadian investment in and association with the islands.[5] Over the course of three months, the Tory committee interviewed politicians, business people, and union lobbyists in Canada and the islands, as well as External Affairs officials. Its report, released in September 1987, echoed the same concerns the department had outlined the previous year. The committee also worried that an association with the TCI would complicate efforts to negotiate Quebec's constitutional future, which Prime Minister Brian Mulroney revived at Meech Lake at the end of April 1987. Neither Quebec's status nor the spectre of neo-colonialist charges deterred Conservative MP Sinclair Stevens, who surveyed his York-Peel constituents on union with the TCI in 1988. Of the 995 responses he received, 92 per cent said Canada should take up the question in Britain and the TCI, and 84 per cent said an association "would not amount to a return to colonialism."[6] With insufficient interest in Ottawa and Cockburn Town, however, the issue was a non-starter.

There was little discussion of union in the 1990s, aside from the occasional lament over the failed efforts of past unionists and some satirical suggestions about the need to have the TCI on the ready if Quebec seceded.[7] The idea gained traction once again in the early twenty-first century when Alliance (later Conservative) MP Peter Goldring championed it for over a decade. Private and public interest groups from Vancouver to Halifax lobbied the federal government. Nova Scotia's provincial parliament passed a resolution to explore union, and Canadian MPs visited the islands to stir up support. Two Ottawa executives launched a (now defunct) website, aplaceinthesun.ca, that encouraged Canadians to write to their MPs in support of "annexation."[8] Union proposals returned to the headlines in 2009 when the UK government seized control of the Turks and Caicos' government in the wake of corruption allegations, in 2014 when TCI premier Rufus Ewing visited Ottawa, in 2016 when a resolution to consider union was put forward at the NDP convention in Edmonton, and in 2017 when the NDP member for Regina, Erin Weir, created an online survey to solicit Canadian opinion on the question.[9]

The persistence of the union idea since the 1860s and the regional, political, and professional diversity of its proponents are difficult to dismiss. Union's allure was not limited to Maritime fishermen, Montreal businessmen, nor Toronto sun seekers. Enthusiasts were intellectuals, civil servants, politicians, teachers, lawyers, business people, writers, bankers, doctors, students, and tourists. They were Conservative, Liberal, and, from the 1960s, New Democrat. They hailed from big cities and small towns from Victoria to Halifax. They were principally English speakers of British descent, although many French-speaking Canadians promoted union or were open to exploring the idea. Some were well familiar with the British Caribbean, having commercial, familial, or tourist ties to the region, while others would have struggled to locate the Caribbean on a map.

Most understood union as a political or constitutional association, although the terms of association were much contested. Some favoured a customs union only, or saw a customs arrangement as a stepping-stone to a future political association. The territory on which they focused varied from a single colony (Jamaica in the 1880s, the Bahamas in the 1910s, British Guiana in the 1920s, the Turks and Caicos in the 1970s) to territorial groupings (the "Little Eight" islands of the eastern Caribbean in the 1960s) to more ambitious plans to annex the British Caribbean as a whole. Some unionists travelled extensively in Canada, the Caribbean, and the UK conducting research and promoting their agenda. Some drafted detailed plans for union that included everything from post-office revenues to the administration of penitentiaries. Others were armchair imperialists who wrote longingly about a "tropical Canada" without considering the practical implications. Sometimes their campaigns sustained media attention for a year or two; at other times, their efforts attracted interest in intermittent bursts over the course of two, five, or ten years. Sometimes union was front-page news, at other times buried several pages deep. When it did emerge, it almost always crossed national boundaries. It was a subject of considerable debate in the Caribbean and the UK.

Unionism tells us much about Canada's history, despite – and because of – its failure. Unionists were a disparate, ever-changing bunch who took up the idea with varied interests and intensity, but they had much in common. In contemplating Canada's economic development, sovereignty, and purpose in the world, they looked to the Caribbean. They were preoccupied with Canada's lack of climatic variation and were convinced that the country's economic independence and continued growth hinged on unrestrained access to the tropics. They believed that taking on formal responsibilities in the Caribbean would boost Canada's autonomy and stature in the Empire-Commonwealth, temper American power, and enhance Canada's international profile. Their campaigns reiterate the enduring significance of Britain and the United States to Canada's engagement with the world, while pointing to a new way in which Canadians negotiated these relationships. The North Atlantic context of Canada's becoming was deeply entwined with the Caribbean.

Dominion over Palm and Pine joins the growing body of studies that have reclaimed Canada's role as an imperial actor in its own right, a role long muffled by Canada's own subjugation in the British and American empires.[10] While considerable work has focused on the post-1945 period, a reconceptualization of imperialism in the first half of the twentieth century, one that takes for granted Canada's active role in a capitalist world system, is long overdue. Our understanding of Canadian imperialism, particularly before the First World War, continues to be based on the seminal work of Carl Berger, who characterized Canadian imperialism as "one variety of Canadian nationalism."[11] To be an imperialist or imperial-minded Canadian generally meant you were a proud British subject with an abiding faith in the empire's purpose to bring order, enlightenment, and civilization to the world. Imperialists furthered British principles and the cause of empire at home and abroad: they pushed westward to the Pacific and connected the empire along the All Red Route, supported imperial commerce, privileged British immigrants above all others, and sent soldiers abroad to defend British values. Many – perhaps most – Canadians of British descent identified themselves as imperialists in these terms well into the middle decades of the twentieth century. To be sure, British-Canadian sentiment for the empire was a powerful force in Canadian society. But the enduring tendency to reduce Canadian imperialism to a sentiment or identity – "Britishness" – risks minimizing histories of aggrandizement within and beyond Canada's borders.[12] The Canadian quest for territory in the Caribbean underscores the need to interrogate other "varieties" of imperialism in the period before the Second World War. While British identity and empire cohesion were important to early unionists, they were only part of the story.

The pursuit of a Canadian Caribbean reminds us that US power could be inspiring as well as domineering. Characterizations of Canada as a nation in America's shadow, as an "errand boy" or "semi-colony," elide the envy and spirit of rivalry that US imperialism often stimulated in Canada. Indeed, US expansion was a perennial impetus for union. Unionists believed that America's push across the continent during the course of the nineteenth century, its debut as a global imperial power in the wake of the Spanish-American War, and the widening scope of its imperial engagements in the twentieth century positioned the republic in a privileged and enviable position among nations. It was no coincidence that unionism emerged soon after the United States seized Cuba and Puerto Rico in 1898, intervened in Haiti and the Dominican Republic and purchased the Danish Virgin Islands during the First World War; and contemplated absorbing Britain's Caribbean colonies in payment of its war debt. As America's Caribbean presence continued to expand amidst the strategic concerns of the Cold War, unionists rallied again, though many did so in a spirit of both geopolitical cooperation and commercial rivalry.

Unionism was implicated in imperial and hemispheric concerns, but in many ways it was a global story too. In the late nineteenth and early twentieth centuries, Canadian designs on the Caribbean were part of the expansionist fever sweeping the globe. Europe's scramble for Africa, Antipodean designs on the South Pacific, and American exploits in Hawaii and the Philippines, Cuba, and Puerto Rico stimulated a preoccupation with the commercial potential of tropical regions and galvanized Canadian interest in the Caribbean. The union idea often loomed up in the midst of weighty geopolitical developments: Germany's challenge to British naval and industrial supremacy in the early twentieth century, (anticipation of) the Panama Canal's opening in 1914, the redistribution of former German colonies during and immediately following the First World War, the shift in global power from Europe to America and Soviet Russia after 1945, decolonization, and the threat of global communism. Moreover, unionism was born in and nourished by a global cadre of self-styled "white men's countries" and was challenged, again and again, by an evolving, global community of Black activists.

The history of union foregrounds the centrality of race to Canada's international history.[13] Unionists' shared vision in the Caribbean derived its meaning from Canada's asymmetrical and deeply racialized relationships within and beyond the country's borders. Their designs on the Caribbean were one strategy in a broader repertoire of settler Canadian efforts to secure Canada's privileged position in a capitalist world system that generated and sustained uneven power relations between metropoles and colonies on the one hand and between colonies on the other. The same sense of entitlement, nurtured since slavery, animated their varied impulses to intervene in the Caribbean, avail themselves of the region's resources, and dictate the terms on which Caribbean peoples' would inhabit the new union.

The white supremacist logic that fuelled this entitlement was central to union's recurring failure. It was a resilient logic that adapted to evolving settler priorities, African-Caribbean struggles for self-determination, the decline of imperialism and the rise of human rights as normative aspects of international relations, and decolonization. Union was hopelessly incompatible with the settler state's commitment to a white Canada from Confederation through most of the twentieth century, compelling unionists to devise strategies to keep African Caribbeans at a physical and political distance. Well into the 1950s, unionists wielded pseudo-science about Canada's climatic unsuitability for peoples of African descent – codified in the country's immigration legislation – to reassure white Canadians that union would not prompt a Black influx into Canada. They relied on the tenets of racial liberalism, casting African-Caribbean peoples astern in a temporalizing universalism that allowed them to circumscribe African-Caribbean rights and rationalize Canadian intervention in the region. This latter strategy was not viable after 1945, at least not explicitly. Race continued to order international relations, but in the shifting postwar order marked by decolonization, racial justice movements, and the growing diversity of the world's councils, it lost its rhetorical purchase. Unionists de-emphasized race and reframed their designs as a Commonwealth obligation and a geopolitical priority, yet racial paternalism prevailed in their failure to conceive Caribbean independence as either practical or imperative. Unionism's persistence into the 1970s reflected the continued salience of race-thinking and an unfulfilled reckoning with colonialism and its legacies.

Caribbean peoples were often the first to point out the impracticality and distastefulness of union campaigns in the context of white Canadian racism. They situated their union critiques in the racial and colonial indignities of particular historical moments, from the virulent assault on Black immigration in 1910–11 and the markedly different wartime experiences of Canada's white and Black servicemen to the interwar trials of African-Caribbean workers on Canadian National Steamships, the exploitative conduct of Canadian corporations in the Caribbean, and the Sir George Williams University affair. Whether through the Black press, labour organizations and protective associations, missive protests to London and Ottawa, or physical demonstrations in Montreal and Port of Spain, the message was the same: white Canadian racism made union repugnant and even absurd. While some African-Caribbean planters and merchants entertained union in the late nineteenth and early twentieth centuries, from the interwar period Black interest in union was increasingly difficult to find. White racism was a continuing source of offence, but the growing momentum for self-determination and independence in the Caribbean was more decisive in scuttling union.

As the union idea continues to pop up year after year, it is worth reflecting on its colonial roots. Contemporary iterations are uncomfortably familiar. Union is regarded as a benevolent Canadian overture, a mutually beneficial scheme that will rescue Caribbean peoples from their stagnant economies and finally give Canada "a place in the sun." How such arguments escape critical scrutiny are important questions. Why is the language of "annexing" Caribbean islands still used in the twenty-first century? How is it that articles with headlines such as "Canada's Caribbean Ambition," "Should Canada Adopt Turks and Caicos as Its 11th Province?" and "Will We Finally Get Our Islands in the Sun?" are still published by major Canadian news outlets?[14] The answers lie in the national mythologies that continue to shape our understandings of Canada's history and role in the world. As a *Washington Times* correspondent put it in August 2019, "Canadian proposals to absorb new territories usually have an air of whimsy to them, but it's a playfulness rooted in a chauvinistic assumption that Canada is a country of such self-evident goodness and purity, virtually anything it could imagine doing in the realm of foreign policy would be morally justifiable."[15] To be sure, presumptions of Canadian morality and goodness have justified unionist designs since the nineteenth century. More often, though, those who hold such idealistic notions of Canada respond to the union idea with humour, wonder, or disbelief.

In 1987, long-time unionist Heath Macquarrie told the Senate he was perplexed as to why the union idea frequently elicited amusement. "I do not remember anyone ha, hah, hahing about Newfoundland joining Canada," he said.[16] The difference, as Macquarrie was probably aware, was a function of white assumptions about how Canada – as an idea – was racially and geographically constituted. Newfoundlanders were perceived as white, their territory was contiguous to Canada, and their entry was long anticipated and "natural." African Caribbeans, on the other hand, were seen as racially and geographically remote. With the shifting demographic and ideological contours of Canadian society over the past several decades – the country's substantial populations of African and African-Caribbean descent, the legal and cultural import of multiculturalism, and settler Canadians' nascent reckoning with the country's histories of colonialism and racism – one might expect the satirical hold of a Canadian Caribbean to have evaporated. Yet over the many years in which I prepared this book, sharing my research in myriad contexts across Canada and abroad, I frequently encountered confused or surprised expressions, sometimes laughter. Canadians wanted to annex Jamaica? What? Really? Not Canada! Scholars and activists have long challenged whitewashed images of Canada as the beacon of racial egalitarianism at home and the moral superpower abroad, but the extent to which these critiques have resonated in the broader public consciousness is questionable. If they had resonated more broadly, the union idea and its capacity to amuse would have disappeared long ago. Talk of a Canadian Caribbean elicits laughter because it is seen as antithetical to Canada. As I hope this book has demonstrated, unionism was not a novelty or aberration in Canadian history. It was a phenomenon that cohered with the imperial impulses on which Canada was founded, subsequently developed, and continues to flourish.

NOTES

Introduction

1 Amor De Cosmos, "Union of the Dominion of Canada with the British West Indies," *Victoria Daily Standard*, 9 March 1871.

2 The idea continues to attract media attention. See, for example, Ishaan Tharoor, "Canada's Strange Quest for Its Own Hawaii," *Washington Post* (online), 8 April 2016; "Some Canadians Still Want Turks and Caicos to Become Canada's 11th Province," *Narcity*, 18 July 2018; Michael Hiscock, "Why Making the Turks and Caicos Our 11th Province Is a Horrible Idea," *Loop*, 6 April 2019.

3 On the history of Canadian banking and commercial enterprises in the Caribbean in the late nineteenth and early twentieth centuries, see Duncan McDowall, *Quick to the Frontier*; Neil Quigley, "Bank of Nova Scotia in the Caribbean"; Christopher Armstrong and H.V. Nelles, *Southern Exposure*; R.A. Shields, "Canada, The Foreign Office and the Caribbean Market"; Peter Newman, "Canada's Role in West Indian Trade before 1912."

4 On industrial labourers in Nova Scotia, see Elizabeth Beaton, "An African-American Community in Cape Breton." On sleeping-car porters, see Sarah-Jane Mathieu, *North of the Color Line*. On farmers on the prairies, see Katrina Vernon, "Black Civility"; Bruce Shepard, *Deemed Unsuitable*. On domestic workers, see Agnes Calliste, "Race, Gender and Canadian Immigration Policy."

5 Kari Levitt and Alister McIntyre, *Canada-West Indies Economic Relations*, 24.

6 G. Glazebrook, DEA memorandum, 5 February 1962, and Commonwealth division memorandum to Glazebrook, 6 March 1962, LAC, RG 25, G-2, vol. 3322, file 10824-A-40, pt. 5.

7 Subsequent aid contributions were made by way of the Canadian International Development Agency, established in 1968.

8 Levitt and McIntyre, *Canada-West Indies Economic Relations*, 24; Statistics Canada, CANSIM table 427-0004, accessed 5 May 2021, https://www150. statcan.gc.ca/n1/pub/11-630-x/11-630-x2017001-eng.htm; Statistics Canada, *Travel between Canada and Other Countries* [various years (1946 to 1971)].

9 James W. St G. Walker, *West Indians in Canada*, 9.

10 Charmaine Nelson, *Slavery, Geography, and Empire in Nineteenth-Century Marine Landscapes of Montreal and Jamaica*, 3–6. Catherine Beaudette, "Bonavista Biennale," 81–2. On slavery in Canada, see also Marcel Trudel, *L'esclavage au Canada français*; Afua Cooper, *Hanging of Angelique*, 7–11; Harvey Amani Whitfield, *North to Bondage*; Ken Donovan, "Slavery and Freedom in Atlantic Canada's African Diaspora," 110; Maureen G. Elgersman, *Unyielding Spirits*. On the building of slave ships in Newfoundland, see Camille Turner, Bonavista Biennale 2019, accessed 20 September 2020, https://bonavistabiennale.com/catalogue/artists/camille-turner/.

11 Canada, 1911 Census, as cited in "A Hundred Years of Immigration to Canada," Canadian Council for Refugees, accessed 11 September 2020, https://ccrweb.ca/en/hundred-years-immigration-canada-1900-1999; James C. Saku, "Aboriginal Census Data in Canada," 370. Of course, as Saku observes, p. 365, this census data should be interpreted cautiously, recognizing that there are significant structural and administrative problems in the collection of this data.

12 F.R. Augier, *Making of the West Indies*, 91.

13 In the nineteenth century, the Cayman Islands were a Jamaican dependency, and the Turks and Caicos Islands were administered by the Bahamas and later Jamaica.

14 K.O. Laurence, *A Question of Labour*; Lomarsh Roopnarine, *Indo-Caribbean Indenture*; Walton Look Lai, *Indentured Labor, Caribbean Sugar*.

15 Patrick E. Bryan, *Jamaican People*, 67; G.W. Roberts, "Some Observations on the Population of British Guiana," 186. The Chinese population accounted for 0.9 per cent of British Guiana's total population.

16 Richard Eves, "Unsettling Settler Colonialism," 308–9.

17 Bridget Brereton, "White Elite of Trinidad"; Michael Craton, "Bay Street, Black Power"; Patrick Bryan, "White Minority in Jamaica."

18 On the different ways that Canada and Jamaica were integrated into the global economy, see Jenny Burman, *Transnational Yearnings*, 26–9.

19 Thomas C. Holt, *Problem of Freedom*, 233–43.

20 Ibid., 307–9. Catherine Hall, *Civilising Subjects*. See also Uday Singh Mehta, *Liberalism and Empire*.

21 See, for example, Paula Hastings, "'Our Glorious Anglo-Saxon Race.'"

22 India was represented at the Imperial War Conferences (and in the Imperial War Cabinet) in 1917–18 and at the imperial conferences in the interwar

period, but representation beyond the "white dominions" was otherwise scarce. A representative of Southern Rhodesia (Zimbabwe) attended the Imperial Economic Conference in Ottawa in 1932, and Southern Rhodesia and Burma (Myanmar) were represented at the Imperial Conference of 1937.

23 I borrow the concept of a "project of rule" from Ian McKay, "Liberal Order Framework," and take up David Meren's call in "Tragedies of Canadian International History" to reflect on the international manifestations of this project.

24 See, for example, Doug Owram, *Promise of Eden*; Morris Zaslow, *Northward Expansion of Canada*; Berger, *Sense of Power*. Berger briefly mentions Canadian interest in a political connection with the British Caribbean in the context of his discussion of the Canada First movement in the 1870s (71).

25 On the intersections of sovereignty and colonialism, see Partha Chatterjee, *Nationalist Thought and the Colonial World*; Michael Hardt and Antonio Negri, *Empire*; Antony Anghie, *Imperialism, Sovereignty and the Making of International Law*; Jonathan Elmer, *On Lingering and Being Last*; Edward Keene, *Beyond the Anarchical Society*. In the Canadian context, I draw from the rich body of postcolonial and anti-racist scholarship that underscores the constitutive function of exclusionary rhetoric and practices to Canada's national formation(s). As a starting place, see Eva Mackey, *House of Difference*; Himani Bannerji, *Dark Side of the Nation*; Sunera Thobani, *Exalted Subjects*.

26 Ikuko Asaka, *Tropical Freedom*, 7.

27 Felix Driver and Luciana Martins, "Views and Visions of the Tropical World," introduction to *Tropical Visions in an Age of Empire*, 14.

28 Mehta, *Liberalism and Empire*, 162.

29 Following philosopher Charles Mills, I contend that liberalism has "historically been predominantly a racial liberalism." See Mills, *Black Rights/ White Wrongs*, 29. On the racially exclusive history of the "liberal order" in the Canadian context, see Adele Perry, "Women, Racialized People, and the Making of the Liberal Order in Northern North America."

30 Daniel Gorman, "Race, the Commonwealth, and the United Nations," 140–1.

31 Barrington Walker, H-Diplo Roundtable 20–23.

32 David Webster, "Foreign Policy, Diplomacy, and Decolonization," 156.

33 The topic has been addressed in several articles, most of which focus on a short time frame, usually before 1921. These studies rely primarily on Canadian perspectives. I engage these studies, when relevant, in chapters 1 through 3. See Robin Winks, *Canadian-West Indian Union*; Alice Stewart, "Canadian-West Indian Union"; Brinsley Samaroo, "The Politics of Disharmony"; P.G. Wigley, "Canada and Imperialism"; Paula Hastings, "Territorial Spoils"; Andrew D. Smith, Thomas Bassett Macaulay and the

Bahamas"; Paula Hastings, "Rounding off the Confederation"; the subject
has also received marginal attention in larger narratives of Canadian-British
Caribbean relations, which include Trevor Carmichael, *Passport to the
Heart*, and Robert Chodos, *Caribbean Connection*. In general, the literature
that explores Canada's relationship with the British Caribbean focuses on
commerce and trade. See Brian Tennyson, "The British West Indies and
Mackenzie King's National Policy in the 1920s"; Quigley, "Bank of Nova
Scotia in the Caribbean"; Selwyn Carrington, "United States and Canada";
R.A. Shields, "Canada, The Foreign Office and the Caribbean Market";
Newman, "Canada's Role in West Indian Trade before 1912."

34 See, for example, David Webster, *Fire and the Full Moon*; John Price,
    Orienting Canada; Sean Mills, *A Place in the Sun*; Robin S. Gendron,
    Towards a Francophone Community; Ryan Touhey, *Conflicting Visions*; Laura
    Madokoro, Francine McKenzie, and David Meren, *Dominion of Race*; Karen
    Dubinsky, Sean Mills, and Scott Rutherford, *Canada and the Third World*;
    Robert Wright and Lana Wylie, *Our Place in the Sun*; Renisa Mawani, *Across
    Oceans of Law*; John Zucchi, *Mad Flight*; Eric Fillion, "Experiments in
    Cultural Diplomacy"; Paula Butler, *Colonial Extractions*; Todd Gordon and
    Jeffrey R. Webber, *Blood of Extraction*.

35 On the importance and possibilities of a multi-perspective approach
    to Canada's international history, see Meren, "Tragedies of Canadian
    International History," 562–5.

36 Marilyn Lake and Henry Reynolds. *Drawing the Global Colour Line*, 3, 6–7.
    See also Harold Winant, *The World Is a Ghetto*; Erika Lee, "'Yellow Peril,'" 545.

Chapter One

1   "Y.M.E.C. Association: Lecture by Mr. R.G. Haliburton," *Ottawa Citizen*,
    4 March 1871.

2   Robert Grant Haliburton, *Mr. Haliburton's Speech on the Young Men of the
    New Dominion; from the Ottawa Citizen, January 27, 1870*, Thomas Fisher
    Rare Book Library, University of Toronto.

3   Owram, *Promise of Eden*; Kenneth Coates, *Canada's Colonies*; Zaslow,
    Northward Expansion of Canada; Berger, *Sense of Power*.

4   Jane Burbank and Frederick Cooper, *Empires in World History*, 11, 50–77.

5   Alan MacEachern, "The Large and Lovelier Canada," 49.

6   As Indigenous studies scholar Adam Gaudry argues in "Fantasies of
    Sovereignty," these assumptions invalidate or ignore the Indigenous political
    authority and proprietary claims to land that pre-existed the imposition of
    white settler governance, thereby sustaining what he calls "the fantasy of
    sovereignty," 46–7.

7   Peter Price, *Questions of Order*, 50–77; Duncan Bell, *Idea of Greater Britain*.

8   Hastings, "'Our Glorious Anglo-Saxon Race,'" 92–110; Donald F. Warner, *Idea of Continental Union*.

9   William Foster, Charles Mair, Henry Morgan, and George Taylor Denison comprised the original membership of what would become Canada First. See David P. Gagan, "Relevance of 'Canada First'" and "William Alexander Foster."

10 Bonnie Huskins, "Robert Grant Haliburton."

11 Benjamin Pine, as cited in Haliburton, *Mr. Haliburton's Speech on the Young Men of the New Dominion*.

12 Alex W. Moir to Lieutenant-Governor Mundy (Tortola), June 1870, *Reports on the Present State of Her Majesty's Colonial Possessions*, transmitted with Blue Books for the Year 1870, Pt. 1, West Indies, c. 523, British Parliamentary Papers (London: W. Cloves & Sons, 1872), 155.

13 William A. Foster, *Canada First*, 8; Haliburton to Foster, 29 April 1878, William A. Foster Papers, Provincial Archives of Ontario, F70-MU1058, box B299654.

14 Berger, *Sense of Power*, 62–4.

15 Foster, *Canada First*, 8.

16 Berger, *Sense of Power*, 70, notes that Smith and Denison believed Foster wrote the platform, but Berger speculates that it may have been the work of several contributors. The other planks included electoral reform, immigration to the Northwest, tariffs and the promotion of domestic industry, and a strengthened militia under the leadership of Canadian officers.

17 Gagan, "William Alexander Foster"; Owram, *Promise of Eden*, 127–8.

18 These population estimates are based on census data from 1871. On Canada see Statistics Canada, CANSIM table 051-0001, accessed 15 March 2022, https://www150.statcan.gc.ca/n1/pub/11-402-x/2009/3867/tbl/cybac3867_2009_000_t01-eng.htm; on the British Caribbean see Juanita De Barros, *Reproducing the British Caribbean*, 46.

19 Patrick Wolfe, "Land Labor, and Difference," 867.

20 R.G. Haliburton to J.A. Macdonald, 7 October 1870, and Haliburton to Macdonald, 8 October 1870, LAC, MG 26-A, vol. 342; "By Telegraph," *Ottawa Daily Citizen*, 7 July 1870.

21 His critique of the "French question" intensified while in London, where he railed against the dangerous impact of ultramontanism in Canada and also in Europe. See Haliburton, "Queen and the United Empire," January 1874, LAC, MG29, E29, vol. 18, no. 51.

22 Haliburton, *Men of the North*, 10.

23 Ibid., 2.

24 Haliburton, "Black and Brown Landholders of Jamaica," 85.

25 Ibid., 85–7.

26 Norman Knowles, "George Taylor Denison."

27 George T. Denison, *Review of the Judgments of the Bench.*

28 Allan Levine, *Toronto: Biography of a City.* On Denison, see also James M. Pitsula, *Keeping Canada British*, 183.

29 On the periodical's ties to Canada First, see Gagan, "Canada First," 95.

30 "Current Events," *Canadian Monthly and National Review* 10, no. 5 (1876): 449–50.

31 "Current Events," *Canadian Monthly and National Review* 6, no. 4 (1874): 380.

32 "The West Indies," *Nation*, 12 November 1874.

33 *Bystander*, May 1881, 252.

34 James W. St G. Walker, "African Canadians," 142–5, 148. From 1628 to British Emancipation in 1834, hundreds of Africans and Indigenous peoples were enslaved in French and later British North America, though these numbers had declined considerably before Emancipation. Prior to the Conquest in 1760, there were approximately 1,400 African and 2,692 Indigenous slaves in New France. In addition to the loyalist migration after the American Revolutionary War, six hundred Jamaican Maroons were sent to Halifax in 1796. Prior to their relocation to Sierra Leone in 1800, they were put to work reinforcing the Halifax Citadel. On Black loyalists, see James W. St. G. Walker, *The Black Loyalists.*

35 Gagan, "William Alexander Foster." For a representative critique, see "Canada First," *Globe*, 9 January 1874. The depression marked a low point for immigration and a rise in emigration to the United States. As a result, in the 1870s and for much of the 1880s, population growth fell to little more than 1 per cent per year. Rapid urbanization and industrialization occurring in the United States, and the continuing availability of land in the American West in the 1870s and 1880s, led many immigrants to favour the American over the Canadian West. On this decline in population growth, see Jean-Claude Robert, "The People," 77–9.

36 J. Castell Hopkins, *Canada: An Encyclopedia of the Country*, vol. 1, 484.

37 On Jones's connection to Vogel, see Stewart, "Canadian-West Indian Union," 372.

38 "Agricultural Labourers," *Times* (London), 12 January 1875; "News from Canada," *Reynolds Newspaper*, 13 June 1875; "Another Colonization Scheme," *Winnipeg Free Press*, 8 February 1876.

39 Jones, letter to the editor, *Toronto Mail*, 3 June 1882.

40 Ibid.

41 Jones to Macdonald, 22 May 1883, Macdonald fonds, LAC, MG 26A, vol. 393.

42 Brian D. Tennyson, "Canada and the Commonwealth Caribbean," 4–7.

43 "Notes on the Admission of the British West Indies and British Guiana into the Dominion," enclosed in Jones to Macdonald, 2 August 1884, Macdonald fonds, LAC, MG 26A, vol. 393.

44 R.A. Shields, "Canada, the Foreign Office and the Caribbean Market," 703–4.

45 "The Jamaica Question," *Ottawa Free Press*, 28 August 1884.

46 "Jamaica and the Sugar Trade," *Morning Herald*, 30 August 1884.

47 See, for example, "The Jamaica Question," 2 August 1884, "The 'Hegemony' of Jamaica," 23 August 1884, and "The Jamaica Question," 2 September 1884, *Globe*; "The West Indies Crisis," 11 September 1884, and "The Jamaican Question," 15 September 1884, *Gazette* (Montreal); "West Indian Federation," *Journal of Commerce* 19, no. 7 (1884): 230–1, "The West India Question," *Journal of Commerce* 19, no. 12 (1884): 410–11, and "The Jamaica Question," *Journal of Commerce* 19, no. 13 (1884): 443–4; Editorial, *Morning Chronicle*, 4 September 1884.

48 "The Jamaica Scheme," *Globe*, 18 August 1884; "The Annexation of the West Indies," *Ottawa Gazette*, 9 September 1884.

49 "The Jamaica Scheme," *Journal of Commerce*, 19, no. 9 (1884): 304–5; Editorial, *Morning Chronicle*, 2 September 1884.

50 Editorial, *Morning Chronicle*, 2 September 1884. Opponents of union also argued that Canadian flour did not fare well in the tropics, there was scarce demand for coffee in Canada, and, contrary to the contention of union advocates, Newfoundland would not be compelled to enter Confederation if Canada annexed Jamaica because Newfoundland did not rely heavily on the Jamaican market for its fish exports.

51 Jones, letter to the editor, *Toronto Mail*, 3 June 1882.

52 James Patterson Smith, "The Liberals, Race, and Political Reform," 131–46; Holt, *Problem of Freedom*, 215–309; Brian L. Moore and Michele A. Johnson, *Neither Led nor Driven*, 1–13; Hall, *Civilising Subjects*, 406–24, 435–41.

53 Holt, *Problem of Freedom*, 278–9.

54 Smith, "Liberals, Race, and Political Reform," 135.

55 Under the charter of a Venezuelan general, the *Florence* was transporting armaments from Venezuela to St Thomas in 1877 when it docked at Kingston's harbour for repairs. Suspicious of the vessel's purpose, Jamaican Governor Anthony Musgrave ordered its detention. In *Musgrave v. Pulido*, the British Privy Council ruled in favor of Pulido and ordered the Jamaican government to pay half the expenditure resulting from the detention. See Jamaica, *Correspondence Respecting the Case of the Ship Florence*, 1882, C. 3453; West Indies, *Report of the Royal Commission Appointed in 1882*, 1884, C. 3840; Jamaica, *Petition from the Inhabitants of Jamaica for a Change in the Constitution of that Colony*, 1884, C. 3854; Jamaica, *Further Correspondence Respecting the Constitution of the Legislative Council in Jamaica*, 1884, C. 4140; Ernest Thomas

and Charles Attenborough, *Leading Cases in Constitutional Law Briefly Stated*, 87–8; Joseph Ford, *Handbook of Jamaica*, 55.

56 Dennis Benn, *Caribbean*, 65–6.

57 Holt, *Problem of Freedom*, 340–1. The literacy requirement was waived during the first elections. See Holt, 469n87. Of Jamaica's total population of 580,805 in 1884, those registered included 98 Indians, 2,578 "mulattoes," 3,766 "African," and 1,001 European voters.

58 *Colonial Standard and Jamaica Despatch*, 4 April 1883.

59 *Colonial Standard and Jamaica Despatch*, 13 April 1883.

60 Editorial, *Colonial Standard*, 12 March 1884.

61 *Trelawny Advertiser*, as cited in editorial in *Colonial Standard*, 12 March 1884.

62 "Michael Solomon," Biographical Notes, National Library of Jamaica (hereafter NLJ).

63 "Death of Mr. Michael Solomon," *Daily Gleaner*, 6 May 1892.

64 Tupper to Macdonald, 8 July 1884, in Tupper, *Life and Letters of the Rt. Hon. Sir Charles Tupper*, 34.

65 Minutes of a Meeting of Jamaican Proprietors and Merchants, 17 June and 7 August 1884, West India Committee Records, Special Collections, UWI St Augustine Library; "Memorandum on the Proposal for the Entrance of Jamaica as a Province into the Dominion of Canada," enclosed in "Jamaica Re: Annexation by Canada," undated, George Baden-Powell Papers 13/102, Parliamentary Archives (hereafter PA).

66 Memorandum on the Proposal for the entrance of Jamaica as a Province into the Dominion of Canada, enclosed in "Jamaica Re: Annexation by Canada," undated, George Baden-Powell Papers, PA, GBP 13/102.

67 Ibid. The government services listed included the lieutenant governor's office, the militia, hospitals, a penitentiary, judicial and customs offices, and telegraphic and postal services.

68 "Lord Derby on the West Indies," *Times* (London), 29 August 1884. The deputation included Solomon, James Ohlson (chairman of the Jamaica Board of the West India interest), Neville Lubbock (chairman of the West India Committee), George H. Chambers, Ernest Tinne (chairman of the West India Association of Liverpool), Captain S. Bridges (representing the Bristol West India interest), A.P. Pittman and F. Lubbock (representing Demerara and Trinidad), and C. Washington Eaves.

69 "Jamaica Question," *Grip*, 18 October 1884.

70 *Ottawa Free Press*, 18 September 1884.

71 Macdonald to Hincks, 18 September 1884, Macdonald Papers, vol. 526 LAC, MG 26-A; Hincks to Macdonald, 20 September 1884, vol. 224, LAC, MG 26-A.

72 During a Jamaica-wide revolt of enslaved peoples in 1832, Bernard's St James property, on which thirty-nine persons were enslaved, was burned

to the ground. With emancipation two years later, Bernard received
£1,723 from the British government for the loss of his enslaved workforce.
Reynolds, *Agnes*, 6–7. See also "Thomas James Bernard of Bernards Lodge,"
Legacies of British Slave Ownership database, University College London,
LBS Centre; Waldie, "Sir John A. Macdonald Had Family Ties to Slave
Trade," *Globe and Mail* (online), 1 March 2013. John A. Macdonald,
*Canada, the West Indies, and British Guiana: Paper Read before the Board
of Trade of Toronto* (Toronto, 1889), at https://www.canadiana.ca/view/
oocihm.09403/6?r=0&s=1.

73 Macdonald to Solomon, 25 September 1884, Macdonald Papers, vol. 323,
LAC, MG 26-A.

74 Henry Berkeley, letter to the editor, *Times* (London), 12 August 1884;
"Resolution of the Sub-Committee of Jamaica Proprietors and Merchants,"
enclosed in Henry Berkeley to O.C. Chipman, 15 September 1884, Department
of External Affairs fonds (hereafter DEA), LAC, RG 25, series A-I, vol. 36.

75 The three-quarter of a million consumers that Berkeley cited included
Jamaica and the Leeward Islands. According to the Census of 1881, Jamaica's
population was 580,804, and the Leeward Islands, which included the British
Virgin Islands, Anguilla, St Kitts, Nevis, Barbuda, and Antigua, was 114,112.
See Berkeley to Chipman, 15 September 1884, Macdonald Papers, series A-I,
vol. 36, LAC, MG 26-A.

76 "Confederation with Canada," *Port of Spain Gazette*, 25 October 1884;
Charles Levy to J.J. Stewart, editor of the *Halifax Daily Chronicle*; Levy to
Spencer Jones, 24 January 1885, in Levy, *Correspondence on Confederation
with the Dominion of Canada*, 5–6, 15–16.

77 *New York Herald*, 14 January 1882.

78 Albert P. Marryat, letter to the editor, *Times* (London), 21 August, 30 August
1884. The 21 August article was reprinted in Trinidad's *Port of Spain Gazette*,
13 September 1884. It is unknown on which island Marryat resided or
carried on his commercial activities. He wrote these letters to the *Times* from
a London address, but his reference to himself as a "colonist" suggests he was
not (always) an absentee planter.

79 P.N. Barnard, letter to the editor, *Times* (London), 21 August 1884.

80 West Indies, *Report of the Royal Commission appointed in December 1882, to
inquire into the public revenues, expenditure, debts, and liabilities of the islands
of Jamaica, Grenada, St. Vincent, Tobago, and St. Lucia, and the Leeward
Islands*, 1884, C. 3840.

81 "Canadian Annexation of West Indian Islands," 2 October 1884, enclosed in
George Baden-Powell Papers, PA, GBP 12/99A.

82 Baden-Powell, letter to the editor, *Times* (London), 1 October 1884. Baden-
Powell thought complications might also arise if Canada absorbed the public

debts of the Caribbean colonies. These debts accrued from money advanced
by British capitalists on the understanding that the Caribbean colonies
were under the direct administration of the Crown. This capital might be
compromised if these colonies passed from British to Canadian hands.

83 *Minutes of the Legislative Council of Jamaica*, 28 October 1884 (Kingston:
Government Printing Establishment, 1885), 81; *Daily Gleaner* (Jamaica),
29 October 1884; Robert G.W. Herbert to the British High Commissioner
at Ottawa, 1 November 1884, DEA, series A-1, vol. 36, LAC, RG 25. Eight
Legislative Council members voted against the motion.

84 F.A. Autey, letter to the editor, *Daily Gleaner*, 31 March 1884.

85 Editorial, *Daily Gleaner*, 23 September 1884.

86 Owram, *Promise of Eden*, 170–1, 173.

87 *Bulletin* (Edmonton), 1 November 1884, as cited in Owram, *Promise of
Eden*, 177.

88 Judith Fingard, "The 1880s: Paradoxes of Progress," 83, 82; T.W. Acheson,
"National Policy and the Industrialization of the Maritimes," 3–31; Kris
Inwood, "Maritime Industrialization from 1870 to 1910," 149–70. For a
concise summary of the social, economic, and political contours of the 1880s,
see Fingard, "The 1880s," 82–116.

89 Daniel Cronan, paraphrased in the *Morning Chronicle*, 29 August 1884.

90 As reproduced in "Canadian Confederation," *Daily Gleaner*, 23 September
1884.

91 As cited in "Jamaica Annexation," the *Daily Gleaner*, 26 November 1884;
Morning Chronicle, 4 September 1884.

92 Editorial, *Manchester Guardian*, 3 October 1884.

93 Published extract dated 17 October 1884, enclosed in file titled "America –
West Indies, Canadian Annexation of West Indian Islands 1884, George
Baden-Powell Papers, PA, GBP 12/99A; West Indies, *Report of the Royal
Commission appointed in December 1882, to inquire into the public revenues,
expenditure, debts, and liabilities of the islands of Jamaica, Grenada, St. Vincent,
Tobago, and St. Lucia, and the Leeward Islands*, 1884, C. 3840.

94 I draw here from Frederick Cooper's discussion of the "poles of incorporation
and differentiation" in different imperial contexts. See his *Colonialism in
Question*, 154.

95 James Daschuk, *Clearing the Plains*, 99–180; John S. Milloy, *National Crime*,
23–186.

96 Esyllt Jones and Adele Perry, *People's Citizenship Guide*, 26.

97 George Baden-Powell, *Times* (London), 2 October 1884; Internal Minutes,
2 October 1884, The National Archives (hereafter TNA), CO 137/518.

98 Cole Harris, *Making Native Space*, 178. See also Alicja Muszynski, *Cheap
Wage Labour*, 129–79; Rolf Knight, *Indians at Work*.

99   David Goutor, *Guarding the* Gates, 35–59. The English Canadian labour movement's distinction between Blacks and Chinese is elaborated in Goutor, "Drawing Different Lines of Color."

100 As cited in Gouter, *Guarding the Gates*, 45. On Sheppard, see Hann, "Brainworkers and the Knights of Labor," 35–57. On the Knights of Labor, see Gregory Kealey and Bryan Palmer, *Dreaming of What Might Be*.

101 See Dean Pavlakis, "Development of British Overseas Humanitarianism," para. 9.

102 Baden-Powell, *Times* (London), 2 October 1884.

103 Andrew Porter, "Trusteeship, Anti-Slavery, and Humanitarianism," 213–14.

104 Ibid., 214; Holt, *Problem of Freedom*, 307–9; Hall, *Civilising Subjects*.

105 Karuna Mantena, "Crisis of Liberal Imperialism," 114. This argument is elaborated in Mantena, *Alibis of Empire*, 307–9. On the nature of liberal imperialism more generally, see Jennifer Pitts, *Turn to Empire*; Mehta, *Liberalism and Empire*.

106 Hincks to Macdonald, 20 September 1884, Macdonald fonds, LAC, MG 26-A, vol. 222.

107 C. Colville Malton, *Reminiscences*, 2.

108 Mary Louise Pratt, *Imperial Eyes*, 4; Susan Bassnett, "Empire, Travel Writing, and British Studies," 1–21.

109 Malton, *Reminiscences*, 4–5, makes only passing reference to representative institutions in Barbados.

110 Malton, *Reminiscences*, 8.

111 Bassnett, "Empire, Travel Writing, and British Studies," 17.

112 Robert Hornback, *Racism and Early Blackface Comic Traditions*, 144. While the image of "Sambo" has a long, protean genealogy in African American history, it can be argued that its function in Malton's narrative actually counters the popular notion that "subject races" require strict governance. As the "natural, contented subordinate," "Sambo" accepts his location in the racial hierarchy and is less likely to disrupt the status quo of white dominance. See Luther W. Spoehr, "Sambo and the Heathen Chinee," 194n26.

113 Eric Williams, "Massa Day Done," 727.

114 Leland Ware, *Century of Segregation*, 160; McWhorter, "There's Nothing Wrong with Black English," *Atlantic* (online), 6 August 2018.

115 "The New Confederacy," *Grip*, 20 September 1884.

116 Malton, *Reminiscences*, 37. Nineteenth-century literature often represented the image of the ignorant African Caribbean as "Quashi."

117 Malton, *Reminiscences*, 37.

118 Moore and Johnson, *Neither Led nor Driven*, 15–33, at 15; Kenneth Bilby and Jerome Handler, "Obeah," 153–83; Monica Schuler, "*Alas, Alas, Kongo*,"

36; Mary Turner, *Slaves and Missionaries*, 54–9; Robert Stewart, *Religion and Society in Post-Emancipation Jamaica*, 36–8.

119 Malton, *Reminiscences*, 38.

120 Ibid.

121 Ruby King, "Elementary Education in Early Twentieth-Century Jamaica," 224–46; Ruby King, "Education in the British Caribbean," 25–45; Moore and Johnson, *Neither Led nor Driven*, 205–28.

122 Mariana Valverde, *Age of Light, Soap and Water*, 15.

123 Ibid., 104–5, 110–11.

124 *Acadian Recorder*, 1 April 1884, as cited in Bridglal Pachai, *Nova Scotia Black Experience*, 131–2.

125 Nova Scotia, Debates and Proceedings of the House of Assembly, 2nd sess., 28th parl., 28 March, 1884 (Halifax: Charles Annand, 1884), 140.

126 Ibid., 140–1.

127 As cited in the *Daily Gleaner*, 26 November 1884.

128 Murray's interview can be found in the *Morning Herald*, 21 October 1884; *Morning Chronicle*, as cited in the *Daily Gleaner*, 26 November 1884.

129 *Morning Chronicle*, 27 August 1884.

130 Interview of "A Gentleman," paraphrased in the *Morning Chronicle*, 29 August 1884.

131 James Butler interview, as paraphrased in the *Morning Chronicle*, 29 August 1884.

132 E.C. Dacosta interview, as paraphrased in the *Morning Chronicle*, 29 August 1884.

133 Daniel Cronan interview, as paraphrased in the *Morning Chronicle*, 29 August 1884. Timothy Stanley, *Contesting White Supremacy*, 89, discusses a similar racialization of Chinese in British Columbia, though with different implications. In protesting Asian immigration to Canada, for example, the Dominion Trades and Labor Congress claimed that "Asian workers did not provide fair competition, since 'a white man cannot subsist on a handful of rice; a white man must have a house, not a shack to live in; a home to bring up his children in; a school to send them to.'"

134 Walker, "African Canadians," 148.

135 W.B. McSweeney interview, paraphrased in the *Morning Chronicle*, 29 August 1884.

136 "Jamaicans and Their Island," *Morning Herald*, 27 August 1884.

137 As cited in "Jamaica," *Morning Herald*, 25 August 1884.

138 Watson Griffin, *Provinces and the States*, 70. Universal male suffrage was not, in fact, practised in Nova Scotia. In 1884, men aged twenty-one years or older were required to own or in good faith occupy property valued at a minimum of $150, or own at least $300 in combined real and personal property; Government of Canada, *History of the Vote in Canada*, 46.

139 Levy, *Morning Chronicle*, 29 November 1884, reprinted in Levy, *Correspondence*, 15. According to the Census of 1881, Jamaica's population was 14,432 white, 109,946 "coloured or half-breed," and 444,186 Black. These figures can be found in Frederick Martin, *The Statesman's Year-Book*, 221.

140 Jones, letter to the editor, *Toronto Mail*, 3 June 1884.

141 Jones, "Advantages to the Conservative Party of WI Confederation," enclosed in Jones to Macdonald, 2 August 1884, Macdonald fonds, LAC, MG 26-A, vol. 323. See also Jones to Macdonald, 20 September 1883, vol. 396; Jones to Macdonald and enclosures, 1 November 1883, vol. 277; Jones to Macdonald, 2 August 1884, vol. 393, and enclosure, "Notes on the Admission of the British West Indies and British Guiana into the Dominion," all at LAC, MG 26-A.

142 Levy, *Daily Gleaner*, 15 November 1884; Levy, *Morning Chronicle*, 29 November 1884. On the trade negotiations between Washington and London, see John B. Moore, *Digest of International Law*, 269; Alpheus Todd, *Parliamentary Government in the British Colonies*, 272–3.

143 *Minutes of the Legislative Council of Jamaica*, 8.

144 Minutes, Legislative Council of Jamaica, 11 June 1885, enclosed in vol. 521, TNA, CO 137.

145 Sarah Carter, *Aboriginal People and Colonizers of Western Canada to 1900*, 151–5.

146 Jones to Macdonald, 8 January 1885, Macdonald fonds, LAC, MG 26-A, vol. 323. Jones wrote, "I would feel greatly obliged if you consider that I have any claim moral or equitable for expenses incurred in this West Indies business, that you would send by award me such a sum as you may consider reasonable for the devotion of nearly a year of my time & several journeys between Toronto and Ottawa." See also Office of the Privy Council, Order in Council, 6 August 1885, LAC, RG 2.

147 Macdonald to Baden-Powell, 18 October 1884, George Baden-Powell Papers, PA, GBP 12/97. A Jamaican deputation visited Ottawa in June 1885 to discuss trade reciprocity, but these negotiations floundered as well. The delegates met with various trade groups in eastern and Maritime Canada, including the Halifax Chamber of Commerce, the Toronto Board of Trade, and the Montreal Board of Trade. The negotiations were hampered by Macdonald's inability to meet with the delegates, the absence of Finance Minister Tilley, and, most importantly, the imperial government's refusal to sanction a trade agreement that did not include all the British Caribbean colonies. On these negotiations, see "Reciprocity with Jamaica," *Globe*, 11 June 1885; "Jamaica and Canada," *Gazette*, 17 June 1885; Macdonald to H.H. Hocking, 25 June 1885, enclosed in Henry Norman to Frederick Stanley, 22 July 1885, TNA, CO 137/522.

Chapter Two

1 George Johnson, "Canada's Opportunity," *Ottawa Evening Citizen*,
   25 August 1898.
2 "Canada and the West Indies," *Mail and Empire* (Toronto),
   30 November 1898.
3 Johnson, "Canada's Opportunity."
4 Angus Maddison, *The World Economy in the 20th Century*, 43.
5 Michael Bliss, *Northern Enterprise*, 313–43. Jaydeep Balakrishnan, Janice
   B. Eliasson, and Timothy R.C. Sweet, "Factors Affecting the Evolution of
   Manufacturing in Canada," 265, 268, 273–4. See also H.V. Nelles, *Politics
   of Development*.
6 On the expansion of Canadian banking in the Caribbean, see Quigley, "Bank
   of Nova Scotia in the Caribbean"; Duncan McDowall, *Quick to the Frontier*.
   Canadian involvement in the development of Trinidad's petroleum industry
   is outlined in "The Petroleum Industry," Randolph Rust Collection, Rec. 1,
   Special Collections, UWI St Augustine Library, West Indiana. The history
   of Canadian utilities companies in the region is treated in Christopher
   Armstrong and H.V. Nelles, *Southern Exposure*, and McDowall, *The Light*.
   On Canada-Caribbean trade in the early twentieth century, see Newman,
   "Canada's Role in West Indian Trade before 1912"; Robert Falconer, "Canada
   and the West Indies," 165–7.
7 On this unbridled optimism, see Robert Craig Brown and Ramsay Cook,
   Canada, 1896–1921, 49–82; Bliss, *Northern Enterprise*, 313–14. In a speech
   at Massey Hall on 14 October 1904, Wilfrid Laurier said, "The twentieth
   century shall be the century of Canada and Canadian development." Laurier,
   "Canada's Century," 300.
8 Stephen Leacock, "Greater Canada," 135.
9 The few studies that address unionism in this period consider only briefly the
   broader international and imperial contexts that animated its proponents.
   Nor do they situate unionism in the wave of settler optimism that generated
   lofty expectations about Canada's future greatness. See Winks, *Canadian-West
   Indian Union*, and Samaroo, "Politics of Disharmony." The most recent study
   is Andrew Smith's 2009 "Thomas Bassett Macaulay and the Bahamas: Racism,
   Business and Canadian Sub-Imperialism," which focuses on Macaulay's
   interest in union with the Bahamas in 1911. Smith's argument that Macaulay
   was an imperialist but not a racist differs from the findings presented in this
   chapter. Peter James Hudson, "Imperial Designs," is an important challenge
   to the narrative of Canadian benevolence in the Caribbean. The article briefly
   mentions early twentieth-century unionism but focuses primarily on the
   period after 1914.

10 The seminal study on the world-systems framework is Wallerstein, *Modern World System*.

11 See for example Marius B. Jansen, "Japanese Imperialism"; Bradley Naranch, "Made in China." Roger C. Thompson, *Australian Imperialism in the Pacific*, does not directly link Australian expansion in the South Pacific to nationalism or nation building, but the connection is implicit. See also Paul Kramer, *Blood of Government*, 308.

12 While the United States' authority in Cuba, Puerto Rico, Guam, and the Philippines was not officially recognized until the Treaty of Paris on 10 December 1898, the islands had been under US control during the summer of 1898.

13 "A New Situation," *The Guardian* (Charlottetown), 29 August 1898.

14 Bonham Richardson, "The Importance of the 1897 British Royal Commission," 17–28; C.Y. Shephard, "The Sugar Industry of the British West Indies and British Guiana," 151. Of course, the experience across the region was not uniform. With the assistance of private capital, new methods were introduced in British Guiana and Trinidad in the final decades of the nineteenth century to modernize sugar production. See H.A. Will, "Colonial Policy and Economic Development in the British West Indies," 129.

15 Dobson, as cited in "United British America," *Daily Gleaner*, 26 May 1899.

16 Letter to the editor, *Montreal Weekly Witness*, 22 June 1899.

17 "The West Indies and Canada," *Charlottetown Guardian*, 17 September 1898.

18 See, for example, Audley Gosling, "Central America and Its Resources," 96–102; Arthur Curtiss James, "Advantages of Hawaiian Annexation," 758–60; Josiah Strong, *Expansion under New World-Conditions*; J. Russell Smith, "Western South America and Its Relation to American Trade," 56–78; James H. Wilson, *Address on Our Trade Relations with the Tropics*; E.R. Johnson, "The Trade and Industries of Western South America," 109–22; O.P. Austin, "Our Trade with Hawaii and Porto Rico," 47–52.

19 Warwick Anderson, *Colonial Pathologies*; John Farley, *Bilharzia*; Helen J. Power, *Tropical Medicine in the Twentieth Century*.

20 Felix Driver and Luciana Martins, "Views and Visions of the Tropical World."

21 Bryan, *Jamaican People*, 3; Bonham Richardson, "Depression Riots and the Calling of the 1897 Royal Commission," 169–91.

22 Murdoch, as cited in *Daily Gleaner*, 16 June 1899. Murdoch was originally from Saint John.

23 Ibid.

24 Chamberlain, as cited in "Canada in the West Indies," *Mail and Empire*, 30 November 1898; "M. Chamberlain," *Journal des campagnes*, 17 September 1898.

25 George Johnson, as cited in "Canada and the West Indies," *Mail and Empire*, 30 November 1898.

26 "Jamaica's Trade Future," *New York Times*, 14 September 1898; "Jamaican Annexation," *Ottawa Citizen*, 9 December 1898.

27 "Shall We Join Canada?" *Daily Gleaner*, 12 October 1898.

28 See, for example, *The Voice* (St Lucia), as reproduced in the *Ottawa Evening Citizen*, 25 November 1898; *The Federalist* (Grenada) and *Daily Gleaner* (Jamaica), as cited in "The West Indies," *Globe*, 31 December 1898; "West Indies Negotiations," *Globe*, 18 November 1898.

29 "West Indian Loyalty," *Monetary Times*, 22 August 1902; Edward Morrison, "The British West Indies," *Ottawa Evening Citizen*, 22 July 1902.

30 Carrington, "United States and Canada," 81–4.

31 W.D. Taunton, *To the British West Indies via Halifax*. While tourist traffic to the Caribbean increased in the first decade of the twentieth century, the commodities trade remained a more lucrative enterprise. Canadians more commonly travelled to European or North American destinations. As Duncan McDowall, *Another World*, 3, writes, "When the century dawned, travel was still largely the preserve of the affluent classes who wandered the beaten paths of Europe and North America." See also Cecilia Morgan, *Happy Holiday*.

32 Canada, *House of Commons Debates*, 15 March 1901, 1530 (Adam Bell, MP). J. Castell Hopkins, ed., *Morang's Annual Register, 1902*, 161–2. Also available at https://parl.canadiana.ca/browse?show=eng_s_debates.

33 Minutes of the Maritime Board of Trade, 16 and 17 August 1905, Yarmouth, Nova Scotia, as cited in the *Halifax Chronicle*, 17, 18 August 1905. Other board members who spoke were W.S. Fisher of Saint John, NB, Melville G. DeWolfe of Kentville, NS, Captain Reid of Summerside, PEI, and E.B. Elderkin. As of 1900, there were 138 boards of trade in Canada, with thirty-nine in the Maritime provinces (twenty-six in Nova Scotia, ten in New Brunswick, and three in Prince Edward Island). These numbers were collected from the Minutes of the Sixth Annual Session of the Board of Trade of the Maritime Provinces, Kentville, Nova Scotia, August 1900, George Major Creed fonds, Dalhousie University Archives and Special Collections, MS-2.241, file 4.23.

34 Minutes of the Maritime Board of Trade, 17 August 1905, as cited in the *Halifax Chronicle*, 18 August 1905.

35 Minutes of the Convention of the Canadian Manufacturers' Association, 20 September 1905, as cited in Hopkins, *Canadian Annual Review for 1905*, 492. See also "Ouvriers et Patrons," *La Vérité*, 30 September 1905. William Kirkpatrick McNaught seconded Fisher's resolution. Fisher owned the Enterprise Foundry in Sackville, New Brunswick.

36 Canada, *House of Commons Debates*, 9 June 1905, 7187 (George Foster, MP).

37 G.A. Newman, as cited in Carrington, "Struggle for the British West Indian Trade," 94.

38 Canada, *House of Commons Debates*, 9 June 1905, 7192 (Robert Borden, MP).

39 Canada, *House of Commons Debates*, 19 March 1906, 334 (Wilfrid Laurier, PM). The subject of annexation was raised by the MP for Queen's, PEI, Alexander Martin (Conservative). See also *Toronto Daily Star*, 20 March 1906; *Pall Mall Gazette*, 20 March 1906.

40 Carrington, "United States and Canada," 87; "Canada and the West Indies," *Toronto Daily Star*, 2 October 1909. Hemming's company, Hemming Manufacturing Co., made jewelry and regalia.

41 James Hutchison to Laurier, 19 July 1909, and Laurier to Hutchison, 20 July 1909, Laurier fonds, LAC, MG 26-G, series A, vol. 582.

42 "Territories General" file, *The Sun Life of Canada Almanac: A Chronicle of Company and World Events 1865–1946*, box 289, Corporate Archives of the Sun Life Insurance Company of Canada, Mississauga. Branches were opened in the Bahamas, British Guiana, Barbados, and Trinidad in 1880; in Bermuda in 1881; and in British Honduras (Belize) in 1886. Winks, *Canadian-West Indian Union*, 24.

43 "L'entrée des Iles Bahama dans la Confédération canadienne," *La Presse*, 25 March 1911.

44 Macaulay to Laurier, 20 February 1911, Laurier fonds, LAC, MG 26-G, series A, vol. 668.

45 Joseph Levitt, *Henri Bourassa and the Golden Calf*; Henry Bourassa, *Henri Bourassa on Imperialism and Biculturalism, 1900–1918*. Bourassa later sanctioned the creation of a Canadian navy, though he insisted that it should be under Canadian rather than British control.

46 "L'entrée des Iles Bahama dans la Confédération canadienne," *La Presse*, 25 March 1911; "Le Dominion du Canada comptera-t-il bientôt une dixième province?," *La Presse*, 2 March 1911.

47 "Canada and the Bahamas," *Nassau Guardian*, 22 February 1911; "The Great Public Meeting at Nassau," *Sunshine* 16, no. 5 (1911): 50.

48 "Great Public Meeting at Nassau," *Sunshine* 16, no. 5 (1911): 50.

49 Macdonald, letter to the editor, *Nassau Guardian*, 11 March 1911.

50 "Great Public Meeting at Nassau," *Sunshine* 16, no. 5 (1911): 55–6, at 52.

51 For information on the Bahamian economy in the nineteenth and early twentieth centuries, see Michael Craton, *A History of the Bahamas*, 225–44; Jan Rogozinski, *A Brief History of the Caribbean*, 343; Howard Johnson, *The Bahamas in Slavery and Freedom*, 168–9.

52 The members selected included three white Bahamians, Dr. G.H. Johnson, W.C.B. Johnson, and T.G. Brice, and two Black Bahamians, G.R. Evans and Ernest L. Bowen; *Nassau Guardian*, 22 February 1911. Occupation

information on Cole and Rae was found in Gail Saunders and Michael Craton, *Islanders in the Stream*, 2:211, and Howard S. Pactor, *Colonial British Caribbean Newspapers*, 27.

53   William Christopher Barnett Johnson's address to the House of Assembly, as cited in "The Bahamas Legislature. House of Assembly," *Nassau Guardian*, 15 March 1911. According to Craton and Saunders, *Islanders in the Stream*, 2:234, Johnson was a white Bahamian and the deputy speaker of the Assembly. He was also a onetime member of the Bank of Nassau's board of directors. When the bank folded in 1916 (leaving the Royal Bank of Canada with a monopoly on the island), Johnson and the other directors were accused of illegal activities and brought to trial.

54   Minutes of the Legislative Assembly, copied in "The Bahamas Legislature: House of Assembly," *Nassau Guardian*, 15 March 1911. G.R. Evans, who was originally selected to sit on the Ways and Means Committee, was absent. According to Governor Grey-Wilson, Evans supported the resolution. William Grey-Wilson to Lewis Harcourt, 4 April 1911, TNA, CO 23/267.

55   Macaulay to Laurier, 11 May 1911, Laurier fonds, LAC, MG-26-G, series A, vol. 681.

56   Enclosure in Elwyn P. Mousir to Wilfrid Laurier, 21 April 1911, Laurier fonds, LAC, MG-26-G, series A, vol. 677.

57   "The Canadian and West Indian League – Names of Some Members Who Have Joined during July," *Canada-West Indies Magazine*, no. 1 (August 1911): 11.

58   T.C. Keenleyside to Laurier, 7 April 1911, Laurier fonds, LAC, MG-26-G, series A, vol. 675. Hutchings was involved in saddlery companies and several other enterprises. See Don Nerbas, "Wealth and Privilege."

59   Macaulay to Laurier, 11 May 1911, Laurier fonds, LAC, MG-26-G, series A, vol. 681; Hopkins, *Canadian Annual Review of Public Affairs*, 599; *Globe*, 11 December 1923.

60   Falconer's family was close with the family of Nova Scotian reverend Kenneth J. Grant, who helped found the Trinidad mission in 1870. Grant was also a prosperous merchant who encouraged closer commercial and constitutional relations with Canada. To his mind the British Caribbean "geographically belong[ed] to Canada," and it was only a matter of time before they were "politically one." James G. Greenlee, *Sir Robert Falconer*, 12; Kenneth J. Grant, as cited in Samaroo, "Politics of Disharmony," 51.

61   Bélanger, "Robert Alexander Falconer."

62   Falconer, "Canada and the West Indies," 165–8, 170, at 168 and 170. Duncan MacIntyre (the Whitby judge who campaigned for union in the Bahamas with Macaulay, Macdonald, and Nicholson in February 1911) sat on the board of the University of Toronto's Presbyterian college (Knox) and may have found a union ally in Falconer.

63   Winks, *Canada-West Indies Union*; Laurier, as cited in ibid., 26.

64   Laurier to Lord Grey, 7 April 1911, TNA, CO 42/947.

65   Richard Jebb to Laurier, 23 May 1911, Laurier fonds, LAC, MG-26-G, series A, vol. 682.

66   Macaulay to Laurier, 20 April 1911, Laurier fonds, LAC, MG-26-G, series A, vol. 677; Laurier to Grey, 7 April 1911, TNA, CO 42/947.

67   Macdonald, letter to the editor, *Nassau Guardian*, 11 March 1911. See also "Une Annexion au Canada," *L'Étoile du Nord*, 6 April 1911. Manitoba businessman T.C. Keenleyside similarly argued that nothing was likely "to develop the Canadian national sentiment more than absorbing into confederation adjacent British territories." Keenleyside's list included territories that were neither British nor adjacent: Greenland, Newfoundland and Labrador, St Pierre and Miquelon in the St Lawrence, and, "last but not least," the British Caribbean colonies. T.C. Keenleyside to Laurier, 7 April 1911, Laurier fonds, LAC, MG-26-G, series A, vol. 675.

68   T.B. Macaulay, "The Bahamas and Canada," address before the Canadian Club, Montreal, 3 April 1911, copied in *Sunshine* 16, no. 5 (1911): 47–8.

69   "Canada's Future Is in Hands of People," *Brandon Weekly Sun*, 25 April 1912. "The British Empire Is Made for Canada," *Daily Gleaner*, 3 May 1928. "Sir James Aikins on His Trip to the West Indies," *Daily Gleaner*, 16 February 1929. Predictions of a shifting centre of imperial power was common in the years before 1914. See, for example, *Edmonton Bulletin*, 2 August 1911; "Says Canada Will Become Centre of British Empire," *Brandon Weekly Sun*, 4 July 1912; "An Imperial Council," *Daily Colonist* (Victoria), 19 September 1913; "Britannia's Destiny," *Daily Colonist*, 23 February 1913; "Honored with Civic Reception," *Daily Colonist*, 14 December 1911; "Lord Provost of Glasgow Predicts Canada Will Be Centre of the Empire," *Manitoba Free Press*, 16 August 1913; "Report by Arthur Hawkes on Immigration Work," *Winnipeg Free Press*, 1 June 1912.

70   Benjamin Kidd, *Control of the Tropics*. The content of this book first appeared as a series of articles in the London *Times*, on 29 July, 13 August, and 15 August 1898. On Kidd's influence, see Rod Edmond, "Returning Fears," 178–9.

71   W.P. Livingstone, "The Future of the British West Indies," 428.

72   Geoffrey R. Searle, *The Quest for National Efficiency*, 8–12, 173.

73   Bernard Porter, *Britannia's Burden: The Political Evolution of Modern Britain, 1851–1990*, 158–62.

74   On the international impact of the South African War, see Donal Lowry, "'The Boers Were the Beginning of the End?,'" 203–46. See also Ronald Hyam, "The British Empire in the Edwardian Era," 49–51; A.P. Thornton, *The Imperial Idea and Its Enemies*, 108–52.

75   Lake and Reynolds, *Drawing the Global Color Line*, 2.

76   *Toronto Daily Star*, 21 August 1905.

77   See Minutes, 5 March 1912, TNA, CO 23/268. On British enthusiasm about
the opening of the Panama Canal, see *West India Committee Circular*, 14
February, 1 August, 15 August, 10 October, and 24 October 1911; *Pall
Mall Gazette*, as cited in the *West India Committee Circular*, 12 September
1911; Robert Porter, *London Magazine*, as cited in the *West India Committee
Circular*, 28 May 1911.

78   See Bradford Perkins, *The Great Rapprochement: England and the United
States, 1895–1914;* Stuart Anderson, *Race and Rapprochement: Anglo-Saxonism
and Anglo-American Relations*.

79   John Herd Thompson and Stephen J. Randall, *Canada and the United States:
Ambivalent Allies*, 65–9; Stephen Azzi, *Reconcilable Differences: A History of
Canada-US Relations*, 75–7.

80   Samuel F. Wells, "British Strategic Withdrawal from the Western
Hemisphere, 1904–1906," 335–56; War Office to Colonial Office, 20 March,
12 July, and 3 August 1905, TNA, CO 318/313.

81   Petition of the Barbados House of Assembly, cited in the *West India
Committee Circular*, 6 June 1905.

82   *West India Committee Circular*, 9 May 1905. White residents and absentee
planters also feared the implications of this withdrawal on domestic order in the
colonies. Blacks were "acknowledged to be excitable," the *West India Committee
Circular* warned, "and when their passions are roused neither reason nor interest
will keep them in check." Not surprisingly, members of London's West India
Committee worried that the removal of British troops would compromise
their property and investments in the region. *West India Committee Circular*,
28 February 1905, 14 September 1905, and 18 August 1907.

83   Edward R. Davson, letter to the editor, *West India Committee Circular*,
31 January 1905; Davson, "British Guiana and Its Development," 229.

84   J. Kemplay, "The Balance of Power in the Caribbean," letter to the editor,
West India Committee Circular, 14 March 1905.

85   Alfred Thayer Mahan, *Mahan on Naval Warfare*, 109. The changed Anglo-
American power dynamic in the Caribbean was laid bare once again in
January 1907 when the US Marines landed in Jamaica without British
consent, following a devastating earthquake that claimed the lives of
approximately one thousand people and destroyed most of Kingston.
Jamaica's governor, Alexander Swettenham, sent the rear admiral
commanding the marines a note rebuking the intervention, which leaked to
the press and caused an international stir. The British quickly apologized to
the US, and Swettenham soon resigned. See William N. Tilchin, "Theodore
Roosevelt, Anglo-American Relations, and the Jamaica Incident of 1907,"
385–406.

86 Hyam, "British Empire in the Edwardian Era," 49–51.

87 W.R. Lawson, *Canada and the Empire*, 2–14, 20–1.

88 Ibid., 28–31.

89 "Centre of the Empire Will Move to Canada, Says Halford J. Mackinder,"
    Richmond Hill Liberal, 9 April 1908; "Centre of the Empire," *Saturday Sunset*
    (Vancouver), 25 September 1909; "Canada as Centre of the Empire," *Banner*
    (Russell, Manitoba), 19 January 1911; "Canada as the Seat of Imperial Rule,"
    Globe, 5 January 1911; "Canada's Great Future," *Scotsman*, 7 November
    1911; "Canada of the Future," *Weekly Irish Times*, 10 August 1912; "Canada
    and Imperial Federation: The Future Heart of the Empire," *Manchester
    Guardian*," 20 May 1912; "Divergent Views on Navy Question Expressed,"
    Daily Province, 11 March 1910; "Centre of the Empire," *Scotsman*, 22 March
    1911. See also J. Ellis Barker, *Great and Greater Britain*.

90 Griffin, "Imperial Alliance," 415–22.

91 Peter Price, "Steppingstones to Imperial Unity? The British West Indies in the
    Late-Victorian Imperial Federation Movement," 240–63.

92 De Léry Macdonald, *Nassau Guardian*, 11 March 1911; Macaulay to Laurier,
    20 February 1911, Laurier fonds, LAC, MG 26-G, series A, vol. 668; Macaulay,
    "The Bahamas and Canada," address before the Canadian Club, Montreal, 3
    April 1911, reproduced in *Sunshine* 16, no. 5 (1911): 48.

93 Bell, *Idea of Greater Britain*, 8–10.

94 S.R. Mehrotra, "Imperial Federation and India, 1868–1917," 29–30.

95 "Shall We Join Canada?" *Daily Gleaner*, 12 October 1898.

96 "A New Link of Empire," *Canadian Magazine* 12, no. 6 (1899): 479.

97 "The Bahamas Legislature," *Nassau Guardian*, 15 March 1911.

98 Jebb, as paraphrased in "Empire Depends on Individual Action," *Winnipeg
    Free Press*, 2 November 1905.

99 Simon Potter, "Richard Jebb, John S. Ewart and the Round Table,
    1898–1926," 105.

100 Brown and Cook, *Canada, 1896–1921*, 162–73.

101 Earl Grey, "Notes on Canada," c. 1911, Durham University Special
    Collections (hereafter DUSC), GREY 171/4; William Grey-Wilson to Grey,
    31 March 1905, and Grey to Grey-Wilson, 24 August 1905, DUSC, GREY
    174/4; J. Wodehouse to Grey, 10 April 1908, DUSC, GREY 179/7; Wodehouse
    to Grey, 3 July 1908, DUSC, GREY 179/13; Grey to Argyll, 13 February 1911,
    DUSC, GREY 178/16. The quotation from Grey's Calgary speech can be found
    in the *Christian Science Monitor* (Boston), 11 October 1909.

102 "The Empire's Future. A Policy Outline by the Duke of Marlborough,"
    Manchester Guardian, 9 November 1910.

103 "Lord Milner and Ourselves," *Daily Gleaner*, 1 July 1910.

104 Ibid.

105 Anthony Howe, *Free Trade and Liberal England, 1846–1946*, 248; Michael
     Ashley Havinden and David Meredith, *Colonialism and Development: Britain
     and its Tropical Colonies, 1850–1960*, 45.

106 Herbert Musgrave, *United Empire*, vol. 2 (May 1911), as cited in "Bahamas
     and Canada," *Nassau Guardian*, 22 November 1911.

107 Grey-Wilson to Harcourt, 4 April 1911, TNA, CO 23/267. Grey-Wilson told
     the Colonial Office that hard times on the islands had made the prospect of
     union particularly attractive to Bahamians. The hurricanes of 1908 and the
     calamitous droughts that followed prompted large numbers of the labouring
     population to migrate to Florida, where wages more than doubled those
     in the Bahamas. The impact of out-migration and endemic poverty on the
     islands' commerce was nothing short of disastrous. Internal correspondence,
     15 March 1911, TNA, CO 23/268. On Colonial Office concerns about trade,
     see, for example, Internal Correspondence, 4 April and 15 April 1911, TNA,
     CO 23/267.

108 Internal Correspondence, 6 May 1911, TNA, CO 23/267.

109 Ibid.

110 Ibid.

111 Ibid.

112 Harcourt, "Suggested Reconstruction of the Colonial Office," April 1911,
     Lewis Harcourt Papers, Bodleian Library, Oxford, UK, vol. 503.

113 Minutes, 4 April 1911, TNA, CO 23/267. See also Minutes, 5 March 1912,
     TNA, CO 23/268.

114 Minutes, 4 April 1911, TNA, CO 23/267.

115 On the ways in which the principle of trusteeship functioned to sustain
     and obscure imperial power relations during the interwar period, see Susan
     Pedersen, "Modernity and Trusteeship," especially 204, 217.

116 Berger, *Sense of Power*, 128–33, at 129, 133.

117 Arnold Haultain, "A Winter's Walk in Canada," *Nineteenth Century and After*
     (September 1901), 558, as cited in Berger, *Sense of Power*, 130.

118 Kidd, *Control of the Tropics*, 52.

119 I borrow the term *racelessness* from Constance Backhouse, *Colour-Coded: A
     Legal History of Racism in Canada, 1900–1950*.

120 John Millar, *Canadian Citizenship*, 68.

121 W.L. Grant, "Geographical Conditions Affecting the Development of
     Canada," 373. Grant was a professor of colonial history at Queen's University
     in Kingston.

122 G.R. Parkin, "Presidential Address," 193. Parkin was recounting the remarks
     he had made to a Montreal journalist c. 1908.

123 Winks, *Blacks in Canada*, 484–96.

124 See Walker, *West Indians in Canada*. On industrial labourers in Nova Scotia,
     see Elizabeth Beaton, "An African-American Community in Cape Breton,

1901–1904." On sleeping-car porters, see Sarah-Jane Mathieu, *North of the Color Line*. On farmers on the prairies, see Karina Vernon, "Black Civility: Black Grammars of Protest on the Canadian Prairies 1905–1950"; Bruce R. Shepard, *Deemed Unsuitable*. On domestic workers, see Calliste, "Race, Gender and Canadian Immigration Policy," 131–48.

125 "High Water-Mark," *Toronto Weekly Sun*, 31 August 1905.

126 "Union with Canada," *Nassau Tribune*, 16 November 1911.

127 On the exteriorization of blackness, see David Theo Goldberg, *The Racial State*, 120.

128 George Johnson, "Canada's Opportunity," *Ottawa Evening Citizen*, 25 August 1898.

129 Of course the techniques and outcomes of this erasure varied across racialized populations, but all derived from the white supremacist logic upon which Canada's settler society was founded.

130 W.D. Taunton, "Should Canada Annex the British West Indies," *Canadian Magazine*, as cited in the *Nassau Tribune*, 28 February 1912.

131 Ibid.

132 CalvinJohn Smiley and David Fakunle, "From 'Brute' to 'Thug': The Demonization and Criminalization of Unarmed Black Male Victims in America," 353.

133 Grey-Wilson, "Bahamas, West Indies, Canada," *Empire Club of Canada Addresses*, 25 October 1911, https://speeches.empireclub.org/details.asp?ID=62316&n=4.

134 Macaulay, address before the Canadian Club, Montreal, 3 April 1911, reproduced in *Sunshine* 16, no. 5 (1911): 46–47. Bahamian society was deeply divided by race and class in the early twentieth century. In Nassau especially, all aspects of society – housing, education, employment, and social life – were racially segregated. Race relations in the Bahamas, as historian Gail Saunders, *Race and Class in the Colonial Bahamas*, 41, 39, observes, were "perhaps not as harsh as in the southern United States with its inflexible and legislated color line," but neither did they conform to the more flexible norm in the West Indies. In the main, elite whites ruled the colony and, like whites elsewhere in the empire, they believed people of African descent were "subhuman, ignorant, and savages." But in a way distinct from the United States and Canada, there was a significant socioeconomic division in the Bahamas between Blacks and those of mixed African-European descent. Although the historically contingent and constructed nature of race meant that these differences were always contested, ambiguous, and mutable, the latter generally straddled an "intermediate" position in society, and many were identified with the colony's rising middle class. They often worked as craftsmen, merchants, or teachers, and by the early twentieth century many owned land. Black Bahamians, on the other hand, were largely confined to

positions in manual labour. Of course, as Craton and Saunders point out in *Islanders in the Stream*, 89–100, people of mixed European and African descent occupied a somewhat ambiguous position. While some gained a measure of respectability among upper-class whites, others worked as labourers. See also Saunders, "The Role of the Coloured Middle Class in Nassau, Bahamas," 77–112.

135 "Jamaica and Canada: A Detailed Scheme of Political Union," *Montreal Weekly Witness*, 22 June 1899.

136 "Canada and the West Indies," *Globe*, 9 September 1905.

137 On the Foraker Act, see Pedro A. Cabán, *Constructing a Colonial People: Puerto Rico and the United States, 1898–1932*.

138 "Union with Canada," *Nassau Guardian*, 11 March 1913.

139 "An American Visitor," letter to the editor, *Nassau Guardian*, 17 February 1912; Robert Bailey, letter to the editor, *Nassau Guardian*, 21 February 1912.

140 "Canada and the Bahamas," *Nassau Guardian*, 22 February 1911; "Union with Canada," *Nassau Tribune*, 25 April 1911; T.B. Macaulay, "Union with Canada," *Nassau Guardian*, 12 April 1911.

141 Macaulay to Laurier, 20 June 1911, Laurier fonds, LAC, MG 26-G, series A, vol. 684.

142 Vernon, in "Black Civility," 85, estimates that 1,650 Black Americans settled on the Canadian prairies from 1905 to 1911.

143 See, for example, "The white residents of Junkins" to Laurier, 18 April 1911, Laurier fonds, LAC, MG 26-G, series A, vol. 677; Miss Jessie H. Edmonds, to Laurier, 18 April 1911, vol. 678; F. Maclure Solanders, Saskatoon Board of Trade, to Laurier, 27 April 1911, R. Gordon Fraser, Fort Saskatchewan Board of Trade, 28 April 1911, F.M. Crosskill to Laurier, 28 April 1911, Morinville Board of Trade to Laurier, 29 April 1911, all vol. 679; Leduc Board of Trade to Laurier, 1 May 1911, G.H. Bradbrook, Yorkton District Board of Trade, to Laurier, 2 May 1911, F.T. Fisher, Edmonton Board of Trade, to Laurier, 3 May 1911, A. Wetmore, Edmonton Builders' Exchange, to Laurier, 4 May 1911, Edmund T. Baines, Strathcona Board of Trade, to Laurier, 5 May 1911, W.W. Smith, Battleford, Board of Trade, 8 May 1911, all vol. 680; Lacombe Board of Trade to Laurier, 26 April 1911, N.C. Lyster, Lloydminster Board of Trade, to Laurier, 25 May 1911, both vol. 681; Fred J. Powell, United Farmers of Alberta (Edwell), to Laurier, 6 June 1911, IODE Head Office, to Laurier, no date, all vol. 682.

144 Canada, An Act Respecting Immigration, assented to 4 May 1910, Statutes of Canada, SC 9–10, Edward VII, chap. 27.

145 Calliste, "Race, Gender and Canadian Immigration Policy," 140–3.

146 Winks, *Blacks in Canada*, 298–313.

147 Robert Bailey, "Union with Canada," letter to the editor, *Nassau Guardian*, 29 March 1911.

148 Ibid.

149 "A Bahamian – and Proud of It," letter to the editor, *Nassau Guardian*, 18 March 1911.

150 Grey-Wilson to Harcourt, 6 May 1911, TNA, CO23/267.

151 D.A. Corinaldi, letter, *Daily Gleaner*, 8 August 1911. Corinaldi wrote the letter on 1 July. Jacob H. De Jonge, a member of British Guiana's executive council, made a similar argument when union came up in 1905. He stated that the race prejudice of "the Canadian is even more pronounced than the Yankee." The union of Canada and the British Caribbean would not make for a "happy family." While Ottawa would "rule and snub," the Caribbean colonies would "sulk and feel dissatisfied." De Jonge was quite sure that the majority of Caribbeans would "prefer an existence of poverty with happiness to that of financial success if coupled with social ostracism." See *Barbados Recorder*, as cited in "The Proposed Confederation," *Daily Gleaner*, 20 October 1905. De Jonge died of malarial fever the following year.

152 Meikle, *Confederation of the British West Indies versus Annexation to the United States of America*, 59–60, 114.

153 Walter Reece, letter to the editor, *Daily Gleaner*, 12 April 1911.

154 On imperial citizenship, see Daniel Gorman, "Wider and Wider Still?" On the ways in which Indians mobilized notions of citizenship within the empire, see Sukanya Banerjee, *Becoming Imperial Citizens: Indians in the Late-Victorian Empire*.

155 Radhika Viyas Mongia, "Race, Nationality, Mobility: A History of the Passport," 199–204. Immigrants also had to be in possession of at least $200 and undergo medical and sanitary examinations; labour conditions also had to be favourable.

156 As cited in Hugh Tinker, *Separate but Unequal: India and the Indians in the British Commonwealth, 1920–1950*, 28. See also Mongia, "Race, Nationality," 196–214; Gorman, *Imperial Citizenship*, 158–71.

157 Lake and Reynolds, *Drawing the Global Color Line*, 166–89.

158 See Lee, "'Yellow Peril' and Asian Exclusion in the Americas," 553–4.

159 Smith, *Reminiscences by Goldwin Smith*, 422–3.

160 Meikle, *Confederation of the British West Indies versus Annexation to the United States of America*, 59.

161 "The Cry for Annexation to Canada," *Daily Gleaner*, 29 June 1911.

162 *Daily Gleaner*, 30 June 1911.

163 Minutes, 5 March 1912, TNA, CO 23/268; Minutes, 6 May 1911, TNA, CO 23/267.

164 Winks, *Canadian-West Indian Union*, 23.

165 Grey-Wilson, "Bahamas, West Indies, Canada," address to the Empire Club, Toronto, 25 October 1911, http://speeches.empireclub.org/62316/data?n=4.

166 Harcourt, as cited in Samaroo, "Politics of Disharmony," 54.

167   Bailey, *Nassau Guardian*, 18 November 1911.

168   "An American Visitor," letter to the editor, *Nassau Guardian*, 17 February 1912; Bailey, *Nassau Guardian*, 21 February 1912; "Canada and the Bahamas," *Daily Gleaner*, 23 March 1912; "Canada and the Bahamas," *Nassau Guardian*, 17 February 1912.

169   "Union with Canada," *Nassau Tribune*, 25 February 1911.

170   Editorials, *Nassau Tribune*, 28 October, 21 November, 28 November, and 9 December 1911. The *Tribune* represented Black Bahamians.

171   Lorenzo Brice, George Cole, Daniel Moseley, William Johnson, James Sands, George Weech, Eric Solomon, and G.H. Johnson.

172   Robert Sawyer, Harcourt Malcolm, James Culmer, Charles Bethell, and *Nassau Guardian* proprietor Mary Moseley.

173   Grey-Wilson to Harcourt, 6 May 1911, TNA, CO 23/267.

174   *Nassau Tribune*, 25 February 1911.

175   Craton and Saunders, *Islanders in the Stream*, 89–100; Gail Saunders, *Bahamian Society after Emancipation: Essays in Nineteenth and Early Twentieth Century Bahamian History*, 77–112.

176   *Agreement between Canada and Certain West Indian Colonies, Dated 9th April 1912; and Correspondence Relating Thereto*, June 1912, Cd. 6092; "Canadian Preference and American Retaliation," *Daily Gleaner*, 10 April 1912.

177   Editorial, *Nassau Guardian*, 13 April 1912.

178   "Want Canada to Annex them," *Gazette* (Montreal), 2 March 1911. See also "Bahamas want to be Annexed," *Globe*, 12 April 1911; "Annexation to Canada favoured in Bahama," *Globe*, 15 March 1911. On the reported four hundred to five hundred in attendance at the February 1911 meeting, see *Nassau Guardian*, 14 March 1911.

179   "Canada Should Annex the West Indies," *Globe*, 30 March 1911; Mackay, *Daily Gleaner*, 18 April 1911. "Wider Canada," *Toronto World*, 27 October 1911.

180   Minutes, 12 September 1912, TNA, CO 23/270.

181   George Haddon-Smith to Harcourt, 12 April 1913, TNA, CO 23/271.

182   This argument is informed by Goldberg, *Racial State*, 120.

Chapter Three

1   Committee on Territorial Changes, Committee of Imperial Defence, 1916–1917, Reports, Proceedings and Memoranda, TNA, CAB 16/36. Reports of the Mallet Committee were released on 25 January, 22 March, 28 March, and 17 July 1917.

2   Joseph Pope, *Confidential Memorandum upon the Subject of the Annexation of the West India Islands to the Dominion of Canada*, 2–3. While the provenance of this document was likely the Department of External Affairs (LAC,

RG 25), it is catalogued separately in the library collections of Library and Archives Canada.

3 Pope, *Confidential Memorandum*, 4–5; Borden to George Perley, 3 June 1916, Borden fonds, LAC, MG 26-H, OC series, vol. 70.

4 W. David McIntyre, *Commonwealth of Nations*, 181.

5 Robert Holland, "The British Empire and the Great War, 1914–1918," 119.

6 John Herd Thompson, "Canada and the 'Third British Empire,'" 97–8. Norman Hillmer and J.L. Granatstein, *Empire to Umpire*, 58–64. L.W. White and W.D. Hussey, *Government in Great Britain, the Empire, and the Commonwealth*, 264.

7 See for example, Michael Adas, "Contested Hegemony: The Great War and the Afro-Asian Assault on the Civilizing Mission Ideology," 31–63; Judith M. Brown, *War and the Colonial Relationship*; John Gallagher, "Nationalisms and the Crisis of Empire, 1919–1922," 355–68; Frederick Cooper, *Colonialism in Question*, 175–6.

8 *Canadian Observer*, 14 April 1917.

9 Wigley, "Canada and Imperialism," 215–55. See also Winks, *Canadian-West Indian Union*; Samaroo, "Politics of Disharmony"; Hudson, "Imperial Designs," 33–48.

10 Wigley, "Canada and Imperialism," 215–55.

11 *Halifax Herald*, 13 July 1895; "Harry Judson Crowe Passes in Toronto," *Globe*, 26 May 1928; J.K. Hiller, "The Origins of the Pulp and Paper Industry in Newfoundland," 42–68; J.K. Hiller, "The Politics of Newsprint," 3–39; and Melvin Baker, "Harry Judson Crowe."

12 Harry Judson Crowe, "Commercial Union with the West Indies or Confederation?," 629. Crowe's interest in bringing Newfoundland into Canadian Confederation was long-standing. In the years before the war, he corresponded with the former Canadian governor general Earl Grey, who similarly supported Newfoundland's entry into Confederation as well as stronger ties between Canada and the Caribbean. Harry J. Crowe to Grey, 4 February 1911, DUSC, Grey, 174/4.

13 Crowe, "Canada and the West Indies," 430.

14 Crowe to Borden, 29 April 1916, Borden fonds, LAC, MG 26-H, OC series, vol. 70.

15 Borden to Perley, telegram, 2 June 1916, Borden to Perley, 3 June 1916, Perley to Borden, 27 June 1916, in Canada, *Documents on Canadian External Relations*, vol. 1, 714–75, 716–17; George Foster to Andrew Bonar Law, 19 June 1916, TNA, CO 318/345.

16 Pope, "Confidential Memorandum," 2.

17 Ibid., 4, 5.

18 Ibid., 4, 5.

19 Ibid., 4.
20 Sensitive to the distinct lack of empire zeal in Quebec, Borden was never too
    quick to commit Canadian resources to the Royal Navy. But he did identify
    a national navy of modest size and strength as a long-term goal. Hillmer
    and Granatstein, *Empire to Umpire*, 45–9. The addition to Canada of several
    territories in the Caribbean would accelerate these plans.
21 Pope, "Confidential Memorandum," 5.
22 Ibid., 2–3.
23 Hillmer and Granatstein, *Empire to Umpire*, 52–4.
24 Committee of the Imperial War Cabinet on Territorial Desiderata in the
    Terms of Peace, TNA, CAB 21/77. In 1919–20, there was also talk of
    Canada taking on a League of Nations mandate in Armenia, though the
    Canadian government was not keen on the idea; see Webster, "Foreign Policy,
    Diplomacy, and Decolonization," 161–2.
25 Thompson and Randall, *Canada and the United States*, 66–9; Hillmer
    and Granatstein, *Empire to Umpire*, 61. The British Foreign Office
    entertained the possibility of exchanging British Honduras for a strip of
    the panhandle – an idea Borden later took up with Lloyd George in April
    1918 – but the Colonial Office objected strenuously. As Wigley observes
    in "Canada and Imperialism," 220–1, relinquishing British Honduras to a
    country with deplorable race relations would violate the Colonial Office's
    frequently avowed commitment to protect Black and other racialized peoples
    throughout the empire. On Borden's interest in the proposal to trade British
    Honduras for a strip of the Alaska panhandle, see Borden to Lloyd George,
    29 April 1919, and John J. O'Gorman to Borden, 26 April 1919, David
    Lloyd George Papers, PA, LG F/35/3.
26 Committee of the Imperial War Cabinet on Territorial Desiderata in the
    Terms of Peace, TNA, CAB 21/77. In 1907, the Canadian government had
    expressed similar concerns to the Colonial Office about the future of St Pierre
    and Miquelon. See Committee of Imperial Defence, Committee on Territorial
    Changes, Reports, Proceedings and Memoranda 1916–1917, TNA, CAB 16/36.
27 "Greenland and the Danish Islands," *New York Times*, 21 August 1916.
28 Report of the Sub-Committee of the Imperial War Cabinet," April 1917, as
    cited in Governor General of Canada to the Colonial Secretary, 28 September
    1919, TNA, FO 608/120, file 419/1/4.
29 Peace Congress, Minutes, Danish Claims to Sovereignty over Greenland, 18
    August 1919, Charles Tufton [for Balfour] to M. Berhoft [Danish Minister
    at Paris], 26 August 1919, Curzon to Tufton [for Balfour], 26 August 1919,
    Gerald Spicer [for Curzon] to Eyre Crowe, 15 November 1919, TNA, FO
    608/120, file 419/1/4.
30 Lansing, as cited in Délégation de Danemark, 9 July 1919, TNA,
    FO 608/120, file 419/1/4.

31 Peace Congress, Minutes, Danish Claims to Sovereignty over Greenland, 18 August 1919, TNA, FO 608/120, file 419/1/4.

32 Committee of the Imperial War Cabinet on Territorial Desiderata in the Terms of Peace, TNA, CAB 21/77.

33 John Kendle, *Round Table Movement and Imperial Union.*

34 Borden, 14 August 1918, as cited in Riddell, *Documents on Canadian Foreign Policy, 1917–1919,* 56.

35 Amery to Borden, 19 August 1918, Leo Amery Papers, Churchill Archives Centre, Cambridge, UK (this repository hereafter abbreviated as CAC), AMEL 2/1/1. This correspondence is reproduced in Canada, *Documents on Canadian External Relations,* vol. 1, *1909–1918,* 717–18.

36 Ibid.

37 Susan Pedersen, "Modernity and Trusteeship," 203–20. As Margaret MacMillan observes in *Paris 1919,* Borden's "real dream was always a partnership between the United States and the British empire"; the "main Canadian concern ... was to keep on good terms with the United States and to bring it together with Britain" (93, 47).

38 Crowe, "Canada and the West Indies," 430; Kidd, *Control of the Tropics.*

39 Crowe, "Canada and the West Indies," 430.

40 Lansing, as cited in "Let Us Buy the Dutch West Indies," *Independent,* 21 July 1917.

41 Ibid.

42 *New York Evening Mail,* 2 April 1917. Bahamas governor William Allardyce assured the Colonial Office that while such "editorial effusion" was "doubtless significant as reflecting the thoughts and wishes of a certain class of people in the United States ... no real importance need to be attached [to it]." With few exceptions, Allardyce stated, "all sections" of the Bahamian population opposed annexation to the United States. William Allardyce to Walter H. Long, 11 April 1917, TNA, CO 23/279.

43 *Nassau Tribune,* 5 and 7 June 1917.

44 *New York Evening Mail,* cited in the *Nassau Tribune,* 25 October 1917.

45 *Nassau Guardian,* 27 October, 3 November, 7 November 1917.

46 On the Royal Bank's expansion in the Caribbean, see McDowall, *Quick to the Frontier.*

47 "Canadian Bankers Busy: Financiers Tour West Indies on Yacht to Plan Expansion," *New York Times,* 3 March 1916; "Royal Bank of Canada Planning to Put Branch Houses in West Indies," *Washington Post,* 3 March 1916.

48 *Financial Times,* 26 August 1916.

49 McDowall, *Quick to the Frontier,* 163–202. "Given Canada's fledgling presence on the world stage," McDowall argues, the Royal Bank "habitually donned the *de facto* identity of other nationalities. Hence, the Platt

Amendment had allowed it to assume American protection in Cuba, Puerto Rico, and the Dominican Republic. In the British West Indies, it was a 'British' bank. In Guadeloupe, it was a 'French' bank. Only in South America did it develop a more autonomous identity" (188). See also Joseph Schull and J. Douglas Gibson, *Scotia Bank Story*, 67–78.

50   John Gallagher and Ronald Robinson argued in "Imperialism of Free Trade," 6, that it is "only when the polities of these new regions fail to provide satisfactory conditions for commercial or strategic integration and when their relative weakness allows, that power is used imperialistically to adjust those conditions."

51   H.V. Nelles and Christopher Armstrong, *Southern Exposure*, 287–92. See also McDowall, *The Light*.

52   Nelles and Armstrong, *Southern Exposure*, 290.

53   Hudson, "Imperial Designs."

54   Edwin M. Borchard, "Commercial and Financial Interests of the United States in the Caribbean," 193. Borchard was a professor of law at Yale. The historiography dealing with dollar diplomacy and American economic imperialism in the Caribbean and Latin America more generally is voluminous. See, for example, Emily Rosenberg, *Financial Missionaries to the World*; Cyrus Veeser, *A World Safe for Capitalism*; Michael Gobat, *Confronting the American Dream*.

55   Gallagher and Robinson, "Imperialism of Free Trade," 6.

56   "Canadian Trade would Benefit," *Ottawa Gazette*, 28 August 1916

57   Crowe, "Commercial Union with the West Indies or Confederation?," 630–1.

58   *Agreement between Canada and Certain West Indian Colonies, Dated 9th April 1912*, June 1912, Cd. 6092.

59   Crowe, "Commercial Union with the West Indies or Confederation?," 630–1.

60   James Carson, "Commercial and Financial Agencies of Pan-American Union," 270.

61   Pope, "Confidential Memorandum," 4.

62   Ibid., 4, 5.

63   Gideon Murray, "Canada and the British West Indies," 58; Murray, who argued that a federation of the British Caribbean colonies should be a prerequisite to Canada-Caribbean union, was an exception.

64   In the nineteenth and early twentieth centuries, the Colonial Office intermittently entertained the idea of a Caribbean federation. The subject was often raised in Britain's House of Commons and subsequently considered in several royal commissions on the Caribbean. Amalgamating the island governments under one administration was thought not only financially expedient but an important stage toward regional development and, ultimately, independence. But these plans were hampered by a lack

of adequate support in the islands. Ever sensitive to the appearance of despotism, the British government did not force the issue. Yet as Thomas Holt has pointed out, some members of the Colonial Office were reluctant to endorse a Caribbean federation on the grounds that it might inspire agitation for more popular (specifically non-white) control over the administration of the region. See Holt, *Problem of Freedom*, 361–2. Samuel J. Hurwitz, "The Federation of the West Indies," 139–68, Colin A. Hughes, "Experiments towards Closer Union in the British West Indies," 85–104, and Jesse H. Proctor, "Development of the Idea of Federation of the British Caribbean Territories," 61–105, though somewhat dated, continue to offer useful summaries of the federation debate in the nineteenth and twentieth centuries.

65 Pope, "Confidential Memorandum," 5.

66 Crowe, "Canada and the West Indies," 427; Canada, *House of Commons Debates*, 13 June 1917, 2289–90 (George Foster, MP).

67 *Journal of Commerce*, cited in "Concerning Us," *Daily Gleaner*, 29 July 1918.

68 George Perley to Robert Borden, 27 June 1916 and 15 September 1916, Borden fonds, LAC, MG 26-H, OC series, vol. 70.

69 "Mr. Crowe Returns to His Advocacy of Canada-West Indian Federation," *Daily Gleaner*, 29 August 1919.

70 *Daily Gleaner*, 29 August 1919.

71 Patriot, "The Proposed Union between the West Indies and Canada," *Daily Gleaner*, 16 May 1919.

72 "Address to the Manchester Branch of the Jamaica League," *Daily Gleaner*, 10 June 1919.

73 J. Kissock Graham, letter to the editor, *Daily Gleaner*, 3 May 1919.

74 Crowe to Borden, 13 September 1916, and Crowe to Loring Christie, 26 November 1919, Borden fonds, LAC, MG 26-H, OC series, vol. 70.

75 Crowe, "Commercial Union with the West Indies or Confederation?," 632.

76 Crowe, "Canada and the West Indies," 428.

77 On the First World War as a watershed in political protest and organization in the Caribbean, see Glenford Howe, *Race, War and Nationalism*; Richard Smith, *Jamaican Volunteers in the First World War*.

78 John R. Reid, "Canada's Future Relations with the West Indies," *Canada-West Indies Magazine* 7, no. 3 (1919): 66.

79 Crowe, "Commercial Union with the West Indies or Confederation?," 632.

80 Pope, "Confidential Memorandum," 4.

81 Borden to George Perley, 3 June 1916, Borden fonds, LAC, MG 26-H, OC series, vol. 70.

82 Borden to Keefer, 1 January 1919, ibid.

83 Watson Griffin, "Why Canada Should Pay Attention to the West Indies," *By-Water Magazine* 1, no. 8 (1916): 30.

84   Sarah-Jane Mathieu, "Jim Crow Rides This Train," 124, 129–30; Senate, Meeting Minutes, 4 September 1917, Dalhousie University Archives (hereafter DUA); *Daily Gleaner*, 2 May 1914, 24 April 1915, "The Movement Closer," 12 April 1916, 12 April 1917. Canada's immigration policy did not explicitly exclude Blacks, but the superintendent of immigration at Ottawa instructed immigration inspectors to restrict Black migration as much as possible. Inspectors could thus deny entry to Black immigrants who, in the inspector's assessment, had poor health, questionable "moral character," or were presumed unsuited to Canada's climate. Inspectors also used the "continuous passage" regulation liberally when they encountered non-white migrants. If African Caribbeans docked in New York or Newfoundland before proceeding to Canada, for example, they were refused entry because they did not arrive by continuous passage. See, for example, W.D. Scott to J. Russell Smith, 26 January 1917, Scott to L.F. St. Bernard, 8 February 1917; Scott to J.W. Gallway, 3 February 1917; Scott to C.E. Donald Horton, 2 April 1917; and Scott to D. Vallancey, 30 April 1917, all at LAC, RG 76, vol. 566, pt. 2, file 810666.

85   Howe, *Race, War and Nationalism*, 29–40.

86   Robin Winks, *Blacks in Canada*, 314–15.

87   James W. St. G. Walker, "Race and Recruitment in World War I," 1. On British concerns about employing Black soldiers in combat, see Howe, *Race, War and Nationalism*, 46–7. In the French context, see Sally Marks, "Black Watch on the Rhine: A Study in Propaganda, Prejudice, and Prurience," 297–334. On concerns about the use of Black South African troops, see B.P. Willan, "The South African Native Labour Contingent, 1916–1918," 61–86. In the American context, see Adriane Lentz-Smith, *Freedom Struggles*; Chad L. Williams, *Torchbearers of Democracy*.

88   Interview with George Fells, Yarmouth, NS, 9 September 1982, as cited in Calvin W. Ruck, *Canada's Black Battalion*, 12; Winks, *Blacks in Canada*, 314.

89   Willan, "The South African Labour Contingent, 1916–1918," 63; Walker, "Race and Recruitment," 7, has identified a similar phenomenon regarding Japanese would-be recruits in Canada.

90   C.J. Doherty to Colonel E.A. Stanton, 7 January 1916, "Memorandum for the Minister of Justice," 25 January 1916, W. Stuart Edwards to E.A. Stanton, 31 January 1916, all LAC, RG 13, series A-2, vol. 199, file 148; Canada, *House of Commons Debates*, 24 March 1916, 2114–15 (William Pugsley, MP).

91   Mathieu, *North of the Color Line*, 100–12. Melissa Shaw, "'Most Anxious to Serve Their King and Country,'" is an excellent study of the dynamics of this activism in Ontario.

92   *Atlantic Advocate*, April 1915; Wilfred DeCosta's birthplace is listed as Kingston, Jamaica, on his son's birth certificate. See Wilfred Alleyne DeCosta,

b. 1908, Halifax, Halifax County, registered in 1908, Vital Statistics of Nova Scotia, Birth Registry, p. 56300313, Nova Scotia Archives and Records Management (hereafter NSARM). Additional bibliographical material on DeCosta can be found in Philip Hartling, "*The Atlantic Advocate*, Nova Scotia's First Black Magazine," unpublished history with biographical notes of *Advocate* staff, 1992, NSARM.

93 Hartling, "*Atlantic Advocate*."

94 *Atlantic Advocate*, April 1917.

95 On the history of conscription in Canada, see J.L. Granatstein and J. Mackay Hitsman, *Broken Promises*.

96 "Conscription and the Colored Man," *Canadian Observer*, 8 September 1917; "Colored Engineer Refused Exemption, Volunteered 3 Times," *Canadian Observer*, 17 November 1917; "Is This British Fair Play," *Canadian Observer*, 1 December 1917.

97 "Conscription Was Debated by the Shareholders of the West Indian Trading Co.," *Canadian Observer*, 24 November 1917. Winks, *Blacks in Canada*, 414.

98 "A.E. King Pres. West Indies Trading Association Answers Attacks Made on Name of Association," *Canadian Observer*, 9 December 1916; "Successful Publicity Meeting of West Indies Trading Association," *Canadian Observer*, 16 December 1916; and "Montreal Buying Shares of West Indies Trading Co., Ltd.," *Canadian Observer*, 23 December 1916.

99 "Montreal Buying Shares of West Indies Trading Co., Ltd.," *Canadian Observer*, 23 December 1916.

100 "Conscription Was Debated by the Shareholders of the West Indian Trading Co.," *Canadian Observer*, 24 November 1917.

101 J.L. Granatstein, *Canada's Army*, 117, 123–4.

102 Ruck, *Canada's Black Battalion*, 37–8.

103 Stanley Mackenzie to J.C. Connell, 3 May 1918, and Connell to Mackenzie, 8 May 1918, President's Office fonds, DUA, UA3, file 310.10.

104 Scane to the Acting Colonial Secretary, Jamaica, 10 June 1918, reproduced in "McGill College and Our Students," *Daily Gleaner*, 13 July 1918 and 22 May 1917.

105 John W. Scane to Stanley Mackenzie, 6 May 1918, President's Office fonds, DUA, UA3, file 310.10.

106 "Colored Students [at] McGill University Form Medical League," *Canadian Observer*, 11 December 1916. The elected officers of the Gamma League were R.S. Hall (president, Med. '17), R.B. Taylor (vice-president, Med. '18), P.M. Savory (secretary, Med. '19), C. Chandler Jones (assistant secretary, Med. '20), H.L. Ellis (treasurer, Med. '20), and Julius Jordan (chaplain, Arts '16, Med. '20). The University Corporation, according to the 1821 Charter of McGill College, consisted of college faculty, governors, and prominent

members of the Montreal community. See Stanley Brice Frost, *McGill University for the Advancement of Learning: 1801–1895*, vol. 1, 79.

107 "Colored Students [at] McGill University Form Medical League," *Canadian Observer*, 11 December 1916.

108 Peterson, as cited in *Canadian Observer*, 11 December 1916.

109 Ibid.

110 Scane to unnamed McGill medical school graduate, as cited in "Colour Line," *Daily Gleaner*, 22 May 1917.

111 A detailed description of the league's activities from September 1916 through July 1917 can be found in the *Daily Gleaner*, 2 March 1918.

112 Gamma Medical League, letter to the editor, *Daily Gleaner*, 14 June 1917.

113 *Jamaica Times*, as cited in "The Weakness of McGill on the Color Question," *Canadian Observer*, 16 March 1918.

114 G.M. Wortley to J.A.G. Smith, 6 July 1918, and J.A.G. Smith, letter to the *Daily Gleaner*, 10 July 1918, all cited in *Daily Gleaner*, 13 July 1918. On Smith, see Bakan, *Ideology and Class Conflict in Jamaica*, 99.

115 Scane to the Acting Assistant Colonial Secretary, Jamaica, 10 June 1918, reproduced in the *Daily Gleaner*, 13 July 1918.

116 Ibid.

117 "Medical Doors of Queen's Closed to Colored Students," *Canadian Observer*, 2 February 1918.

118 Letter to the editor, *Canadian Observer*, 9 February 1918.

119 The West Indian Club of Queen's University to the Officer Administering the Government of the Colony of Barbados, 15 April 1918, enclosure in T.E. Fell to Walter H. Long, 4 June 1918, TNA, CO 28/293.

120 James Willcocks to the Colonial Secretary, 15 May 1918, TNA, CO 37/262.

121 T.E. Fell to Walter H. Long, 4 June 1918, and enclosure: The West Indian Club of Queen's University to the Officer Administering the Government of the Colony of Barbados, 15 April 1918, TNA, CO 28/293.

122 Internal correspondence, 14 May 1918, TNA, CO 37/262; Internal correspondence, 4 June 1918, TNA CO 28/293. On British Caribbean soldiers in the war, see Howe, *Race, War and Nationalism*.

123 As cited in Tinker, *Separate but Unequal*, 28.

124 "The Prohibition," *Daily Gleaner*, 15 June 1917.

125 ITALEAN [pseud.], letter to the editor, *Daily Gleaner*, 16 April 1917.

126 *Daily Chronicle*, 4 August 1916.

127 Annual Report of the Georgetown Chamber of Commerce, 1917, as cited in the *West India Committee Circular*, 4 October 1917.

128 *Barbados Advocate*, 26 June 1917, enclosed in O'Hara to Scott, 17 July 1917, LAC, RG 76, vol. 566, file 810666, pt. 2.

129 Scott to O'Hara, 30 July 1917, LAC, RG 76, vol. 566, file 810666, pt. 2.

130 "Canada and the Colour Question," *West India Committee Circular*, 4 October 1917.

131 *United Empire*, as reproduced in "West Indies," *Daily Gleaner*, 8 November 1917. Union was a recurring subject in *United Empire*. See Evans Lewin, "Canada and the West Indies," *United Empire* 7, no. 11 (1916): 704–6; T.H. MacDermot, "The British West Indies and Their Future," *United Empire* 8, no. 9 (1917): 550–1; W.R. Hunt, "The British West Indies," *United Empire* 8, no. 12 (1917): 707–8; Harry J. Crowe, "Canada and the West Indies," *United Empire* 9, no. 10 (1918): 426–31. The Royal Colonial Institute was founded in 1868 (originally named the Colonial Society) to provide a forum for discussion of empire-related topics. Focused on intellectual exchange of a non-partisan nature, the institute's central endeavour was the establishment and expansion of a colonial library. See T.R. Rees, *The History of the Royal Commonwealth Society, 1868–1968*.

132 "West Indies Must Join Canada or U.S. Says Judge Rowan-Hamilton," *Canadian Observer*, 16 March 1918.

133 "Shall West India Islands Be United with Canada?" *Canadian Observer*, 8 March 1919.

134 Winks, *Blacks in Canada*, 486–7.

135 Letters to the editor, *Canadian Observer*, 1 and 11 March 1919.

136 Lake and Reynolds, *Drawing the Global Colour Line*, 306–8.

137 "Pan-African Congress to Safe-Guard Race Interest," *Canadian Observer*, 22 February 1919; "Race Topics of To-Day," *Canadian Observer*, 1 March 1919. Thoughtful summaries of the peace negotiations can be found in Lake and Reynolds, *Drawing the Global Colour Line*, and Pedersen, "Settler Colonialism at the Bar of the League of Nations."

138 As cited in Lake and Reynolds, *Drawing the Global Colour Line*, 289. See also Thomas W. Burkman, *Japan and the League of Nations*, 80–6.

139 As cited in Lake and Reynolds, *Drawing the Global Colour Line*, 291.

140 Lake and Reynolds, *Drawing the Global Colour Line*, 297–8. MacMillan, "Canada and the Peace Settlements," 400.

141 Mathieu, *North of the Color Line*, 108–17, at 114.

142 Ibid., 119–20; Howe, *Race, War and Nationalism*, 172–99.

143 Howe, *Race, War and Nationalism*, 200.

144 Stimpson, letter to the editor, *Daily Gleaner*, 28 May 1917.

145 Stimpson, letter to the editor, *Daily Gleaner*, 12 May 1919. On these contradictions, see Mehta, *Liberalism and Empire*.

146 Stimpson, letter to the editor, *Daily Gleaner*, 12 May 1919.

147 Erez Manela, *The Wilsonian Moment*, 13.

148 Liddelow, letter to the editor, *West India Committee Circular*, 11 December 1919; Liddelow wrote the letter on 17 October.

149   "Canada and the West Indies," *West India Committee Circular*, 26 June
      1919; Edward Davson, letter to the editor, *Times* (London), 2 August 1919;
      Gideon Murray, letter to the editor, *Times* (London), 11 August 1919;
      Jamaica Imperial Association to the Colonial Office, December 1919, TNA,
      CO 318/352; Wigley, "Canada and Imperialism," 244.
150   Crowe to Borden, 1 March 1919, Keefer to Borden, 14 March 1919; Borden
      to Keefer, 14 March 1919, Borden fonds, LAC, MG 26-H, OC series, vol. 70.
151   Borden to Keefer, 1 January 1919, LAC, MG 26-H, OC series, vol. 70.
152   Valerie Knowles, *Strangers at Our Gates*, 98–107; Gregory S. Kealey, *Workers
      in Canadian History*, 289–328; Craig Heron, *The Worker's Revolt in Canada,
      1917–1925*; David J. Bercuson, *Confrontation at* Winnipeg, 217–31.
153   R.A. Boutilier, "Ten Years of Non-Existence," 65.
154   "The Movement Closer," *Daily Gleaner*, 12 April 1916.
155   "What Does Lord Milner Mean?" *Daily Gleaner*, 24 October 1919.
156   Howe, *Race, War, and Nationalism*, 200–1.
157   Adas, "Contested Hegemony," 31–63.

Chapter Four

1   Arthur Sears Henning, "New American Empire Headed by Canada Seen,"
      Chicago Tribune, 27 January 1928. The report was discussed in several US
      newspapers, including in Drew Pearson, "U.S. Opposes Canada in Pan-
      American Union," *Canton Daily News*, 29 January 1928; A.M. Brayton, "The
      Week," *La Crosse Tribune*, 29 January 1928; "Canada May Be Empire," *Los
      Angeles Times*, 27 January 1928; and "Canadian Empire in N.A. Envisioned,"
      Marion Star, 4 February 1928. It received less attention in Canadian
      newspapers. See "Hear West Indies to Be Put under Canadian Guardianship,"
      Winnipeg Free Press," 29 January 1928.
2   The report was likely the work of a Latin American or Canadian interest group
      committed to seeing Canada join the Pan-American Union. Latin Americans,
      Iowa's *Sioux City Journal* claimed on 27 January 1928, "would welcome the
      Canadians all the more warmly if the Dominion were to acquire control of the
      British colonial possessions in the Americas." Canada did not officially join the
      Organization of American States (the Pan American Union's successor) until
      1990. On this history, see Peter McKenna, *Canada and the OAS*.
3   "Report of Inter-Imperial Relations Committee," *Imperial Conference, 1926,
      Summary of Proceedings*, 1926, Cmnd. 2768, at 14.
4   Robert J. Alexander, *History of Organized Labor in the English-Speaking West
      Indies*, 4–5.
5   R.A. Falconer, letter to the editor, *Globe*, 4 March 1920.
6   Robert Bothwell, "The Canadian Isolationist Tradition," 79; James Eayrs,

In Defence of Canada; H. Blair Neatby, *The Politics of Chaos*; P.B. Waite, "French Canadian Isolationism and English Canada." More recent studies, biographies of prominent isolationists, include Norman Hillmer, *O.D. Skelton: A Portrait of Political Ambition*; R. Douglas Francis, *Frank Underhill: Intellectual Provocateur*; J.L. Granatstein, "Becoming Difficult: Escott Reid: Diplomat and Scholar." Of course, historians generally agree that despite these isolationist tendencies, in the 1920s and 1930s the question of whether Canada would provide military support to Britain in the event of another major conflict was not in doubt (a sentiment demonstrated in 1939). See J.L. Granatstein and Robert Bothwell, "'A Self Evident National Duty.'"

7   "Special Luncheon Meeting in Honour of His Excellency, Viscount Willingdon, Governor-General," Royal York Hotel, Toronto, 28 March 1930, Empire Club of Canada Addresses, http://speeches.empireclub.org/61019/data?n=7.

8   Ibid.

9   "Viceroy's Suggestion as to Indies under Fire," *Toronto Daily Star*, 29 March 1930.

10 "Governor's Opinion. His Personal View," *Globe*, 29 March 1930.

11 John Darwin, "A Third British Empire?" 65.

12 Darwin, "Third British Empire?" 66–7. Holland, *Britain and the Commonwealth Alliance*, argues that this interwar emergence of the "Commonwealth system" was not an assertion of imperial strength but of insecurity and weakness.

13 Harry J. Crowe, "Suggested Union of Jamaica and Canada," *Daily Gleaner*, 10 February 1921.

14 Leopold Amery, "The British League of Nations," address delivered by Leopold S. Amery before the Empire Club of Canada, *Empire Club Addresses*, June 1920, http://speeches.empireclub.org/62374/data?n=1.

15 Amery, "British League of Nations."

16 Charles Lucas, "Balance of Power within the Empire," 17–26.

17 Ibid., 23.

18 George V. Fiddes, *Dominions and Colonial Offices*, 275.

19 British Parliamentary Papers, *Summary of Proceedings, Conference of Prime Ministers and representatives of the United Kingdom, the Dominions, and India, held in June, July, and August, 1921*, Cmd. 1474, 36.

20 "Prince and West Indies: Mr. Churchill on Links with Canada," *Times*, 25 June 1921; "To Link up Canada with West Indies," *Globe*, 27 June 1921; "Links Canada and Indies. Churchill Urges Close Union of Dominion and Islands," *Washington Post*, 27 June 1921; "Canadian-West Indian Co-operation Is Urged," *New York Times*, 27 June 1921.

21 *Appendix II: Statement by the Secretary of State for the Colonies as to the Colonies, Protectorates and Mandated Territories, October 3, 1923, Appendices to the Summary of Proceedings*, BPP, Cmd. 1988.

22   Holland, *Britain and the Commonwealth Alliance*, 41. J.A. Cross, "Whitehall and the Commonwealth," 190. A Dominions department was established within the Colonial Office in 1907, but its monopoly on dominion communications was increasingly undercut by the interests of other government bodies in dominion affairs – such as the Foreign Office and the Committee for Imperial Defence. And a precedent had been set in the Imperial War Cabinet in 1918 for dominion premiers to circumvent the Colonial Office and correspond directly with the British prime minister. When the UK Cabinet Secretariat assumed responsibility for the Imperial Conferences following its founding in 1916, the Colonial Office's function in dominion affairs was again called into question.

23   Fiddes, *Dominions and Colonial Offices*, 277–8.

24   Baldwin, as cited in J.A. Cross, *Whitehall and the Commonwealth*, 47.

25   Amery, as cited in Cross, *Whitehall and the Commonwealth*, 47.

26   Walter Runciman, as cited in Cross, *Whitehall and the Commonwealth*, 47.

27   Amery, *My Political Life*, 2:335–7.

28   Harcourt, "Suggested Reconstruction of the Colonial Office," April 1911, Lewis Harcourt Papers, Bodleian Library, vol. 503.

29   *Appendices to the Summary of Proceedings*, Imperial Conference, 1926, Cmd. 2768, 115.

30   *Summary of Proceedings*, Imperial Conference, 1926, Cmd. 2768, 31–2.

31   *Appendices to the Summary of Proceedings*, Cmd. 2768, 112.

32   Ibid., 116.

33   Anthony H.M. Kirk-Greene, "'Taking Canada into Partnership in 'The White Man's Burden,'" 38.

34   As cited in Jonathan A. Moore, "The Transformation of the British Imperial Administration, 1919–1939," 137.

35   *Appendices to the Summary of Proceedings*, Imperial Conference, 1926, Cmd. 2768, 115.

36   Moore, "Transformation of the British Imperial Administration," 72. Low salaries in the colonial service deterred some Canadians. See Charles Orr to L.S. Amery, 21 February 1928, L.B. Freeston to Charles Orr, 13 April 1928, and Orr to R.D. Furse, 30 April 1928, TNA, CO 23/375.

37   On the conference of 1921, see P.G. Wigley, *Canada and the Transition to Commonwealth*, 98.

38   *Summary of Proceedings*, Imperial Conference, 1937, Cmd. 5482, 22–3.

39   "The Next Imperial Conference," *Round Table* 16, no. 62 (1926): 228.

40   C.P. Stacey, *Mackenzie King and the Atlantic Triangle*, 33.

41   "The Next Imperial Conference," *Round Table* 16, no. 62 (1926): 232.

42   Harry J. Crowe to C.J. Doherty, 13 April 1921, LAC, RG 13, series A-2, vol. 258, file 880; "Suggested Union of Jamaica and Canada," *Daily Gleaner*, 10 February 1921.

43 "Canada and the West Indies," *Globe*, 29 March 1930.

44 "Sir James Aikins on His Trip to the West Indies," *Daily Gleaner*, 16 February 1929.

45 "The British Empire Is Made for Canada," *Daily Gleaner*, 3 May 1928.

46 J. Calvin Reid to R.B. Bennett, 24 March 1934, R.B. Bennett fonds, LAC, MG 26-K, Political Series, section F, vol. 465.

47 A.E. Miller to Reid, 8 May 1934, ibid.

48 "Bennett Statement on Place of Empire to Be Contentious," *Globe*, 7 May 1930.

49 Hillmer and Granatstein, *Empire to Umpire*, 116–17.

50 "Bennett Statement on Place of Empire to be Contentious," *Globe*, 7 May 1930.

51 King Diary, 8 March 1923, 67, Mackenzie King fonds, LAC, MG 26-J13.

52 King Diary, 25 January 1929, 25, ibid. With the expansion of Canadian National's steamship service to the Caribbean in the latter half of the 1920s, Thornton visited the Caribbean regularly and was a driving force behind the Canada-West Indies Hotels Company. He accompanied King to Bermuda in April 1930 for a brief holiday and then travelled on to Jamaica to lay the ceremonial foundation stone for a new hotel at Constant Spring. The stated purpose of King's Bermuda trip was rest and relaxation, but rumours circulated on the island and beyond that his visit was inspired by recent discussions in Ottawa about the expansion of imperial trade, a subject Canadian Parliament would soon take up in its discussion of the new federal budget. King's activities in Bermuda likely fuelled these rumours. He met with members of the island government and, with Canadian senators Andrew Haydon and Wilfrid McDougald, sat in on a meeting of the House of Assembly, which happened to be discussing Bermuda's trade relations with Canada. See "Bermuda Visit of the Canadian Prime Minister," *Daily Gleaner*, 5 May 1930; "One of the World's Greatest Railroad Men," *Daily Gleaner*, 2 May 1929.

53 King Diary, 26 May 1928, 147, Mackenzie King fonds, LAC, MG 26-J13.

54 King Diary, 28 January 1930, 28, ibid.

55 R.A. Falconer, *The United States as a Neighbor from a Canadian Point of View*.

56 Ibid., 129.

57 Ibid., 132.

58 "Canada and the West Indies," *New York Times*, 26 May 1929.

59 "Canada in the Caribbean," *Chicago Daily Tribune*, 25 April 1930.

60 The Colonial Office sent Canada's Department of External Affairs the Jamaican and British Guianian resolutions on 13 January 1920. See LAC, RG 25, series A3 (G1), vol. 1260, file 193-1920.

61 Ibid.

62 Ibid.

63   "Favors U.S. Buying British West Indies," *St Louis Globe-Democrat*, 26
February 1920; U.S. Senate Resolution 315, 66th Congress, 2D Session,
27 February 1920, enclosed in R.C. Lindsay, British Embassy, Washington,
to the Duke of Devonshire, Governor General of Canada, 1 March 1920,
LAC, RG 25, series A3a (G1), vol. 1263, file 365.

64   "Favors U.S. Buying British West Indies," *St Louis Globe-Democrat*,
26 February 1920.

65   "U.S. Peace Treaty," *Times* (London) 24 November 1920.

66   "West Indies Not to Be Ceded to U.S.," *Manitoba Free Press*, 21 February
1921; Harry N. Price, "President Opposes Island Debt Deal," *Washington
Post*, 17 January 1923.

67   U.S. Senate Resolution 396, 67th Congress, 4th Session, enclosed in
Marchant M. Mahoney to Under-Secretary of State for External Affairs,
Ottawa, 23 February 1923, LAC, RG25, series A3a (G1), vol. 1343, file 148.
Prohibitionist senators were particularly interested in the resolution. With
the British Caribbean under American administration, the illicit liquor
traffic from these islands could be minimized and prohibition would be
easier to enforce. But the opposition, led by President Warren Harding
and Republican leader Henry Cabot Lodge, prevailed. Both thought it
impractical. Acquiring new territories was against Harding's anti-imperialist
policy, and the examples of Puerto Rico and the Philippines were instructive.
"Those in touch with the executive difficulties in dealing with Porto Rico, and
with the never-ending problems in the Philippines," reported the *Washington
Post*, would understand fully why the Harding administration opposed the
acquisition of new territory. See Price, "President Opposes Island Debt Deal,"
Washington Post, 17 January 1923.

68   "Britain Will Not Trade W. Indies," *Brandon Daily Sun*, 22 February 1921;
"Britain Has No Intention of Selling West Indies," *Globe*, 26 June 1923.

69   Canada, *House of Commons Debates*, 19 May 1920, 2543 (W.K. Baldwin, MP).

70   Ibid., 19 March 1926, 1736 (W.K. Baldwin).

71   "Suggested Union of Jamaica and Canada," *Daily Gleaner*, 10 February 1921.

72   Harry J. Crowe to C.J. Doherty, 13 April 1921, LAC, RG 13, series A-2,
vol. 258, file 880.

73   Ibid.

74   "Jamaica Opposes Union with Canada," *Globe*, 5 August 1921;
"Confederation of West Indies," *Times*, 29 August 1921.

75   T.B. Macaulay, "Never Give Up the Colonies!," *Maclean's* 35, no. 5 (1922): 36.

76   T.B. Macaulay to Robert Borden, 27 June 1919, LAC, RG 20-A-3, vol. 957,
file 7-984.

77   Ibid.

78   Ibid.

79 Ibid.
80 "Finds West Indies Anxious for Union with This Dominion," *Globe*, 16 April 1925.
81 Tennyson, "British West Indies and Mackenzie King's National Policy," 68.
82 Ibid., 79.
83 Ibid., 68. The two services that plied the trade, the Canadian Government Merchant Marine and the Royal Mail Steam Packet Company, were slow and inefficient. In the years 1920–24, the latter service operated at a loss of $1.1 million, and many of the Caribbean colonies refused to pay the agreed-upon subsidies because the service proved inadequate.
84 Ibid., 79.
85 "Finds West Indies Anxious for Union with This Dominion," *Globe*, 16 April 1925.
86 Canada, *House of Commons Debates*, 5 April 1929, 1296 (Charles Cahan, MP).
87 Blanca G. Silvestrini, "Contemporary Puerto Rico," 147–51, at 148.
88 The Jones-Shafroth Act replaced the Foraker Act in 1917. It granted US citizenship to Puerto Ricans, created a local senate and bill of rights, and made the resident commissioner an elected rather than an appointed position.
89 Hume Wrong, *Government of the West Indies*, 5.
90 Ibid., 18. Bermuda, Barbados, and the Bahamas were the exception, as they remained under the old representative system. Newfoundland would present an exception to the course of constitutional development in the dominions in 1933, when, in a state of fiscal and political crisis, it voluntarily gave up self-government in favour of crown colony government.
91 Wrong, *Government of the West Indies*, 171.
92 Ibid., 179.
93 Andrew T. Drummond, "West Indies and the Dominion," *Daily Gleaner*, 30 May 1919. See also Drummond, *Gazette* (Montreal), 15 March 1920; Andrew T. Drummond, "Canada and the British West Indies," 29–34. Drummond advocated a customs union rather than a political union. See Canada, *House of Commons Debates*, 28 May 1920, 2845 (W.F. Cockshutt, MP), and 19 April 1921, 2254 (George Foster, MP); A.M. Belding, *Willison's Monthly*, as cited in "Relationship with Canada and West Indies," *Daily Gleaner*, 7 June 1929; "Canada and B.W.I.," *Financial Post*, 3 April 1930.
94 Harry Crowe, "British West Indies," *Times* (London), 25 June 1923.
95 As cited in "Relationship with Canada and West Indies," *Daily Gleaner*, 7 June 1929.
96 "West Indies Look to Canada for Economic Salvation," *Toronto Daily Star*, 12 May 1930.
97 E.H.B. Stafford to O.D. Skelton, 29 September 1939, LAC, RG 25, vol. 1978, file 1939-955.

98 Lionel North, "Songs of the Afro-Indian," *Canada-West Indies Magazine* 21, no. 3 (1932): 96–7.

99 "Dead Frog," *Canada-West Indies Magazine* 23, no. 10 (1934): 311.

100 Cover of *Canada-West Indies Magazine* 25, no. 4 (1936).

101 On the concept of trusteeship in the British context, see Pedersen, "Modernity and Trusteeship," 204, 217.

102 "Urges Commercial Union to Break American Grip," *Toronto Daily Star*, 7 December 1927. "West Indies Look to Canada for Economic Salvation," *Toronto Daily Star*, 12 May 1930.

103 Bernard Porter, *The Lion's Share*, 278.

104 Robert Stokes, *New Imperial Ideals*, 94.

105 Sharon C. Sewell, *Decolonization and the Other*, 13–18.

106 Dennis Benn, *The Caribbean: An Intellectual History*, 72–3.

107 West India Royal Commission Report, June 1945, Cmd. 6607, British Parliamentary Papers. The commission travelled to all the colonies and completed its report in 1939. The social and economic conditions outlined in the report were so deplorable that the Colonial Office delayed its publication until 1945 for fear it might be used against the British during the war. While conditions varied significantly across the region, the report highlighted many disturbing trends: overpopulation and inadequate social and health services, high infant mortality, poor drainage and irrigation, unregulated labour markets rife with child labour, paltry wages, unsafe workplaces, squalid living conditions in rural areas, and dilapidated, overcrowded schoolhouses.

108 Jay R. Mandle, "British Caribbean Economic History: An Interpretation," 239–40. In the early 1920s, the British government did send E.F.L. Wood, parliamentary undersecretary for the colonies, to the region on a fact-finding mission. Wood's report recommended a small modification of the colonial legislatures but "stopped short of pointing the way to the ultimate transfer of responsibility from London to the West Indies." Wood's recommendations were consistent with opinion at Whitehall. The British government had no intention of transferring political authority to its Caribbean colonies. See Gordon K. Lewis, *The Growth of the Modern West Indies*, 122–3.

109 Winks, *Blacks in Canada*, 423–5.

110 Sarah-Jane Mathieu, *North of the Color Line*, 186–7.

111 Amoaba Gooden, "Community Organizing by African Caribbean People in Toronto, Ontario," 413–26, provides an excellent overview of the various ways that African Caribbeans organized during the twentieth century.

112 "China and the League of Nations," *Dawn of Tomorrow*, 9 September 1930.

113 Thomas Holt, *Problem of Freedom*, 392.

114 Franklin W. Knight, *The Caribbean: The Genesis of a Fragmented Nationalism*, 289.

115 On the Canadian context of Pan-Africanism in the interwar period, see Wendell Nii Laryea Adjetey, "In Search of Ethiopia: Messianic Pan-Africanism and the Problem of the Promised Land, 1919–1931."

116 "Trade Treaty between Canada and the West Indies," *Daily Gleaner*, 21 January 1926.

117 Mathieu, *North of the Color Line*, 176–7.

118 R.P. Edwards, "Franklin – the Race," *Dawn of Tomorrow*, 9 February 1924.

119 "Ontario or Mississippi?," *Dawn of Tomorrow*, 1 August 1925.

120 "Hotel London Discharges Colored Help and Replaces Them with White Ex-Service Men," *Dawn of Tomorrow*, 16 June 1934.

121 F.C. Blair to James Cormack, 24 April 1925, LAC, RG 76, vol. 566, file 810666, pt. 3.

122 "Are West Indian Negroes British Subjects?," *Dawn of Tomorrow*, 26 August 1929.

123 The incident was first reported in the *Toronto Daily Star* and subsequently picked up by the British Caribbean press. "Immigrant Girl Held Virtually as Prisoner," *Toronto Daily Star*, 21 August 1925; "Jamaica Girl Held the Same as Prisoner," *Daily Gleaner*, 23 September 1925.

124 "Information Wanted," *Daily Gleaner*, 24 September 1925. For more on the Holness incident, see Paula Hastings, "The Limits of 'Brotherly Love,'" 46–8, 49–50.

125 "Hold Mass Meeting RE Ban on Colored Students at U.W.O.," *Dawn of Tomorrow*, 29 August 1931.

126 T.A. Marryshow, *West Indian*, as cited in "Union with B.W.I. Impossible," *Saturday Night*, 5 September 1925.

127 "B.G. Electives Entertain Hon. T.A. Marryshow," *Daily Gleaner*, 7 August 1928; F.L. Casserly to F.C.T. O'Hara, 11 March 1929, LAC, RG20-A-3, vol. 951, file 7-769; "Echo of West Indian Press Conference," *Port of Spain Gazette*, 5 April 1929; *Voice of St Lucia*, 23 March 1929; "Coloured Man Ordered off Canadian Ship," *West Indian*, 29 November 1929.

128 "Coloured Man Ordered off Canadian Ship," *West Indian*, 29 November 1929.

129 "Unpleasant," *Daily Gleaner*, 10 August 1928.

130 "Great Expectations," *Daily Gleaner*, 8 August 1928.

131 Ibid.; "Unpleasant," *Daily Gleaner*, 10 August 1928.

132 "Unpleasant," *Daily Gleaner*, 10 August 1928.

133 F.L. Casserly to F.C.T. O'Hara, 11 March 1929, LAC, RG 20-A-3, vol. 951, file 7-769.

134 "Unpleasant," *Daily Gleaner*, 10 August 1928.

135 R.C. Vaughan to C.D. Howe, 28 December 1938, enclosed in "Memorandum for the Prime Minister," 31 December 1938, LAC, RG 25, series A-2 (d1), vol. 749, file 175 (1-w-26).

136 Colin A. Palmer, *Freedom's Children*, 124.

137 W.B. Armit to R.B. Teakle, 24 December 1938, enclosed in "Memorandum
     for the Prime Minister," 31 December 1938, LAC, RG25, series A2 (d1),
     vol. 749, file 175 (1-w-26).

138 Bryan D. Palmer, *Working Class Experience*, 296; Craig Heron, "Communists,
     Gangsters, and Canadian Sailors," 231–7.

139 Judgement of Maritime Relations Board, 12 April 1945, LAC, RG 145,
     vol. 23, file 751:212:45.

140 W.B. Armit to R.B. Teakle, 24 December 1938, enclosed in Memorandum
     for the Prime Minister, 31 December 1938, LAC, RG25, series A2 (d1),
     vol. 749, file 175 (I-W-26).

141 R.C. Vaughan to C.D. Howe, 28 December 1938, ibid.

142 W.B. Armit to R.B. Teakle, 24 December 1938, ibid.

143 "Case of Men Fired Off 'Lady [Rodney]' to Be Discussed," *Daily Gleaner*,
     28 March 1939.

144 "All Hands on Strike against Canadian National Steamships," *Daily Gleaner*,
     3 January 1939.

145 "Refuse to Load Liner: Jamaica Workers Will Not Handle Lady Rodney,"
     Gazette (Montreal), 7 January 1939; "Strikes Called Off, New Arbitration
     Board to Settle Disputes," *Daily Gleaner*, 5 January 1939. The *Lady Rodney*
     was notified by wireless of the arbitration settlement and returned to the
     harbour to unload, but the dispute delayed the ship's northbound schedule.
     See "Port of Boston, Lady Rodney to Arrive Today: Delayed by Strike," *Daily
     Boston Globe*, 13 January, 1939.

146 Canada, *House of Commons Debates*, 12 April 1948, 2877 (J.F. Pouliot, MP).

147 Tony Martin, *Pan-African Connection*, 65.

148 Carrington, "United States and Canada," 101; Hastings, "Limits of 'Brotherly
     Love,'" 49.

149 Theo McKay was the elder brother of the influential literary figure Claude
     McKay. See Jimmy Carnegie, "Claude McKay's Big Brother, U. Theo McKay
     (1872–1949)."

150 "Information Wanted," *Daily Gleaner*, 24 September 1925; U. Theo McKay,
     Daily Gleaner, 13 July 1925.

151 "The West Indies through a Hunter's Spectacles," *Labour Leader*,
     9 March 1929.

152 Ibid.

153 Lake and Reynolds, *Drawing the Global Colour Line*.

154 Caribbean labourers were instrumental in the construction of the Panama
     Canal in the early twentieth century, and a significant portion remained in
     the canal zone after construction was complete in 1914. Velma Newton, *The
     Silver Men*; Carla Burnett, "'Unity Is Strength.'"

155 W.R. Little to R.T. Rutherford, 5 February 1920, LAC, RG 76, vol. 766, file 810666, pt. 2.

156 Marcus Garvey to Robert Borden, 18 October 1921, Robert Borden fonds, LAC, MG 26-H1, vol. 284.

157 A.W. Merriam to H.V. Tennant, 15 November 1921, LAC, MG 26-H1, vol. 284.

158 H.V. Tennant to A.W. Merriam, 15 November 1921, LAC, MG 26-H1, vol. 284.

159 Barbara Roberts, *Whence They Came*, 65–75.

160 Jerome Teelucksingh, *Labour and the Decolonization Struggle in Trinidad and Tobago*, 38–42.

161 "Marcus Garvey Held by Immigration Men," *Globe*, 31 October 1928; "Garvey, Ordered Deported, Leaves for Jamaica Today," *Globe*, 7 November 1928; "Garvey Forced out of Canada Wednesday," *Baltimore Afro-American*, 10 November 1928; "Canada Balks Garvey," *Baltimore Afro-American*, 24 November 1928.

162 "Again, Marcus Garvey," *Dawn of Tomorrow*, 30 November 1928.

163 A.M. Wendell Malliet to W.D. Herridge, 11 July 1934, enclosed in W.D. Herridge to O.D. Skelton, 13 July 1934, LAC, RG25, series A2 (d1), vol. 749, file 175 (1-w-26). For more on A.M. Wendell Malliet, a Jamaican immigrant who worked for the *New York Amsterdam News*, see Eric D. Duke, "The Diasporic Dimensions of British Caribbean Federation in the Early Twentieth Century," 242–3.

164 W.D. Herridge to O.D. Skelton, 13 July 1934, LAC, RG25, series A2 (d1), vol. 749, file 175 (1-w-26).

165 O.D. Skelton to W.D. Herridge, 16 July 1934, ibid.

166 See, for example, "Riot Probe Ordered," *Globe and Mail*, 4 May 1938; "Jamaica Riot Traced to Strike Attempt," *Globe and Mail*, 25 May 1938; "Riots Renewed in Jamaica," *Globe and Mail*, 4 June 1938; "Jamaica Labor Men Freed; Crowds Cheer," *Globe and Mail*, 16 June 1938; "West Indians Clamor for Self-Rule," and "Disorder in British Guiana," *Globe and Mail*, 18 June 1938.

167 "Poverty in West Indies May Cause Revolt," *Globe*, 24 October 1935.

168 "West Indian Strike Quelling Is Protested," *Globe and Mail*, 22 June 1938.

169 "Colonies Secretary Studies Jamaica Riot Cause," *Globe and Mail*, 26 May 1938.

170 Revolt Predicted among Islanders," *Globe*, 24 October 1935.

171 King Diary, 27 October 1938, 811–12, Mackenzie King fonds, LAC, MG 26-J13. When the subject was raised during his visit, he responded, somewhat deceptively, that the idea "had not been even thought of by Canada and probably would not be for quite some time." The labour turmoil in the Caribbean may have partly influenced King's evasiveness. The prime minister did not want an official Canadian representative sitting on the Royal (Moyne) Commission to investigate the labour disturbances, let alone a union of Canada and the British Caribbean. Aware that the commission would

be arriving on 1 November, King may have planned his departure on 27 October accordingly. Had his visit overlapped with that of the commission, speculation might have run rampant about Canadian involvement in the region's future. King was interested in the commission's findings because he valued Canada's relationship with the Caribbean. But he was not interested in discussing union, likely for many of the same reasons that dampened his interest in 1929: a depressed economy, the expenditure, his general distaste for British efforts to define Canada's imperial obligations (in the Caribbean or elsewhere), and the racist dilemma of incorporating African Caribbeans in the Canadian federation. King's commitment to maintaining the white racial "character of Canada's population" persisted throughout his time in office. On this latter point, see Ninette Kelley and Michael Trebilcock, *Making of the Mosaic*, 317.

172 Manela, *Wilsonian Moment*.
173 I borrow this term from Lake and Reynolds, *Drawing the Global Color Line*.

Chapter Five

1 Canada, *House of Commons Debates*, 11 April 1946, 787 (Jean-François Pouliot, MP); "Un vif débat sur le prêt à l'Angleterre," *La Presse*, 12 April 1946.
2 Canada, *House of Commons Debates*, 18 March 1948, 2351 (Jean-François Pouliot, MP); "Le Canada paie trop cher le sucre qu'il achète de la Grande-Bretagne," *Le Soleil*, 19 March 1948.
3 Canada, *House of Commons Debates*, 18 March 1948, 2351–2 (Jean-François Pouliot, MP); 4 July 1947, 5110–14; 29 April 1948, 3467–8.
4 Ibid., 17 November 1949, 1900.
5 London Declaration, 26 April 1949, as cited in Amitav Banerji, "The 1949 London Declaration," 4. The declaration allowed republics and Indigenous monarchies to be Commonwealth members, and the British Commonwealth was renamed the Commonwealth of Nations. Canadian support for an expanded Commonwealth in the late 1940s is detailed in Hector Mackenzie, "An Old Dominion and the New Commonwealth," 84.
6 John Holmes, "Impact on the Commonwealth of the Emergence of Africa," 299.
7 King Diary, 21 September 1943, Mackenzie King fonds, LAC, MG 26–J13. President Roosevelt had assured King the previous year that his government had no designs on either the British Caribbean or Newfoundland. Acquiring the British Caribbean, in Roosevelt's view, would only saddle the United States with "an additional negro problem," while Newfoundland was "not even a Crown colony." It was a "bankrupt concern in the hands of a commission" that he had no interest in taking on; King Diary, 5 December 1942.

8   King Diary, 27 December 1946.

9   T.G. Major to G.R. Heasman, 12 August 1949, and Director, Information Division, DEA, to Leslie Brown, Dept. of Trade and Commerce, 18 February 1953, LAC, RG 20-A-3, vol. 957, file 7-984.

10 "Smallwood Aide Urges West Indies Be 11th Province," *Globe and Mail*, 29 July 1949. Smallwood offered similar encouragement during a trip to Jamaica in 1953. "Jamaica-Canada Union? 'Someone Should Find Out' Says Premier of Newfoundland," *Daily Gleaner*, 17 January 1953.

11 James Eayrs, *Northern Approaches*, 92–3.

12 Canada, *House of Commons Debates*, 18 March 1948, 2349–54 (Jean-François Pouliot, MP), and 31 March 1948, 2351–2; "Le Canada paie trop cher le sucre qu'il achète de la Grande-Bretagne," *Le Soleil*, 19 March 1948; D'Arcy O'Donnell, "Transfer West Indies to Canada's Control, Pouliot's Suggestion," *Globe and Mail*, 19 March 1948.

13 Alexander Brady, "Canada and the West Indies," enclosed in Commonwealth Division to Mr Dier, DEA, 7 January 1963, LAC, RG25, G-2, vol. 3322, file 10824-A-40, pt. 6.

14 Canada, *Senate Debates*, 16 November 1949, 283 (Neil McLean).

15 Hutton, "West Indies Want to Join Us," 8.

16 Canada, *House of Commons Debates*, 24 April 1950, 1852 (George Fulford, MP).

17 Hutton, "West Indies Want to Join Us," 9.

18 E.C. Ertl, "Are We Developing a Crop of Imperialists in Canada?," *Financial Times*, 24 April 1953.

19 Hutton, "West Indies Want to Join Us," 74.

20 Ibid.

21 Ibid., 9, 73–4.

22 "Beat USA to Adoption of Indies," and "British West Indies Tired of Colony Rule Eyes Canada – Senator, *Toronto Daily Star*, 4 April 1952; "Bermuda's Future," *Daily Gleaner*, 15 August 1952; "Canada and Us," talk given on George Hunte's Barbados radio program *Rediffusion*, enclosed in O.W. Dier to USSEA [Under-Secretary of State for External Affairs, Canada], 7 May 1952, LAC, RG 20-A-3, vol. 957, file 7-984.

23 Canada, *House of Commons Debates*, 3 December 1952, 295 (Alfred Brooks, MP).

24 Canada, *House of Commons Debates*, 27 February 1953, 2496 (Harry White, MP).

25 On the impact of the destroyers-for-bases deal, see Steven High, *Base Colonies in the Western Hemisphere, 1940–1967*. On the Anglo-American Caribbean Commission, see Charlie Whitham, *Bitter Rehearsal*. On American anti-communism in relation to the British Caribbean, see Jason Parker, *Brother's Keeper*, 94–116.

26 High, *Base Colonies*, 101–3.

27 *Daily Argosy*, as cited in Hutton, "The West Indies Want to Join Us," 75.

28 Both cited in Hutton, "West Indies Want to Join Us," 75.

29 "Canada and West Indies Union Is No Longer Small Talk, Says Ralph Vignale," *Trinidad Guardian*, 1 May 1952.

30 Hutton, "West Indies Want to Join Us." 9.

31 "See West Indies as Canada Province," *Daily Gleaner*, 8 October 1952.

32 Phrase borrowed from Lake and Reynolds, *Drawing the Global Color Line*.

33 Clause 28, *Canadian Citizenship Act*, 1946.

34 Tinker, *Separate and Unequal*, 357–8.

35 Ibid., 358.

36 Canada, P.C. 1950-2856, Order re. Landing of Immigrants in Canada, 9 June 1950.

37 "Canada Abridges Commonwealth," *Canadian Labour Reports*, November 1951, enclosed in Jean Boucher to the Deputy Minister, Immigration Branch, Dept. of Immigration and Citizenship, 8 January 1952, LAC, RG26, series AIC, vol. 124, file 3-33-6, pt. 1.

38 Purba Fernandez, "Asian Indian Immigration to Canada," 75.

39 Knowles, *Strangers at Our Gates*, 170–1.

40 To be eligible for the scheme, women had to be single, aged eighteen to thirty-five, have at least a grade-eight education, and pass a medical examination. These women received landed immigrant status upon their arrival in Canada and were free to go to school or pursue other careers or training in Canada after one year of domestic service. The quotas increased in subsequent years (up to 280 by 1967), and the scheme expanded to include women from British Guiana and the Windward Islands. The Canadian government terminated the quota system in 1968, but domestic workers continued to gain entry to Canada by applying directly to Ottawa. See Frances Henry, "West Indian Domestic Scheme in Canada."

41 Ciprian Bolah, "Excellent Workers but Wrong Colour of Skin," 27.

42 Memorandum, Department of Trade and Commerce, 14 January 1955, LAC, RG26, series AIC, vol. 124, file 3-33-6, pt. 1.

43 "West Indian Students Said under Pressure to Quit Canada Soon," *Globe and Mail*, 7 August 1957.

44 R.R. Parlour to DEA, 3 October 1956, LAC, RG 25, G2, vol. 3322, file 10824-A-40, pt. 1.

45 Jules Léger, memorandum for the Minister on the Exclusion of the Prime Minister of Barbados from the Windsor Hotel, 12 November 1954, ibid.

46 L.B. Pearson to Grantley Adams, 12 November 1954, ibid.

47 "Legislature Condemns Racial Discrimination," *Port of Spain Gazette*, 11 January 1947.

48 As cited in Hutton, "West Indies Want to Join Us," 9, 72. On the expectation
    of equality upon union, see also Jamaica, *House of Representatives Debate*,
    20 May 1952, as reported in the *Daily Gleaner*, 21 May 1952; and Malcolm
    Barcant, "Some Reasons Why West Indies Should Link Up with Canada,"
    Trinidad Guardian, 4 August 1949. A white Trinidadian, Barcant was a well-
    known lepidopterist and founder of the Angostura Barcant Butterfly Sanctuary.

49 *Daily Gleaner*, "These Leaders," 8 October 1952.

50 O.W. Dier to USSEA, 7 May 1952, LAC, RG 20-A-3, vol. 957, file 7-984.

51 "Canada-West Indies Federation," *Barbados Advocate*, 5 April 1952; "Canada-
    BW.I.," *Daily Gleaner*, 13 February 1950; "Sees BWI Stopping at Economic
    Ties," *Toronto Daily Star*, 11 April 1953; "Canada-B.W.I. Relations," *Port of
    Spain Gazette*, 24 November 1950.

52 Knight, *The Caribbean*, 300.

53 The West Indies (Federation) Order in Council 1957, 31 July 1957,
    Section 53(1).

54 Hugh. W. Springer, *Reflections on the Failure of the First West Indian
    Federation*; Elisabeth Wallace, "The West Indies Federation, Decline and Fall."

55 Greg Donaghy and Bruce Muirhead, "'Interests but No Foreign Policy,'"
    280–1.

56 See Jason Parker, "Remapping the Cold War in the Tropics"; Wright and
    Wylie, *Our Place in the Sun*.

57 Excerpt concerning aid to underdeveloped countries from an address by
    Louis St Laurent at Victoria, BC, 4 May 1957, LAC, RG 2, accession 1990-
    91/154, box 103, file W15 1952-58.

58 Molly Kane, "Canada and the Third World: Development Aid," 94–5. On
    the relationship between anti-communism, aid, and Canadian foreign policy
    in the postwar decades, see Cranford Pratt, "Ethical Values and Canadian
    Foreign Aid Policies"; Gendron, "Canada's University: Father Lévesque,
    Canadian Aid, and the National University of Rwanda."

59 A.F.W. Plumptre to R.B. Bryce, 24 May 1957, and an excerpt concerning aid to
    underdeveloped countries from an address by Louis St Laurent at Victoria, BC,
    4 May 1957, LAC, RG 2, accession 1990-91/154, box 103, file W15 1952-58;
    Donaghy and Muirhead, "Interests but No Foreign Policy," 275–6.

60 Donaghy and Muirhead, "Interests but No Foreign Policy," 283–5. Canada
    had repeatedly declined invitations from the US and the other American
    republics to join the Organization of American States (OAS), primarily to
    avoid the hemispheric tensions and increased US influence that might arise
    from Canadian membership. As a confidential External Affairs memorandum
    summarized in 1960, if Canada voted with the Latin American nations
    against the United States on any given issue, this might create friction in the
    Canada-US relationship. On the other hand, by siding with the US, Canada

might be seen as a US satellite or a recipient of special favours from the US; Confidential Memorandum, DEA, 12 May 1960, LAC, RG 25, vol. 5398, file 10824-F-40, pt. 5. Canadian officials also hoped that a Colombo-style plan might attract US funds to the Commonwealth Caribbean, as the original Colombo Plan had done in Asia. Concerned with the spread of communism in Asia, the US became involved in the Colombo Plan soon after its launch in 1950; Donaghy and Muirhead, "Interests but No Foreign Policy," 292n49.

61 L.B. Pearson, Memorandum to Cabinet, 10 April 1957, LAC, RG 2, Accession 1990-91/154, box 103, file W15 1952-58.

62 Donaghy and Muirhead, "Interests but No Foreign Policy," 280.

63 Graeme Mount and Stephen Randall, *The Caribbean Basin*, 86–92, 104–111.

64 G. Glazebrook, DEA memorandum, 5 February 1962, and memorandum, Commonwealth division, to Glazebrook, 6 March 1962, LAC, RG 25, G-2, vol. 3322, file 10824-A-40, pt. 5; Isaiah A. Litvak and Christopher J. Maule, "Nationalisation in the Caribbean Bauxite Industry," 45–7.

65 Memorandum to Cabinet, 14 December 1961, LAC, RG 25, G-2, vol. 3322, file 10824-A-40, pt. 5.

66 Memorandum to Cabinet, 14 December 1961, LAC, RG 25, vol. 5398, file 10824-F-40, pt. 5; R.G.C. Smith to USSEA, 1 June 1960, 12 July 1960, and 5 October 1960, and L.A.D. Stephens, internal correspondence summarizing the visit of Sir John Mordecai, former deputy governor general of the West Indies Federation, LAC, RG25, G-2, vol. 3322, file 10824-A-40, pt. 6.

67 Deborah A. Thomas, "Rastafari, Communism, and Surveillance in Late Colonial Jamaica," 65.

68 Henry's followers claimed that the letter was not written by Henry but by a police informant working undercover. Ibid., 79n72.

69 R.G.C. Smith to USSEA, 1 June 1960, 12 July 1960, and 5 October 1960, LAC, RG 25, vol. 5398, file 10824-F-40, pt. 5; "Jamaica Drama: Bullets, Intrigue, Marijuana," *Globe and Mail*, 4 July 1960; "Blood, Dope Sect Bulwarks," *Toronto Daily Star*, 4 July 1960; "Jamaica and Marxism," *Globe and Mail*, 4 August 1960; Ross Willmot, "Wild Sect Worries West Indies," *Brandon Sun*, 12 January 1961; "Bearded Jamaican Sect Poses Large Problem for Island Authorities," *Brandon Sun*, 15 August 1960; "Jamaicans Kill Two Soldiers," *Toronto Daily Star*, 22 June 1960; "Aim of Ex-'Political Bad Boy,'" *Toronto Daily Star*, 3 August 1962. On British constructs of the Mau Mau, see John Lonsdale, "Mau Maus of the Mind"; A.S. Cleary, "The Myth of Mau Mau in Its International Context."

70 E.P.W. Guy, "Best Ways to Help West Indians," *Globe and Mail*, 11 October 1958.

71 Ibid.

72 Ibid.

73　See Hakim Adi, *Pan-Africanism and Communism*; J. Callaghan, "Communists and the Colonies"; Susan Campbell, "'Black Bolsheviks'"; Evan Smith, "Against Fascism, for Racial Equality."

74　"UN Best Hope for Peace," *Daily Gleaner*, 11 January 1961.

75　Mathieu, *North of the Color Line*, 212.

76　As cited in Ross Lambertson, "'The Dresden Story,'" para. 50.

77　D.S. Dainton, "Canada and 'The Eight,'" *New Commonwealth*, May 1962.

78　E.P.W. Guy, "Best Ways to Help West Indians," *Globe and Mail*, 11 October 1958.

79　Note on Motion received from Mr. H.H. Shah on the Hardships West Indian Students are Reported to Be Suffering in Canada, enclosed in R.G.C. Smith to SSEA [Secretary of State for External Affairs, Canada], 10 January 1962, LAC, RG 25, vol. 5009, file 232-AM-40, pt. 4.

80　R.F. Renwick to USSEA, 16 August 1961, LAC, RG25, vol. 3322, file 10824-A-40, pt. 4.

81　R.G.C. Smith to SSEA, 10 January 1962, LAC, RG25, vol. 5009, file 232-AM-40, pt. 4.

82　"West Indians Look to Canada as New Home or for Training," *Montreal Star*, 21 February 1958.

83　*West Indian Economist*, c. December 1961, as cited in "Economic Union between Canada and West Indies Seen," *Canada-Caribbean Affairs* 3, no. 50 (1962): unpaginated.

84　Memo, Commonwealth Division, DEA, 27 March 1961, LAC, RG 25, G-2, vol. 3322, file 10824-A-40, pt. 4.

85　Triadafilopoulos Triadafilos, "Global Norms, Domestic Institutions and the Transformation of Immigration Policy in Canada and the US," 180–1.

86　Ray Greenidge, "The Emigration of West Indians," *Globe and Mail*, 17 September, 1958. Greenidge was responding to "In Place of Emigration," *Globe and Mail*, 5 September 1958. On the connections between immigration, development aid, and Canada's international reputation, see also David C. Corbett, *Canada's Immigration Policy: A Critique*, 177–200; "Color Bar: As Others See It," *Toronto Daily Star*, 1 November 1958; "Aid West Indies by Immigration, Anglicans Urge," *Globe and Mail*, 14 November 1958.

87　A.F.W. Plumptre to R.B. Bryce, 5 February 1957, LAC, RG 2, acc. 1990-91/154, box 103, file W15 1952-58; John W. Graham, Memorandum, DEA, 9 October 1957, LAC, RG 25, G-2, vol. 3322, file 10824-A-40, pt. 2.

88　This clause of the regulations was intended to limit Asian immigration; Kelley and Trebilcock, *Making of the Mosaic*, 332–3.

89　As cited in Triadafilos, "Global Norms," 182.

90　Triadafilos, "Global Norms," 182–3; Knowles, *Strangers at Our Gates*, 187–90.

91　"A Little Brown Sister Joins Commonwealth," *Toronto Daily Star*, 4 January

1958. "Indies Canada's Problem," *Toronto Daily Star*, 3 May 1958. "West Indies Good-Will," *Toronto Daily Star*, 28 July 1958; R.R. Parlour to Dept. of Trade and Commerce, 20 August 1956, LAC, RG 25, series A-2, vol. 3322, file 10824-A-40, pt. 1.

92   Brady, "Canada and the West Indies," enclosed in Commonwealth Division to Mr Dier, DEA, 7 January 1963, LAC, RG25, G-2, vol. 3322, file 10824-A-40, pt. 6.

93   Ibid.

94   Harold MacMillan's Conservative government saw EEC membership as a way to gain greater access to European markets and re-establish the UK's leadership role in Western Europe. The UK applied for membership in the EEC in 1961 and 1963 but was rejected over concerns (especially in France) of US influence on the UK. The UK finally became a member in 1973. Alex May, "The Commonwealth and Britain's Turn to Europe, 1945–73."

95   Charles Lynch, "Canada Has Chance to Help the Indies," *Hamilton Spectator*, 10 February 1962.

96   Eayrs, *Northern Approaches*, 90.

97   Lynch, "Canada Has Chance to Help the Indies"; Charles Lynch, "West Indies Islands as a Province," *Ottawa Citizen*, 10 February 1962.

98   D.G. Dainton, "Canada and 'The Eight,'" *New Commonwealth*, May 1962, enclosed in LAC, RG25, G-2, vol. 3322, file 10824-A-40, pt. 6. Dainton was a playwright and a staff writer for the *Monetary Times*. These biographical details can be found in "Theatre Notes," *Globe and Mail*, 14 May 1960.

99   George E. Brooks to John Diefenbaker, 10 February 1962, LAC, RG25, G-2, vol. 3322, file 10824-A-40, pt. 5.

100   Eayrs, *Northern Approaches*, 89–94.

101   Ibid., 90–1. Simon C. Smith, "Integration and Disintegration: The Attempted Incorporation of Malta into the United Kingdom in the 1950s."

102   Mount and Randall, *Caribbean Basin*, 88.

103   Eayrs, *Northern Approaches*, 93–4.

104   Ibid., 91.

105   Rafael Cox Alomar, *Revisiting the Transatlantic Triangle*, 42–128.

106   Telegram, Canadian Commissioner at Port of Spain to DEA; John M. Hill to J. Diefenbaker, 28 February 1962, enclosed in DEA Memorandum for the Minister, Norman A. Robertson; DEA Memorandum to Glazebrook, 29 March 1962, W. Harris to Howard Green, 2 May 1962, all at LAC, RG25, G-2, vol. 3322, file 10824-A-40, pt. 5; DEA Memorandum on visit of Sir John Mordecai, 17 May 1962; L.A.D. Stephens, DEA Memorandum, 30 May 1962, all at LAC, RG25, G-2, vol. 3322, file 10824-A-40, pt. 6.

107   DEA Memorandum to Glazebrook, 29 March 1962, LAC, RG25, G-2, vol. 3322, file 10824-A-40, pt. 5; DEA Memorandum on visit of Sir John Mordecai, 17 May 1962, L.A.D. Stephens, DEA Memorandum, 30 May

1962, Norman Robertson, Note for the Minister, 16 November 1962, A.G. Campbell to Glazebrook, 28 August 1963, all at LAC, RG25, G-2, vol. 3322, file 10824-A-40, pt. 6.

108 Telegram, Canadian Commissioner at Port of Spain to DEA, 27 March 1962, LAC, RG25, G-2, vol. 3322, file 10824-A-40, pt. 5. The MP was Dennis Healey, who was at the time shadow colonial secretary.

109 L.A.D. Stephens, DEA Memorandum, 30 May 1962, LAC, RG25, G-2, vol. 3322, file 10824-A-40, pt. 6.

110 E.O. LeBlanc to Diefenbaker, 19 September 1962, LAC, RG25, G-2, vol. 3322, file 10824-A-40, pt. 6; Irving W. Andre, *Edward Oliver Leblanc and the Struggle to Transform Dominica*, 139–41.

111 DEA Memorandum, 23 October 1962, LAC, RG25, G-2, vol. 3322, file 10824-A-40, pt. 6.

112 In 1962, the combined population of the "Little Eight" was about 695,000, with Barbados accounting for 245,000 of this total. This information obtained in ibid.

113 Ibid.

114 Diefenbaker to Leblanc, 23 October 1962, LAC, RG25, G-2, vol. 3322, file 10824-A-40, pt. 6.

115 See Article 146, British North America Act, 1867.

116 Diefenbaker to Leblanc, 23 October 1962, LAC, RG25, G-2, vol. 3322, file 10824-A-40, pt. 6.

117 Diefenbaker to John M. Hill, 5 March 1962, enclosed in DEA Memorandum, 29 March 1962, LAC, RG25, G-2, vol. 3322, file 10824-A-40, pt. 5.

118 Norman Robertson, DEA Memorandum, "Proposed Visit to Ottawa by Premier of Barbados," 26 April 1963, LAC, RG 25, vol. 6152, file 50414-40, pt. 1.

119 Barrow, "Role for Canada in the West Indies," 184–5. The conference was titled "Commonwealth Partners in the West Indies."

120 Ibid., 185.

121 For expressions of moral duty and Commonwealth responsibility, see "Pearson's Plan," *Halifax Chronicle*, 25 March 1963; Alexander Brady, "Canada and the West Indies," enclosed in Commonwealth Division, DEA to Mr Dier, 7 January 1963, LAC, RG25, G-2, vol. 3322, file 10824-A-40, pt. 6; Robert Taylor, "Indies Canada Problem," *Toronto Daily Star*, 3 May 1958; Lynch, "Canada Has Chance to Help the Indies."

122 Barrow, "Role for Canada in the West Indies," 186, 180.

123 Ibid., 181.

124 Ibid.

125 Stanley Westall, "Trinidad PM Rules Out Indies as 11th Province but Wants Closer Ties," *Globe and Mail*, 23 April 1964.

126 Donaghy and Muirhead, "Interests but No Foreign Policy," 284–5.

127   Memorandum to Cabinet, Canadian Aid to the Caribbean, 11 May 1963, LAC, RG25, G-2, vol. 3322, file 10824-A-40, pt. 6. In November 1963, Ottawa increased its official development assistance budget to $400 million by 1969. The aid was concentrated on India, Pakistan, Francophone Africa, and the Commonwealth Caribbean.

128   "6 'Associate State' Islands Planned in Caribbean by U.K," *Globe and Mail*, 31 December 1965.

129   John G. Hadwen, Memorandum, 10 December 1965, LAC, RG 25, vol. 6152, file 50414-40, pt. 1.

130   Ibid.

131   Rafael Cox Alomar, "Britain's Withdrawal from the Eastern Caribbean, 1965–1967," 87–90. In its correspondence with Whitehall, the US State Department also hinted that the constitutional status worked out in the eastern Caribbean might complicate ongoing US efforts to clarify its constitutional relationship with Puerto Rico.

132   "'Associate State' Boosted," *Gazette* (Montreal), 9 December 1964; "Federal-Provincial Talks," *Edmonton Journal*, 7 December 1965.

133   These developments are outlined in Canada, *Canada and the Commonwealth Caribbean Conference, Ottawa, July 6–8, 1966*; Eric Williams, "Canada and the West Indies"; Donaghy and Muirhead, "'Interests but No Foreign Policy,'" 66–71.

134   G.V. Doxey, "The Commonwealth in the Americas: Canada Takes the Initiative," 388.

Chapter Six

1   Carl Lumumba, "West Indies and the Sir George Williams Affair."

2   Report of the Standing Committee on Foreign Affairs on Canada-Caribbean Relations," Appendix to Debates of 23 June 1970, *Senate Debates, Second Session, Twenty-Eighth Parliament*, vol. 2 (April 7, 1970, to October 7, 1970), Queen's Printer for Canada, Ottawa, 1970. Also available at https://parl.canadiana.ca/browse?show=eng_s_debates.

3   Eayrs, "Our Neo-Colonialism in the Caribbean," *Toronto Daily Star*, 18 March 1970.

4   "Report of the Standing Committee on Foreign Affairs on Canada-Caribbean Relations," Appendix to Debates of 23 June 1970, 7.

5   Statistics Canada, CANSIM table 427-0004 and *Travel between Canada and Other Countries*, https://www150.statcan.gc.ca/n1/pub/11-630-x/11-630-x2017001-eng.htm.

6   Nicholas Steed, "The Caribbean," 67; Rosie Douglas, "Canadian Racism and Sir George," *Uhuru*, 2 February 1970.

7   On these constitutional developments, see Cox Alomar, *Revisiting the Transatlantic Triangle*, 184–228; Margaret Broderick, "Associated Statehood";

J.H. Parry, Philip Sherlock, and Anthony Maingot, *Short History of the West Indies*, 265–8; Daniel Malcolm Sr, "Constitutional Development (1957–76)," 157–64.

8 Steed, "Caribbean," 67.

9 Canada, *Proceedings of the Senate Standing Committee on Foreign Affairs*, 9 December 1969, 12 (testimony of K.R. Patrick), https://parl.canadiana.ca/ view/oop.com_SOC_2802_2_1/113?r=0&s=1.

10 Steed, "Caribbean," 11, 67, 69.

11 Bird, as cited in Steed, "Caribbean," 67.

12 Clarke, as cited in Steed, "Caribbean," 64, and Compton, as cited in ibid., 65.

13 Macquarrie recounts this history in Canada, *House of Commons Debates*, 5 February 1968, 6378 (Heath Macquarrie, MP).

14 Ibid., 6378–9.

15 "Biographical History," Senator Heath Macquarrie fonds, Archives PEI, acc. no. 368, http://www.archives.pe.ca/atom/index.php/senator-heath-macquarrie-fonds. Macquarrie was appointed to the Senate in 1978.

16 Canada, *House of Commons Debates*, 5 February 1968, 6378–9 (Heath Macquarrie, MP).

17 Ibid., 6383 (Arnold Peters, MP).

18 Ibid., 6384.

19 Ibid.

20 "Report of the Senate Standing Committee on Foreign Affairs on Canada-Caribbean Relations" (1970), Appendix E., 61, appended to the debates of 23 June 1970.

21 Canada, *House of Commons Debates*, 5 February 1968, 6384–5 (Arnold Peters, MP).

22 Ibid. 6382–3 (John Matheson, MP).

23 Ibid. 6382.

24 Ibid., 22 June 1966, 6776–7 (Jean-Eudes Dubé, MP).

25 Ibid., 6777.

26 Ken Patrick to Allard, 26 January 1966, Jean V. Allard fonds, Department of National Defence, Directorate of History and Heritage, 84/126, file 119.

27 Terry Lacey, *Violence and Politics in Jamaica, 1960–1970*, 157–8.

28 Pratt, "Ethical Values and Canadian Foreign Aid Policies," 89.

29 David Austin, "Liberation from Below," 3–7.

30 David Austin, "All Roads Led to Montreal," 521–7. On the wider significance of the Congress of Black Writers, see David Austin, *Moving against the System*.

31 Ibid., 527.

32 Lacey, *Violence and Politics in Jamaica 1960–70*, 94–6.

33 Austin, "All Roads Led to Montreal," 527. The American civil rights and Black Power movements had a significant impact on Black communities elsewhere in Canada, notably in Toronto and Halifax. Observes Agnes

Calliste in "The Influence of the Civil Rights and Black Power Movement in Canada," 129, the Black Power movement was instrumental in the "ideological mobilization of African-Canadians which increased their militancy, political consciousness and identity." See also Chris Harris, "Canadian Black Power, Organic Intellectuals and the War of Position in Toronto, 1967–1975"; Gooden, "Community Organizing by African Caribbean People in Toronto, Ontario"; Rosanne P. Waters, "March from Selma to Canada."

34 The events and immediate aftermath of the Sir George Williams affair are documented and critically assessed in Dennis Forsythe, ed., *Let the N—— Burn!*

35 Calliste, "Influence of the Civil Rights and Black Power Movement in Canada," 132; Austin, "All Roads Led to Montreal," 531; Marcel Martel, "'Riot' at Sir George Williams."

36 David Austin, *Fear of a Black Nation*, 178.

37 Harris, "Canadian Black Power," 328.

38 Austin, *Fear of a Black Nation*, 178.

39 "What of the Anderson Affair," *Contrast*, 7 March 1969.

40 "Interview with Dave (Darbeau) and Geddes Granger," *Uhuru*, 2 March 1970; Yvonne Baboolal, "Daaga Remembered," *Trinidad & Tobago Guardian* online, 9 August 2016, accessed 13 October 2018, http://www.guardian. co.tt/article-6.2.356863.64c65ac643.

41 "Sir George Williams U. Administration 'Buried,'" *Daily Gleaner*, 10 March 1969.

42 "Sir George Williams Students Raise Funds in Jamaica," *Contrast*, 7 March 1969; "Sir George Williams University Affair," *Star* (Roseau, Dominica), 15 March 1969.

43 Lacey, *Violence and Politics in Jamaica*, 145–6; Rosie Douglas, "Canadian Racism and Sir George," *Uhuru*, 2 February 1970.

44 Lacey, *Violence and Politics in Jamaica*, 157–8.

45 Ibid., 149.

46 Rosie Douglas, "Where Do We Go from Here?," *Uhuru*, 23 March 1970; Douglas, "Canadian Racism and Sir George," *Uhuru*, 2 February 1970; Levitt and McIntyre, *Canada-West Indies Economic Relations*, 24.

47 Sean Maloney, "Maple Leaf over the Caribbean," 163.

48 Douglas, "Canadian Racism and Sir George," *Uhuru*, 2 February 1970.

49 "Interview with Dave (Darbeau) and Geddes (Granger)."

50 "Guyana the Lost Revolution?" *Black Liberation News* 1, no. 2 (1969).

51 George I. Brizan, "Canada and the Commonwealth Caribbean Economic Relations, 1966–74," 117; "Tourism and the West Indies," *Black Liberation News*, February 1970.

52 William Demas, *Economics of Development in Small Countries with Special Reference to the Caribbean*; Norman Girvan and Cherita Girvan, "Dependency Economics in the Caribbean and Latin America."

53 Caribbean economists published a series of studies exploring the possibilities of regional integration, most notably Bridget Brewster and Clive Thomas, *The Dynamics of West Indian Economic Integration*.

54 Lloyd Best and Kari Levitt, *Externally Propelled Industrialization and Growth in the Caribbean*. See also Lloyd Best, "Outlines of a Model of Pure Plantation Economy." Following the work of Best and Levitt, a number of economists turned their attention to the role of foreign investment, MNCs, and the persistence of plantation societies in perpetuating Caribbean underdevelopment, such as Norman Girvan, *Foreign Capital and Economic Underdevelopment in Jamaica*, and George L. Beckford, *Persistent Poverty*.

55 Levitt and McIntyre, *Canada-West Indies Economic Relations*, 24.

56 Norman Girvan, "The Guyana-Alcan Conflict and the Nationalization of DEMBA," 90–5. The Aluminum Company of America (Alcoa), which had established Demba in 1916 shortly after the discovery of bauxite along the Demerara River, handed over its Guyanese operations to Alcan in 1929. With the onset of an international recession the same year, the bauxite industry suffered in the years that immediately followed but then thrived during the Second World War.

57 Litvak and Maule, "Nationalisation in the Caribbean Bauxite Industry," 45–7.

58 "The Caribbean: The People Rebel against Canadian Control," *Last Post* 1, no. 3 (1970): 46, 49.

59 As cited in ibid., 49.

60 Fran Reid, "Cost of Eden," 3.

61 Oswald Larcher, "The Politics of Canadian Aid to the Commonwealth Caribbean," 121.

62 Trevor Turner, "Canadian Involvement in the Development of the West Indies," 1–3.

63 Levitt and McIntyre, *Canada-West Indies Economic Relations*, 26; Larcher, "Politics of Canadian Aid," 122.

64 "The Caribbean, the People Rebel against Canadian Control," 47.

65 Douglas, "Canadian Racism and Sir George," *Uhuru*, 2 February 1970.

66 "Sir George Williams," *Uhuru*, 31 July 1969.

67 Hudson, "Imperial Designs," 35.

68 "Interview with Dave (Darbeau) & Geddes (Granger)."

69 "Trinidad to Pay $33,500 Fines for 8 Guilty in Sir George Riot," *Toronto Daily Star*, 14 March 1970.

70 Calliste, "Influence of the Civil Rights and Black Power Movement in Canada," 132. After his release, Douglas was under RCMP surveillance until 1975, when he was branded a national security threat and deported to Dominica.

71 Lumumba, "West Indies and the Sir George Williams Affair," 183–9. The impact of the SGWU affair on the Black Power movement, while important, should not be overstated. The affair provided emerging Black Power leaders and groups with an issue to rally around and further mobilize their agendas. As "Deep Ramifications," *Uhuru*, 16 February 1970, described it, revolutionary leaders in the Caribbean identified the events at SGWU as a "microcosm of their general struggle." Lloyd Best, "February Revolution: Origins," *Tapia* (Tunapuna, Trinidad), 20 December 1970, described Black Power in the late 1960s as the "culmination of a long confrontation that has been going on in the political and social system of the West Indies from the very start" between white capitalist interests (and their local abettors) and the region's poor, labouring populations. At the same time, Black Power did not constitute the whole of Caribbean resentment toward expatriate ownership.

72 "Report of the Standing Committee on Foreign Affairs on Canada-Caribbean Relations," Appendix to Debates of 23 June 1970, xiv–xv.

73 Canada, *Proceedings of the Senate Standing Committee on Foreign Affairs*, 21 April 1970, 8–10 (testimony of George Eaton), https://parl.canadiana.ca/view/oop.com_SOC_2802_2_1/341?r=0&s=1, and 25 February 1969, 22–5 (testimony of William G. Demas), https://parl.canadiana.ca/view/oop.com_SOC_2801_2_1/40?r=0&s=1.

74 Canada, *Senate Debates*, 23 June 1970, 1321 (John B. Aird).

75 "Report of the Standing Committee on Foreign Affairs on Canada-Caribbean Relations," Appendix to Debates of 23 June 1970, xiv.

76 Ibid., 1–52.

77 Canada, *Senate Debates*, 23 June 1970, 1321 (John B. Aird).

78 Canada, *Proceedings of the Senate Standing Committee on Foreign Affairs*, 19 November 1969, 12 (testimony of Mitchell Sharp) https://parl.canadiana.ca/view/oop.com_SOC_2802_2_1/45?r=0&s=1. The DEA brief is cited by Senate Committee member Allister Grosart.

79 Canada, *Senate Debates*, 22 October 1969, 1873 (Allister Grosart).

80 Ibid., 1 October 1968, 151 (Allister Grosart).

81 Ibid., 22 October 1969, 1874–75 (Allister Grosart).

82 Ibid., 1 Oct 1, 1968, 152 (Allister Grosart).

83 Ibid., 22 October 1969, 1876–78 (Paul Martin, John Connolly, and John B. Aird)

84 Canada, *Proceedings of the Standing Senate Committee on Foreign Affairs*, 19 November 1969, 14 (testimony of Mitchell Sharp), and 4 November 1969, 17–18 (testimony of Maurice Strong).

85 Ibid., 17–18 (testimony of Maurice Strong).

86 Stephen Azzi, *Walter Gordon and the Rise of Canadian Nationalism*, 34–65, 133–66.

87 Early versions included Kari Levitt, "Dependence and Disintegration in Canada," published in *New World Quarterly* in 1968; the following year it was published in Winnipeg by *Canadian Dimension* editor Cy Gonick. See Michèle Rioux and Hugues Brisson, "Interview with Kari Levitt: 'Bring the State Back In!'"

88 Lloyd Penner, "The Foreign Policy of the New Democratic Party, 1961–1988," 208n496.

89 Canada, *Senate Committees*, Standing Committee on Foreign Affairs – Special Joint Meeting with the House of Commons External Affairs and National Defence Committee, 16 March 1971, 18 (Allister Grosart), https://parl. canadiana.ca/browse?show=eng_s_debates.

90 Grosart, November 1971, as cited in John Fayerweather, *Foreign Investment in Canada: Prospects for National Policy*, 46–7.

91 "Report of the Standing Committee on Foreign Affairs on Canada-Caribbean Relations," Appendix to Debates of 23 June 1970, 6.

92 Ibid., 53–4.

93 In view of centuries of colonial knowledge production that racialized expertise, the omission of Caribbean experts is less striking. Whiteness, as well as education, training, and experience, was a key criterion in the determination of expert status. See Uma Kothari, "An Agenda for Thinking about 'Race' in Development"; White, "The 'Gender Lens': A Racial Blinder?" 14–17, 62–4. On the racialization of expertise in Canada's relations with the Third World with respect to aid, see Kane, "Canada and the Third World: Development Aid," 120.

94 *Report of the Senate Committee on Foreign Affairs Respecting Canadian Relations with the Caribbean Area*, 35, appended to *Proceedings of the Standing Senate Committee on Foreign Affairs*, 9 and 12 June 1970.

95 Canada, *Proceedings of the Senate Standing Committee on Foreign Affairs*, 25 February 1969, 22–5 (testimony of William G. Demas), https://parl. canadiana.ca/view/oop.com_SOC_2801_2_1/40?r=0&s=1, and 21 April 1970, 6–12 (testimony of George Eaton), https://parl.canadiana.ca/view/oop. com_SOC_2802_2_1/341?r=0&s=1.

96 Eayrs, "Our Neo-Colonialism in the Caribbean," *Toronto Star*, 18 March 1970.

97 Canada, *House of Commons Debates*, 10 January 1974, 9223 (Max Saltsman, MP). Before Saltman introduced his private members bill on 10 January, the union idea was already in the media. On 6 January, CBC's nightly news program, *The National*, included a feature on the proposal.

98 Resolution of the TCI State Council, 14 March 1973, reproduced in "The Courtship Continues," *Contrast*, 8 February 1974.

99 Max Saltsman to Liam Maguire, 11 January 1974, TNA, FCO 44/1120.

100   A.G. Mitchell, Governor of the TCI, to the Secretary of State for Foreign and Commonwealth Affairs, 1 February 1974, TNA, FCO 44/1120.

101   Glen Allen, "Great Turk Land Rush Is On as Investors Descend on Island," *Toronto Star*, 20 February 1974.

102   Display ad, *Globe and Mail*, 6 February 1974, 9.

103   Anonymized to Saltsman, 31 January 1974, fols. 3–5, Saltsman fonds, LAC, MG 32, C 15, vol. 34, file 5. Following copyright guidelines for this volume of the Saltsman fonds, I have anonymized all the letter writers.

104   Ibid., files 1–11, 14–16.

105   Daphne James, as cited in Glen Allen, "Carpet-Baggers Ready to Pull the Rug on Paradise," *Gazette* (Montreal), 16 February 1974.

106   Allen, "Carpet-Baggers."

107   "Place in the Sun," *Time*, 18 February 1974.

108   Canada, *House of Commons Debates*, 11 March 1974, 396; 16 May 1975, 5901; 19 November 1976 (Stanley Knowles, MP); anonymized to Saltsman, April 1974, fol. 146, Saltsman fonds, LAC, MG32, C15, vol. 34, file 1. Douglas's interest in a Canadian association with one or more Caribbean islands dated back to at least 1964. See Locksley G.E. Edmonston, "Canada and the West Indies: Trends and Prospects," 192–3; Canada, *Senate Debates*, 3 May 1974, 378 (Hazen Argue); Akerman to Liam Maguire, 21 January 1974, TNA, FCO 44/1120. Saltsman was particularly pleased to gain Akerman's support because he thought the best way for the TCI to join Canada was through an extension of Nova Scotia's provincial boundaries. Saltsman to Maguire, 11 January 1974, TNA, FCO 44/1120.

109   Azzi, *Reconcilable Differences*, 198–201.

110   Penner, "Foreign Policy of the New Democratic Party, 1961–1988."

111   Canada, *House of Commons Debates*, 11 March 1974, 396 (Max Saltsman).

112   Ibid.

113   Anonymized to Saltsman, 3 May 1974, fols. 34–6, Saltsman fonds, LAC, MG 32, C15, vol. 34, file 8.

114   Anonymized to Saltsman, April 1974, fol. 146, ibid., file 1.

115   Anonymized to Saltsman, 14 January 1974, fol. 110, ibid., file 5.

116   Réal Lalonde, "Vive le commonwealth canadien!," *La Presse*, 2 March 1974.

117   Anonymized to Saltsman, c. May 1974, fols. 5–6, Saltsman fonds, LAC, MG 32, C15, vol. 34, file 1.

118   Anonymized to Saltsman, 19 March 1974, fols. 49–51, ibid., file 2.

119   Anonymized to Saltsman, c. April 1974, fol. 146, ibid., file 1.

120   Anonymized to Saltsman, 11 January 1974, fol. 140, ibid., file 5.

121   Anonymized to Saltsman, 12 January 1974, fol. 134, ibid.

122   A.G. Mitchell to FCO, 9 January and 1 February 1974, TNA, FCO 44/1120.

123 W.T.A. Cox to E.N. Larmour (FCO), 4 March 1974, and E.N. Larmour (FCO) to Peter Hayman (British High Commission, Ottawa), 6 March 1974, TNA, FCO 44/1120.

124 W.T.A. Cox to E.N. Larmour, 4 March 1974, ibid.

125 Mitchell Sharp, as cited in United Nations General Assembly, "Turks and Caicos Islands," 1 May 1974, working paper A/AC.109/L.931/Add.1.

126 Text of Sharp interview, enclosed in Peter Hayman to Foreign and Commonwealth Office, 1 February 1974, TNA, FCO 44/1120.

127 As cited in Colin Rickards, "Seeking a Sunny Place," *Share*, 4 February 1987.

128 Trudeau's conversations with Barrow, Pindling, and Manley are referenced in ibid.

129 Stephen Azzi, *Walter Gordon and the Rise of Canadian Nationalism*, 169–70; Hillmer and Granatstein, *Empire to Umpire*, 294–5.

130 Susan Mann, *Dream of Nation*, 326–7.

131 This image of a young Canada – uncorrupted by a history of imperial exploits and colonial violence and thus well positioned to lend a helping hand on the world stage – had gained considerable currency in the postwar decades. It was not unusual to hear of Canada's unique qualifications to tackle Third World problems. The roots of this image arguably pre-dated the Second World War. In the late nineteenth and early twentieth centuries, British Canadians relished their country's status as the empire's senior dominion and a model of constitutional progress and nation building. And it was this narrative of national becoming, reiterated and refined into the post-1945 period, that obscured the history of colonial violence and dispossession upon which Canada was built. Quebec's founding narrative was similarly based on denial and distortion, most notably in its sanitized rendering of colonial relations in New France. See David Austin, "Narratives of Power," 24. On the contradictions in the fashioning of Canada's postwar image, see Webster, "Foreign Policy, Diplomacy, and Decolonization," 155–92.

132 Canada, *Senate Debates*, 30 April 1974, 350 (Jean-Paul Deschatelets).

133 Canada, *House of Commons Debates*, 16 May 1975, 5900–1 (Claude-André Lachance, MP).

134 The need for a multicultural policy was first recognized in the Royal Commission on Bilingualism and Biculturalism (1963–1970).

135 Anonymized to Saltsman, 14 May 1974, fol. 15, Saltsman fonds, LAC, MG 32, C15, vol. 34, file 14.

136 Anonymized to Saltsman, 6 May 1974, fol. 60, ibid., file 1.

137 Anonymized to Saltsman, 4 March 1974, fol. 104, ibid., file 2.

138 Rinaldo Walcott, "Shame: A Polemic," 276. See also Katherine McKittrick, "Wait Canada Anticipate Black."

139	Joseph Mensah, *Black Canadians*, 203.
140	Anonymized to Saltsman, 4 March 1974, fols. 85–6, Saltsman fonds, LAC, MG 32, C15, vol. 34, file 2.
141	Ken Thomas, "Hands off Turks and Caicos," *Contrast*, 18 January 1974.
142	"Turks and Caicos Islands," *Black Voice*, February 1974.
143	Letter to the editor, *Contrast*, 22 February 1974.
144	Chaka Lumumba, "Political Economy of Liberation in Southern Africa," *Spear*, September 1974.
145	Alex Brown, "Canada's Role in South Africa," *Contrast*, 8 February 1974.
146	Anonymized to Saltsman, May 1974, fol. 118, Saltsman fonds, LAC, MG 32, C15, vol. 34, file 14.
147	Anonymized to Saltsman, May 1974, fols. 103–4, ibid.
148	Anonymized to Saltsman, 13 April 1974, fol. 16, ibid., file 1.
149	Anonymized to Saltsman, c. January 1974, fol. 137, ibid., file 6.
150	See, for example, Anonymized to Saltsman, c. May 1974, fol. 72, ibid., file 14.
151	See Austin, "Narratives of Power"; Scott Rutherford, Sean Mills, and David Austin, editorial, 4–5; Scott Rutherford, "Colonialism and the Indigenous Present"; Aziz Choudry, "What's Left?"; Thobani, *Exalted Subjects*, 1–7.
152	See, for example, Sean Carleton, "Colonizing Minds"; Ken Montgomery, "Imagining the Anti-Racist State."
153	Walter Rodney, *How Europe Underdeveloped Africa*. For a survey of the literature on underdevelopment in the late 1970s, see Richard Higgott, "Competing Theoretical Perspectives on Development and Underdevelopment," 26–41.
154	William Easterly, *White Man's Burden*, 20–2, 24; J.R. Miller, *Skyscrapers Hide the Heavens*, 226, observes a similar denial of colonialism in the *Statement of the Government of Canada on Indian Policy* (1969).
155	See Webster, "Foreign Policy, Diplomacy, and Decolonization," 156.

Conclusion

1	Internal correspondence, 30 May 1980, LAC, RG 25, series A3C, vol. 27624.
2	"Local P.C.'S Propose Union with Caicos," *Whitby Free Press*, 26 March 1986; Henry R. Beer, "Canada Could Have Its Own Place in the Sun," *Toronto Star*, 16 January 1987.
3	"Trade Winds Trade Dreams," *Gazette* (Montreal), 27 April 1987; "Canada Eyes Islands in the Sun," *Windsor Star*, 9 May 1987.
4	"Senate Committee on Foreign Affairs: Notes for the Briefing on the Turks and Caicos Islands," 7 May 1987, Roméo Leblanc fonds, LAC, R-12069-10-9-E, vol. 376, file no. 5.

5   "Island Delegation Tempts Tories with Tropics," *Ottawa Citizen*, 22 April 1987; "Islands-Canada Link Causes Confusion," *Windsor Star*, 22 April 1987. "Islands Want Canadian Ties – but How?," *Gazette* (Montreal), 22 April 1987; Statement and Membership Application, brochure, Turks & Caicos Development Organization of Canada, enclosed in LAC, R12069-10-9-E, vol. 376, file 5; Ralph L. Higgs to Senator Leblanc and members of the Senate, undated letter, c. late 1987, LAC, R12069-10-9-E, vol. 376, file 5. The idea attracted limited interest in the islands, too. In April, two representatives of the Turks and Caicos Development Organization visited Ottawa to promote closer links with Canada. They were Ralph Higgs, a junior customs agent, and Dalton Jones, a community development officer. While in Canada, Jones and Higgs shared the results of a recent poll conducted by their organization. Of 289 islanders surveyed, 90 per cent favoured a stronger relationship with Canada, but of these 90 per cent, only 19 per cent wished to explore the possibility of a political association. The large majority supported stronger economic, educational, and cultural links only.

6   Brian Dexter, "Canadians Would Vacation in the Turks and Caicos Islands," *Toronto Star*, 17 May 1988.

7   "Changes Would Likely Come at Separation Time," *Brandon Sun*, 29 November 1991; Richard Cairney, "Of All the Mistakes of Our Ex-PM, the Most Galling Is This: 'It Might Have Been,'" *Globe and Mail*, 29 January 1994. "February Fantasy," *Globe and Mail*, 10 February 1998. "Pity … We Lost Our Place in the Sun," *Ottawa Citizen*, 9 January 1999; "Imagine Hot Winter Holiday in Canada," *Windsor Sun*, 9 January 1998. "Dear Chairman Spicer," *Ottawa Citizen*, 18 December 1990; "It Could Have Been Ours," *Ottawa Citizen*, 10 April 1999.

8   See "Canada's Caribbean Ambition," CBC *News Online*, 16 April 2004; R. Remiorz, "Canada Could Ditch Winter Blues by Annexing Caribbean Paradise," USA *Today* (online), 26 March 2004.

9   "Canada's Place in the Sun," *Gazette* (Montreal), 13 June 2003; D. Smith, "Task Force Should Study Turks and Caicos Pitch," *Calgary Herald*, 14 February 2004; "Caribbean Canada? 'It Would Be Very Hard,'" *Edmonton Journal*, 21 January 2004; J. Wingrove, "Baird Says No to Annexing 'Saskatchewarm,'" *Globe and Mail*, 27 May 2014.

10 Some studies documenting the international exploits and racialized practices of Canadian corporations, individuals, and the state have challenged the image of a benevolent, disinterested Canada and apply the concept of imperialism in a more critical sense. These include Sherene H. Razack, *Dark Threats and White Knights*; Price, *Orienting Canada*; Todd Gordon, *Imperialist Canada*; Yves Engler, *Left, Right*; Gordon and Webber, *Blood of Extraction*;

and many of the chapters in Dubinsky, Mills and Rutherford, *Canada and the Third World*.

11   Berger, *Sense of Power*, 1–2.

12   See Stuart Ward, "Transcending the Nation," 45.

13   I build here on a growing body of scholarship that explores how race thinking shaped Canada's international relations. See, for example, Price, *Orienting Canada*; Madokoro, McKenzie, and Meren, *Dominion of Race*; Asa McKercher, *Canada and the World since 1867*, especially 181–206.

14   "Canada's Caribbean Ambition," CBC *News Online*, 16 April 2004; Andrew Russell, "Reality Check: Should Canada Adopt Turks and Caicos as its 11th Province?," 6 April 2016, *Global News* (online); M. Vallis, "Will We Finally Get Our Island(s) in the Sun?," *Windsor Star*, 15 July 2003.

15   J.J. McCullough, "Think Trump Sounds Absurd on Greenland? Canada Has Entertained Crazier Ideas," *Washington Post* (online), 22 August 2019.

16   Canada, *Senate Debates*, 17 March 1987, 639 (Heath Macquarrie).

BIBLIOGRAPHY

Archival and Library Collections

Bodleian Library (Oxford)
    Lewis Harcourt papers (Modern Political MSS)
Centre for the Study of the Legacies of British Slavery, University College London
    Legacies of British Slave Ownership database (online). https://www.ucl.ac.uk/lbs/
    person/view/20012
Churchill Archives Center, Cambridge University
    Leopold Amery Papers
Dalhousie University Archives
    Minutes of the University Senate
    President's Office fonds
Dalhousie University Library, Special Collections
    George Major Creed fonds
Durham University Library, Archives and Special Collections, Palace Green Section
    Albert Henry George Grey Correspondence (Earl Grey)
Library and Archives Canada, Ottawa
    Government Records
        Department of Citizenship and Immigration
        Department of Immigration
        Department of External Affairs
        Department of Industry, Trade and Commerce
        Labour Relations Board
        Department of Justice
        Privy Council Office
    Private Manuscript Records
        R.B. Bennett fonds
        Robert Laird Borden fonds
        Roméo Leblanc fonds
        W.L. Mackenzie King fonds
        Wilfrid Laurier fonds

John A. Macdonald fonds
Max Saltsman fonds
National Archives of the United Kingdom (Kew) (TNA)
Cabinet Records (CAB)
Colonial Office Records (CO)
Foreign Office Records (FO)
Foreign and Commonwealth Office (FCO)
National Library of Jamaica, Kingston (NLJ)
Michael Solomon (Biographical Notes)
Parliamentary Archives, House of Lords (London)
David Lloyd George Papers
George Baden-Powell Papers
Provincial Archives of Ontario
William A. Foster fonds
Sun Life Insurance Company of Canada Corporate Archives (Mississauga)
Divisions and Territories, box 289
University of the West Indies, St Augustine, Alma Jordan Library Special Collections
Randolph Rust Collection, Photographic series, rec. no. 1
West India Committee Records, SC89

Parliamentary Papers

Britain, House of Commons Debates and Command Papers
Canada, House of Commons Debates
Canada, Senate Debates
Jamaica, Legislative Council Debates
Nova Scotia, Debates and Proceedings of the House of Assembly
Trinidad and Tobago, Legislative Council Debates

Newspapers and Magazines

CANADA

Acadian Recorder (Halifax)
The Anglo-Saxon
Atlantic Advocate
The Banner
B.C. Saturday Sunset
Behind the Headlines
Black Liberation News
Black Voice
Brandon Weekly Sun
The Bystander
By-Water Magazine
Calgary Daily Herald
Le Canada
Canada-Caribbean Affairs
Canada-West Indies Magazine
Canadian Century
Canadian Monthly and National Review
Canadian Observer
CBC News (online)
Citizen (Halifax)
Contrast
Daily Colonist (Victoria)
Dalhousie Gazette
Dawn of Tomorrow

Le Devoir
Edmonton Bulletin
Financial Post
Gazette (Montreal)
Globe/Globe and Mail (Toronto)
Grip (Toronto)
Guardian (Charlottetown)
Hamilton Spectator
The Head Quarters
Journal des campagnes
Journal of Commerce
The Loop
Maclean's
Mail and Empire (Toronto)
Maritime Merchant
Medicine Hat News
Montreal Herald
Montreal Witness
Morning Herald (Halifax)
Morning Chronicle (Halifax)
Narcity (online)
The Nation
New Socialist
Ottawa Citizen
Ottawa Evening Journal
Ottawa Free Press
Ottawa Journal
Port Arthur News
Presbyterian Witness
La Presse
Queen's Quarterly
Le Quotidien (Chicoutimi)
Richmond Hill Liberal
Saint John Globe
Share
Spear
Sunshine (Sun Life Insurance Company of
   Canada publication)
Toronto Daily Star
Toronto Mail
Toronto News
Toronto Saturday Night
Toronto Weekly Sun

Toronto World
Uhuru
Vancouver Sun
La Vérité (Quebec)
Victoria Daily Standard
Whitby Free Press
Windsor Star
Windsor Sun
Winnipeg/Manitoba Free Press

BAHAMAS

Inagua Record
Nassau Guardian
Nassau Tribune

BARBADOS

The Bajan
Barbados Advocate
Barbados Agricultural Reporter
Official Gazette

GUYANA

Daily Chronicle

DOMINICA

The Dominican

GRENADA

The Federalist
The West Indian

JAMAICA

Colonial Standard and Jamaica Despatch
Daily Gleaner
Telegraph and Guardian
Trelawny Advertiser

SAINT LUCIA

The Voice

TRINIDAD AND TOBAGO

Labour Leader
Port of Spain Gazette
Tapia
Trinidad Guardian

TURKS AND CAICOS

Conch News

UNITED KINGDOM AND REPUBLIC OF IRELAND

Empire Review
Financial Times (London)
Fortnightly Review
Glasgow Herald
Leeds Mercury
Manchester Guardian
Morning Post (London)
Pall Mall Gazette
Proceedings of the Royal Colonial Institute
Reynolds Newspaper
The Round Table
St James Gazette

St James Magazine and United Empire Review
Scotsman
Spectator
Standard of Empire
Times (London)
United Empire
Weekly Irish Times
West India Committee Circular

UNITED STATES

Atlantic Constitution
Baltimore Afro-American
Buffalo Express
Chicago Daily Tribune
Christian Science Monitor
Daily Boston Globe
Los Angeles Times
McClure's
New York Evening Mail
New York Herald
New York Times
Philadelphia Inquirer
St Louis Globe Democrat
Time
USA Today (online)
Wall Street Journal
Washington Post

Additional Sources

Abu-Laban, Baha. "Arab-Canadians and the Arab-Israeli Conflict." *Arab Studies Quarterly* 10, no. 1 (1988): 104–26.

Acheson, T.W. "The National Policy and the Industrialization of the Maritimes, 1880–1910." *Acadiensis* 1, no. 2 (1972): 3–31.

Adas, Michael. "Contested Hegemony: The Great War and the Afro-Asian Assault on the Civilizing Mission Ideology." *Journal of World History* 15, no. 1 (2004): 31–63.

Adi, Hakim. *Pan-Africanism and Communism: The Communist International, Africa, and the Diaspora, 1919–1939*. Trenton, NJ: Africa World Press, 2013.

Adjetey, Wendell Nii Laryea. "In Search of Ethiopia: Messianic Pan-Africanism and the Problem of the Promised Land, 1919–1931." *Canadian Historical Review* 102, no. 1 (2021): 53–78.

Albertini, Rudolph von. "The Impact of Two World Wars on the Decline of Colonialism." *Journal of Contemporary History* 4, no. 1 (1969): 17–35.

Alexander, Robert J. *A History of Organized Labor in the English-Speaking West Indies.* Westport, CN: Praeger, 2004.

Amery, L.S. "The British League of Nations." Address delivered by Leopold S. Amery before the Empire Club of Canada. *Empire Club Addresses*, June 1920. http:// speeches.empireclub.org/62374/data?n=1

– *My Political Life.* 2 vols. London: Hutchinson, 1953.

Anderson, Stuart. *Race and Rapprochement: Anglo-Saxonism and Anglo-American Relations, 1895–1904.* Rutherford, NJ: Fairleigh Dickinson University, 1981.

Anderson, Warwick. *Colonial Pathologies: American Tropical Medicine, Race, and Hygiene in the Philippines.* Durham: Duke University Press, 2006.

Andre, Irving W. *Edward Oliver Leblanc and the Struggle to Transform Dominica.* Brampton and Roseau: Pont Casse Press, 2004.

Anghie, Antony. *Imperialism, Sovereignty and the Making of International Law.* Cambridge: Cambridge University Press, 2004.

Armstrong, Christopher, and H.V. Nelles. *Southern Exposure: Canadian Promoters in Latin America and the Caribbean, 1896–1930.* Toronto: University of Toronto Press, 1988.

Asaka, Ikuko. *Tropical Freedom: Climate, Settler Colonialism, and Black Exclusion in the Age of Emancipation.* Durham: Duke University Press, 2017.

Augier, F.R. *The Making of the West Indies.* London: Longmans, 1961.

Austin, David. "All Roads Led to Montreal: Black Power, the Caribbean, and the Black Radical Tradition in Canada." *Journal of African American History* 92, no. 4 (2007): 516–39.

– *Fear of a Black Nation: Race, Sex and Security in Sixties Montreal.* Toronto: Between the Lines, 2013.

– "Liberation from Below: The Caribbean Conference Committee of Montreal and the Global New Left." MA thesis, Université de Montréal, 2007.

– "Narratives of Power: Historical Mythologies in Contemporary Québec and Canada." *Race and Class* 52, no. 1 (2010): 19–32.

– ed. *Moving against the System: The 1968 Congress of Black Writers and the Making of Global Consciousness.* Toronto: Between the Lines, 2018.

Austin, O.P. "Our Trade with Hawaii and Porto Rico." *Annals of the American Academy of Political and Social Science* 19, no. 3 (1902): 47–52.

Ayala, César J. *American Sugar Kingdom: The Plantation Economy of the Spanish Caribbean, 1898–1934.* Chapel Hill: University of North Carolina Press, 1999.

Azzi, Stephen. *Reconcilable Differences: A History of Canada-US Relations* (Don Mills, ON: Oxford University Press, 2015), 75–7.

– *Walter Gordon and the Rise of Canadian Nationalism.* Montreal: McGill-Queen's University Press, 1999.

Backhouse, Constance. *Colour-Coded: A Legal History of Racism in Canada, 1900–1950.* Toronto: University of Toronto Press, 1999.

Bakan, Abigail B. *Ideology and Class Conflict in Jamaica: The Politics of Rebellion.* Montreal: McGill-Queen's University Press, 1990.

Baker, Melvin. "Harry Judson Crowe." *Dictionary of Canadian Biography*. Vol. 15, *1921–1930*. http://www.biographi.ca/en/bio/crowe_harry_judson_15F.html.

Balakrishnan, Jaydeep, Janice B. Eliasson, and Timothy R.C. Sweet. "Factors Affecting the Evolution of Manufacturing in Canada: An Historical Perspective." *Journal of Operations Management* 25 (2007): 260–83.

Banerjee, Sukanya. *Becoming Imperial Citizens: Indians in the Late-Victorian Empire*. Durham: Duke University Press, 2010.

Banerji, Amitav. "The 1949 London Declaration: Birth of the Modern Commonwealth." *Commonwealth Law Bulletin* 25, no. 1 (1999): 1–8.

Bannerji, Himani. *The Dark Side of the Nation: Essays on Multiculturalism, Nationalism and Gender*. Toronto: Canadian Scholars' Press Inc., 2000.

Barker, J. Ellis. *Great and Greater Britain*. London: Smith, Elder, & Co., 1910.

Barnes, Felicity. "Bringing Another Empire Alive? The Empire Marketing Board and the Construction of Identity, 1926–33." *Journal of Imperial and Commonwealth History* 42, no. 1 (2014): 61–85.

Barrow, Errol. "A Role for Canada in the West Indies." *International Journal* 19, no. 2 (1964): 184–5.

Bassnett, Susan. "The Empire, Travel Writing, and British Studies." In *Travel Writing and the Empire*, edited by Sachidananda Mohanty. New Delhi: Katha, 2003.

Baum, Daniel Jay. *The Banks of Canada in the Commonwealth Caribbean: Economic Nationalism and Multinational Enterprise of a Medium Power*. New York: Praeger, 1974.

Beaton, Elizabeth. "An African-American Community in Cape Breton, 1901–1904." *Acadiensis* 24, no. 2 (1995): 65–97.

Beaudette, Catherine. "Bonavista Biennale – Art Encounters on the Edge: Contemporary Art in Rural Newfoundland." In *Cultural Sustainability, Tourism and Development: (Re)articulations in Tourism Contexts*, edited by Nancy Duxbury, 69–84. New York: Routledge, 2021.

Beckford, George L. *Persistent Poverty: Underdevelopment in Plantation Economies of the Third World*. New York: Oxford University Press, 1972.

Bélanger, Damien-Claude. "Robert Alexander Falconer." *Quebec History* (2004). http://faculty.marianopolis.edu/c.belanger/quebechistory/bios/robertfalconer.htm.

Bell, Duncan. *The Idea of Greater Britain: Empire and the Future of World Order, 1860–1900*. Princeton: Princeton University Press, 2007.

Benn, Dennis. *The Caribbean: An Intellectual History, 1774–2003*. Kingston, JA: Ian Randle Publishers, 2004.

Bercuson, David J. *Confrontation at Winnipeg: Labour, Industrial Relations, and the General Strike*. Montreal: McGill-Queen's University Press, 1974.

Berger, Carl. *The Sense of Power: Studies in the Ideas of Canadian Imperialism, 1867–1914*. Toronto: University of Toronto Press, 1970.

Best, Lloyd. "Outlines of a Model of Pure Plantation Economy." *Social and Economic Studies* 17, no. 3 (1968): 283–326.

Best, Lloyd, and Kari Levitt. *Externally Propelled Industrialization and Growth in the Caribbean*. Montreal: McGill Centre for Developing Area Studies, 1969.

Bevins, Charles I. *Treaties and Other International Agreements of the United States*. Vol. 4, *1931–1945*. Washington, DC: Department of State, 1970.

Bilby, Kenneth M., and Jerome S. Handler. "Obeah: Healing and Protection in West Indian Slave Life." *Journal of Caribbean History* 38, no. 2 (2004): 153–83.

Bliss, Michael. *Northern Enterprise: Five Centuries of Canadian Business*. Toronto: McClelland & Stewart, 1987.

Bolah, Ciprian. "Excellent Workers but Wrong Colour of Skin: Canada's Reluctance to Admit Caribbean People as Domestic Workers and Farm Labourers." MA thesis, University of Saskatchewan, 2014.

Borchard, Edwin M. "Commercial and Financial Interests of the United States in the Caribbean." *Proceedings of the Academy of Political Science in the City of New York* 7, no. 2 (1917): 191–9.

Borden, Henry, ed. *Robert Laird Borden: His Memoirs*. 2 vols. Toronto: St Martin's House, 1938.

Bothwell, Robert. "The Canadian Isolationist Tradition." *International Journal* 54, no. 1 (1998/99): 76–87.

Bothwell, Robert, Ian Drummond, and John English. *Canada since 1945: Power, Politics, and Provincialism*. Toronto: University of Toronto Press, 1984.

Bourassa, Henri. *Henri Bourassa on Imperialism and Biculturalism, 1900–1918*. Compiled by Joseph Levitt. Toronto: Copp Clark, 1970.

Boutilier, R.A. "Ten Years of Non-Existence: Canadian-West Indian Union, 1911–1920." BA thesis, Mount Allison University, 1971.

Brereton, Bridget. "The White Elite of Trinidad, 1838–1950." In *The White Minority in the Caribbean*, edited by Howard Johnson and Karl Watson, 32–70. Kingston, JA: Ian Randle Publishers, 1998.

Brewster, Havelock, and Clive Thomas. *The Dynamics of West Indian Economic Integration*. Mona: Institute of Social and Economic Research, University of the West Indies, 1967.

Brizan, George I. "Canada and the Commonwealth Caribbean Economic Relations, 1966–74." MA thesis, Carleton University, 1975.

Broderick, Margaret. "Associated Statehood – A New Form of Decolonisation." *International and Comparative Law Quarterly* 17, no. 2 (April 1968): 368–403.

Brouwer, Ruth Compton. *Canada's Global Villagers: CUSO in Development, 1961–86*. Vancouver: University of British Columbia Press, 2013.

Brown, Judith M. *War and the Colonial Relationship:* New Delhi: South Asia Books, 1978.

Brown, Robert Craig, and Ramsay Cook. *Canada 1896–1921: A Nation Transformed*. Toronto: McClelland & Stewart, 1974.

Bryan, Patrick E. *The Jamaican People, 1880–1902: Race, Class and Social Control*. London: Macmillan Education, 1991.

– "The White Minority in Jamaica at the End of the Nineteenth Century." In *The White Minority in the Caribbean*, edited by Howard Johnson and Karl Watson, 116–32. Kingston, JA: Ian Randle Publishers, 1998.

Burbank, Jane, and Frederick Cooper. *Empires in World History: Power and the Politics of Difference*. Princeton: Princeton University Press, 2010.

Burkman, Thomas W. *Japan and the League of Nations: Empire and World Order, 1914–1938*. Honolulu: University of Hawai'i Press, 2008.

Burman, Jenny. *Transnational Yearnings: Tourism, Migration, and the Diasporic City*. Vancouver: University of British Columbia Press, 2010.

Burnett, Carla. "'Unity Is Strength': Labor, Race, Garveyism, and the 1920 Panama Canal Strike." *Global South* 6, no. 2 (2012): 39–64.

Butler, Paula. *Colonial Extractions: Race and Canadian Mining in Contemporary Africa*. Toronto: University of Toronto Press, 2015.

Cabán, Pedro A. *Constructing a Colonial People: Puerto Rico and the United States, 1898–1932*. New York: Routledge, 2018.

Callaghan, J. "The Communists and the Colonies: Anti-Imperialism between the Wars." In *Opening the Books: Essays on the Social and Cultural History of the British Communist Party*, edited by Geoff Andrews, Nina Fishman, and Kevin Morgan, 4–22. London: Pluto Press, 1995.

Calliste, Agnes. "The Influence of the Civil Rights and Black Power Movement in Canada." *Race, Gender and Class: Perspective on Canadian Anti-Racism* 2, no. 3 (1995): 123–40.

– "Race, Gender and Canadian Immigration Policy: Blacks from the Caribbean." *Journal of Canadian Studies* 28, no. 4 (1993–94): 131–48.

Campbell, S. "'Black Bolsheviks' and the Recognition of African-America's Right to Self-Determination by the Communist Party USA." *Science and Society*, no. 58 (1994–95): 440–70.

Canada. *Canada and the Commonwealth Caribbean Conference, Ottawa, July 6–8, 1966: Text of the Committee Issued at the Close of the Conference*. Ottawa: Department of External Affairs, 1966.

Canada. *Documents on Canadian External Relations*. Vol. 1. Compiled by Robert A. MacKay. Ottawa: Queen's Printer, 1967.

Canada. *A History of the Vote in Canada*. Ottawa: Minister of Public Works and Government Services, 1997.

Canada Year Book, 1954. Ottawa: Dominion Bureau of Statistics, Queen's Printer, 1955.

Canada Year Book, 1962. Ottawa: Dominion Bureau of Statistics, Queen's Printer, 1962.

Canada Year Book, 1963–1964. Ottawa: Dominion Bureau of Statistics, Queen's Printer, 1964.

Canada Year Book, 1967. Ottawa: Dominion Bureau of Statistics, Queen's Printer, 1967.

Canada Year Book, 1968. Ottawa: Dominion Bureau of Statistics, Queen's Printer, 1968.

Carleton, Sean. "Colonizing Minds: Public Education, the 'Textbook Indian,' and Settler Colonialism in British Columbia, 1920–1970." *BC Studies* no. 169 (2011): 101–30.

Carmichael, Trevor A. *Passport to the Heart: Reflections on Canada Caribbean Relations*. Kingston, JA: Ian Randle Publishers, 2001.

Carnegie, Jimmy. "Claude McKay's Big Brother, U. Theo McKay (1872–1949)." *Caribbean Quarterly* 38, no. 1 (1992): 5–9.

Carrington, Selwyn. "The United States and Canada: The Struggle for the British West Indian Trade." *Social and Economic Studies*, no. 37 (1988): 69–105.

Carson, James. "Commercial and Financial Agencies of Pan-American Union." *Proceedings of the Academy of Political Science in the City of New York* 7, no. 2 (1917): 260–71.

Carter, Sarah. *Aboriginal People and Colonizers of Western Canada to 1900*. Toronto: University of Toronto Press, 1999.

Carty, Robert, and Virginia Smith. *Perpetuating Poverty: The Political Economy of Canadian Foreign Aid*. Toronto: Between the Lines Press, 1981.

Chamberlain, Joseph. "Recent Developments of Policy in the United States and Their Relation to an Anglo-American Alliance." *Scribner's Magazine* 24, no. 6 (1898): 674–82.

Chapnick, Adam. "Peace, Order and Good Government: The 'Conservative' Tradition in Canadian Foreign Policy." *International Journal* 60, no. 3 (2005): 635–50.

Chatterjee, Partha. *Nationalist Thought and the Colonial World: A Derivative Discourse?* London: Zed Books for the United Nations University, 1986.

Chodos, Robert. *The Caribbean Connection*. Toronto: James Lorimer & Co., 1977.

Choudry, Aziz. "What's Left? Canada's 'Global Justice' Movement and Colonial Amnesia." *Race and Class* 52, no. 1 (2010): 97–102.

Clark, Lovell. "John Christian Schultz." *Dictionary of Canadian Biography*. Vol. 12, *1891–1901*. http://www.biographi.ca/en/bio/schultz_john_christian_12E.html.

Cleary, A.S. "The Myth of Mau Mau in Its International Context." *African Affairs* 89, no. 355 (1990): 227–45.

Clément, Dominique. *Human Rights in Canada: A History*. Waterloo: Wilfrid Laurier University Press, 2016.

Coates, Kenneth. *Canada's Colonies: A History of the Yukon and Northwest Territories*. Toronto: James Lorimer & Co., 1985.

Cooper, Afua. *The Hanging of Angelique*. Athens, GA: University of Georgia Press, 2007.

Cooper, Frederick. *Colonialism in Question: Theory, Knowledge, History*. Berkeley: University of California Press, 2005.

Corbett, David C. *Canada's Immigration Policy: A Critique*. Toronto: University of Toronto Press, 1957.

Courteaux, Olivier. *Canada between Vichy and Free France, 1940–1945*. Toronto: University of Toronto Press, 2013.

Cox Alomar, Rafael. "Britain's Withdrawal from the Eastern Caribbean, 1965–67: A Reappraisal." *Journal of Imperial and Commonwealth History* 31, no. 3 (2003): 74–106.

– *Revisiting the Transatlantic Triangle: The Constitutional Decolonization of the Eastern Caribbean*. Kingston, JA: Ian Randle Publishers, 2009.

Craton, Michael. "Bay Street, Black Power, and the Conchy Joes: Race and Class in the Colony and Commonwealth of the Bahamas, 1850–2000." In *The White Minority in the Caribbean*, edited by Howard Johnson and Karl S. Watson, 71–94. Kingston, JA: Ian Randle Publishers, 1998.

– *A History of the Bahamas*. Waterloo, ON: San Salvador Press, 1986.

Craton, Michael, and Gail Saunders. *Islanders in the Stream: A History of the Bahamian People*, 2 vols. Athens: University of Georgia Press, 2000.

Cross, J.A. "Whitehall and the Commonwealth." *Journal of Commonwealth Political Studies* 2, no. 3 (1964): 189–206.

– *Whitehall and the Commonwealth: British Departmental Organisation for Commonwealth Relations, 1900–1966*. London: Routledge & Kegan Paul, 1967.

Crowe, Harry Judson. "Commercial Union with the West Indies or Confederation?" *Canada-West Indies Magazine* 5, no. 25 (1916–17).

– "Canada and the West Indies," *United Empire* 9, no. 10 (1918).

Darwin, John. "A Third British Empire? The Dominion Idea in Imperial Politics." In *The Oxford History of the British Empire*. Vol. 5, *The Twentieth Century*, edited by Judith M. Brown and Wm. Roger Louis, 64–72. Oxford: Oxford University Press, 1999.

Daschuk, James. *Clearing the Plains: Disease, Politics of Starvation, and the Loss of Indigenous Life*. Regina: University of Regina Press, 2013.

Davson, Edward R. "British Guiana and its Development." *Proceedings of the Royal Colonial Institute* 39 (1908): 229–53.

De Barros, Juanita. *Reproducing the British Caribbean: Sex, Gender, and Population Politics after Slavery*. Chapel Hill: University of North Carolina Press, 2014.

Demas, Walter. *The Economics of Development in Small Countries with Special Reference to the Caribbean*. Montreal: McGill-Queen's University Press, 1965.

Denison, George Taylor. *A Review of the Judgments of the Bench, in the Anderson Extradition Case*. Toronto: Printed for the Publisher, 1861.

Dewitt, David B., and John J. Kirton. *Canada as a Principal Power*. Toronto: John Wiley & Sons, 1983.

Donaghy, Greg, and Bruce Muirhead. "'Interests but No Foreign Policy': Canada and the Commonwealth Caribbean, 1941–1966." *American Review of Canadian Studies* 38, no. 3 (2008): 275–94.

Donovan, Ken. "Slavery and Freedom in Atlantic Canada's African Diaspora: Introduction." *Acadiensis* 43, no.1 (2014): 109–15

Doxey, G.V. "The Commonwealth in the Americas: Canada Takes the Initiative." *Round Table* 56, no. 224 (1966): 387–93.

Driver, Felix, and Luciana Martins. "Views and Visions of the Tropical World," introduction to *Tropical Visions in an Age of Empire*, edited by Felix Driver and Luciana Martins, 3–22. Chicago: University of Chicago Press, 2005.

Drummond, Andrew T. "Canada and the British West Indies," *By-Water Magazine* 5, no. 2 (1920): 29–34.

Easterly, William. *The White Man's Burden: Why the West's Efforts to Aid the Rest Have Done So Much Ill and So Little Good*. New York: Penguin, 2006.

Dubinsky, Karen, Sean Mills, and Scott Rutherford. *Canada and the Third World: Overlapping Histories*. Toronto: University of Toronto Press, 2016.

Duke, Eric D. "The Diasporic Dimensions of British Caribbean Federation in the Early Twentieth Century." *NWIG: New West Indian Guide* 83, nos. 3–4 (2009): 219–48.

Easterly, William, *White Man's Burden: Why the West's Efforts to Aid the Rest Have Done So Much Ill and So Little Good*. New York: Penguin, 2006.

Eayrs, James. *In Defence of Canada: From the Great War to the Great Depression*. Toronto: University of Toronto Press, 1964.

– *Northern Approaches: Canada and the Search for Peace*. Toronto: Macmillan, 1961.

Edmond, Rod. "Returning Fears: Tropical Disease and the Metropolis." In Driver and Martins, *Tropical Visions in an Age of Empire*, 175–96. Chicago: University of Chicago Press, 2005.

Edmondson, Locksley G.E. "Canada and the West Indies: Trends and Prospects." *International Journal* 19, no. 2 (1964): 188–201.

Elgersman, Maureen G. *Unyielding Spirits: Black Women and Slavery in Early Canada and Jamaica*. New York: Garland, 1999.

Elmer, Jonathan. *On Lingering and Being Last: Race and Sovereignty in the New World*. New York: Fordham University Press, 2008.

Engler, Yves. *The Black Book of Canadian Foreign Policy*. Halifax: Fernwood, 2009.

– *Left, Right: Marching to the Beat of Imperial Canada*. Montreal: Black Rose Books, 2019.

– *Propaganda System: How Canada's Government, Corporations, Media and Academia Sell War*. Blackpoint, NS: Fernwood, 2016.

Eves, Richard. "Unsettling Settler Colonialism: Debates over Climate and Colonization in New Guinea, 1875–1914." *Ethnic and Racial Studies* 28, no. 2 (2005): 304–30.

Falconer, R.A. "Canada and the West Indies." In *Proceedings of the Canadian Club, Toronto, 1910–1911*. Toronto: Warwick Bros. & Rutter, 1911.

– *The United States as a Neighbor from a Canadian Point of View*. Cambridge: Cambridge University Press, 1925.

Fanon, Frantz. *Black Skin White Masks*, trans. Charles Lam Markmann. 1952. Reprint, New York: Grove Press, 1967.

– *The Wretched of the Earth*, trans. Constance Farrington. 1961. Reprint, New York: Grove Press, 1963.

Farley, John. *Bilharzia: A History of Tropical Medicine*. Cambridge: Cambridge University Press, 2003.

Fayerweather, John. *Foreign Investment in Canada: Prospects for National Policy*. White Plains, NY: International Arts & Sciences Press, 1973.

Fergus, Howard A. *Montserrat: History of a Caribbean Colony*. London: Macmillan, 1994.

Fernandez, Purba. "Asian Indian Immigration to Canada." In *Geographical Identities of Ethnic America: Race, Space, and Place*, edited by Kate A. Berry and Martha L. Henderson, 64–91. Reno: University of Nevada Press, 2002.

Fiddes, George V. *The Dominions and Colonial Offices*. London: G.P. Putnam's Sons, 1926.

Fieldhouse, David. *The Colonial Empires*. New York: Delacorte Press, 1966.

Fillion, Eric. "Experiments in Cultural Diplomacy: Music as Mediation in Canadian-Brazilian Relations." PhD diss., Concordia University, 2019.

Fingard, Judith. "The 1880s: Paradoxes of Progress." In *The Atlantic Provinces in Confederation*, edited by E.R. Forbes and Delphin A. Muise, 82–116. Toronto: University of Toronto Press, 1993.

Forbes, Ernest R. *The Maritime Rights Movement, 1919–1927: A Study in Canadian Regionalism*. Montreal: McGill-Queen's University Press, 1979.

Ford, Joseph C. *The Handbook of Jamaica*. Kingston, JA: Government Printing Office, 1890.

Forsythe, Dennis, ed., *Let the N—— Burn! The Sir George Williams University Affair and Its Caribbean Aftermath*. Montreal: Black Rose Books/Our Generation Press, 1971.

Foster, William A. *Canada First: A Memorial of the Late William A. Foster, Q.C.* Toronto: Hunter, Rose & Co., 1890.

Francis, R. Douglas. *Frank Underhill: Intellectual Provocateur.* Toronto: University of Toronto Press, 1986.

Frost, Stanley Brice. *McGill University for the Advancement of Learning.* Vol. 1, *1801–1895.* Montreal: McGill-Queen's University Press, 1980.

Gagan, David P. "Canada First: A Bundle of Little Egotisms." MA thesis, University of Western Ontario, 1964.

– "The Relevance of 'Canada First.'" *Journal of Canadian Studies* 5, no. 4 (1970): 36–44.

– "William Alexander Foster." *Dictionary of Canadian Biography.* Vol. 11, *1881–1890.* http://www.biographi.ca/en/bio/foster_william_alexander_11E.html.

Gallagher, John. "Nationalisms and the Crisis of Empire, 1919–1922." *Modern Asian Studies* 15, no. 3 (1981): 355–68.

Gallagher, John, and Ronald Robinson. "The Imperialism of Free Trade." *Economic History Review* 8, no. 1 (1953): 1–15.

Gaudry, Adam. "Fantasies of Sovereignty: Deconstructing British and Canadian Claims to Ownership of the Historic North-West." *Native American and Indigenous Studies* 3, no. 1 (2016): 46–74.

Gendron, Robin S. "Canada's University: Father Lévesque, Canadian Aid, and the National University of Rwanda." *Historical Studies* 1, no. 73 (2007): 63–86.

– "Tempered Sympathy: Canada's Reaction to the Independence Movement in Algeria, 1954–1962." *Journal of the Canadian Historical Association* 9, no. 1 (1998): 225–41.

– *Towards a Francophone Community: Canada's Relations with France and French Africa, 1945–1968.* Montreal: McGill-Queen's University Press, 2007.

Gilmore, William C. "The Associated States of the Commonwealth Caribbean: The Constitutions and the Individual." *University of Miami Inter-American Law Review* 11, nos. 1–2 (1979): 1–41.

Girvan, Norman. *Foreign Capital and Economic Underdevelopment in Jamaica.* Jamaica: Institute of Social and Economic Research, University of the West Indies, 1971.

– "The Guyana-Alcan Conflict and the Nationalization of DEMBA." *International Journal of Politics* 3, no. 3 (1973): 87–111.

Girvan, Norman, and Cherita Girvan. "Dependency Economics in the Caribbean and Latin America: Review and Comparison." *Social and Economic Studies* 22, no.1 (1973): 1–33.

Gobat, Michel. *Confronting the American Dream: Nicaragua under U.S. Imperial Rule.* Durham: Duke University Press, 2005.

Goldberg, David Theo. *The Racial State.* Oxford: Blackwell, 2002.

Gooden, Amoaba. "Community Organizing by African Caribbean People in Toronto, Ontario." *Journal of Black Studies* 38, no. 3 (2008): 413–26.

Gordon, Todd. *Imperialist Canada.* Winnipeg: Arbeiter Ring, 2010.

Gordon, Todd, and Jeffrey R. Webber. *Blood of Extraction: Canadian Imperialism in Latin America.* Black Point, NS: Fernwood, 2016.

Gorman, Daniel. *Imperial Citizenship: Empire and the Question of Belonging.* Manchester: Manchester University Press, 2006.

– "Race, the Commonwealth, and the United Nations: From Imperialism to Internationalism in Canada, 1940–1960." In *Dominion of Race: Rethinking Canada's International History*, edited by Laura Madokoro, David Meren, and Francine McKenzie, 139–89. Vancouver: University of British Columbia Press, 2017.

– "'Wider and Wider Still?': Racial Politics, Intra-Imperial Immigration and the Absence of an Imperial Citizenship in the British Empire." *Journal of Colonialism and Colonial History* 3, no. 3 (2002): 1–24.

Gosling, Audley. "Central America and Its Resources." *North American Review* 162, no. 470 (1896): 96–102.

Goutor, David. "Drawing Different Lines of Color: The Mainstream English Canadian Labor Movement's Approach to Blacks and Chinese, 1880–1914." *Labor: Studies in Working-Class History of the Americas* 3, no. 1 (2005): 55–76.

– *Guarding the Gates: The Canadian Labor Movement and Immigration, 1872–1934.* Vancouver: University of British Columbia Press, 2007.

Granatstein, J.L. "Becoming Difficult: Escott Reid: Diplomat and Scholar." In *Escott Reid: Diplomat and Scholar*, edited by Greg Donaghy, 11–22. Montreal: McGill-Queen's Press, 2004.

– *Canada's Army: Waging War and Keeping the Peace.* Toronto: University of Toronto Press, 2002.

– *Yankee Go Home: Canada and Anti-Americanism.* Toronto: Harper Collins, 1996.

Granatstein, J.L., and J. Mackay Hitsman. *Broken Promises: A History of Conscription in Canada.* Toronto: Oxford University Press, 1977.

Granatstein, J.L., and Robert Bothwell. "'A Self Evident National Duty': Canadian Foreign Policy, 1935–1939." *Journal of Imperial and Commonwealth History* 3, no. 3 (1975): 212–33.

Grant, Cedric H. "Political Sequel to Alcan Nationalization in Guyana: The International Aspects." *Social and Economic Studies* 22, no. 2 (1973): 249–71.

Grant, George. *Lament for a Nation: The Defeat of Canadian Nationalism.* Toronto: McClelland & Stewart, 1965.

Grant, W.L. "Geographical Conditions Affecting the Development of Canada." *Geographical Journal* 38, no. 4 (1911): 362–74.

Greenlee, James G. *Sir Robert Falconer: A Biography.* Toronto: University of Toronto Press, 1988.

Griffin, Watson. "An Imperial Alliance," *Empire Review*, no. 3 (May 1902): 415–22.

– *The Provinces and the States. Why Canada Does Not Want Annexation.* Toronto: J. Moore, 1884.

Gupta, Partha Sarathi. *Imperialism and the British Labour Movement, 1914–1964.* London: Macmillan, 1975.

Haliburton, R.G. "The Black and Brown Landholders of Jamaica: Character and Condition." In *The Crown Colonies of Great Britain. An Inquiry into Their Social*

Condition and Methods of Administration, edited by Charles Spencer Salmon,
   85–100. London: Cassell & Co., 1885.

– *The Men of the North and Their Place in History*. Montreal: John Lovell, 1869.

– *Mr. Haliburton's Speech on the Young Men of the New Dominion*. Thomas Fisher Rare
   Book Library, University of Toronto, 1870.

Hall, Catherine. *Civilising Subjects: Colony and Metropole in the English Imagination,
   1830–1867*. Chicago: University of Chicago Press, 2002.

Hann, Russell. "Brainworkers and the Knights of Labor: E. E. Sheppard, Phillips
   Thompson, and the Toronto News, 1883–1887." In *Essays in Canadian Working
   Class History*, edited by Gregory S. Kealey and Peter Warrian, 35–57. Toronto:
   McClelland & Stewart, 1976.

Hardt, Michael, and Antonio Negri, *Empire*. Cambridge, MA: Harvard University Press,
   2000.

Harris, Chris. "Canadian Black Power, Organic Intellectuals and the War of Position in
   Toronto, 1967–1975." In *The Sixties in Canada: A Turbulent and Creative Decade*,
   edited by M. Athena Palaeologu, 324–39. Montreal: Black Rose Books, 2009.

Harris, Richard Cole. *Making Native Space: Colonialism, Resistance, and Reserves in
   British Columbia*. Vancouver: University of British Columbia Press, 2002.

Hastings, Paula. "The Limits of 'Brotherly Love': Rethinking Canada-Caribbean
   Relations in the Early Twentieth Century." In Madokoro, McKenzie, and Meren,
   Dominion of Race: Rethinking Canada's International History, 38–53. Vancouver:
   University of British Columbia Press, 2017.

– "'Our Glorious Anglo-Saxon Race Shall Ever Fill Earth's Highest Place': The Anglo-Saxon
   and the Construction of Identity in Late Nineteenth-Century Canada." In *Canada
   and the British World: Culture, Migration, and Identity*, edited by Phillip Buckner and
   Doug Francis, 92–110. Vancouver: University of British Columbia Press, 2006.

– "Rounding off the Confederation: Geopolitics, Tropicality, and Canada's 'Destiny'
   in the West Indies in the Early Twentieth Century." *Journal of Colonialism and
   Colonial History* 13, no. 2 (2013). https://muse-jhu-edu.myaccess.library.utoronto.
   ca/article/513260.

– "Territorial Spoils, Transnational Black Resistance, and Canada's Evolving Autonomy
   during the First World War." *Histoire Sociale/Social History* 47, no. 94 (2014): 443–70.

Havinden, Michael Ashley, and David Meredith. *Colonialism and Development: Britain
   and Its Tropical Colonies, 1850–1960*. London: Routledge, 1993.

Henry, Frances. "The West Indian Domestic Scheme in Canada." *Social and Economic
   Studies* 17, no. 1 (1968): 83–91.

Heron, Craig. "Communists, Gangsters, and Canadian Sailors." *Labour/Le Travail*
   (1989): 231–7.

– *The Worker's Revolt in Canada, 1917–1925*. Toronto: University of Toronto Press, 1998.

Higgott, Richard. "Competing Theoretical Perspectives on Development and
   Underdevelopment: A Recent Intellectual History." *Politics* 13, no. 1 (1978): 26–41.

High, Steven. *Base Colonies in the Western Hemisphere, 1940–1967*. New York: Palgrave
   Macmillan, 2009.

Hiller, J.K. "The Origins of the Pulp and Paper Industry in Newfoundland." *Acadiensis*
    11, no. 2 (1981–82): 42–68.
– "The Politics of Newsprint: The Newfoundland Pulp and Paper Industry,
    1915–1939." *Acadiensis* 19, no. 2 (1989–90): 3–39.
Hillmer, Norman. *O.D. Skelton: A Portrait of Political Ambition*. Toronto: University of
    Toronto Press, 2015.
Hillmer, Norman, and J.L. Granatstein. *Empire to Umpire: Canada and the World to the
    1990s*. Toronto: Irwin, 2000.
Holland, Robert. *Britain and the Commonwealth Alliance 1918–1939*. London:
    Macmillan, 1981.
– "The British Empire and the Great War, 1914–1918." In *Oxford History of the British
    Empire*. Vol. 4, *The Twentieth Century*, edited by Judith Brown and Wm. Roger
    Louis, 115–38. Oxford: Oxford University Press, 1999.
Holmes, John. "The Impact on the Commonwealth of the Emergence of Africa."
    International Organization 16, no. 2 (1962): 291–302.
Holt, Thomas C. *The Problem of Freedom: Race, Labor, and Politics in Jamaica and
    Britain, 1832–1938*. Baltimore: Johns Hopkins University Press, 1992.
Hopkins, J. Castell, ed. *Canada: An Encyclopedia of the Century*. Vol. 1. Toronto:
    Linscott Publishing, 1898.
– ed. *Canadian Annual Review for 1905*. Toronto: Annual Review Publishing, 1906.
– ed. *Morang's Annual Register 1902*. Toronto: George Morang & Co., 1902.
Hornback, Robert. *Racism and Early Blackface Comic Traditions: From the Old World to
    the New*. Cham: Palgrave-Macmillan, 2018.
Howe, Anthony. *Free Trade and Liberal England, 1846–1946*. New York: Oxford
    University Press, 1998.
Howe, Glenford. *Race, War and Nationalism: A Social History of West Indians in the First
    World War*. Kingston, JA: Ian Randle Publishers, 2002.
Hudson, Peter James. "Imperial Designs: The Royal Bank of Canada in the Caribbean."
    Race and Class 52, no. 33 (2010): 33–48.
Hughes, Colin A. "Experiments towards Closer Union in the British West Indies."
    Journal of Negro History 43, no. 2 (1958): 85–104.
Hurwitz, Samuel J. "The Federation of the West Indies: A Study in Nationalisms."
    Journal of British Studies 6, no. 1 (1966): 139–68.
Huskins, Bonnie. "Robert Grant Haliburton." *Dictionary of Canadian Biography*, no. 13
    (1901–10). http://www.biographi.ca/en/bio/haliburton_robert_grant_13E.html.
Huttenback, Robert A. *Racism and Empire: White Settlers and Colored Immigrants in the
    British Self-Governing Colonies, 1830–1910*. Ithaca: Cornell University Press, 1976.
Hyam, Ronald. "The British Empire in the Edwardian Era." In *The Oxford History of the
    British Empire*. Vol. 4, *The Twentieth Century*, edited by Judith M. Brown and Wm
    Roger Louis, 48–64. Oxford: Oxford University Press, 1999.
Idema, Ralph. Interview, *Liquid Lunch with Hugh Reilly and Miranda Hill*,
    11 November 2012. https://www.youtube.com/watch?v=3U2k5O37NNM.

Igartua, J.E. *The Other Quiet Revolution: National Identities in English Canada, 1945–1971*. Vancouver: University of British Columbia Press, 2005.

Inwood, Kris. "Maritime Industrialization from 1870 to 1910: A Review of the Evidence and Its Interpretation." In *Farm, Factory and Fortune: New Studies in the Economic History of the Maritime Provinces*, edited by Kris Inwood, 149–70. Fredericton: Acadiensis Press, 1991.

Jamaica. *Minutes of the Legislative Council of Jamaica*. Kingston: Government Printing Establishment, 1885.

James, Arthur Curtiss. "Advantages of Hawaiian Annexation." *North American Review* 165, no. 493 (1897): 758–60.

James, C.L.R. *Party Politics in the West Indies*. San Juan, Trinidad: Vedic Enterprises, 1962.

Jansen, Marius B. "Japanese Imperialism: Late Meiji Perspectives." In *The Japanese Colonial Empire, 1895–1945*, edited by Ramon H. Myers and Mark R. Peattie, 61–79. Princeton: Princeton University Press, 1984.

John, Tamanisha Jennifer. "Canada's Financial Dominance in the Former English Caribbean Colonies (FECC)." *Council on Hemispheric Affairs* (online), 9 January 2018. https://www.coha.org/canadas-financial-dominance-in-the-former-english-caribbean-colonies-fecc/.

Johnson, E.R. "The Trade and Industries of Western South America." *Journal of Geography* 1, no. 3 (1902): 109–22.

Johnson, Gregory A., and David A. Lenarcic. "The Decade of Transition: The North Atlantic Triangle during the 1920s." In *The North Atlantic Triangle in a Changing World: Anglo-American Relations, 1902–1956*, edited by B.J.C. McKercher and Lawrence Aronsen, 81–109. Toronto: University of Toronto Press, 1996.

Johnson, Howard. *The Bahamas in Slavery and Freedom*. Kingston, JA: Ian Randle Publishers, 1991.

Jones, Delton. "Turks & Caicos Islands' Economic Structure, Challenges and Prospects." In *History of the Turks and Caicos Islands*, edited by Carlton Mills, 222–32. Oxford: Macmillan Education, 2008.

Jones, Esyllt, and Adele Perry. *People's Citizenship Guide: A Response to Conservative Canada*. Winnipeg: Arbeiter Ring Publishing, 2011.

Kane, Molly. "Canada and the Third World: Development Aid." In Dubinsky, Mills, and Rutherford, *Canada and the Third World: Overlapping Histories*, 88–119. Toronto: University of Toronto Press, 2016.

Kealey, Gregory S. *Workers in Canadian History*. Montreal: McGill-Queen's University Press, 1995.

Kealey, Gregory S., and Bryan D. Palmer. *Dreaming of What Might Be: The Knights of Labor in Ontario, 1880–1900*. Cambridge: Cambridge University Press, 2005.

Keene, Edward. *Beyond the Anarchical Society: Grotius, Colonialism and Order in World Politics*. Cambridge: Cambridge University Press, 2002.

Kelley, Ninette, and Michael Trebilcock. *The Making of the Mosaic: A History of Canadian Immigration Policy*. Toronto: University of Toronto Press, 2000.

Kendle, John. *The Round Table Movement and Imperial Union*. Toronto: University of Toronto Press, 1975.

Kidd, Benjamin. *The Control of the Tropics*. New York: Macmillan, 1898.

King, Ruby. "Education in the British Caribbean: The Legacy of the Nineteenth Century." In *Educational Reform in the Commonwealth Caribbean*, edited by Errol Miller, 25–45. Washington, DC: Organization of American States, 1999.

– "Elementary Education in Early Twentieth-Century Jamaica." *Caribbean Journal of Education* 16, no. 3 (1989): 224–46.

Kirk-Greene, Anthony H.M. "Taking Canada into Partnership in 'The White Man's Burden': The British Colonial Service and the Dominion Selection Scheme of 1923." *Canadian Journal of African Studies* 15, no. 1 (1981): 33–54.

Klassen, Jerome, and Greg Albo. *Empire's Ally: Canada and the War in Afghanistan*. Toronto: University of Toronto Press, 2013.

Knight, Franklin W. *The Caribbean: The Genesis of a Fragmented Nationalism*. New York: Oxford University Press, 1990.

Knight, Rolf. *Indians at Work: An Informal History of Native Labour in British Columbia, 1848–1930*. Vancouver: New Star Books, 1996.

Knowles, Norman. "George Taylor Denison." *Dictionary of Canadian Biography*. Vol. 15, *1921–30*. http://www.biographi.ca/en/bio/denison_george_taylor_1839_1925_15E.html.

Knowles, Valerie. *Strangers at Our Gates: Canadian Immigration and Immigration Policy, 1540–1990*. Toronto: Dundurn Press, 1992.

Kothari, Uma. "An Agenda for Thinking about 'Race' in Development." *Progress in Development Studies* 6, no.1 (2006): 9–23.

Kramer, Paul A. *The Blood of Government: Race, Empire, the United States, and the Philippines*. Chapel Hill: University of North Carolina Press, 2006.

Lacey, Terry. *Violence and Politics in Jamaica, 1960–70: Internal Security in a Developing Country*. London: Frank Cass, 1977.

Lake, Marilyn, and Henry Reynolds. *Drawing the Global Colour Line: White Men's Countries and the International Challenge of Racial Equality*. Cambridge: Cambridge University Press, 2008.

Lambertson, Ross. "'The Dresden Story': Racism, Human Rights, and the Jewish Labour Committee of Canada." *Labour/Le Travail* 47 (Spring 2001), 43–82.

Larcher, Oswald. *The Politics of Canadian Aid to the Commonwealth Caribbean*. MA thesis, University of Waterloo, 1973.

Laurence, K.O. *A Question of Labour: Indentured Immigration into Trinidad and British Guiana, 1875–1917*. New York: St Martin's Press, 1994.

Laurier, Wilfrid. "Canada's Century." In *Canada Always: The Defining Speeches of Wilfrid Laurier*, edited by Arthur Milnes, 299–300. Toronto: McClelland & Stewart, 2016.

Lawson, W.R. *Canada and the Empire*. Edinburgh: William Blackwood & Sons, 1911.

Leacock, Stephen. "Greater Canada." *University Magazine* (McGill), no. 6 (1907): 132–41.

Lee, Erika. "The 'Yellow Peril' and Asian Exclusion in the Americas." *Pacific Historical Review* 76, no. 4 (2007): 537–62.

Lentz-Smith, Adriane. *Freedom Struggles: African Americans and World War I*. Cambridge, MA: Harvard University Press, 2009.

Levine, Allan. *Toronto: Biography of a City.* Madeira Park, BC: Douglas & McIntyre, 2014.

Levitt, Joseph. *Henri Bourassa and the Golden Calf: The Social Program of the Nationalistes of Quebec, 1900–1914.* Ottawa: Les Editions de l'Université d'Ottawa, 1972.

Levitt, Kari. "Dependence and Disintegration in Canada." *New World Quarterly* 2, no. 2 (1968): 57–139.

– *Reclaiming Development: Independent Thought and Caribbean Community.* Kingston, JA: Ian Randle Publishers, 2005.

– *Silent Surrender: The Multinational Corporation in Canada.* Toronto: Macmillan, 1970.

Levitt, Kari, and Iqbal Gulati. "Income Effect of Tourist Spending: Mystification Multiplied." *Journal of Social and Economic Studies* 19, no. 3 (1970): 326–43.

Levitt, Kari, and Alister McIntyre. *Canada-West Indies Economic Relations.* Montreal: Canadian Trade Committee and the Centre for Development Studies, McGill University, 1967.

Levy, Charles. *Correspondence on Confederation with the Dominion of Canada.* Kingston, JA: DeCordova & Co., 1885.

Lewis, Gordon K. *The Growth of the Modern West Indies.* New York: Monthly Review Press, 1968.

Liberation Support Movement. *Getting Hip to Imperialism: Alcan, Jamaica, and Cabora Bassa.* Richmond, BC: Information Center/The Movement, 1972.

Litvak, Isaiah A., and Christopher J. Maule. "Nationalisation in the Caribbean Bauxite Industry." *International Affairs* 51, no.1 (1975): 43–59.

Livingstone, W.P. "The Future of the British West Indies." *North American Review* 182, no. 592 (1906): 426–32.

Lonsdale, John. "Mau Maus of the Mind: Making Mau Mau and Remaking Kenya." *Journal of African History* 31, no. 3 (1990): 393–421.

Look Lai, Walton. *Indentured Labor, Caribbean Sugar: Chinese and Indian Migrants to the British West Indies, 1838–1918.* Baltimore: Johns Hopkins University Press, 1993.

Lowry, Donal. "'The Boers Were the Beginning of the End'? The Wider Impact of the South African War." In *The South African War Reappraised,* edited by Donal Lowry, 203–46. Manchester: Manchester University Press, 2000.

Lucas, Charles. "Balance of Power within the Empire." *United Empire* 13, no. 12 (1922): 17–26.

Lumumba, Carl. "The West Indies and the Sir George Williams Affair: An Assessment." In *Let the N—— Burn! The Sir George Williams University Affair and Its Caribbean Aftermath,* edited by Dennis Forsythe, 144–92. Montreal: Black Rose Books/Our Generation Press, 1971.

Macaulay, T.B. "Never Give Up the Colonies!" *Maclean's* 35, no. 5 (1922): 36.

Macdonald, John A. *Canada, the West Indies, and British Guiana: Paper Read before the Board of Trade of Toronto.* Toronto: n.p., 1889.

MacEachern, Alan. "The Large and Lovelier Canada." *Canadian Issues/Thèmes Canadiens* (Fall 2014): 46–50.

Mackey, Eva. *The House of Difference: Cultural Politics and National Identity in Canada.* London: Routledge, 1999.

Mackenzie, Hector. "An Old Dominion and the New Commonwealth: Canadian
    Policy on the Question of India's Membership, 1947–1949." *Journal of Imperial and
    Commonwealth History* 27, no. 3 (1999): 82–112.
MacMillan, Margaret. "Canada and the Peace Settlements." In *Canada and the First
    World War: Essays in Honour of Robert Craig Brown*, edited by David Mackenzie,
    379–408. Toronto: University of Toronto Press, 2005.
– *Paris 1919: Six Months That Changed the World*. New York: Random House, 2001.
Maddison, Angus. *The World Economy in the 20th Century*. Paris: OECD Publishing, 1989.
Madokoro, Laura, and Francine McKenzie. "Introduction: Writing Race into Canada's
    International History." In Madokoro, McKenzie, and Meren, *Dominion of Race:
    Rethinking Canada's International History*, 3–24. Vancouver: University of British
    Columbia Press, 2017.
Madokoro, Laura, Francine McKenzie, and David Meren. *Dominion of Race: Rethinking
    Canada's International History*. Vancouver: University of British Columbia Press, 2017.
Mahan, Alfred Thayer. *Mahan on Naval Warfare: Selections from the Writings of Rear
    Admiral Alfred T. Mahan*. Mineola, NY: Courier Dover Publications, 1999.
Malcolm, Daniel, Sr. "Constitutional Development (1957–76)." In *History of the Turks and
    Caicos Islands*, edited by Carlton Mills, 157–64. Oxford: Macmillan Education, 2008.
– "Party Politics since 1976 and the Blom-Cooper Report." In Mills, *History of the Turks
    and Caicos Islands*, 178–87. Oxford: Macmillan Education, 2008.
Maloney, Sean. "Maple Leaf over the Caribbean: Gunboat Diplomacy Canadian Style."
    In *Canadian Gunboat Diplomacy: The Canadian Navy and Foreign Policy*, edited by
    Ann L. Griffiths, Richard Howard Gimblett, and Peter T. Haydon, 147–83. Halifax:
    Dalhousie University Centre for Foreign Policy Studies, 2000.
Malton, C. Colville. *Reminiscences of a Tour through the West Indies*. Saint John, NB: E.J.
    Armstrong, c. 1885.
Mandle, Jay R. "British Caribbean Economic History: An Interpretation." In *The
    Modern Caribbean*, edited by Franklin W. Knight and Colin A. Palmer, 229–58.
    Chapel Hill: University of North Carolina Press, 1989.
Manela, Erez. *The Wilsonian Moment: Self-Determination and the International Origins of
    Anticolonial Nationalism*. New York: Oxford University Press, 2007.
Mann, Susan, *Dream of Nation: A Social and Intellectual History of Quebec*. Montreal:
    McGill-Queen's University Press, 2002.
Mantena, Karuna. *Alibis of Empire: Henry Maine and the Ends of Liberal Imperialism*.
    Princeton: Princeton University Press, 2010.
– "The Crisis of Liberal Imperialism." In *Victorian Visions of Global Order: Empire and
    International Relations in Nineteenth-Century Political Thought*, edited by Duncan
    Bell, 113–35. Cambridge: Cambridge University Press, 2011.
Marano, Carla. "'Rising Strongly and Rapidly': The Universal Negro Improvement
    Association of Canada, 1919–1940." *Canadian Historical Review* 91, no. 2 (2010):
    233–59.
Marks, Sally. "Black Watch on the Rhine: A Study in Propaganda, Prejudice, and
    Prurience." *European Studies Review* 13 (1983): 297–334.

Martel, Marcel. "'Riot' at Sir George Williams: Giving Meaning to Student Dissent."
    In *Debating Dissent: Canada and the Sixties*, edited by Lara Campbell, Dominique
    Clément, and Gregory S. Kealey, 97–114. Toronto: University of Toronto Press, 2012.

Martin, Frederick. *The Statesman's Year-Book*. Vol. 28. New York: St Martin's Press, 1891.

Martin, Ged. "Empire Federalism and Imperial Parliamentary Union, 1820–1870."
    Historical Journal 16, no. 1 (1973): 65–92.

Martin, Paul. *Hell or High Water: My Life in and out of Politics*. Toronto: McClelland &
    Stewart, 2008.

Martin, Tony. *The Pan-African Connection: From Slavery to Garvey and Beyond*. Dover,
    MA: Majority Press, 1984.

Mathieu, Sarah-Jane. "Jim Crow Rides This Train: The Social and Political Impact of
    African American Sleeping Car Porters in Canada, 1880–1939." PhD diss., Yale
    University, 2001.

– *North of the Color Line: Migration and Black Resistance in Canada, 1870–1955*. Chapel
    Hill: University of North Carolina Press, 2010.

Mawani, Renisa. *Across Oceans of Law: The Komagata Maru and Jurisdiction in the Time
    of Empire*. Durham: Duke University Press, 2018.

May, Alex. "The Commonwealth and Britain's Turn to Europe, 1945–73." *Round Table*
    102, no. 1 (2013): 29–39.

McDowall, Duncan. *Another World: Bermuda and the Rise of Modern Tourism*. London:
    MacMillan Education, 1999.

– *The Light: Brazilian Traction, Light and Power Company Limited, 1899–1945*. Toronto:
    University of Toronto Press, 1988.

– *Quick to the Frontier: Canada's Royal Bank*. Toronto: McClelland & Stewart, 1993.

McGrath, P.T. "The Newfoundland Fishery Dispute." *North American Review* 183, no.
    604 (1906): 1134–43.

McIntyre, W. David. *The Commonwealth of Nations: Origins and Impact, 1869–1971*.
    Minneapolis: University of Minnesota Press, 1977.

– *Winding up the British Empire in the Pacific Islands*. Oxford: Oxford University Press,
    2014.

McKay, Ian. "The Liberal Order Framework: A Prospectus for a Reconnaissance of
    Canadian History." *Canadian Historical Review* 81, no. 4 (2000): 617–45.

McKenna, Peter. *Canada and the OAS: From Dilettante to Full Partner*. Montreal:
    McGill-Queen's University Press, 1995.

McKercher, Asa. *Canada and the World since 1867*. London: Bloomsbury, 2019.

– "Sound and Fury: Diefenbaker, Human Rights, and Canadian Foreign Policy."
    Canadian Historical Review 97, no. 2 (2016): 165–94.

McKittrick, Katherine. *Demonic Grounds: Black Women and the Cartographies of Struggle*.
    Minneapolis: University of Minnesota Press, 2006.

– "Wait Canada Anticipate Black." *CLR James Journal* 20, no.1 (2014): 243–49.

McWhorter, John. "There's Nothing Wrong with Black English." *Atlantic*, 6 August
    2018. https://www.theatlantic.com/ideas/archive/2018/08/who-gets-to-use-black-
    english/566867/.

Mehrotra, S.R. "Imperial Federation and India, 1868–1917." *Journal of Commonwealth and Comparative Politics* 1, no. 1 (1961): 29–30.

Mehta, Uday Singh. *Liberalism and Empire: A Study in Nineteenth-Century British Liberal Thought.* Chicago: University of Chicago Press, 1999.

Meikle, Louis. *Confederation of the British West Indies versus Annexation to the United States of America.* London: S. Low, Marston & Co., 1912.

Mensah, Joseph. *Black Canadians: History, Experiences, Social Conditions.* Winnipeg: Fernwood, 2002.

Meren, David. "The Tragedies of Canadian International History." *Canadian Historical Review* 96, no. 4 (2015): 534–66.

– *With Friends Like These: Entangled Nationalisms and the Canada-Quebec-France Triangle, 1944–1970.* Vancouver: University of British Columbia Press, 2012.

Millar, John. *Canadian Citizenship: A Treatise on Civil Government.* Toronto: William Briggs, 1899.

Miller, J.R. *Skyscrapers Hide the Heavens: A History of Indian-White Relations in Canada.* Toronto: University of Toronto Press, 1991.

Milloy, John S. *A National Crime: The Canadian Government and the Residential School System, 1879–1986.* Winnipeg: University of Manitoba Press, 1999.

Mills, Charles. *Black Rights/White Wrongs: The Critique of Racial Liberalism.* Oxford: Oxford University Press, 2017.

Mills, Sean. *Empire Within: Postcolonial Thought and Political Activism in Sixties Montreal.* Montreal: McGill-Queen's University Press, 2010.

– *A Place in the Sun: Haiti, Haitians, and the Remaking of Quebec.* Montreal: McGill-Queen's University Press, 2016.

Mongia, Radhika Viyas. "Race, Nationality, Mobility: A History of the Passport." In *After the Imperial Turn: Thinking with and through the Nation*, edited by Antoinette Burton, 196–214. Durham: Duke University Press, 2003.

Montgomery, Ken. "Imagining the Antiracist State: Representations of Racism in Canadian History Textbooks." *Discourse: Studies in the Cultural Politics of Education* 26, no. 4 (2005): 427–42.

Moore, Brian L., and Michele A. Johnson. *Neither Led nor Driven: Contesting British Cultural Imperialism in Jamaica, 1865–1920.* Kingston: University of the West Indies Press, 2004.

Moore, John B. *A Digest of International Law.* Vol. 5. Washington, DC: Government Printing Office, 1906.

Moore, Jonathan A. "The Transformation of the British Imperial Administration, 1919–1939." PhD diss., Tulane University, 2016.

Morgan, Cecilia. *A Happy Holiday: English Canadians and Transatlantic Tourism, 1870–1930.* Toronto: University of Toronto Press, 2008.

Mount, Graeme S., and Stephen J. Randall, *The Caribbean Basin: An International History.* London: Routledge, 1998.

Moyles, R.G., and Doug Owram. *Imperial Dreams and Colonial Realities: British Views of Canada, 1880–1914.* Toronto: University of Toronto Press, 1988.

Munro, J.A., ed. *The Alaska Boundary Dispute.* Toronto: Copp Clark, 1970.

Murray, David. "Garrisoning the Caribbean: A Chapter in Canadian Military History." In *Canada and the Commonwealth Caribbean*, edited by Bryan Douglas Tennyson, 279–97. Lanham, MD: University Press of America, 1988.

Murray, Gideon. "Canada and the British West Indies." *United Empire* 10, no. 2 (1919).

Muszynski, Alicja. *Cheap Wage Labour: Race and Gender in the Fisheries of British Columbia*. Montreal: McGill-Queen's University Press, 1996.

Naranch, Bradley. "Made in China: Austro-Prussian Overseas Rivalry and the Global Unification of the German Nation." *Australian Journal of Politics and History* 56, no. 3 (2010): 366–80.

Naylor, R.T. *The History of Canadian Business, 1867–1914*. Montreal: McGill-Queen's University Press, 2006.

Neatby, H. Blair. *The Politics of Chaos: Canada in the Thirties*. Toronto: Macmillan, 1972.

Nelles, H.V. *The Politics of Development: Forests, Mines and Hydro-Electric Power in Ontario, 1849–1911*. Toronto: Macmillan, 1974.

Nelles, H.V., and Christopher Armstrong. *Southern Exposure: Canadian Promoters in Latin America and the Caribbean, 1896–1930*. Toronto: University of Toronto Press, 1988.

Nelson, Charmaine A. *Slavery, Geography and Empire in Nineteenth-Century Marine Landscapes of Montreal and Jamaica*. London: Routledge, 2016.

Nerbas, Don. "Wealth and Privilege: An Analysis of Winnipeg's Early Business Elite." *Manitoba History*, no. 47 (2004): 42–64.

Newman, Peter K. "Canada's Role in West Indian Trade before 1912." *Inter-American Economic Affairs* 14, no. 1 (1960): 25–49.

Newton, Velma. *The Silver Men: West Indian Labour Migration to Panama, 1850–1914*. Kingston, JA: Institute of Social and Economic Research, University of the West Indies, 1984.

Owram, Doug. *Promise of Eden: The Canadian Expansionist Movement and the Idea of the West, 1856–1900*. Toronto: University of Toronto Press, 1980.

Pachai, Bridglal. *The Nova Scotia Black Experience through the Centuries*. Halifax: Nimbus, 2007.

Pactor, Howard S. *Colonial British Caribbean Newspapers: A Bibliography and Directory*. New York: Greenwood Press, 1990.

Palmer, Bryan D. *Working Class Experience: Rethinking the History of Canadian Labour, 1800–1991*. Toronto: McClelland & Stewart, 1992.

Palmer, Colin A. *Freedom's Children: The 1938 Labor Rebellion and the Birth of Modern Jamaica*. Chapel Hill: University of North Carolina Press, 2014.

Parker, Jason C. *Brother's Keeper: The United States, Race, and Empire in the British Caribbean, 1927–1962*. New York: Oxford University Press, 2008.

– "Remapping the Cold War in the Tropics: Race, Communism, and National Security in the West Indies." *International History Review* 24, no. 2 (2002): 318–47.

Parkin, G.R. "Presidential Address." *Geographical Teacher* 6, no. 4 (1912): 189–98.

Parry, J.H., Philip Sherlock, and Anthony Maingot. *A Short History of the West Indies*. New York: St Martin's Press, 1987.

Pavlakis, Dean. "The Development of British Overseas Humanitarianism and the Congo Reform Campaign." *Journal of Colonialism and Colonial History* 11, no. 1 (2010).

Pedersen, Susan. "Modernity and Trusteeship: Tensions of Empire in Britain between the Wars." In *Meanings of Modernity: Britain from the Late-Victorian Era to World War II*, edited by Martin J. Daunton and Bernard Rieger, 203–20. Oxford: Berg Publishers, 2001.

– "Settler Colonialism at the Bar of the League of Nations." In *Settler Colonialism in the Twentieth Century: Projects, Practices, Legacies*, edited by Caroline Elkins and Susan Pederson, 113–34. New York: Routledge, 2005.

Penlington, N. *The Alaska Boundary Dispute: A Critical Reappraisal.* Toronto: McGraw-Hill Ryerson, 1972.

Penner, Lloyd. "The Foreign Policy of the New Democratic Party, 1961–1988." PhD diss., University of Manitoba, 1994.

Perkins, Bradford. *The Great Rapprochement: England and the United States, 1895–1914.* New York: Atheneum, 1968.

Perry, Adele. "The State of Empire: Reproducing Colonialism in British Columbia, 1849–1871." *Journal of Colonialism and Colonial History* 2, no. 2 (2001).

– "Women, Racialized People, and the Making of the Liberal Order in Northern North America." In *Liberalism and Hegemony: Debating the Canadian Liberal Revolution*, edited by Jean-François Constant and Michel Ducharme, 274–97. Toronto: University of Toronto Press, 2009.

Pitsula, James M. *Keeping Canada British: The Ku Klux Klan in 1920s Saskatchewan.* Vancouver: University of British Columbia Press, 2013.

Pitts, Jennifer. *A Turn to Empire: The Rise of Imperial Liberalism in Britain and France.* Princeton: Princeton University Press, 2005.

Platt, Elizabeth R. "The Determinants of Canada's South African Policy." MA thesis, McMaster University, 1986.

Pope, Joseph. *Confidential Memorandum upon the Subject of the Annexation of the West India Islands to the Dominion of Canada.* Ottawa: Dominion of Canada, 1917.

Porter, Andrew. "Trusteeship, Anti-Slavery, and Humanitarianism." In *The Oxford History of the British Empire.* Vol. 3, *The Nineteenth Century*, edited by Andrew Porter, 198–221. Oxford: Oxford University Press, 1999.

Porter, Bernard. *Britannia's Burden: The Political Evolution of Modern Britain, 1851–1990.* London: Edward Arnold, 1994.

– *The Lion's Share: A Short History of British Imperialism, 1850–1983.* New York: Longman, 1984.

Porter, John. *The Vertical Mosaic: An Analysis of Social Class and Power in Canada.* Toronto: University of Toronto Press, 1965.

Posluns, Michael W. *Speaking with Authority: The Emergence of the Vocabulary of First Nations' Self-Government.* London: Routledge, 2007.

Potter, Simon. "Richard Jebb, John S. Ewart and the Round Table, 1898–1926." *English Historical Review* 122, no. 495 (2007): 105–32.

Power, Helen J. *Tropical Medicine in the Twentieth Century: A History of the Liverpool School of Tropical Medicine, 1898–1990*. London and New York: Kegan Paul, 1999.

Pratt, Cranford. "Ethical Values and Canadian Foreign Aid Policies." *Canadian Journal of African Studies* 37, no. 1 (2003): 84–101.

Pratt, Mary Louise. *Imperial Eyes: Travel Writing and Transculturation*. London: Routledge, 1992.

Price, John. *Orienting Canada: Race, Empire, and the Transpacific*. Vancouver: University of British Columbia Press, 2011.

Price, Peter. *Questions of Order: Confederation and the Making of Modern Canada*. Toronto: University of Toronto Press, 2021.

– "Steppingstones to Imperial Unity? The British West Indies in the Late-Victorian Imperial Federation Movement." *Canadian Journal of History* 52, no. 2 (2017): 240–63.

Proctor, Jesse H., Jr. "The Development of the Idea of Federation of the British Caribbean Territories." *Revista de Historia de América*, no. 39 (1955): 61–105.

Quigley, Neil C. "The Bank of Nova Scotia in the Caribbean, 1889–1940." *Business History Review* 63, no. 4 (1989): 797–838.

Rawlyk, G.A. "Canada's Immigration Policy, 1945–1962." *Dalhousie Review* 42, no. 3 (1962): 288–99.

Razack, Sherene H. *Dark Threats and White Knights: The Somalia Affair, Peacekeeping, and the New Imperialism*. Toronto: University of Toronto Press, 2004.

Rees, T.R. *The History of the Royal Commonwealth Society, 1868–1968*. London: Oxford University Press, 1968.

Regan, Paulette. *Unsettling the Settler Within: Indian Residential Schools, Truth Telling, and Reconciliation in Canada*. Vancouver: University of British Columbia Press, 2010.

Reid, Fran. "The Cost of Eden." In *Third World File 5: Canada in the Caribbean*, 1–10. Toronto: Development Education Centre, 1974.

Reid, John R. "Canada's Future Relations with the West Indies." *Canada-West Indies Magazine* 7, no. 3 (1919): 66.

Reynolds, Louise. *Agnes: The Biography of Lady Macdonald*. Ottawa: Carleton University Press, 1990.

Richardson, Bonham. "Depression Riots and the Calling of the 1897 Royal Commission." *New West Indian Guide* 66, nos. 3–4 (1992): 169–91.

– "The Importance of the 1897 British Royal Commission." In *Caribbean Land and Development Revisited*, edited by Jean Besson and Janet Momsen, 17–28. New York: Macmillan, 2007.

Riddell, W.A. *Documents on Canadian Foreign Policy, 1917–1919*. Toronto: Oxford University Press, 1962.

Rioux, Michèle, and Hugues Brisson. "Interview with Kari Levitt: 'Bring the State Back In!'" *Papers in Political Economy* 45 (2012). https://doi.org/10.4000/interventionseconomiques.1686.

Robert, Jean-Claude. "The People." In *Historical Atlas of Canada*. Vol. 2, *The Land Transformed, 1800–1891*, edited by R. Louis Gentilcore, 77–94. Toronto: University of Toronto Press, 1993.

Roberts, Barbara. *Whence They Came: Deportation from Canada, 1900–1935*. Ottawa: University of Ottawa Press, 1997.

Roberts, G.W. "Some Observations on the Population of British Guiana." *Population Studies* 2, no. 2 (1948): 185–218.

Rodney, Walter. *How Europe Underdeveloped Africa*. London: L'Ouverture Publications, 1972.

Rogozinski, Jan. *A Brief History of the Caribbean: From the Arawak and the Carib to the Present*. New York: Plume, 2000.

Roopnarine, Lomarsh. *Indo-Caribbean Indenture: Resistance and Accommodation, 1838–1920*. Kingston, JA: University of the West Indies Press, 2007.

Rosenburg, Emily. *Financial Missionaries to the World: The Politics and Culture of Dollar Diplomacy, 1900–1930*. Durham: Duke University Press, 2003.

Ruck, Calvin W. *Canada's Black Battalion: No. 2 Construction, 1916–1920*. Halifax: The Society for the Protection and Preservation of Black Culture in Nova Scotia, 1986.

Rutherford, Scott. "Colonialism and the Indigenous Present: An Interview with Bonita Lawrence." *Race and Class* 52, no. 1 (2010): 9–18.

Rutherford, Scott, Sean Mills, and David Austin. Editorial. *Race and Class* 52, no. 1 (2010): 1–7.

Saku, James C. "Aboriginal Census Data in Canada: A Research Note." *Canadian Journal of Native Studies* 19, no. 2 (1999): 365–79.

Samaroo, Brinsley. "The Politics of Disharmony: The Debate on the Political Union of the British West Indies and Canada, 1884–1921." *Revista Interamericana* 7, no. 1 (1977): 46–59.

Sapoznik, Karlee. "Where the Historiography Falls Short: Le Vérendrye through the Lens of Gender, Race and Slavery in Early French Canada, 1731–1749." *Manitoba History*, no. 62 (2009): 22–32.

Saul, S.B. "The British West Indies in Depression, 1880–1914." *Inter-American Economic Affairs* 12, no. 3 (1958): 3–25.

Saunders, Gail. "The Role of the Coloured Middle Class in Nassau, Bahamas, 1890–1942." *Ethnic and Racial Studies* 10, no. 4 (1987): 448–65.

– *Bahamian Society after Emancipation: Essays in Nineteenth and Early Twentieth Century Bahamian History*. Kingston, JA: Ian Randle Publishers, 2003.

– *Race and Class in the Colonial Bahamas, 1880–1960*. Gainesville: University Press of Florida, 2016.

Schabas, William A. "Canada and the Adoption of the Universal Declaration of Human Rights." *McGill Law Journal* 43, no. 2 (1998): 403–44.

Schuler, Monica. *"Alas, Alas, Kongo": A Social History of Indentured African Immigration into Jamaica, 1841–1865*. Baltimore: Johns Hopkins University Press, 1980.

Schull, Joseph, and J. Douglas Gibson. *The Scotia Bank Story: A History of the Bank of Nova Scotia, 1832–1982*. Toronto: Macmillan, 1982.

Searle, Geoffrey R. *The Quest for National Efficiency: A Study in British Politics and Political Thought, 1899–1914*. Berkeley: University of California Press, 1971.

Sewell, Sharon C. *Decolonization and the Other: The Case of the British West Indies*. Newcastle upon Tyne: Cambridge Scholars Publishing, 2010.

Shaw, Melissa. "'Most Anxious to Serve Their King and Country': Black Canadians' Fight to Enlist in wwi and Emerging Race Consciousness in Ontario, 1914–1919." *Histoire sociale/Social History* 49, no. 100 (2016): 543–80.

Shepard, R. Bruce. *Deemed Unsuitable: Blacks from Oklahoma Move to the Canadian Prairies in Search of Equality in the Early 20th Century Only to Find Racism in Their New Home*. Toronto: Dundurn Press, 1997.

Shephard, C.Y. "The Sugar Industry of the British West Indies and British Guiana with Special Reference to Trinidad." *Economic Geography* 5, no. 2 (1929): 149–75.

Sheridan, Richard B. "Temperate and Tropical: Aspects of European Penetration into Tropical Regions." *Caribbean Studies* 3, no. 2 (1963): 3–21.

Shields, R.A. "Canada, the Foreign Office and the Caribbean Market, 1884–1895." *Dalhousie Review* 58, no. 4 (1978–79): 703–22.

Silvestrini, Blanca G. "Contemporary Puerto Rico: A Society of Contrasts." In *The Modern Caribbean*, edited by Franklin W. Knight and Colin A. Palmer. Chapel Hill: University of North Carolina Press, 1989.

Simpson, Erika. "The Principles of Liberal Internationalism according to Lester Pearson." *Journal of Canadian Studies* 34, no. 1 (1999): 75–92.

Sinha, Mrinalini. "Whatever Happened to the Third British Empire? Empire, Nation Redux." In *Writing Imperial Histories*, edited by Andrew S. Thompson, 168–87. Manchester: Manchester University Press, 2013.

Smiley, CalvinJohn, and David Fakunle. "From 'Brute' to 'Thug': The Demonization and Criminalization of Unarmed Black Male Victims in America." *Journal of Human Behavior in the Social Environment* 26, nos. 3–4 (2016): 350–66.

Smith, Andrew. "Thomas Bassett Macaulay and the Bahamas: Racism, Business and Canadian Sub-Imperialism." *Journal of Imperial and Commonwealth History* 37, no.1 (2009): 29–50.

Smith, Evan. "Against Fascism, for Racial Equality: Communists, Anti-racism and the Road to the Second World War in Australia, South Africa and the United States." *Labor History* 58, no. 5 (2017): 676–96.

Smith, Goldwin. *Reminiscences by Goldwin Smith*. Edited by Arnold Haultain. Toronto: Macmillan, 1910.

Smith, James Patterson. "The Liberals, Race, and Political Reform in the British West Indies, 1866–1874." *Journal of Negro History* 79, no. 2 (1994): 131–46.

Smith, J. Russell. "Western South America and Its Relation to American Trade." *Annals of the American Academy of Political and Social Science*, no. 18 (November 1901): 56–78

Smith, M.G. *The Plural Society in the British West Indies*. Berkeley: University of California Press, 1965.

Smith, Richard. *Jamaican Volunteers in the First World War: Race, Masculinity and the Development of National Consciousness*. Manchester: Manchester University Press, 2010.

Smith, Simon C. "Integration and Disintegration: The Attempted Incorporation of Malta into the United Kingdom in the 1950s." *Journal of Imperial and Commonwealth History* 35, no. 1 (2007): 49–71.

Spoehr, Luther W. "Sambo and the Heathen Chinee: Californians' Racial Stereotypes in the Late 1870s." *Pacific Historical Review* 42, no. 2 (1973): 185–204.

Springer, Hugh. W. *Reflections on the Failure of the First West Indian Federation.* Cambridge, MA: Center for International Affairs, Harvard University, 1962.

Stacey, C.P. *Mackenzie King and the Atlantic Triangle.* Toronto: Macmillan, 1976.

Stairs, Dennis. "Of Medium Powers and Middling Roles." In *Statecraft and Security: The Cold War and Beyond*, edited by Ken Booth, 270–86. Cambridge: Cambridge University Press, 1998.

Stanley, Timothy J. *Contesting White Supremacy: School Segregation, Anti-Racism, and the Making of Chinese Canadians.* Vancouver: University of British Columbia Press, 2011.

Steed, Nicholas. "The Caribbean: Our Sunny New Frontier." *Maclean's* 80, no. 2 (1967): 11–15, 62–4, 67, 69.

Stewart, Alice. "Canadian-West Indian Union, 1884–1885." *Canadian Historical Review* 31, no. 4 (1950): 369–89.

Stewart, Gordon T. "'An Objective of US Foreign Policy since the Founding of the Republic': The United States and the End of Empire in Canada." In *Canada and the End of Empire*, edited by Phillip Buckner, 94–116. Vancouver: University of British Columbia Press, 2005.

Stewart, Robert J. *Religion and Society in Post-emancipation Jamaica.* Knoxville: University of Tennessee Press, 1992.

Stokes, Robert. *New Imperial Ideals: A Plea for the Association of the Dominions in the Government of the Dependent Empire.* London: John Murray, 1930.

Strong, Josiah. *Expansion under New World-Conditions.* New York: Baker & Taylor, 1900.

Taunton, W.D. *To the British West Indies via Halifax: The All Canadian Route.* Halifax: Pickford & Black, c. 1902.

– "Should Canada Annex the British West Indies." *Canadian Magazine*, February 1912, 6.

Teelucksingh, Jerome. *Labour and the Decolonization Struggle in Trinidad and Tobago.* Basingstoke: Palgrave Macmillan, 2015.

Teigrob, Robert. "Glad Adventures, Tragedies, Silences: Remembering and Forgetting Wars for Empire in Canada and the United States." *International Journal of Canadian Studies*, nos. 45–6 (2012): 441–65.

– "'Which Kind of Imperialism?': Early Cold War Decolonization and Canada–US Relations." *Canadian Review of American Studies* 37, no. 3 (2007): 403–30.

Tennyson, Brian. "The British West Indies and Mackenzie King's National Policy in the 1920s." *Journal of Caribbean History* 24, no. 1 (1990): 65–88.

– "Canada and the Commonwealth Caribbean: The Historical Relationship." In *Canadian-Caribbean Relations: Aspects of a Relationship*, edited by Brian Tennyson, 1–57. Sydney, NS: Centre for International Studies, Cape Breton University, 1990.

Thobani, Sunera. *Exalted Subjects: Studies in the Making of Race and Nation in Canada.* Toronto: University of Toronto Press, 2007.

Thomas, Deborah A. "Rastafari, Communism, and Surveillance in Late Colonial
    Jamaica." *Small Axe* 21, no. 3 (2017): 63–84.
Thomas, Ernest C., and Charles L. Attenborough. *Leading Cases in Constitutional Law
    Briefly Stated.* London: Stevens & Haynes, 1908.
Thompson, John Herd. "Canada and the 'Third British Empire.'" In *Canada and the
    British Empire,* edited by Phillip Buckner, 88–107. Oxford: Oxford University Press,
    2008.
Thompson, John Herd, and Stephen J. Randall. *Canada and the United States:
    Ambivalent Allies.* Athens: University of Georgia Press, 2008.
Thompson, Roger C. *Australian Imperialism in the Pacific: The Expansionist Era,
    1880–1920.* Carlton: Melbourne University Press, 1980.
Thornton, A.P. *The Imperial Idea and Its Enemies: A Study in British Power.* London:
    Macmillan, 1985.
Tilchin, William N. "Theodore Roosevelt, Anglo-American Relations, and the Jamaica
    Incident of 1907." *Diplomatic History* 19, no. 3 (1995): 385–406.
Tinker, Hugh. *Separate but Unequal: India and the Indians in the British Commonwealth,
    1920–1950.* Vancouver: University of British Columbia Press, 1976.
Todd, Alpheus. *Parliamentary Government in the British Colonies.* London: Longman's,
    1894.
Touhey, Ryan. "Commonwealth Conundrums: Canada and South Asia during the
    Pearson Era." In *Mike's World: Lester B. Pearson and Canadian External Affairs,* edited
    by Galen R. Perras and Asa McKercher, 251–74. Vancouver: University of British
    Columbia Press, 2016.
– *Conflicting Visions: Canada and India in the Cold War World, 1946–76.* Vancouver:
    University of British Columbia Press, 2015.
– "Dealing in Black and White: The Diefenbaker Government and the Cold War in
    South Asia, 1957–1963." *Canadian Historical Review* 92, no. 3 (2011): 429–54.
Triadafilos, Triadafilopoulos. "Global Norms, Domestic Institutions and the
    Transformation of Immigration Policy in Canada and the US." *Review of
    International Studies* 36, no. 1 (2010): 169–94.
Trudel, Marcel. *L'esclavage au Canada français: Histoire et conditions de l'esclavage.*
    Quebec: Presse de L'Université Laval, 1960.
Tunnicliffe, Jennifer. "A Limited Vision: Canadian Participation in the Adoption of the
    International Covenants on Human Rights." In *Taking Liberties: A History of Human
    Rights in Canada,* edited by David Goutor and Stephen J. Heathorn, 166–87. Don
    Mills, ON: Oxford University Press, 2013.
Tupper, Charles. *The Life and Letters of the Rt. Hon. Sir Charles Tupper.* Edited by E.M.
    Saunders. London: Cassell & Co., 1916.
Turner, Mary. *Slaves and Missionaries: The Disintegration of Jamaican Slave Society,
    1787–1834.* Kingston, JA: University of the West Indies, 1998.
Turner, Trevor. "Canadian Involvement in the Development of the West Indies." In
    Third World File 5: Canada in the Caribbean, 1–3. Toronto: Development Education
    Centre, 1974.

Valverde, Mariana. *The Age of Light, Soap and Water: Moral Reform in English Canada, 1885–1925*. Toronto: University of Toronto Press, 2008.

Veeser, Cyrus. *A World Safe for Capitalism: Dollar Diplomacy and America's Rise to Global Power*. New York: Columbia University Press, 2002.

Vernon, Karina. "Black Civility: Black Grammars of Protest on the Canadian Prairies, 1905–1950." *CLR James Journal* 20, no. 1–2 (2014): 83–96.

Waite, P.B. "French Canadian Isolationism and English Canada: An Elliptical Foreign Policy, 1935–1939." *Journal of Canadian Studies* 18, no. 2 (1983): 111–43.

Walcott, Rinaldo. "The End of Diversity." *Public Culture* 31, no. 2 (2019): 393–408.

– "Shame: A Polemic." *CLR James Journal* 20, nos. 1–2 (2014): 275–79.

Walker, Barrington. H–Diplo Roundtable 20–23 on *Dominion of Race: Rethinking Canada's International History*, edited by Laura Madokoro, Francine McKenzie, and David Meren. Vancouver: University of British Columbia Press, 2017, 4 February 2019. https://networks.h-net.org/node/28443/discussions/3642968/h-diplo-roundtable-xx-23-laura-madokoro-francine-mckenzie-and.

Walker, James W. St G. "African Canadians." In *Encyclopedia of Canada's Peoples*, edited by Paul Robert Magosci, 142–50. Toronto: Published for the Multicultural Society of Ontario by the University of Toronto, 1999.

– *The Black Loyalists: The Search for a Promised Land in Nova Scotia and Sierra Leone, 1783–1870*. Toronto: University of Toronto Press, 1992.

– "Race and Recruitment in World War I: Enlistment of Visible Minorities in the Canadian Expeditionary Force." *Canadian Historical Review* 70, no. 1 (1989): 1–26.

– *The West Indians in Canada*. Canadian Historical Association Ethnic Groups Series, no. 6. Saint John, NB: Keystone Publishing, 1984.

Wallace, Elisabeth. "The West Indies Federation, Decline and Fall." *International Journal* 17, no. 3 (1962): 269–88.

Wallerstein, Immanuel. *The Modern World System*. New York: Academic Press, 1974.

Ward, Stuart. "Transcending the Nation: A Global Imperial History?" In *After the Imperial Turn: Thinking with and through the Nation*, edited by Antoinette M. Burton, 44–56. Durham, NC: Duke University Press, 2003.

Ware, Leland. *A Century of Segregation: Race, Class, and Disadvantage*. Lanham, MD: Lexington Books, 2018.

Warner, Donald F. *The Idea of Continental Union: Agitation for Annexation of Canada to the United States, 1849–1893*. Lexington: University of Kentucky Press, 1960.

Waters, Rosanne P. "A March from Selma to Canada: Canada and the Transnational Civil Rights Movement." PhD diss., McMaster University, 2015.

Webster, David. *Fire and the Full Moon: Canada and Indonesia in a Decolonizing World*. Vancouver: University of British Columbia Press, 2010.

– "Foreign Policy, Diplomacy, and Decolonization." In Dubinsky, Mills, and Rutherford, *Canada and the Third World: Overlapping Histories*, 155–92. Toronto: University of Toronto Press, 2016.

Wells, Samuel F. "British Strategic Withdrawal from the Western Hemisphere, 1904–1906." *Canadian Historical Review* 49, no. 4 (1968): 335–56.

White, L.W., and W.D. Hussey. *Government in Great Britain, the Empire, and the Commonwealth*. Cambridge: Cambridge University Press, 1961.

White, Sarah C. "The 'Gender Lens': A Racial Blinder?" *Progress in Development Studies* 6, no. 1 (2006): 55–67.

Whitfield, Harvey Amani. *North to Bondage: Loyalist Slavery in the Maritimes*. Vancouver: University of British Columbia Press, 2016.

Whitham, Charlie. *Bitter Rehearsal: British and American Planning for a Post-War West Indies*. Westport, CT: Praeger, 2002.

Wigley, P.G. "Canada and Imperialism: West Indian Aspirations and the First World War." In *Canada and the Commonwealth Caribbean*, edited by Brian Douglas Tennyson, 215–55. Lanham, MD: University Press of America, 1988.

– *Canada and the Transition to Commonwealth: British-Canadian Relations, 1917–1926*. Cambridge: Cambridge University Press, 1977.

Will, H.A. "Colonial Policy and Economic Development in the British West Indies, 1895–1903." *Economic History Review* 23, no. 1 (1970): 129–43.

Willan, B.P. "The South African Native Labour Contingent, 1916–1918." *Journal of African History* 19, no. 1 (1978): 61–86.

Williams, Chad L. *Torchbearers of Democracy: African American Soldiers in the World War I Era*. Chapel Hill: University of North Carolina Press, 2013.

Williams, Eric. "Canada and the West Indies." *Round Table* 57, no. 225 (1967): 57–60.

– *Capitalism and Slavery*. Chapel Hill: University of North Carolina Press, 1944.

– "Massa Day Done." Public Lecture at Woodford Square, 22 March 1961. *Callaloo* 20, no. 4 (1997): 724–30.

Wilson, James H. *An Address on Our Trade Relations with the Tropics*. Boston: George H. Ellis, 1901.

Winks, Robin. *The Blacks in Canada: A History*. Montreal: McGill-Queen's University Press, 1997.

– *Canadian-West Indian Union: A Forty-Year Minuet*. London: Athlone Press, 1968.

Winant, Harold. *The World Is a Ghetto: Race and Democracy since World War II*. New York: Basic Books, 2001.

Wolfe, Patrick. "Land, Labor, and Difference: Elementary Structures of Race." *American Historical Review* 106, no. 3 (2001): 866–905.

Wright, Robert, and Lana Wylie, eds. *Our Place in the Sun: Canada and Cuba in the Castro Era*. Toronto: University of Toronto Press, 2009.

Wrong, Hume. *Government of the West Indies*. London: Oxford University Press, 1923.

Zaslow, Morris. *The Northward Expansion of Canada, 1914–1967*. Toronto: McClelland & Stewart, 1988.

Zucchi, John. *Mad Flight: The Quebec Emigration to the Coffee Plantations of Brazil*. Montreal: McGill-Queen's University Press, 2018.

INDEX